Wallace K. Harrison, Architect

Wallace K. Harrison, Architect

Victoria Newhouse

RIZZOLI
NEW YORK

First published in the United States of America in 1989 by
Rizzoli International Publications, Inc.
597 Fifth Avenue, New York, NY 10017

Grateful acknowledgement is made for permission to reprint
the following:

"The Promised Land of Mr. Moses," by Ogden Nash.
Reprinted by permission of Curtis Brown, Ltd.
Copyright © 1964 by Ogden Nash.

World's Fair by E. L. Doctorow (New York, 1985), p. 250.
Reprinted by permission of Random House, Inc.

Library of Congress Cataloging-in-Publication Data

Newhouse, Victoria.
  Wallace K. Harrison, architect.

  Includes index.
  1. Harrison, Wallace K. (Wallace Kirkman), 1895–1981
2. Architects—United States—Biography.   3. Architecture,
Modern—20th century—United States.   I. Title.
NA737.H32N49   1989   720'.92'4   [B]   85–42951
ISBN 0–8478–0644–8
ISBN 0–8478–1071–2 (pbk.)

Designed by Sylvia Steiner
Type composed by Rainsford Type, Danbury, CT
Printed and bound in Spain

Contents

Acknowledgements

The idea for this book came into being eight years ago at an impromptu luncheon given by Hester Diamond and her late husband, Harold, mutual friends of Wallace Harrison's and mine. Three people were essential to realizing the idea. Ellen Harrison's patience in answering innumerable questions and her entrustment to me of many important drawings and documents greatly facilitated my research. Adolf K. Placzek helped me give form to a large mass of undifferentiated information. Finally, Edgar Kaufmann, jr., provided important insight and editing.

I am indebted to Mosette Glazer Broderick, who researched with painstaking care the long and varied historical context within which Harrison worked; to David De Long, Carol Herselle Krinsky, Leo Lerman, and my husband, Si, for their comments; to Brenda Gilchrist and Sara Blackburn for their editorial suggestions; to Katrina Thomas for her editing of the chapters on Lincoln Center; and to Deborah Kirk for her checking of facts. Thanks must also go to Carol Herselle Krinsky and Gregory Gilmartin for their invaluable help in providing a number of illustrations.

The project provided the opportunity to meet regularly with Harrison and with a multitude of his friends and colleagues (cited in the relevant notes), to whom I am indebted for generous help, especially Max Abramovitz, George Dudley, and Harmon Goldstone. Bernadette O'Toole, Harrison's secretary for over forty years, provided many facts about his life and work. James W. Aston, Dr. David Axelrod, Colonel Frederick C. Badger, Sam Bleecker, Anthony Bliss, Flora Brennan, Gordon Bunshaft, John Byron, Dr. Donald Campbell, Brad Clark, Fritz Close, Thaddeus Crapster, Martha Dalrymple, Richard Dana, Cliff Dodge, Cyril Harris, the late Michael Harris and his wife, Rosalyn, Alexander Hood, Arthur Houghton, Jr., Grant Indorf, Barry Isenberg, Steven Izenour, Philip Johnson, Robert Klein, the late Irving Kolodin, John Kossman, Morris Lapidus, Emmerich Levatich, Rushmore H. Mariner, Thomas McCormick, Porter McCray, Carl Morse, Michael Mostoller, Oscar Nitzchke, Perry Prentice, Walter Relihan, Richard Rose, William Schuman, Mr. and Mrs. Charles Spofford, Frank Stanton, Julian Street, Jr., General William W. Wanamaker, Robert White, Malcolm Wilson, Edgar Young, and William Zeckendorf, Jr., all were helpful. Further thanks go to the staff at the following institutions and offices: at Columbia University's Avery Library, Herbert Mitchell and Janet Parks; at Dartmouth College, Jacqueline Baas, Werner Bentley, and Churchill Lathrope; at Davis, Polk, Wardwell, Jean Kelly; at the Metropolitan Opera Archive, Robert Tuggle; at the *New Yorker*, Helen Stark; at the New York Public Library, John Stinson; at the Rockefeller Family Archive Center, Joseph Ernst; at Rockefeller University, Richard Dana; at Time, Inc., Elaine Felsher; and at the United Nations Archive, Alf M. E. Erlandsson.

To my mother and the memory of my father

Chapter 1

In Worcester and Boston

"That nook of the world smiles for me beyond all others."

Quoted by Harrison from *Horace, Odes,* II.6.13–14

"Show your teeth Teddy or they won't know you!"[1] From the lofty perch of his father's shoulders, the seven-year-old Wallace Kirkman Harrison heard the shout of the crowd and watched the dashing figure of President Theodore Roosevelt as he rode his horse on past. The year was 1902, and the place was Worcester, Massachusetts. Roosevelt had just succeeded the murdered McKinley as president and was in Worcester to attend the New England Fair. The Roosevelt incident was Harrison's first memory of the city where he was born on September 28, 1895, and where he spent his first twenty-one years. For him Worcester was "wonderful, because you were free to do anything you pleased as long as you didn't interfere with your neighbor" (Fig. 1).

Worcester was a manufacturing city fifty miles west of Boston, where, after the Civil War, four major industries developed: wire, textiles, grinding wheels, and envelopes. These and other, smaller manufacturers were home-owned, and so successful that by the latter part of the nineteenth century Worcester's population had reached 118,000, making it the second largest city in Massachusetts and the third largest in New England.

By the time the new president appeared in the city, most of its streets had been paved with the exception of Harrison's modest neighborhood in the southern part of town, where there were still dirt roads lit by gas lamps. Traffic consisted mainly of horses and buggies and many bicycles: the quietness of early evening was broken only by the shouts of children playing.

Worcester had been settled in the latter part of the seventeenth century by a handful of English-born Puritans from Boston, where a strict work ethic and religious intolerance had earned them considerable dislike. Whatever they lacked in popularity, however, was compensated by hard work and efficiency. In the small Massachusetts communities that became mill towns, they quickly set up authoritative groups to monitor living conditions. In time, they accepted the presence in their midst of other religious and ethnic groups, notably the Scotch-Irish Presbyterians, but the Congregationalist legacy survived in Worcester well into the twentieth century. It would have a profound effect on Harrison.

1. W. K. Harrison (far left) with schoolmates in Worcester, Massachusetts (c. 1905).

In notes for *The Ambassadors*, Henry James said of Worcester: "an American city of the second order—not such a place either as New York, as Boston or as Chicago, but a New England important local centre... an old and enlightened Eastern community."[2] By the 1890s, this "enlightened community" boasted a small opera house, an art museum, a new free library, several educational institutions, and a theater in which Edwin Booth and Sarah Bernhardt performed.

At the time of Harrison's third birthday, Worcester was preparing to celebrate its fiftieth as a member of the commonwealth of Massachusetts. The most important of the events scheduled was the dedication of a handsome, new pink granite city hall, built to replace the original wooden building. Not surprisingly for a city of Worcester's cultural sophistication, the competition for the city hall had been won by one of Boston's leading architectural firms, Peabody and Stearns.[3] In the style of a Renaissance palazzo, it was intersected at its center by a replica of Florence's Palazzo Vecchio Campanile, at the bottom of which a baroque double stairway curved gracefully down from the main entrance. The building was typical of the eclectic, Beaux-Arts manner that prevailed during Harrison's youth (Fig. 2). The contractor for the building was O. W. Norcross, with whom Harrison would begin his precocious professional life just eleven years later.

Harrison's home in Worcester was far removed from the city's distinguished public buildings and great mansions. He grew up in one of the innumerable triple-decker clapboard houses built throughout New England between the end of the Civil War and the 1930s for new workers, often European immigrants, who came to settle in industrial areas.[4] His parents paid fifteen dollars a month for the second floor. Harrison remembered a parlor—used only for celebrations and funerals; it contained a matching set of furniture and a machine-made copy of a French tapestry; a kitchen, a living room, two bedrooms, and a bath completed the floor. Like its neighbors, the house had front porches at each level, modest front and side yards, and a larger back yard in which four or five fruit trees received plenty of sun and protection

from the wind. It was inexpensive housing that provided ample light and air, and Harrison often looked back to it as an ideal when later he struggled with the problems of low-cost housing in New York City (Fig. 3).

Harrison was the only child of middle-aged parents; his mother, Rachel, was over forty and his father, James, was fifty when he was born. The families of both parents had come from Yorkshire, England, where Rachel Kirkman, her brother, and three sisters worked in factories related to the textile industries of Yorkshire and Lancashire. The Kirkmans had emigrated to America in the 1870s at a time of extensive mill strikes in England.

Harrison's father was born in Worcester, where he started out as a molder in a local iron foundry and rose to become superintendent of a machine and iron company, Rice, Barton and Fales, "builders of modern, fast running and heavy fourdrinier and cylinder machines for making paper and drying pulp."[5] The two grand passions of his life were horses and the Elks fraternal order. Harrison recalled that though a poor man, his father would save up to buy some tired old racer he could run for the fun of it. And a few times a year, he treated himself to a day at White City, a summer pleasure resort on Lake Quinsigamond near Worcester that was looked upon by the locals as a place of perdition; and indeed, there he indulged his tendency to drink.

In the early 1900s life seemed simple in Worcester. The streets in many places were still bordered by fields and there was a pond where children skied on old hockey sticks in winter and swam and fished for pickerel and perch in summer.[6] This child's paradise ended abruptly for Harrison at the age of fourteen when his mother died from a stroke. Rachel Harrison's death was a tragedy for father and son. It was the second time James was widowed; his first marriage had left him with a son twenty years older than Wallace, with whom the latter had little in common. But in addition to the emotional loss Wallace suffered, the death of his mother had a dramatic effect on the circumstances of his life.

Without his wife's restraining influence, James succumbed quickly to a life of dissipation. One day he simply disappeared, leaving Wallace, then only a freshman in high school, to fend for himself. He could not possibly

2. Peabody & Stearns, City Hall, Worcester (1898).

3. Tenement housing, Worcester (c. 1900).

remain in school; he had to find a job. Rather than take the first opportunity that came along, the young man chose to consider his options. Harrison realized the advantage of living in a relatively small city like Worcester, where "you met everybody—at the skating rink in winter, or in the free public parks, or perhaps church." It was at the Episcopalian church that Harrison had met the well-liked and respected Louis N. Wilson, to whom he turned for advice.

The remarkable "Dr." Wilson, a self-taught Englishman in his fifties—like Harrison's family, from Yorkshire—had risen from workman in a New Jersey woolen mill to the prestigious position of librarian at Worcester's Clark Institute (later Clark University). Wilson suggested two fields for career possibilities: chemistry, which was regarded as the up-and-coming science of the day, and architecture, which Wilson believed to be the leading art form. Harrison claimed that he didn't even know how to spell "architect" at the time, but with a letter from Wilson he got a three-dollar-per-week job as office boy at O. W. Norcross, one of the most important construction companies in the country.[7]

Harrison moved to simpler lodgings—a room he rented from the mother of Norcross's head office boy, Harry Winchester. The two young men got up every morning at 6:30 and walked two miles to their place of work, where they spent every weekday from 8:00 to 5:00, and Saturday mornings, in fierce competition with one another. At night they put their feet up on the big stove in the dining room, reading everything they could get their hands on that might be taught in the high-school classes they were unable to attend.

James and Orlando Norcross, two brothers from Maine, had formed their partnership in 1864. By 1897, when James retired, Orlando was running the firm. Ironically, in view of Harrison's later career, his first employer had no interest in skyscrapers, and his failure to adapt to the new building type eventually led to the firm's closing in 1923. Harrison remembered the heavy, walrus-moustached Orlando as a "four-foot-high-by-four-foot-wide terror, who was always running in order to impress the others and keep them on their toes." Even at his young age, Harrison sensed the firm would go out

of business, because it relied too heavily on the owner alone. Orlando was a prolific inventor of new techniques of building, with a serious claim to the creation of the beamless flat-slab system of reinforced concrete, but his brother had been the businessman, and without him Orlando never managed to capitalize on his innovations.[8] On the rare occasions when they came into direct contact, Orlando never failed to tell Harrison that only fools practiced architecture; the single, most honest occupation was that of the farmer.[9]

Harrison began his apprenticeship operating the blueprint machine. After he had worked diligently with blueprints for over a year he had his first real architectural experience: drawing diagrams for the local stone-cutting shop to indicate the size and shape of stones for a Gothic church in Fall River. Once he had mastered the technique, he went on to make similar drawings for other projects that may well have included Carrère and Hastings's New York Public Library, which Norcross was completing at this time.

Despite his progress at Norcross, Harrison believed the world was passing him by. The fact that the contractor merely executed architects' plans disturbed him, for he longed to be among those who decided not just how but *what* to build. He determined at least to ask for a raise, approaching Norcross's son-in-law, Harry Gross, who responded by taking him into his office and, carefully explaining that his timing was inopportune, advised him to "wait until a nice cool day comes and I have a cigar in my mouth after a good lunch."

Harrison tired of waiting. Throughout his life he would be able to act quickly and decisively under difficult circumstances, an ability that he exercised now. He applied for a position as junior draftsman with Frost & Chamberlain, a leading Worcester architectural firm. Harrison got the nine-dollar-a-week job, having arrived with the following letter of recommendation, dated March 12, 1913:

To Whom It May Concern:

The bearer, Wallace Harrison, has been employed by Norcross Bros. Co. for several years and for two years has been making shop drawings and diagrams for stonework. He is a man of good habits and a willing worker, anxious to learn everything that will benefit both himself and his employers.

Chief Draughtsman, Stone Dept.—
Very truly yours, C. P. Tabor————

Chief Draughtsman, Construction Dept.—
John S. Allen————

Appraised: Henry J. Gross, Secretary[10]—

The Frost & Chamberlain offices were in the State Mutual Building, and Harrison enjoyed being one of five or six young draftsmen working in what he described as "a beautiful office building on a top floor where the sun came in on your back as you leaned over the drafting board. Nobody pushed. The bosses had their two games of golf a week, and the men, sometimes with a lady, took long lunch hours to see an occasional show at the art museum."

After he joined Frost & Chamberlain, Harrison enrolled in a series of night courses in structural engineering at Worcester Polytechnic, a tuition-free institute created in the mid-nineteenth century to meet the industrialized city's need for technicians. Among other courses he took were those taught by Arthur W. French, who had worked extensively on the problem of flat-slab concrete buildings. The classes were perfect preparation for some of the commissions then at Frost & Chamberlain—a number of large factories at Niagara Falls and other sites along the Canadian border—and Harrison was given a relatively free hand to design the concrete frames for these large mill structures.

Concrete is reinforced by pouring it around steel rods. At the time Harrison was working on factories for Frost & Chamberlain, however, there were few rules for what has now become a standard procedure, and only when he had completed his drawings did he realize he had specified so much steel that no room remained for the concrete! He never forgot this practical lesson.

At Frost & Chamberlain, Harrison's work was limited mainly to drafting. He continued to ask the why and how of architecture, but to his disappointment he received few answers. His restlessness led him to Boston, a two-hour, fifty-cent trolley ride away. In the elegant Back Bay area, the open-sided trolley stopped within a few blocks of Copley Square, with its two architectural masterpieces: H. H. Richardson's dramatic Trinity Church (1877) and McKim, Mead & White's graceful, classicizing Boston Public Library (1895).

The Boston Public Library was one of two Boston institutions (the other was the Boston Architectural Club) that exerted a powerful influence on the young man. Among the finest of the buildings produced by McKim, Mead & White, the library is a remarkably successful realization of the Beaux-Arts ideal of integrating architecture with the fine arts. Charles Follen McKim designed it in the grand Beaux-Arts manner; he selected with great care both the materials to be used for the building and the artists to decorate it. Louis Saint-Gaudens sculpted the marble lions on the yellow Siena marble grand staircase, for which the celebrated French artist Puvis de Chavannes painted allegorical murals. Daniel Chester French cast bronze doors for the main entrance, and Edwin Austin Abbey painted a frieze, *The Quest of the Holy Grail*, to adorn the book delivery room. John Singer Sargent created his most ambitious mural, *Judaism and Christianity*, for the third floor.[11] In this grandiose setting Harrison spent hours studying books on architecture, diligently copying their illustrations.

Until the latter part of the nineteenth century, no formal school curricula or professional standards existed for architects in America; anyone could call himself an architect and go into practice.[12] Aspiring architects usually served an apprenticeship with an established firm to learn the rudiments of the profession. Those who could afford to went abroad to the Ecole des Beaux-Arts in Paris, which had been in existence for more than two hundred years. (Its structure modified in 1968, the school continues to this day.) Compared with what was available in America, it was a model of order, discipline, and excellence. By 1894 the Society of Beaux-Arts Architects had been founded in the United States and maintained ateliers in various cities based on the teaching methods of the Paris Ecole.

One such atelier was set up in the Boston Architectural Club, which Harrison began to attend in 1914 at the recommendation of his employers at Frost & Chamberlain. The club had been founded in 1889 by a select group of Boston architects to encourage those interested in the profession with lectures, exhibitions, entertainment, and instruction provided by members. In 1911 the club acquired a building near the State House, for which the noted neo-Gothicist Ralph Adams Cram designed a two-story great hall for lectures and exhibition space. There was also a library and several studios.[13]

The club's membership included Boston's outstanding young architects of the day, among them Guy Lowell (architect of a distinguished building for the Museum of Fine Arts), William G. Perry, Thomas Mott Shaw, and Andrew H. Hepburn. The club's president, Henry R. Shepley, was the son of a member of the H. H. Richardson office. Almost without exception the members were from Boston's Brahmin families—most had graduated from Harvard and had attended the Ecole des Beaux-Arts for at least a year. In their late twenties and early thirties at the time Harrison knew them, Shepley and his peers somehow appeared older to the twenty-year-old from Worcester. To Harrison the group was typified by Shepley, with "his older Boston look, restricted conversation and slow-moving but thorough approach to things"; even more important to Harrison, Shepley was "a completely good person in every way." These men "lived architecture. You learned more from your contact with them than you could have in any other way."

Harrison learned "more" in the broadest sense of the word—he learned how commissions were obtained and how they were carried out. His teachers combined high cultural and intellectual standards with strict principles of professional conduct set by the Puritan work ethic. But their designs were as conservative as their backgrounds, consisting in large part of institutional buildings rigorously planned according to Beaux-Art precepts.

As important to Harrison as the classes was his introduction to the Museum of Fine Arts by one of the club's members. The experience of looking at the Old Master paintings with someone who shared his interests and who could discuss the works knowledgeably was a revelation: "I felt I had not really been able to penetrate the world of art until I went to Boston."

Harrison worked full time at Frost & Chamberlain. Besides his job he attended night classes at the Worcester Polytechnic, and in Boston he was enrolled at the Architectural Club studio and spent his Saturdays at the library, copying elevations and sections from the works on architecture. The schedule was demanding, but for Harrison it was a marvelously exciting adventure that provided him with a constant stream of new discoveries. The more he learned, the more questions there seemed to be: "Classic architecture—yes, he now knew what that meant, but what had been the civilization that produced this architecture, and if you were trying to do it yourself, where did you put a column or a cornice, and why?" To the end of his life Harrison never stopped asking the questions he asked as a student: "How do you draw a cornice—as it is or as it looks? From the street, a cornice looks like two equal curves, but it is really *flatter* at the top and *deeper* at the bottom. The flatness does all sorts of things to the way light hits the cornice and the shadows it casts. . . . This is the sort of stuff I don't know much about still."

The answer to one of his questions became evident with completion of the imposing twelve-story Park Office Building designed by Cross & Cross of New York at Worcester's prime downtown location. The new building made Harrison realize that "when you wanted a big office building, they picked a big New York architect. . . . I wanted to be with the people who did that sort of work."[14]

And so in July 1916, at the age of twenty-one and with all of thirty-five dollars in savings, Harrison went to New York, where he moved into a boarding house on West Twenty-third Street. With no professional introductions to the big city and only his skills, personality, and clean-cut good-looks to recommend him, he did not hesitate to make his first application for work at the offices of McKim, Mead & White, unquestionably the era's leading American architects.

Chapter 2

In New York; World War I

In 1916 the cheapest way to go from Worcester to New York was by water. At about 10:30 in the evening a boat picked up passengers at Fall River and sailed out of Rhode Island Sound, along the coasts of Rhode Island and Connecticut, back of Long Island, and under the construction of Hell Gate Bridge (1917), to dock at the New York fish market by 5:30 the following morning. Harrison remembered that

> you bought your ticket when you got aboard; it entitled you to the privacy of a tiny space behind a closed door with a single bed in it; there were public toilets in the passageway; they didn't give you dinner or breakfast. My first impression of the city was the awful smell of the fish market. I had expected New York to be more vertical than it was; it was horizontal.[1]

New York in 1916 was *not*, of course, all horizontal. It had over a thousand buildings of eleven stories or more and a number of soaring towers. Among these were the fifty-six-story Woolworth Building (1913) and the thirty-story Equitable Building (1915), which for years held the titles respectively of the tallest and the biggest buildings in the world. Most of the tall buildings were in lower Manhattan. Mid- and uptown Manhattan were filled with brownstones and other town houses, interspersed with new apartment buildings for the well-to-do.

In 1916 the city's population was just under six million, and the elevated railways daily took in three million five-cent fares. Subways were under construction according to contracts later proved fraudulent. Double-decker buses ran on Fifth Avenue and Riverside Drive, but the ubiquitous electric trolleys were all on strike during the last half of the year.

McKim, Mead & White had lost the original partners to death or senility; a new group was in charge. The office was completing some of its outstanding buildings in New York, the Municipal Building[2] and the imposing additions to the Metropolitan Museum of Art among them. Others, scattered throughout the northeastern states, were rising; notable among them today, the New York Racquet and Tennis Club (1919). These buildings exemplify the firm's work, predominantly styled in a version of the American Neo-renaissance manner, based on motifs from Imperial Roman and Italian Renaissance architecture, and usually carried out in rich materials intricately detailed. McKim, Mead & White's architectural preeminence was matched by its wealth, the result of the firm's practice of taking a portion of fees in the stocks of its commercial clients. Thus it worked with plutocratic and official clients on an equal footing and, with similarly oriented colleagues, dominated the architecture, planning, and landscaping of the country.[3] The firm and its works were solidly based on standards set by the Ecole des Beaux-Arts and this also determined the effective, imposing drawings produced for clients in flawlessly precise plans, elevations, perspectives, and sections brilliantly inked and colored.[4]

Harrison was interviewed at McKim, Mead & White by William Kendall, who had been a partner for ten years and would become a senior partner three years later. As McKim's chief assistant, he had been responsible for a large part of the design and construction of some of the firm's most important buildings.[5] Kendall was known for the perfect little sketches he made at exceptionally small scale, which allowed him to see the entirety of whatever he was working on.[6]

Kendall, scion of a prominent New England family, was educated at Harvard and the Massachusetts Institute of Technology School of Architecture, followed by three years' study and travel in France and Italy. He was affiliated as trustee or member with institutions such as the American Academy in Rome whose building he designed. A widower, Kendall chose to live at the Mansfield Hotel on West Forty-fourth Street, which described itself as "a unique residence for men of taste and discrimination." The hotel was across the street from the Harvard Club, where Kendall took all his meals. His life followed a systematic path from hotel to office to club and back. On first meeting him, Harrison decided he was "the most distinguished guy I ever saw.... The strongest expletive he ever uttered was 'oh my goodness goodness!'"

The job interview took place on a Friday at the end of July. Predictably, a few hours study at the Boston Architectural Club studio did not measure up to Kendall's standards for a McKim, Mead & White draftsman. But Harrison prevailed on Kendall to look at some of his drawings. When he returned on Monday, Kendall simply said, "I found you a job." One of the partners, Teunis Van der Bent, "a very nice middle-class Dutchman who wore a wing collar, a big tie and a long three-quarter-length coat that made him look like a burgher in one of Rembrandt's paintings," had just finished two wings of Bellevue Hospital and had decided to write a book on hospital design. He needed a draftsman to help him, and if Harrison worked satisfactorily without pay for three weeks he would be engaged for twenty dollars per week.

At the offices of McKim, Mead & White, in the Architects' Building at 101 Park Avenue, Harrison became one of almost a hundred draftsmen, none of whom seemed to remain with the firm for very long. One well-to-do young architect, Frederick King, arrived at work daily in a chauffeur-driven car; in later years King was to become a good friend of Harrison. But, at the time, it was Henry Bacon, an older man, who attracted Harrison's attention. An architect who had worked for the firm in the 1890s, he now had his own office on the same floor.[7] Harrison described him as

> a little fellow in one room, with just a drawing board and a chair. He came in early every morning and worked all day with a stubby cigarette in the corner of his mouth.... he drew every detail for the Lincoln Memorial [dedicated 1922], *alone.* He spent a great part of his adult life on it.

The effort was recognized, for in 1923 Bacon was awarded the American Institute of Architects' gold medal in a torchlit ceremony during which he was pulled on a barge by architectural students down the Mall's reflecting pool!

Harrison quickly learned what jobs to avoid. Making innumerable "change drawings" for the Municipal Building (adapting space for new occupants) was one; another was detailing double doors between which to hang clothes for pressing at the Pennsylvania Hotel (1919; now the Penta).

4. Harvey Wiley Corbett.

One of Harrison's early jobs was on the Racquet and Tennis Club (1919), a commission that came to the firm around the time of his arrival. Kendall had designed an Italianate palazzo complete with a rusticated base and an arched loggia inspired by the garden façade of the Palazzo Farnese in Rome. Harrison made full-scale cardboard models showing every stone in the building's high ground floor.

Soon after he joined the firm, Harrison was urged by colleagues to train further at one of the ateliers active in New York directed by Harvey Wiley Corbett (Fig. 4). As he climbed the four flights of stairs above Keen's Chop House at Thirty-sixth Street east of Sixth Avenue to Corbett's atelier, not even his most ambitious fantasies included eventual partnership with this architect, who would provide the commission that launched Harrison's career.

Tall, handsome, and gray haired, Corbett was forty-three at the time, with a gift of the gab and a lilt to his voice. As Harrison soon found out, "he knew what he was talking about. But he was convinced you could have a good time if you wanted to, even if the other fellows were bastards; all you had to do was bawl them out."

Corbett had received a B.S. in engineering from the University of California in 1895 and his diploma from the Ecole des Beaux-Arts in Paris five years later, with awards for architecture, mathematics, modeling, and freehand drawing. His first job had been in the office of Cass Gilbert in 1901. In 1903 he had formed his own firm with F. Livingston Pell and in 1912 had gone into partnership with a tough midwesterner of German origin, Frank J. Helmle.

From 1907 to 1909 Corbett had directed an atelier for the Columbia University School of Architecture. Continuing as critic and lecturer at Columbia from 1909 to 1935, he set up his own atelier, on West Thirty-sixth Street, which was open to anyone he approved. As in France, membership in the New York ateliers consisted of *anciens*, upperclassmen who had been attending the studio for at least a couple of years, and *nouveaux*, newcomers who were subjected to the kind of hazing typical of student life. The atelier was dominated by the *maître*, in this case Corbett, with the assistance of a *massier*, an upperclassman elected by his peers.

There were about twenty men in Corbett's atelier. Harrison described the assignment of a project:

> On Saturday, they gave you a program that was like a letter from a client (the kind of letter an architect might receive telling him what the client expected of the building he was commissioning). You made as many schemes as possible and judged your own scheme by the end of the day. You then made one formal sketch of this particular scheme from which you developed the project.

During this period, Harrison's workday at McKim's would end at five o'clock with the scramble to get something to eat before arriving at Corbett's atelier thirty minutes later, where he would spend three to four hours at his drawing board. He claimed that Corbett

> was the first person to give me the answers I'd been looking for. He taught us the why of drawings, and if there wasn't any good reason for things being as tradition ruled they should be, he said so. You couldn't get that kind of answer at McKim's. McKim, Mead & White was the best—and the end—of the Renaissance. The firm stopped there. You don't learn architecture just by doing it, you learn by talking with people—anybody who is cultivated and knows his history. It's the personal contact that counts.[8]

The young architect struck up a friendship with Corbett and discovered he could learn most from him when they walked through the city together. At the suggestion of his minister in Worcester, Harrison had moved to the parish house of the Calvary Episcopal Church, just a few blocks away from Corbett's home.[9] At the end of the evening's work they often left the atelier in each other's company. Their route took them past McKim's monumental Pennsylvania Station (1911), where Corbett often tarried to talk heatedly about some aspect of the building, punctuating his remarks with a gesture of his cane. Corbett showed, for example, how McKim had followed Roman precedent by planning the columns at either end of the great façade colonnade two to three inches closer to each other than those in between, and he questioned the use of columns that were aesthetically pleasing but created severe traffic problems for the taxis that swarmed through them daily.[10]

Harrison began to spend some time with young students from Corbett's atelier. Together with young churchmen from the parish house where he lived, they were his first companions in New York. Both groups attracted him for the same reason: "They were people you could talk to and learn from."

Harrison was learning, and learning quickly, from his new experiences. He did not have time to visit the New York art galleries, but he made one significant exception: the Léon Bakst show that had opened at the Scott & Fowles Gallery in February 1916. Bakst had designed a number of sets for Diaghilev's Ballets Russes, which performed its second season in New York that year. The exotic, brightly colored sets and costumes and the startling, unfamiliar music by Stravinsky, Prokofiev, and Satie were a revelation to Harrison. He attended the dance as often as possible, and saw Nijinsky perform in *Petrouchka* and *Schéhérazade*, recalling that Nijinsky generated such excitement that in the middle of the ballet a woman stood up and shouted, "Leap again, beautiful creature, leap again!"

Harrison also began to make a weekly excursion to the Metropolitan Museum of Art, where he remembered being particularly attracted to the rooms that included paintings by Manet, Cézanne, and Degas.

The handsome young man was apparently cool to the city's more frivolous institutions—"Castle House," where Manhattan's youth flocked to learn the steps of the two new dance crazes, the tango and the turkey trot; the many popular cabarets and vaudeville theaters; the Ziegfeld Theater with its Follies; or the jazz clubs packed with people. The most profound experience, which had important implications for his future, was his first visit to the Metropolitan Opera. The 1916–17 season opened under the menacing cloud of World War I. Giulio Gatti-Casazza, the renowned manager of the company, stated publicly that "if the war continues another year or two, it may be impossible to give opera."[11] The opening-night performance was Bizet's *Les Pêcheurs de Perles*, with Enrico Caruso and Frieda Hempel, a production that enjoyed enormous success. Harrison was overwhelmed and intrigued by the idea that several art forms—music, dance, theater, and design—could be represented simultaneously. Many years later he claimed it was this visit to the opera that made him realize how little he knew at this period of his life: "I was like a clear glass bowl into which nothing had yet been put."

When the United States entered World War I in the spring of 1917, it was a matter of course for Harrison to enlist in the armed services. He first signed up for a weekly class in navigation at Columbia University and joined the Naval Coastal Defense Reserve. In July 1917, he was called to active duty as a quartermaster second class (Fig. 5). Within a few months he had been commissioned ensign and shipped out of New London, Connecticut. Harrison was assigned to Submarine-Chaser 80, the N.M.S. *Glasgow*, as second-in-command to Lieutenant Walter Blumenthal, a recent Yale graduate; Blumenthal and Harrison struck up a warm friendship that persisted through their two years of duty together.

The subchaser was a wooden ship, 110 feet long, with a fifteen-foot beam, and a maximum speed of seventeen knots. It held twenty-six officers and men. In September 1917, two convoys of subchasers were dispatched to Europe: one took the north route around England to Iceland; the other, Harrison's convoy, headed for the Mediterranean via Bermuda and the Azores. The formation was under the command of Rear Admiral "Juggy" Nelson, remembered by Harrison as having a reputation for getting lost. The crew consisted largely of firemen and policemen from Chicago, whose lack of experience contributed to a number of problems. Harrison recalled this episode in his life with good humor despite a series of mishaps.

In Bermuda, he was struck by "all the houses in white stone cut with a handsaw and giving a wonderful

5. Harrison (center), Quartermaster Second Class (1917).

12

feeling of cleanliness." Nineteen years later, a house in Bermuda—for his brother-in-law, David Milton—was to be his first commission as an independent architect. The Azores provided Harrison with his first sight of European architecture. In the port town of Ponta Delgada he noted baroque churches with elaborately carved door pilasters and window surrounds in dark volcanic stone contrasting dramatically with the whitewashed walls.

After a short stop at Lisbon the convoy proceeded to Gibraltar, where Harrison's first direct encounter with war left a vivid image. Convoys of merchant vessels with supplies for India and Japan were anchored in the harbor. From time to time, a German submarine managed to sink a few ships:

> The boats always shone brightly in the sun in sharp contrast to the dull rocks guarding the harbor's entrance. When a boat was hit, it always went down stern first, with the bow up; it just slid down, and a million dollars sank away.

The SC 80 took about a month to reach her destination at Otranto, where American, French, and English vessels patrolled the Strait—a forty-five-mile strip between Cape Linguetta (Kepi Gjuhëzës) in Albania and the tip of Italy's heel. The operation was designed to prevent Austrian submarines based four hundred miles north from breaking out of the Adriatic into the Mediterranean.[12]

It was a bittersweet time. Harrison described the thrill of being on the sea at daybreak, looking across at the silhouetted hills that divided the brilliant blues of sky and sea; he savored the gentleness of the Mediterranean, its bright colors, and the scent of unfamiliar herbs. But he also experienced enemy shells and mines near the ship. Finally, the subchaser entered the Bay of Cattaro (Kotor), where a large party of the Austrian Navy was anchored. Access to the wide, natural harbor was a passage of about eighty feet, protected by enemy guns on both sides, which fired warning shots at the approaching Americans. As Harrison's ship started down the passage with other American vessels, the *Waldeck Rousseau*, a

French cruiser, signaled them to wait until she had cleared the way. When they penetrated the harbor, they received another signal from the French cruiser, the announcement they all had been awaiting: "*L'armistice est signée*" (November 11, 1918).

The SC 80 was immediately ordered to proceed along the Dalmatian coast to Spalato (Split), where Harrison encountered Roman architecture for the first time. The emperor Diocletian had built a sumptuous fortified palace here (293–305), and the young architect was deeply affected by the grandeur of its remains.

From Spalato, the SC 80 was sent back to Cattaro, where Harrison and Blumenthal acted as American representatives at the armistice talks until experienced diplomats could take over. Because he spoke German, Blumenthal received the top commission; Harrison received a working commission. Their immediate priority was to organize a quick takeover of the Austrian ships. Three days after the Americans arrived at Cattaro the German, Austrian, and American navy officers mingled freely. Harrison's success as a negotiator forecast his subsequent mastery of this role.

After a pleasant two months in Cattaro, their mission was over. The ship was ordered to wait until spring for the home crossing and the SC 80 put in at Marseille for a week. Harrison and Blumenthal received four-day leaves. They decided to separate, with Harrison choosing Paris, where his prime interest was to visit the Ecole des Beaux-Arts. The trip had a decisive influence on his life.

The French capital had suffered little physical damage and relatively few deaths during the war. The Red Cross had set up canteens in the major railroad stations, and dormitories for the soldiers who had survived. True to form, Harrison shunned the city's hedonistic temptations. Instead he investigated how the Ecole des Beaux-Arts functioned, for he was determined to attend it as soon as possible.

Chapter 3

To Paris and back

Following his discharge from the Navy, Harrison returned to his room at the Calvary parsonage and his job at McKim, Mead & White. But his prospects were bleak. His exposure to Europe made him realize that he had to escape the office routine and see more of what he had glimpsed all too briefly. McKim, Mead & White had an excellent architectural library, and he had continued to learn a great deal from Corbett, but he now felt the need to examine things for himself. His one thought was to return to Paris:

> For the first time in my life I wasn't broke. I'd saved up over a thousand dollars in the Navy. The only catch would be getting into the Beaux-Arts. The admission exam has always been pretty brutal. In my day, it lasted twelve hours, and you had to make a grade of seventy to pass. Most of the candidates spent six months in a preparatory atelier before they took the exam. Apparently the object of the school was to see not how many students it could get, but how few.[1]

In preparation for his entry examination, Harrison took classes in mathematics at Columbia and added to the interminable hours he spent in Corbett's atelier. His frugal life paid off. By October of 1920, he had saved enough money to go to Paris, where he joined an atelier—the first step toward admission to the Ecole des Beaux-Arts.

The tuition-free Ecole was the descendant of Louis XIV's Académie Royale d'Architecture; it was based on the belief that universal principles of architecture could be established that would produce perfect designs. The paradigms of these principles were the great buildings and texts of Roman antiquity and the Italian Renaissance. The academic structure was like that of a step-pyramid: the top big enough for only one man, the *patron*; below him the competitors for the Grand Prix; then the first-class students; the second-class students; and, at the base of the pyramid, the *aspirants*, those who were preparing for admission. An *aspirant* had to be between fifteen and thirty years of age and sponsored by the *patron* of an atelier. The school's written and oral entrance exams tested mathematics, descriptive geometry, history, drawing—usually of an ornament cast—and architectural design.[2]

Attendance at the Ecole des Beaux-Arts was considered mandatory for serious American architects at this time. It was one of several factors attracting Americans to Paris, where the English-speaking colony in the early 1920s was large enough to support publication of no fewer than three daily English-language newspapers. Architecture students met at the Café Flore, a block behind the Ecole on the boulevard Saint-Germain, or for dinner at the Pré-aux-Clercs, near the Law School, and talked about architecture, from the allotment of closet space at the ateliers to the use of extensive glazing on ground floors and, of course, the work of the rising modernists—Le Corbusier, Gropius, Mies. These men were presenting new ideas contradicting all established rules, challenging the hierarchical, axial plans of the Beaux-Arts and its traditional ornamented façades with asymmetry, plain surfaces, and sleek, machine-like detailing.

The most famous atelier in Paris was that of Victor Laloux, architect of the Gare d'Orsay—the overblown railroad station and hotel complex (now transformed into a museum) spread along the Seine's Left Bank, between the Esplanade des Invalides and the Ecole des Beaux-Arts. Harrison felt no affinity to this kind of design; besides, he suspected that the Laloux atelier would be far too crowded for the *patron* to provide individual criticism.

Shortly after arriving in Paris, Harrison met Robert ("Bobby") Perry Rodgers, who had graduated from Harvard three years earlier. Rodgers suggested the atelier of Gustave Umbdenstock, an Alsatian, who was less influential than the Paris-born *patrons*. Because of his formidable military bearing and reputation as a severe disciplinarian, Umbdenstock was referred to as "the Colonel." Harrison went to see him and liked him immediately: "He had his own style, his own method of expression and he was so sure of everything."[3] The *patron*'s certainty was particularly appealing to the New England beginner, who was sure of nothing.

Umbdenstock was in his early fifties at this time. To the young American he appeared a gruff old man, with a shaggy Clemenceau mustache and a dented derby ever-present on his head. His atelier was located above a quiet courtyard just a block from the Ecole. Umbdenstock did not attract many Americans, but his atelier was made colorful by the presence of numerous Rumanian students—uninhibited, often talented—who considered France their intellectual home but lived for the day when, studies completed, they could return to their own country. In addition, the ground floor of Umbdenstock's building was occupied by Raymond Duncan, Isadora's eccentric brother, and a group of his disciples who had adopted a way of life they believed imitated ancient Greece. Both men and women wore full-length robes, their feet shod in sandals and their heads crowned with long, flowing locks. Nothing could have been more alien to the conservative old Colonel, who walked sternly around the studio instilling discipline in his thirty students.

Of the modernists discussed by his peers, Harrison was particularly intrigued by Le Corbusier, who had set up office in Paris in 1917. Harrison read his revolutionary ideas in Le Corbusier's magazine, *L'Esprit Nouveau*, which first appeared in 1920. Umbdenstock was unwavering in his animosity toward Le Corbusier and modernism in general. He was devoted to the Beaux-Arts belief that the solution to every plan lay in sculptural mass rather than in the modern linear approach to design. He would point to the Paris Opéra and the Bibliothèque Nationale, for him (as they were to become for Harrison) the best examples of Beaux-Arts architecture.[4] At the time, Harrison rebelled inwardly against his *patron*'s intransigence, only later admitting that "the old Beaux-Arts things allowed you to straighten out plans into something easy to build." Eventually, at Rockefeller Center, the Rockefeller Institute, Lincoln Center, and the Albany Mall, Harrison was to work repeatedly with plans which had Beaux-Arts order, as indeed did many American architects at this time.

After entering Umbdenstock's atelier, Harrison enrolled at the Ecole des Beaux-Arts as an *aspirant* in October 1920. He was allowed to attend lectures, use the school's library, and sketch casts. He finally passed the tough Ecole examination and was formally admitted in

March 1921 (Figs. 6, 7). But the conservatism of the Ecole, the restrictions of its methodology, and the conceptual nature of the education it offered were difficult for Harrison to accept. He realized that many of his questions about architecture would remain unanswered, as they had been in the ateliers and offices in which he had worked in the United States. He became impatient to see more of the European architecture he had spent so much time studying in books and, after only a few months as a student, abandoned the idea of obtaining a degree from the Ecole.

Harrison began to make increasingly frequent trips with new American friends Bobby Rodgers and Paul Nelson. Rodgers was a plain, gangling man, awkward in his speaking manner, whose homespun ways belied his distinguished origins: he was a direct descendant of the naval hero Oliver Hazard Perry and the son of Admiral John Rodgers. In 1924 Rodgers and Harrison formed a partnership—the first for both of them—and remained long-term friends. Nelson, a Chicagoan who had graduated from Princeton two years before, also came from a wealthy family. Each man had comfortable lodgings on the Left Bank—Rodgers near the Panthéon, in a typical eighteenth-century house situated between courtyard and garden; Nelson in a hotel room that overlooked the Luxembourg Gardens. Nelson always claimed that the only person he really wanted to talk to was Gertrude Stein, but he must have made a few exceptions because he became friendly with Braque and eventually married a French woman. Rodgers introduced Harrison to the artists he knew, sparking Harrison's lifelong interest in personal contact with creative people.

Accompanied by Rodgers or Nelson, or both, Harrison set off in pursuit of Gothic towers. The spires and belfries of cathedrals—Chartres, Reims, Beauvais, and Bourges in France, Antwerp, Brussels, and Bruges in Belgium—interested him most. Harrison's natural affinity for height and scale was an early clue to the direction he would take later.

Post-war depreciated European currencies made travel less expensive for Americans. Harrison did not wait long before he embarked upon a train trip to Rome.

He had planned the trip even before he left New York, and the Eternal City exceeded his greatest expectations. To the end of his life, he claimed that it was the imposing architecture of imperial and Renaissance Rome that he prized above all other historical examples.

By spring of 1921, Harrison's relatively carefree life in Europe was over. His meager savings were exhausted and he had no choice but to return to New York. The depressed postwar city he had left just over a year before was eagerly shedding inhibitions and pursuing pleasure. The Jazz Age was in full swing.

Harrison's New York social life began to reach beyond his work and residence. The personable and handsome, blond, blue-eyed six-footer made an ideal escort for well-bred, affluent young women he met through friends like Bobby Rodgers, and he was soon invited to some of the city's most luxurious homes. One of these was the Cornelius Vanderbilt 2d house. It was designed by Richard Morris Hunt and George B. Post (1883 and 1892), an enormous red brick and white stone pile located at Fifth Avenue between Fifty-seventh and Fifty-eighth streets, the site now occupied by Bergdorf Goodman. Staffed by a platoon of servants uniformed in bright red coats, the Vanderbilt house symbolized a waning lifestyle. By the end of the decade practically all the great mansions on Fifth Avenue had been replaced by apartment houses.

Harrison also became a welcome guest of Walter and Margaret Damrosch. Walter and his brother Frank (both born in Breslau) were distinguished conductors, and their father, Leopold, was a pillar of the city's musical community. Walter and Margaret thought nothing of inviting thirty or forty dinner guests, who usually included outstanding figures of the art world. Harrison was of the same generation as the four Damrosch daughters, who brought to the family brownstone on East Sixty-first Street some of the new jazz musicians—one of whom, George Gershwin, became a frequent visitor. Harrison remembered Gershwin often playing the piano for the assembled company and his dignified host occasionally joining him in an after-dinner duet.[5]

6. Pen and ink drawing made by Harrison at the Ecole des Beaux-Arts.

7. Watercolor painted by Harrison at the Ecole des Beaux-Arts.

With some time at the Beaux-Arts to his credit, Harrison's reception at McKim, Mead & White was more enthusiastic than it had been five years before. Kendall was delighted to again have the services of this bright beginner and even asked him to work as his personal second draftsman. Harrison preferred to function on a free-lance basis, keeping his options open. Even though Kendall's insistence on discipline now seemed a pale copy of what he had encountered in Paris, Harrison had little tolerance for the limitations imposed on him. He longed for a situation where he would have more freedom of expression. Bertram Grosvenor Goodhue (1869–1924) provided him with that freedom:

> There was one office that was doing an entirely different kind of thing. I['d] been in McKim's office on the classic, and I always had one eye looking over to Goodhue's office, 'What are those fellows doing over there? How can I see another side of life?' I'd been in the meantime to Paris, and you know, had seen a little bit of Europe and what not, and then Goodhue offered me a job and... gee.... [6]

"Next to McKim, the most powerful influence on the aesthetics of Eclectic architecture was the firm of Cram and Goodhue." [7] Goodhue strongly opposed Beaux-Arts principles, favoring the apprentice system associated with medieval architecture. He believed that an architect should be not only designer, draftsman, and construction supervisor but composer, poet, playwright, and even actor.

Goodhue's mother had tried to awaken artistic instincts by acquainting her son with the works of the Pre-Raphaelites. Whether as a result of this or not, Goodhue became a superb draftsman. He began his apprenticeship in architecture at the age of fifteen with Renwick, Aspinwal & Russell in New York, soon leaving to work for Cram & Wentworth in Boston, and becoming a partner in 1892. Wentworth died in 1897 and in 1898 the firm became Cram, Goodhue & Ferguson, who were to build some of the most important neo-Gothic churches in the country, including the West Point Chapel (1910) and Saint Thomas's in New York (1920). In 1903, Goodhue was asked to open a branch of the Cram office in New York. He was an instant success, professionally and socially. Impulsive, opinionated, witty, and gregarious, Goodhue seemed always to have been the center of a circle of debonair friends who admired, respected, and loved him despite his frequent moodiness. [8]

In New York, Goodhue's attitude toward architecture began to diverge from Cram's. Cram favored strict adherence to historical precedent, and especially to English Gothic; Goodhue was more interested in aesthetic impact. As early as 1902 he designed a house in the manner of a Mediterranean villa, and thereafter he began to use Spanish Colonial models as frequently as he did medieval ones. In 1913, in a gesture of rebellion against the restraints imposed by the senior partner in Boston, Goodhue set up his own office. One of his designers was a wisp of a man from Cornwall named Ernest Thomas Jago, who taught Harrison a good deal about Gothic architecture. [9]

The 1920 commission for the National Academy of Sciences in Washington, D.C., further broadened Goodhue's design. The official requirement that government buildings in the nation's capital be in the classical tradition troubled him at first but—like many architects—he was prepared to switch styles. Once he had accepted a Greek ideal without specific historical basis for the National Academy of Sciences building, he went on to refine the style for his next important government commission, the Nebraska State Capitol. [10] In the summer of 1921, Harrison and his friend Rodgers—having decided in Paris that they wanted to practice together—went to work in the small Goodhue office on Fifth Avenue in the upper Forties. Harrison therefore was given the opportunity to work on both the National Academy and the Nebraska State Capitol. He had acquired a new assurance in Europe, and immediately became one of Goodhue's favorites, thereby provoking the jealousy of some senior staff members.

The National Academy was only three stories high, but its rectilinear classicism included the abundant use of

8. Bertram Grosvenor Goodhue, perspective of competition entry for Chicago Tribune Tower (1922).

sculpture. In October 1924, when it was nearing completion, Harrison published a short article about it in *Architecture* magazine in which he stated:

> The sculpture, which constitutes almost the only decoration, is by Lee Lawrie, who has collaborated with Mr. Goodhue on most of his important work. This combination of architect and sculptor, so vital in the production of great buildings, has rarely been equalled in modern times, and has produced what should prove to be an enduring contribution to the beauty of Washington.[11]

Harrison would always maintain this conviction that sculpture and painting were important complements to architecture.

The Nebraska State Capitol was the crowning point of Goodhue's career. Harrison attempted to do some of the working drawings for the project, but he soon learned that precise drafting was not among the skills he had acquired during his years in the ateliers. He could not seem to satisfy his demanding employer, who

> had a way of putting things together that I just couldn't. I'd put up columns with a pediment that simply didn't work. I should have gone back to the little drawings I was used to; but Goodhue had no use for small-scale drawings. He sketched everything with all the details. In fact, he once almost fired me because I accidentally threw out some of those drawings! He ended up doing all the drawings himself.

If Harrison failed at this point in his career as a draftsman, he succeeded in learning a great deal from Goodhue's need to innovate, a need that continually preoccupied Harrison himself. Goodhue believed that his new phase of modern classicism connected him with Frank Lloyd Wright. Although the work of the two architects has little in common, Goodhue did share with Wright an interest in creative, complex spaces.[12]

While he was in Goodhue's employ, Harrison continued to take on independent work, in particular for

Raymond Hood, who, like Goodhue, had begun his career in Cram's office. In 1905–1906 Hood had spent the obligatory year at the Beaux-Arts in Paris; he then worked for a few years in Pittsburgh for Henry Hornbostel. After another year abroad, he had formed a partnership in New York with Rayne Adams, which received few commissions and accomplished little of note. Hood's fortunes sank so low that he became best known for presiding over the "Four-Hour Lunch Club" that met every Friday at Placido Mori's restaurant on Bleecker Street; the restaurant owner paid in kind for Hood's redesign of the premises. Flourishing architects Joseph Urban, Ely Jacques Kahn, and Ralph Walker were regulars, with occasional appearances by such non-architects as designer Tony Sarg and John H. Finley, an editor of the *New York Times*.

On June 10, 1922, a competition was announced for the design of a new building for the *Chicago Tribune*. Goodhue was one of the ten architects invited to compete and his design is interesting in its relationship to the buildings which would soon be built at Rockefeller Center (Fig. 8). Also invited to participate was John Mead Howells, who asked Hood to join him. The *Chicago Tribune* competition was the most important single architectural event of the decade. When Howells and Hood won it on Christmas Eve, 1922, Hood was catapulted to prominence.

Harrison worked for Hood during the feverish preparations for the *Tribune* competition. At one point he drew a Gothic doorway for the building's main entrance that was based on measured drawings Hood had made of Amiens Cathedral. The result looked narrow, and nobody was happy with it. When a model was made in an attempt to solve the problem, it became obvious to Harrison that the door was out of scale with the tremendous structure it was to serve. "It looked like a little addition to a private house; nobody in the group had realized that Amiens Cathedral was much too small in scale for the United States. They had to double everything." It was a lesson that taught Harrison the importance of looking at a building in context rather than as an isolated phenomenon.

Chapter 4

The Grand Tour

Harrison's time in Europe had not begun to satisfy his searching curiosity, and while he was employed by Goodhue and free-lancing for Hood, the young architect filed applications for stipends that would enable him to travel abroad. One was the Traveling Scholarship, founded in 1883 by Arthur Rotch, the architect to whom Goodhue's former partner Ralph Adams Cram had apprenticed. Candidates had to be under thirty and to have worked for at least two years in the employ of an architect resident in Massachusetts; the winner received fifteen hundred dollars a year for two years, which were to be spent in the study of foreign architecture.[1] Early in 1922, on his second try, Harrison won the Rotch Scholarship and "spent two years of travel looking at monuments and copying drawings, from Michelangelo in the British Museum to Leonardo in Rome."[2] He also saw and was deeply affected by Near Eastern architecture.

His first stop, in the spring of 1922, was Paris, where for a few months he enjoyed the company of his old friends at Umbdenstock's atelier. From there he set out leisurely, on a meandering route south, stopping for several days in each place where monuments interested him. He studied and partially measured the Gothic cathedrals in Chartres, Bourges, and Toulouse, the Roman remains in Nîmes, and the great Romanesque churches in Arles and St. Gilles-du-Gard.[3] Finally, after short stays in Genoa and Florence, he arrived in Rome early in the new year. Rather than wander casually amidst its wonders, as he had done on his first visit, Harrison—thanks to the Rotch—resided as a guest of the American Academy in Rome. The massive palazzo that houses the Academy overlooks the city from its own stately park on the slope of Janiculum hill, a position suitable to the self-image of its founders, who considered themselves ultimate arbiters of artistic taste and intellectual excellence. McKim had established the Academy in 1894, in the conviction that Rome was the best place to transmit the principles of classicism to future generations of American artists. He died in 1909, five years before his firm completed the handsome neo-Renaissance building.[4]

The Academy had a record of distinguished supporters. William A. Boring, Dean of Columbia's School of Architecture; Royal Cortissoz, the well-known architectural critic; William M. Kendall, Harrison's mentor at McKim, Mead & White; and Samuel Trowbridge, member of the Society of Beaux-Arts Architects, made up the board of directors, presided over by William R. Mead, McKim's former partner. Gorham Stevens, another architect associated with the firm, was the director, and Harrison remembered that Stevens seemed to encourage the distinction that had been made from the beginning between the school of classical studies and the other disciplines. Harrison could not sympathize with classicists' insistence on scholarly accuracy, and for him Stevens looked exactly the part he played: "He was a thin, little wizened-up old fellow with glasses who got very sore when someone stepped in and suggested doing something differently from the way he did it."

Rome affected Harrison more deeply this time. The monumental architecture fascinated him, particularly the Pantheon. And citing a criterion of the Beaux-Arts, he observed that "Michelangelo knew what he was doing at Saint Peter's—the building is out of scale with what surrounds it, but it is in scale with the crowds who throng it. That is why it works."

As a visiting scholar rather than an official resident of the Academy, Harrison felt like an outsider, encroaching on the reserve of an inner circle. The institution's atmosphere was claustrophobic: it was only a few months before the Mussolini takeover and this might have affected the Academy's policies. Whatever its causes, the straitlaced, reclusive mood was evident to others besides Harrison. Not long before his arrival, Trowbridge had visited the Academy and reported that Stevens had "created an atmosphere which inspires high ideals, which is conducive of creative effort...complete freedom of thought and action but in which there is no taint of that sordid Bohemianism which so often invades artistic communities."

Harrison decided to push on. In Naples he teamed up with Henry French, a Philadelphia architect whom he knew from Paris. They traveled according to whim and the availability of transportation, taking a train south through Calabria and a boat to Sicily. At Palermo they measured the Palatine Chapel, admiring the brilliantly colored mosaics. They then proceeded along the south shore to Girgenti (Agrigento), where Harrison decided that the Greeks chose the most beautiful places in the world to build their cities. In Catania, they embarked as fourth-class deck passengers on a boat to Alexandria; they proceeded immediately to Cairo.

The travelers enjoyed the city's exotic streets made redolent alternately with the sweet scent of magnolias from hidden gardens and the acrid odor of cooking oil at all hours of the day and night. The Pyramids' huge scale attracted Harrison, but he spent the majority of his time at the Egyptian Museum in Cairo. As he remembered it, "Everything here talked to the architect: simple forms created by the men who invented geometry. Explicit drawings explained every conceivable aspect of the tombs—ground plans showing secret passageways that lead several hundred feet underground and bogus passageways to deceive robbers. Wall fragments were articulated by wide, regularly spaced horizontal or vertical lines." He was astounded by the extraordinary quality of the objects displayed and recalled with special pleasure the perfectly preserved leather tent fabrics that were more than a thousand years old.

Sitting on a small camp stool, oblivious to the odd tourist who occasionally wandered through, Harrison sketched for hours in the dusty half-light of the museum. After a week and a half, he and French set off again, up the Nile by steamship as far as Luxor. From here he made side trips to the Great Temple of Amon at Karnak and to the Valley of the Kings.

At Luxor Harrison spent six weeks clambering over the ruins of the temple—also dedicated to Amon—measuring parts, making elaborate, colored drawings, and taking photographs. The temple, with later additions, follows a long, bent axis. The second of the two large, sun-drenched columned courts, joined by a processional colonnade, terminates in an area of massive, narrowly spaced papyrus-bundle columns, creating remarkable effects of light and shade. This in turn leads to a series of smaller, columned rooms culminating in the dimly lit holy of holies that had been dominated by a representation of the god, probably in ithyphallic form. Harrison easily imagined the purpose of the temple's interplay of spaces: "After being manipulated by all these different plays of light and space, by the time you reached the end, you must have felt as if a sphinx were going to spring right at you! It was propaganda architecture, done by architects who wanted to influence people." Harrison later chose to apply the lessons of propaganda architecture in the smaller Corning Glass Center in upstate New York.

Proceeding north from Jerusalem through Haifa to Beirut, Harrison and French traveled into Syria to the ancient sanctuary of Baalbek. Harrison described the approach "across a great long green plain, at the end of which were the six russet-colored columns of the temple, backed by a marvelous screen of purple and white mountains."[5] He marveled at the immense stones in the periphery of the Temple of Jupiter and at its columns, seven feet in diameter and sixty-seven feet high.

From Baalbek the architects journeyed southeast to Damascus, where they decided to part company. French, fascinated by the Middle East, wanted to stay on; Harrison, growing impatient to start back to Europe and the States, proceeded to Alexandria and Constantinople.

In the course of his travels, Harrison had read Flaubert's *Salammbô*, in which Tunisia was described in exotic terms. Assuming that, as another Moslem country, Turkey would be similar in character, he was prepared to spend several weeks in Constantinople, devoting the same attention to Hagia Sophia as he had to other great buildings. But the realities of Asia Minor did not live up to Flaubert's evocations of North Africa, and he was disappointed. Compared with the exquisite sculpture, the rich stained glass, and the mysterious play of light he had found in Gothic cathedrals, the Byzantine

imperial church, still partially whitewashed as a former mosque, with its solid walls and geometrical decorations, seemed anticlimactic.

In Piraeus he happened upon two friends from the American Academy, with whom he continued peregrinations in Greece on foot and by boat. It was the "sense of quiet and simplicity, with nothing to add or to subtract," that he loved about Greek architecture. Arthur Rotch could not have found a more appreciative recipient for his travel allowance. From the time of this trip, Harrison firmly believed that architecture could be understood only experientially—by seeing it, by sitting on it, or by feeling it warmed by the sun.

The three travelers walked from Athens to Daphne, went by sea to Itea, and walked to Delphi, where Harrison's travel notes record:

> Three of the most interesting days it has ever been my pleasure to spend studying architecture—the country here is so beautiful with its great ravine mists floating down and the sea miles below all prove again that the Greeks never will be surpassed in picking sites.[6]

From Delphi they went by mule to Hosios Louka (963), where they spent the night at the monastery:

> We had to make it through the rain and had lunch at a shelter which is provided for the mule teams which go over the trail to the town. . . . As we approached the monastery, which is on a hill in the middle of a large valley, the day cleared and tinkling sheep bells and absolute quiet added, if possible, to the beauty of the setting. After drying out at the open fire while the monks made us a meal of grass [sic] and eggs, we went in to see the monastery for a little while before turning in. The alabaster panels were disappointing but the floor patterns of simple tile inlays in marble strips were the most beautiful I have ever seen.[7]

Harrison returned to Athens, and toured the Peloponnesus and several Greek islands before spending several months in Europe on his way home:

> I grabbed everything I could in order to get something out of it. In America, you're considered crazy if you don't. So I didn't try to make things part of my life. Instead, I thought only in terms of what could advance me and so I missed some of the greatest pleasures, like just sitting somewhere wonderful with a bottle of wine and some cheese.

Whatever he may have missed in terms of personal fulfillment, Harrison had been widely exposed to the lessons of the masters. His travel experiences left him with images to which he referred throughout his career and with a lifelong interest in studying the buildings of the past.

Chapter 5

New York:
the young partner

Late in the fall of 1923, Harrison returned for the third time to New York after an extended stay abroad. The city's population had steadily increased, and Manhattan was at the beginning of a boom.

In lower Manhattan, the Standard Oil Building (1922) by Carrère & Hastings and Shreve, Lamb & Blake made a powerful pair with Benjamin Wistar Morris's Cunard Building (1921) across Bowling Green Park. In midtown, to the west, Raymond Hood was erecting his first major work in New York, the American Radiator Building (1924; now the American Standard Building).

Worcester's skyscraper had fired the young draftsman's ambitions; New York's construction activity was a more heady stimulant. Harrison reentered the Goodhue office to supervise completion of the National Academy of Sciences and to continue his work on the Nebraska State Capitol. He chafed more than ever at having to execute someone else's ideas rather than his own.

1920 marked the beginning of the richest period in Goodhue's career; the office was flooded with commissions, including those for the Los Angeles Public Library and the Honolulu Museum of Art. Unexpectedly, in the midst of this success, Goodhue found himself implicated in a small scandal. On February 23, 1923, George Johnson, a member of the Nebraska Capitol Commission and Acting State Engineer, charged Goodhue with "dishonesty, gross negligence, and gross incompetence."[1] Goodhue apparently had known nothing of the wrongdoing and was exonerated within a month, but the shock of finding himself the subject of a public investigation may have been too great a strain for the architect's fragile health;[2] he died a year later.

For some time the Goodhue office had been divided into antagonistic camps of Gothicist and classicist. Harrison belonged to the latter group. On reaching the office the Monday after Goodhue's death, he found the Gothic group in command, with no room for him. Bobby Rodgers was in the same situation, and the two friends decided that this was the chance to form their own partnership. They set up office in the National Association Building at 25 West Forty-third Street. Their first commission was to remodel the façade of a nearby restaurant, an assignment obtained through a cousin of Rodgers's who sold supplies to restaurants. The front was only eighteen feet high and twelve feet wide, but the partners spent a year on it, meanwhile searching in vain for other commissions. Unlike Rodgers, Harrison had to depend on free-lance jobs to make ends meet. He worked occasionally for Harvey Corbett, his former teacher and mentor, who had helped him get the Rotch Scholarship.

Corbett's own career had not always been smooth. He refused to moderate impractical designs, and was a hopelessly inept businessman. Harrison analyzed the problem simply: "He preferred to talk than to work," and was easy prey for operators with get-rich-quick schemes.[3]

In 1908, Corbett had won the competition for a civic center in Springfield, Massachusetts, with a design for two neoclassical buildings with a campanile between them. While working on this project, Corbett had invested in a country club he had been retained to design in upper New York State; when the venture turned sour, he had been forced into dire financial straits.[4] Fortunately, Frank Helmle, an architect whose experience had been more practical than the impulsive Corbett's, offered him a much-needed job in 1912.

The partnership was the perfect solution for both Corbett and Helmle. The engaging and creative Corbett brought in the commissions and produced the designs; Helmle carried out the jobs. A large part of Helmle's work at the time was coming from Irving Ter Bush, a local businessman. Bush's father had owned an oil refining plant in South Brooklyn, which, upon his death, had become part of the Standard Oil Company. The son had consolidated the family fortune in the 1890s with the creation of a vast terminal in South Brooklyn for rail- and water-borne freight.

The younger Bush went from one success to another, using his profits to commission new buildings. One of these was the Bush Terminal Building, which he asked Corbett to design in 1917 at 130 West Forty-second Street. The thirty-story tower, one of the first high buildings erected after the new zoning rules, presents an intelligent solution to the problem of a tall build-ing on a small site (fifty by two hundred feet).[5] Approximately two-thirds of its façade is articulated with sober vertical fenestration in heavy masonry walls. The top ten floors are expressed in a Gothic idiom; details gradually decrease in size as the building rises to give an impression of great height. Side walls are articulated with "shadow brick," a light and dark brown pattern that simulates the piers of the street facade. The Bush Terminal Building brought Corbett back to Manhattan from Brooklyn and reestablished his reputation.

Corbett became an authority on tall buildings, publishing the first of several articles he would write on the subject in the *American Architect* in 1921.[6] Adapting futuristic concepts of the city current since the turn of the century, in 1925 he predicted that within the next fifty years buildings would be half a mile high; the city would have a population of fifty million; commuters would be shot through pneumatic tubes at ninety miles an hour into the city's center; and streets would be divided into levels: for rapid transit, private vehicles, and pedestrians.[7] Many of Hugh Ferriss's visionary drawings of the city of the future were done in collaboration with Corbett. Clearly, Corbett's futuristic concepts provided Harrison with ideas, many of which were executed later—at Rockefeller Center, at Lincoln Center, and at the Albany Mall. In several unbuilt Harrison projects—among them X City and his early scheme for Lincoln Center—Hugh Ferriss rendered a visionary quality similar to the futuristic cities he had drawn for Corbett.

Harrison described his own work of the period as "not particularly good and not particularly bad. I got along because of Corbett, who was a wonderful man with whom to talk about architecture." But Harrison's free-lance services were soon in demand, not only by Corbett but by Hood, now also famous.

The success of his Chicago Tribune Building (1924) had brought a number of important commissions to Hood and his partner, J. André Fouilhoux. The American Radiator Building, a tower with Gothic detailing set back to meet the code, was distinguished by beveled corners which were clad in clear glass sheathing used later in Helmle, Corbett & Harrison's Riverside (Roerich)

Museum and Master Apartments (now the Master Apartments—Riverside Museum).[8]

After a year of scraping by, Harrison received an offer to become an associate architect for the New York City Board of Education, starting January 1, 1926, at a salary of seventy-five hundred dollars a year. He was happy to abandon independence and his partnership with Rodgers, although he hoped to resume it under more propitious circumstances. However, Rodgers died soon thereafter.

In a fifteen-month period, from May 1924 to July 1925, shortly before Harrison came to the Board of Education, fifty-three new school buildings were erected, a portion of the vast expansion required by New York's population increase (especially in the Bronx, Brooklyn, and Queens). The city government courageously had begun to appropriate the necessary funds.[9]

Harrison's job was to supervise several hundred designers and draftsmen who had been installed in an immense loft in Brooklyn to produce drawings for this mammoth program. It took him almost six months to complete a first inspection of the work; by the time he was ready to check anything, he was dismayed to find that a city official had approved the designs and contractors were already bidding on them.[10] He soon realized that, for the sake of expediency, the city encouraged standardized plans and that these were used even where inappropriate. One large school, he recalled, was built on property owned by the local Democratic office in Jamaica; no public transportation was available within a mile. Faced with more of such political interference, he decided his presence was meaningless and resigned after less than a year. His episode with the Board of Education was Harrison's first experience supervising a team. It was a role for which he would later become famous at the United Nations.

1926 was an important year in the architect's personal and professional life. On February 13, Harrison married Ellen Milton, on her father's side a descendant of Meriwether Lewis of the Lewis and Clark expedition and, on her mother's, a grandchild of Albert Fink, the first engineer to have built an iron suspension bridge in the United States. Ellen's older brother was the husband of Abby, John D. Rockefeller, Jr.'s, only daughter[11] and Harrison's detractors cited this connection as a poor boy's introduction to future clients. But before he met Ellen he seemed at home in Boston and New York social circles; his grace, wit, and straightforward manner endeared him to people of diverse backgrounds. As some men find themselves inexplicably at ease in an adopted foreign country, so Harrison was a born aristocrat, in mind and manner, and well able to seek clients on his own.

Harrison had met his handsome blonde wife in 1924 through Bobby Rodgers. Ellen enjoyed Bobby's wit and charm and often accompanied him to parties. At one such she met Harrison, whom she found "very good looking, with wonderful carriage, like a column; he was unchangeable, he was so straight."[12]

In the course of a marriage that lasted over fifty years, Ellen influenced Harrison in a number of ways. An intelligent woman of keenly independent mind, she had a fine eye for art and architecture. Like many upper-middle-class Americans, the Miltons placed a premium on European culture with which they acquainted their children by spending several winters in Paris.[13] Thus Ellen was her husband's equal in appreciating transatlantic accomplishments.

Just before the Harrisons married, the Exposition des Arts Décoratifs et Industriels Modernes had been held in Paris. Famous as the source of a style, Art Deco, that colored everything from Thermos bottles to skyscrapers, the exhibition intrigued Harrison, who eagerly studied photographs of it. When part of the exhibition came to the Metropolitan Museum of Art in 1926, he and his bride spent many hours there. The French exhibit that interested him most was the Groupe Ruhlmann's L'Hôtel du Collectionneur. Designed by Pierre Patout, it was adorned with bas-reliefs by Joseph Bernard. Harrison cited them as a source of inspiration for the doors of La Maison Française at Rockefeller Center.[14] The architect was drawn to works exhibited in the Austrian Pavilion. But he was critical of Le Corbusier's stark, white, double-height Pavillon de l'Esprit Nouveau, intended for prefabrication: "it looked as if it had left history too far behind, it made a complete cut with the past for Corb's own ideas." It would not be long, however, before Harrison became interested in prefabrication; eventually, he would also use a curvilinear cutout motif, like Le Corbusier's terrace roof, for a house of his own design.

In 1927 the Harrisons made the first of many visits together to the French capital. There he met his wife's friend Mary Callery, whom he remembered thinking was the most beautiful and most elegant woman he had ever seen. He never forgot her apparition in "a green dress, wearing an emerald the size of your fist." Mary and Ellen had been friends since childhood in Oyster Bay, Long Island.[15] Through Mary, Harrison met many of the leading artists working in Paris, including Matisse, Calder, and Maillol. He responded immediately to their work, and became a lifelong friend of Léger and Calder. He later went to considerable length to have some of them contribute to Rockefeller Center.

Mary Callery also introduced the Harrisons to the painter José Maria Sert and his first two wives, Misia and Roussy, a trio that (in various combinations) played a great role in Paris life in the 1920s and 1930s. Diaghilev, Serge Lifar, Francis Poulenc, Georges Auric, Marie Laurencin, Jean Cocteau, Maurice Sachs, and Coco Chanel were Misia's intimates, and to these Roussy added many of the flashier, café society personalities of the day.[16] Ellen Harrison was Roussy's contemporary, and their friendship provided the Harrisons with an introduction to another artistic world. As with so many aspects of his life, this entrée to one of the important cultural milieus came to the architect easily.

The winter of 1925–26 also marked Harrison's first experience as a teacher. In the fall of 1925, through Corbett, he was asked to supervise a studio at Columbia University's School of Architecture. The dean, William A. Boring, was a feisty midwesterner and a board member of the American Academy in Rome. Boring studied at the Ecole des Beaux-Arts in Paris and was one of the founders and first president of the Society of Beaux-Arts Architects (later the Beaux-Arts Institute of Design, BAID), dedicated to maintaining the French system of architectural education in the United States.[17] To avoid producing mere copyists of one instructor or another, Boring provided a number of architects to teach students within

a relatively short time span. In accord with this policy, Harrison taught design.

In his class was Morris Lapidus, a young student from Brooklyn who had enrolled at Columbia to study stage design and who eventually applied his theatricality to such architectural extravaganzas as Miami's Fontainebleau Hotel. Lapidus, a flamboyant would-be actor who became Harrison's assistant, was taken aback by the refined gentility of the architecture department. He wrote a clear account of the school in Harrison's time. According to Lapidus, most students were liberal arts graduates from Ivy League schools, who attached great importance to their image as gentlemen. The exclusively male student body wore vests and jackets to class—even in studio; the only concession made was for particularly demanding work, in which case the removal of jackets was tolerated, but vests were left on. Students were expected to sit silent at the drafting table in a dignified position.[18]

A product of American public education, Lapidus was understandably uncomfortable with this formality; but the department provided more general discontents. By the mid-1920s, Manhattan's proliferation of skyscrapers was famous throughout the world, yet the building type was almost completely ignored at Columbia, as were most of the important new developments taking place in contemporary architecture. The students were eager to understand the ideas of men like Le Corbusier, Mies van der Rohe, and Gropius and wanted to know more about Erich Mendelsohn and Willem Marinus Dudok. The European modernists were preaching a new sense of social responsibility, charging the architect to provide housing for the masses and to design clear, unadorned public buildings. They aimed to make the world a better place to live in. Many American students, shaken by the aftermath of World War I, were ill at ease with the elitist rationale of the Beaux-Arts system. They resented an instructor's simplistic advice to "look at the magazines and copy a house! There is nothing new, gentlemen, so copy a good one."[19]

Lapidus reports that even Corbett, then senior design critic at Columbia, answered student criticism of Raymond Hood's use of Gothic for his *Chicago Tribune*

9. Helmle, Corbett & Harrison, Bush Buildings, London (1927).

design with the statement: "If you dress a Chinese in western clothes he is still an Oriental. So what difference does it make if we dress a structure like the Woolworth Building in Gothic clothes? It is still a modern skyscraper."[20]

For all his ambivalence about modernity, Harrison avoided the doctrinaire attitude of his fellow instructors. He was interested in the new ideas and kept an open mind about them. According to Lapidus, "He was just as confused as the students in the mid-twenties." All he would offer as advice was: "Do a good job and we'll see what comes out."[21] He admitted to having been puzzled by the importance students attached to the competitions sponsored by the BAID, an organization he referred to as "a place for rich men's architects in New York." And although Harrison continued to use elements of Beaux-Arts design throughout his career, by the mid-twenties he believed the system had been dominant too long.

Only in 1931 with the publication of his book *School Buildings of Today and Tomorrow*[22] did Harrison commit himself to modernism—as we shall see the commitment was anything but doctrinaire—calling for a school building type that would be "industrial in character ... a machine for education."[23] New York City's Hunter College (1940, which Harrison excluded from

his list of buildings, claiming the predominance of the associated firm, Shreve, Lamb & Harmon) bears some resemblance to the back elevation of Otto Haesler's Public School at Celle (1925), referred to on the first page of *School Buildings*.[24] Haesler was one of the German architects included in the famous *Modern Architecture* exhibition, organized by Philip Johnson and Henry-Russell Hitchcock at the Museum of Modern Art in 1932.

Troubled by the school's conceptual struggles, and pressed by the increasing demands of work he was forced to take on after leaving the Board of Education, Harrison often forgot to show up for his classes at Columbia. These lapses were frowned upon by the authorities. In a situation that was growing increasingly tense, Frank Helmle again came to the rescue: in January 1927, Helmle invited Harrison to become a junior partner with Corbett and himself, formalizing the loose working association Harrison had already established with Corbett. With this partnership he made the transition from anonymous designer to acknowledged architect. It was a major step forward, followed by many more within a remarkably short time.

Harrison described Helmle & Corbett as "a big small office," with twelve or fourteen men: most important to the new partner, it was "big enough to do a skyscraper." Among the commissions in progress when he joined the firm were One Fifth Avenue and the Riverside (Roerich) Museum and Master Apartments in New York, the Pennsylvania Power & Light Company in Allentown, Pennsylvania, and a large complex in London that had been commissioned by Helmle's Brooklyn client, Irving Ter Bush.

The three Bush Buildings connected by low arcades (1927) occupy a site at the center of London (Fig. 9). The focal point of the complex is the central building, with its tower and great seven-story recessed arch. At the time of construction, the tower (dispensed from normal height limitation) was visible the length of Kingsway, a half-mile down Fleet Street, and on the Strand as far as Trafalgar Square.[25] When Harrison joined the firm, attention had turned to the west wing. By his own account, he participated in its design, though the building is attributed to Helmle and Corbett. It was the first of three

10. Helmle, Corbett & Harrison, Pennsylvania Power and Light
Co. Building, Allentown, Pennsylvania (1928).

11. Helmle, Corbett & Harrison with Sugarman & Berger,
Riverside (Roerich) Museum and Master Apartments Building,
New York City (1929; now the Master Apartments—Riverside
Museum). Rendering by Hugh Ferriss.

buildings outside the United States with which he was involved.[26]

The Bush project aroused enormous interest in London; the important site had stood empty for over eighteen years. *The Architects' Journal and Architectural Engineering* described the project: "This building, besides being one of the largest and most important to be erected in modern times, should, if the promise of preliminary drawings is realized, prove to be also one of the first architecturally."[27] The clarity of form and the sense of urban responsibility conveyed by Helmle, Corbett & Harrison's London complex were unusual for Britain in the late 1920s.[28] The same issue of the *Journal* vehemently protested the idea of American-type skyscrapers in London, and separately analyzed the "great railroad stations of New York." This attention to things American in a leading British architectural journal was impressive.

The firm designed the Pennsylvania Power & Light Company headquarters, a twenty-three-story skyscraper in Allentown (1928; Fig. 10). Along with the neo-Gothic street-level decoration and chamfered corners at the top, the building displays emphatic vertical fenestration and minimal setbacks.

The Riverside (Roerich) Museum and Master Apartments (1929), by Helmle, Corbett & Harrison with Sugarman & Berger, on the northeast corner of New York's 103d Street and Riverside Drive, is the first major building with which Harrison's name was associated. The museum exhibited the paintings of Russian-born Nicholas Roerich, who described himself as artist, designer, philosopher, and explorer. The building also included a school of architecture, painting, sculpture, interior decoration, music, dance, and theater. This complex occupied the main floor, together with a public dining room and a small theater. Revenues from the twenty-nine-story residential hotel, with apartments of one, three, or more rooms plus a service pantry, were intended to support the museum and art school (Fig. 11). (The museum was eventually moved to 107th Street between Broadway and Riverside Drive and its space was divided into studios.)

The Master Apartments' steel frame is clad in interesting patterns of rough brick and terra-cotta. Slim terra-cotta bands run between pairs of windows to emphasize the vertical alignment, which is further accented by brick patterns above and below the windows. Corner windows provide excellent views. Materials were varied in color from black at the base to red and white at the top, a color gradation popular at the time and until World War II.[29] Unfortunately, pollution rapidly changed the black to purple and the white to yellow. One Fifth Avenue echoed the Master Apartments' vertical emphasis within a more conventional design.

The Master Apartments was one of the last buildings to bear Helmle's name; for all practical purposes, Corbett had taken over the practice. Helmle, who appeared older than his sixty-eight years, retired in 1928 and died a year later.

Corbett and Harrison soon realized they had to replace Helmle with someone who, like him, would be willing to invest in the firm and help expedite its work without exerting too much interference in design matters. Fortunately, just such a person appeared on the scene: in April 1929, William H. MacMurray entered into a partnership with Corbett & Harrison that lasted six years; "an old Scotsman who came in to bolster up the office," Harrison called him, but in photographs MacMurray appears only slightly older than Corbett. Certainly his rimless glasses, pursed lips, and heavy tweeds suggest extreme caution where money was concerned.

One of the first works of the new partnership was Bushnell Memorial Hall in Hartford, Connecticut (1929; see Fig. 19). To relate the new building with the city's old State House, the architects decided on a neo-Colonial, red brick and white stone exterior, with gable roofs. This unimaginative envelope enclosed a combination of simple forms that reduces the apparent mass of the large auditorium. Surprisingly, the auditorium is decorated in beige, gold, and magenta Art Deco with stepped-back walls that forecast Radio City Music Hall at Rockefeller Center.[30]

Chapter 6

Rockefeller Center: the beginning

Harrison described the origin of Rockefeller Center in characteristic understatement, as if the project's immensity were slightly embarrassing:

> It began with Otto Kahn's dinner to get Mr. Rockefeller to give $2.5 million to build a plaza in front of an opera house Benjamin Morris had schemed up for this plot of about twelve acres owned by Columbia University.[1]

In fact, John D. Rockefeller, Jr., was one of the few wealthy New Yorkers who did not attend the dinner that had been carefully arranged to interest investors in the midtown property on Fifth Avenue surrounding the Metropolitan Opera's proposed new site. Rockefeller was, however, represented by Ivy Lee, his public relations manager, who joined about forty of the city's most affluent citizens to dine at the Metropolitan Club on May 21, 1928.

There had been talk of building a new opera house since the beginning of the century (see chapter 17). In 1925, Otto Kahn, chairman of Kuhn, Loeb and Company, and chairman of the board of the Metropolitan Opera Company, had assembled property on West Fifty-seventh Street between Eighth and Ninth avenues as a possible site, and had asked Benjamin Wistar Morris and Joseph Urban to produce schemes for it. But the Metropolitan Opera and Real Estate Company rebuffed Kahn's proposal and engaged Morris to produce schemes for alternative sites. Morris proposed designs for several locations, all of which presented problems.[2] Kahn therefore sold the Fifty-seventh Street property and the box-holders formed a committee to search for a new site.[3] In January 1928, the site committee focused on property belonging to Columbia University that extended from Forty-eighth to Fifty-first streets between Fifth and Sixth avenues (minus the northwest corner of Fifth Avenue and Forty-eighth Street, and the Sixth Avenue frontages); for this site Morris conceived the more ambitious project that was presented at the Metropolitan Club dinner. Despite numerous alternative suggestions, Morris's unified treatment of the central Columbia site, with a plaza as its focal point, remained the basic concept for what became Rockefeller Center (Figs. 12, 13).[4]

12. Benjamin Wistar Morris, scheme for the Metropolitan Opera House (April 1928), presented at the Metropolitan Club dinner. Rendering by Chester B. Price.

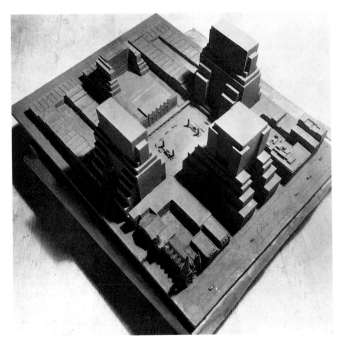

13. Morris, model, Metropolitan Opera House (April 1928).

In the 1920s Fifth Avenue's mansions were being rapidly replaced: above Fifty-ninth Street by twelve-story apartment buildings, below Fifty-ninth Street by commercial buildings. Now, Morris was proposing a mammoth building complex consisting, in addition to the opera house, of several loft or apartment buildings, a hotel, department stores, and a shopping mall that would dominate Fifth Avenue between Forty-eighth and Fifty-first streets. No American city offered a precedent for a commercial venture providing public space like this.[5]

On the basis of Morris's scheme, John D. Rockefeller, Jr., became interested in the project, and shortly after the Metropolitan Club dinner party he pledged the $2.5 million Kahn had needed to purchase the land for the plaza. Rockefeller then set up a syndicate that ensured for himself a part interest to acquire adjacent real estate for the opera. Having made this gift, Rockefeller was expected to act only as leasor to the opera of the land that would be acquired. The concept failed to take into account Rockefeller's personality.

John D. Rockefeller, Jr., learned at an early age that he was not the businessman his father was. His first business transaction failed and he had to ask his father for $1 million to bail him out. For the rest of his life he left all business—other than the acquisition of property—to his father and a series of managers, concentrating his considerable energies on charitable endeavors and buildings. His attention was focused on restoration, maintenance, and construction, the details of which he followed with meticulous interest.

As a student at Brown University, he had come to love the great Gothic cathedrals of England, which he visited in the course of bicycle vacations. Later, Rockefeller became friendly with William Welles Bosworth, an architect who tutored him in the fine arts, particularly architecture. Bosworth eventually built Rockefeller a house at Pocantico Hills, New York, and a townhouse at 10 West Fifty-fourth Street in Manhattan. Rockefeller's marriage to Abby Aldrich, an enthusiastic art lover, served further to endorse his interest in the fine arts; with his wife's encouragement, he continued to collect medieval and antique Chinese arts. In the course of a trip to

Europe with Abby in 1923, Rockefeller was struck by the deterioration of the palaces at Versailles and Fontainebleau, and the cathedral at Rheims. Within a few years, encouraged by Bosworth, who was living in Paris at the time, he gave almost $3 million to the French government for the restoration of these monuments. In these same years he underwrote the revival of colonial Williamsburg, the most ambitious reconstruction and restoration of a historic town in the United States.

By the time the Metropolitan Opera project came his way, Rockefeller had given many additional millions to enterprises that ranged from the construction of public buildings to the creation of some of the country's most important public parks.[6] It is hardly surprising that at the age of fifty-four, with these achievements behind him, Rockefeller chose to be active in the new venture, especially as it was to transform the area where his father, he, and other family members owned houses. Rockefeller Center was to become John D. Rockefeller, Jr.'s, biggest, most famous, and most influential undertaking.

On the recommendation of Thomas M. Debevoise and Charles O. Heydt, his chief legal and real estate advisors, Rockefeller turned for advice on the project to the engineering firm of Todd, Robertson & Todd.[7] The firm had already worked on such large commercial structures in New York as the Cunard Building, the Architects Building, the Equitable Trust Building, and the Graybar Building and was indirectly involved with the Williamsburg restoration through the firm of Todd & Brown. John Todd, in turn, engaged the firm of L. Andrew Reinhard and Henry Hofmeister, two young "rental architects," or building managers, who had done office planning for him. On the basis of Reinhard and Hofmeister's plan of the site, presented on October 1, 1928, Rockefeller formed the Metropolitan Square Corporation to develop the site, and drew up a lease for the entire Columbia property (Fig. 14). Concerned that the best available talent be used to develop this prime midtown area, he then solicited the advice of his brother-in-law, William T. Aldrich, and John Russell Pope, two eminently conservative architects. They proposed an architectural "symposium," to be judged by Cass Gilbert and

Milton B. Medary, Jr., both of whom were firmly rooted in the Beaux-Arts tradition.[8] Invited to participate in the symposium were William T. Aldrich, Charles Adams Platt, Benjamin Wistar Morris, E. H. Bennett, Harvey Wiley Corbett, and the firms of Cross & Cross and York & Sawyer. The architects received plot plans of the Columbia property showing Morris's opera house, plaza, and underground garage, and a plan of the opera's basement level. For a fee of five thousand dollars each, they were asked for specified drawings together with written reports on the project's economic aspects and on the manner in which these could be incorporated into the proposed architectural solution.[9]

Morris wanted to expand the area to be developed to include the northwest corner of Fifth Avenue at Forty-eighth Street and the Sixth Avenue frontage. The added Fifth Avenue lot would allow a broad axial approach to the plaza, a pedestrian walk bordered on Fifth Avenue by two forty-four story office towers, in turn flanked at north and south by low wings. He planned terraced gardens on some setbacks and suggested a ramp that would approach the opera from Fifth Avenue.[10]

Corbett shared Morris's perception about widening the access to the interior plaza. But rather than enlarging the whole plot, he left open the central block front on Fifth Avenue, thereby sacrificing 120 feet of valuable frontage in order to make the other buildings more attractive to potential occupants.[11] In his plan, the opera house stood before the dramatic backdrop of a slim skyscraper; pedestrians would approach it at a second-story level by walking up a long, inclined plane from Fifth Avenue, leading to a plaza flanked by arcaded promenades. Cars would approach the opera at grade level (Fig. 15). What is striking about the Corbett project is its similarity in certain aspects not only to Rockefeller Center as we know it today—the generous access from Fifth Avenue and the plaza backed by a slender skyscraper—but to Lincoln Center as well, especially the broad open area bordered by classical arcades (see Fig. 213). Harrison's subsequent use of an arcaded facade for the Metropolitan Opera House and the Beaux-Arts nature of his general plan for Lincoln Center show the influence of this project, demonstrating an interesting reinterpretation of

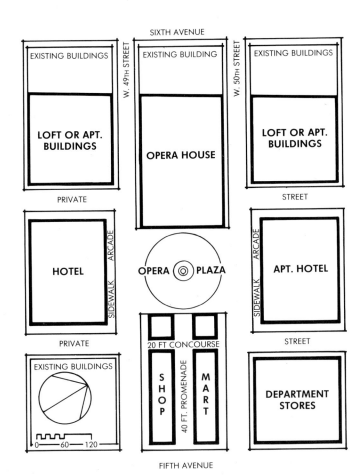

SIXTH AVENUE

| EXISTING BUILDINGS | EXISTING BUILDING | EXISTING BUILDINGS |

LOFT OR APT. BUILDINGS

OPERA HOUSE

LOFT OR APT. BUILDINGS

PRIVATE

STREET

HOTEL

OPERA ⊚ PLAZA

APT. HOTEL

PRIVATE

STREET

EXISTING BUILDINGS

0 — 60 — 120

20 FT CONCOURSE

SHOP

40 FT. PROMENADE

MART

DEPARTMENT STORES

FIFTH AVENUE

W. 49TH STREET
W. 50TH STREET
SIDEWALK ARCADE
SIDEWALK ARCADE

14. L. Andrew Reinhard & Henry Hofmeister, plan for Metropolitan Opera Square (1928).

15. Corbett, Harrison & MacMurray, "Arts Center" scheme for Rockefeller Center (spring 1929).

Corbett's ideas or—possibly—Harrison's greater participation in the early stages of Rockefeller Center design than has been acknowledged.

Gilbert, Medary, and Pope recommended that the project submitted by Corbett, Harrison & MacMurray serve as the basis for a more detailed study. Morris was asked to develop such a study in consultation with the real estate brokers for the site. But after a number of revised proposals, Heydt grew impatient with Morris's participation. He was convinced that work would progress more rapidly if the contractor were in charge. To convince John D. Rockefeller, Jr., of this, Heydt arranged for John Todd to spend three days at Rockefeller's Seal Harbor, Maine, estate. Heydt got what he wanted: Rockefeller took to the conscientious, hardworking contractor (with whom he shared an interest in horses), and on October 1, 1929, he concluded an agreement with Todd for construction of the Center. Todd later said that he came away from his first meeting with Rockefeller feeling that his firm had the same powers as if it owned the land: "We were to build the thing, put it on a profitable basis and sell it to the world."[12]

With the Rockefeller Center contract in hand, Todd's first move was to sign up Reinhard & Hofmeister as general architects, retaining Corbett, Morris, and Raymond Hood as consultants for "architectural style and grouping."[13] Ironically, just twenty-eight days later the stock market crash, which was to put thousands of architects across the country out of work, provided Hood and Corbett with a much larger role at the Center than they had expected. The realization that it was now hopeless to try to finance a new opera house had two major consequences. The first was Morris's decision to bow out of the project. Harrison remembered Morris as being:

> very much of a gent, who handled himself just about the best of any of us. He refused to get into any kind of snap. The rest of us had hung around wondering what would happen next.

What happened was that Corbett, Harrison, and Hood remained the only designers working with the strictly utilitarian architectural firm of Reinhard & Hofmeister.

The commission was a remarkable boon for the Corbett practice. Even though they had earned considerably more for the Bush Building two years before, Harrison remembered the elation he and Corbett felt on signing a contract for Rockefeller Center that guaranteed them annual fees of between eighteen and twenty-five thousand dollars.

The second consequence of the opera's withdrawal was the sudden transformation of a philanthropic, cultural enterprise into a purely commercial venture, the name of which was changed in February 1932 from Metropolitan Square to Rockefeller Center. (It was prophetic that Harrison's first work on a monumental scale began with this abortive project for a new opera house, considering his commission almost thirty years later for the Metropolitan Opera House at Lincoln Center.)

Hood and Corbett were at the time among the most sought-after architects in the city; the historian William Jordy describes them as "two of the most progressive designers of business buildings in New York, each a partner in a leading architectural firm."[14] Since his *Chicago Tribune* competition success, "Hoody," as his friends called him, had abandoned his Greenwich Village lunches at Mori's in favor of the grander facilities of the Architectural League at Park Avenue and Fortieth Street. Many of the old crowd, including Ely Jacques Kahn and Ralph Walker, followed him uptown. Like the group Harrison had known at the Architectural Club in Boston, it was a tight circle of men with similar education and ideas who had access to people who could provide the commissions they wanted. Hood, Kahn, and Walker were referred to in the profession as "the three little Napoleons of architecture,"[15] and Hood's importance is evident from the impact of his Daily News Building (1930) on Rockefeller Center.[16]

In spite of the prominence of such famous practitioners, the days of the individual architect were on the wane. From the start of the century, American architectural practice had begun to assume a new character. The demand for skyscrapers had encouraged the development of large offices in which architects, structural and mechanical engineers, financial advisors, and real estate consultants, played equal parts. As Hood himself put it,

"The day of the one-man show is over...no architect can afford to take risks on a $250 million development."[17] Hood's remarks pertained specifically to Rockefeller Center, in which, by May 1930, the participation of three independent architectural firms had been formalized. Reinhard & Hofmeister; Corbett, Harrison & MacMurray; and Hood, Godley (until 1931) & Fouilhoux agreed to share communal space in the Graybar Building as the Associated Architects.

If the collaboration of several offices was still a novelty, the give and take between professionals in the same office had been increasing for some time. While it was criticized by those who predicted that it would lead inevitably to anonymity and mediocrity, the practice of group design appealed to others. For example, the organizers of the Chicago Century of Progress Exposition of 1933–34 enlisted the coordinated services of eight architects (including Hood, with Corbett as Chairman).[18] Harrison admitted that when he became part of the Associated Architects' collaborative effort, he realized full well that he was taking a decisive step: "If you're alone, you do what you think is right; the more bosses you have, the less you have to say about what you're doing. But I had to eat."

Shortly after the opera's withdrawal, Harrison called his friend Julian Street, Jr., who worked at the National Broadcasting Company and whom he knew through his wife, Ellen. The two men met for lunch, and Street recalls that, upon sitting down, Harrison announced in his usual direct fashion: "The deal on the Metropolitan Opera has fallen through and I think it may be a good thing, because I think it would be very much better from everyone's point of view if it were NBC at Rockefeller Center broadcasting to the world."[19] At the time, NBC and RKO Motion Pictures were controlled by the Radio Corporation of America (RCA), and Mrs. Street's aunt was married to Edward Walker Harden, a director at RCA and chairman of its real estate committee. At the Streets' request, Harden presented the plan for "a radio city broadcasting to the world" to Owen D. Young, chairman of General Electric (parent company of RCA), who responded enthusiastically, calling it "the most marvelous thing he'd ever heard

about."[20] As a result, RCA became the biggest client for Rockefeller Center's central skyscraper with RKO occupying a second building. RCA president David Sarnoff called the complex Radio City.

Connections such as these landed Harrison squarely in the midst of the Rockefeller Center project, to whose principals he was introduced not by his partner, Corbett, but by a friend of David Milton, his brother-in-law. Milton brought him to the attention of Colonel Arthur Woods, a former police commissioner who, as president of the Metropolitan Square Corporation, became the financial manager of Rockefeller Center. Although Todd, among others, responded favorably to Harrison's participation, some of the principals were less receptive. Harrison remembered feeling at first like "a loose nut in the organization." By now, however, he had the personal energy, the architectural qualifications, and the social connections that were to make him indispensable. Of the seven original architects for Rockefeller Center, Harrison became the only one to work on the enormous development from inception to its latest additions in the early 1970s.

Without the opera house, the Center's new focus became a fifty-story office building, and the architects were asked to revise their plans accordingly. One of these, known as G3 (January 1930) and signed only by Reinhard & Hofmeister, established the block layout, channel, and central plaza that were eventually adopted (Fig. 16). Reflecting the change from opera house to offices, G3 placed the tallest, instead of the lowest, building on the western part of the central block. Disposed symmetrically around this central skyscraper were four thirty-story towers. A department store flanked either side of the skyscraper, and a nine-story arcaded building bordered each side of the channel in front of it.[21] The Metropolitan Square Corporation used a modified version of the plan in its negotiations with RCA. After almost a year's discussions with potential financiers and tenants, Todd, Robertson & Todd displayed to the press a model of yet another version of this plan that provided a shopping concourse, bus terminal, and parking in the underground areas that linked the buildings. In this model the plaza was dropped below street level to allow

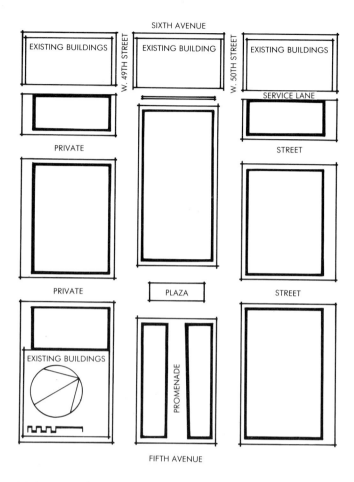

SIXTH AVENUE

EXISTING BUILDINGS | EXISTING BUILDING | EXISTING BUILDINGS

W. 49TH STREET

W. 50TH STREET

SERVICE LANE

PRIVATE | | STREET

PRIVATE | PLAZA | STREET

EXISTING BUILDINGS | PROMENADE |

FIFTH AVENUE

16. Associated Architects, Plan G3 for Rockefeller Center (8 January 1930).

access to the concourse. (The plaza was sealed off in 1936 to make the skating rink.) To accommodate Chase National Bank, a potential client, the promenade leading to the plaza was blocked at Fifth Avenue by an eleven-story oval building that was almost immediately nicknamed the "oil can."[22]

Instead of stimulating interest in Rockefeller Center, the presentation met with a barrage of adverse criticism, among which was the *New York Herald Tribune*'s emphatic judgment that the developers should not make "so immense and so important 'a project' the vehicle for experiment."[23] The architects were convinced they would all lose their jobs until, as Harrison recalled, an unruffled Rockefeller calmly explained that, ever since the press's criticism of his behavior during the brutally repressed miner's strike at Ludlow, Colorado:

> I've learned . . . that I should avoid reading about the things that would be too painful to read, forget about them from that approach, and try to find another one that would be bearable, in which we can repair whatever damage is done.[24]

Rockefeller's attitude was reassuring, but the project faced an even more serious problem in May 1931 when Benjamin Wistar Morris's proposal for a north-south Metropolitan Avenue to be built from Bryant Park to Central Park midway through the Fifth-Sixth Avenue block was endorsed by New York's Fine Arts Federation, the Regional Plan Association, and critic Lewis Mumford. Hood saved the day for Rockefeller Center by concentrating public attention on his proposal (adapted from Morris's earlier design) for elaborate roof gardens on the buildings' lower setbacks. At this time Chase National Bank withdrew, eliminating the offensive oval building. By the fall the basic G3 plan had been reinstated, with two six-story buildings framing the Fifth Avenue entrance to a pleasant promenade sloping gently down to the sunken plaza, backed by the RCA Building (Fig. 17)

With the acceptance of an overall plan by the Rockefeller Center directors, one of the first major design decisions regarding the actual buildings was made: no office space was to be more than twenty-seven and a

17. Raymond Hood, Harrison, and Reinhard inspect model of La
Maison Française and British Empire Building, Rockefeller Center
(c. 1931).

18. The Associated Architects, Eastern Airlines Building,
New York City (1939).

half feet from the windows. The Rockefeller Center developers were determined to offer superior facilities, and at a time when this kind of space normally penetrated thirty feet or more from the exterior of the building without benefit of air-conditioning or sophisticated lighting, the new shallow depth represented an attractive alternative. By July 1931, the City Building Code had been revised to allow the use of new elevators that could rise at a rate of fourteen hundred feet per minute.[25] Because an elevator of this type normally serves only twelve to seventeen floors, at the bottom of a tall building the elevator banks form a thick core that is diminished toward the top as banks are reduced in number. Consequently, if the exterior walls go straight up, floor space extends into the building farther from the windows, leaving a great deal of space without daylight or fresh air. To maintain the approximate twenty-seven-foot standard throughout the RCA Building, setbacks were essential on the flanking walls; Hood proposed setbacks on the east and west walls as well.[26]

Setback buildings had begun to appear in large numbers in New York, as a result of the 1916 zoning law that limited the percentage of the site occupied by a building in relation to its height. The slenderness of the RCA Building and the open space in front of it would have exempted the building from the new law, and Hood's design was purely aesthetic, as were many setbacks at this time.[27] Harrison fought to eliminate these non-essential setbacks, opposing the idea of "cutting out space just for the look of a building."[28] But Hood's proposal won. It was the first of a number of lost battles over design that Harrison weathered in the course of his career.

Because of its setbacks, the RCA Building only approximated the slab form, a term usually designating an exceptionally thin building without breaks or setbacks.[29] With Hood's death in 1934, Harrison was able to exert more influence on design.[30] The Time and Life Building (1937, now 1 Rockefeller Plaza) rises thirty-six stories with setbacks only at the top two floors. The sixteen-story slab Eastern Airlines Building (1939, now 10 Rockefeller Plaza; Fig. 18) showed more than any of the other Rockefeller Center buildings the influence of modernism, particularly in the curved-glass, double-height shop fronts on Forty-ninth Street and the sweeping, semicircular stair connecting the lobby with the underground concourse.[31]

The RCA (1933) and International (1935) buildings seem to have the first examples of elevators of exceptional speed and reach positioned in a new way—in parallel banks, open at either end, in the center of a broad lobby and at right angles to the buildings' axis. The arrangement, allowing a continuous flow of traffic, quick elevator identification, and greater architectural freedom became standard in office-tower lobbies.[32] A big garage at the Eastern Airlines Building, partly underground, was another innovation widely adopted, notably by Harrison. In addition to parking space for 725 cars at the RCA Building, underground facilities for unloading trucks and for warehousing were provided.

Throughout the planning and construction of Rockefeller Center, weekly lunches and dinners were held at the Barclay for the Associated Architects, Rockefeller's advisors, Todd's men, and representatives of the most important leasers. After elaborate meals the group would retire to the Graybar Building, where business discussions would begin in earnest. Although the youngest of the architects at thirty-six, Harrison was nevertheless the first to present his ideas when the meeting was called to order. He failed to understand why he was consistently ignored until he suddenly realized that, their meals consumed, the men shifted their attention to enjoyment of postprandial cigars. Remembering what his first boss at O. W. Norcross had advised him about the importance of timing, Harrison switched from his usual pipe to cigars and from then on waited until he had only a butt in hand before speaking up.[33]

An improved sense of timing was not the only factor that strengthened Harrison's influence at the conferences. In the fall of 1931, John D. Rockefeller, Jr.'s, son, Nelson, began to work with the Metropolitan Square Corporation to lease space at the Center. Harrison's friendship with Nelson, which dates from this time, was to develop into one of the most remarkable relationships between a powerful client and an outstanding architect.

Chapter 7

Rockefeller Center: construction

Work began at Rockefeller Center in September 1931 with the British Empire Building, La Maison Française, the plaza and Radio City (comprising the RCA and RKO buildings, the International Music Hall, and the Center Theater).[1] The Empire State Building and the Chrysler tower had struggled for the title of the world's tallest building; now, with the Empire State just completed, they stood like two giant exclamation points, marking the end of one of the city's most spectacular periods of building activity. By the time riveting began at Rockefeller Center, it was the only sound of major construction in the city.[2]

Architectural Forum, then the nation's leading architectural magazine, featured Rockefeller Center in its January 1932 issue as the outstanding project of the New Year, with articles by several of the participating architects. Reinhard discussed the "financial, functional, and aesthetic" aspects of the buildings, in that order of importance. Hood described the technical advantages of the projected Rockefeller Center buildings in relation to other alternatives, and Harrison presented and analyzed the way in which the Associated Architects worked together. Harrison's article makes it clear—especially when compared with the two other statements—that he was now running the office. The man who had supervised the teamwork in Brooklyn for the New York City Board of Education was obviously good in this role. He began by explaining the Associated Architects' approach to Rockefeller Center: although the project consisted of several buildings, they were considered from all standpoints a single undertaking. Because many of the design features and field conditions of one building were common to the others, specifications could generally be applied throughout. Buildings were designed independently only insofar as this did not interfere with the project as a whole. Architects, designers, draftsmen, modelers, job captains, and assistants worked at the office on two connecting floors of the Graybar Building. Harrison described the intricate connections they formed with structural and mechanical engineers, who worked elsewhere.[3] Many years later he recalled aspects of the design process:

The architect's sketch goes to the designers, who draw up the plan and adapt the elevations and sections to that plan. To start, you've got to have your plans and sections; different heights of the sections will affect the plans, so you have to have both. The two together produce an elevation. There were three great designers at Rockefeller Center: Ed Stone, George Pawley, and Earl Landefeld.[4]

Pawley was an uncouth so-and-so with the damndest ideas. He wanted to create a tapestry effect for the walls of the RCA Building. He used blue bricks for one [part] and brown and red bricks for another to make the whole exterior look like a Persian rug. I thought it was beautiful, but nobody else cared for it.

Landefeld spent his time trying to decide how the windows would go—whether there could be three or four windows to a bay [i.e., discrete, as opposed to continuous, horizontal, fenestration]. Since my days in Worcester, those things have become much more elaborate. In Worcester, you did a window the same as you did the window before it; this was true up to the time of Rockefeller Center. The International Building has a pretty good average window arrangement. I certainly didn't want continuous windows—I wanted the feeling of protecting a wall gives, as well as openness.

Stone was a true Southerner, with a beautiful sense of life in general: he was a friend of William Faulkner, who helped him out on a number of occasions. Unfortunately, he had two handicaps; he drank too much and he had an erratic second wife who influenced him to do all those perforated walls—all that damned stuff.[5]

The importance Harrison attached to these designers is telling: with his volatile imagination and preoccupation with large concepts, he would necessarily rely on others to realize his schemes. In addition, the liking for Pawley's patterned walls and his preference for discrete windows show his resistance to a typically modern aesthetic.

When Reinhard & Hofmeister, Hood, Godley & Fouilhoux, and Corbett, Harrison & MacMurray first found themselves sharing an office, Harrison recalled that it was:

> pure hell for the architects . . . .No businessman, no builder, no architect ever entered a joint operation unless it was necessary. The Architects cooperated on Rockefeller Center not because they wanted to, but because they were paid by Mr. Rockefeller. . . .
>
> Hood's men thought they could run the whole show. There is no doubt that Hood was a capable draftsman and that he contributed a great deal to the big building . . . and we're all conceited.

Harrison's system ensured that each firm was treated equally, with no one of them in charge—a formula he applied later at Lincoln Center. Rockefeller scheduled meetings early each month with executive officers of Todd, Robertson & Todd, the architects, and board members of Rockefeller Center, Inc. (as the Metropolitan Square Corporation was now called). The meetings began promptly at 9:00 a.m. but dapper "Mr. Jr.," as he was called, would arrive in the office at least an hour early, and usually was to be seen on his hands and knees, measuring the proportions of the large presentation drawings with a folding, five-foot, gold-plated ruler. He took intense personal interest in the way the buildings would look. Once he marched the architects to an on-site inspection of the nearly complete RCA Building to find out why the "Gothic effect" for the top, which he had requested at a meeting many months before, had not been executed. The visit resulted in an ornate metal railing that now crowns the building. It was obvious that Mr. Jr. would have liked a great deal more such ornamentation, but the architects managed to persuade him to spend the money it would have cost on the medieval paintings and sculpture he loved.[6] Harrison recalled Rockefeller's decisive role in making the architects' collaboration work:

He was a definite boss. He told you what he wanted. He wasn't a boss that ever pushed his role. I mean, he always had a calming effect on me when he started to talk about [the designs]. He would argue them out with me. . . . He was a diplomat if there ever was one.[7]

John D. Rockefeller, Jr., met with Harrison on innumerable occasions during the planning and building of the Center. He evidently admired and liked the young architect, as is attested by a letter he sent to him on December 16, 1936, accompanied by the gift of a gilded folding ruler similar to the one he himself used.[8] Harrison claimed that Mr. Jr. was unaware of his family connections until several years after they began to work together, when, seated next to Ellen Harrison at a dinner dance, Rockefeller pointed to the tall, gangling figure of her husband and asked, "Is that young man connected with you?" Apparently it was the first time he realized that Harrison was related to him through marriage.

Before construction of the Center began, Rockefeller had tried to persuade numerous big corporations to build headquarters on land leased from the Metropolitan Square Corporation. The idea never caught on; and as the project developed, Rockefeller found himself footing an increasing percentage of construction bills.[9] Rockefeller Center was in large part financed by Standard Oil stock, the price of which remained relatively stable throughout the Depression. According to Harrison, Rockefeller cheerfully explained that he studied large projects by using a thousand-to-one ratio to make the figures more manageable. Thus, for the purposes of his calculations, a $200,000 expense became one of $200.

Like his father, young Nelson Rockefeller was attracted to large, challenging projects. Born in 1908, the third of six children, his struggle throughout childhood and early adolescence to overcome dyslexia led to a keen competitiveness with which he approached every new task.[10] In 1926 he entered Dartmouth College, where he already displayed concerns that characterized his career. He majored in economics, yet tried to stimulate undergraduate interest in the arts by establishing a library of recordings and a guest lecture series for writers and poets. He was particularly interested in architecture,

and, had he not been pressured by his family to concentrate on business, might well have pursued the interest professionally.

After graduation in 1930, Nelson Rockefeller wandered one day into the project's conference room before a meeting of the architects and developers. Seeing architects busily pinning studies of Rockefeller Center to the wall, he asked if he could help. It was Harrison's first encounter with the twenty-three-year-old Rockefeller, whom he remembers as

good-looking and well-built; he asked intelligent questions and gave the impression of a man who could get a job done. He radiated youth and confidence, but there was no side to him.

After studying foreign exchange for a year in London and Paris, Rockefeller formed a rental agency for the Center, Turck and Company—an enterprise launched in partnership with Fenton Turck, vice-president of the American Radiator Company, and Webster Todd, John Todd's son. According to Harrison:

Nelson was a capitalist and a Republican from the word go. Within a year of the creation of Turck and Company [1931], he had bought out his partners and named the company Special Works, Inc. He took to the wheelings and dealings of this enormous project like a duck takes to water.

Nelson's methods as a rental agent were compared to those of "John D. Rockefeller, Sr., at his roughest."[11] In 1934 a successful realtor, August Heckscher, actually brought suit against Nelson for unfair leasing practices. These consisted of offering prospective Rockefeller Center tenants below-market rates and buying out their unexpired leases in former locations. Heckscher died before the suit went to court.[12]

In those early days of the Center's development, Nelson Rockefeller spent most of his time with Todd's people, but he also started to meet the junior architect-on-the-job for midmorning coffee. The young Rockefeller was attracted to Harrison—then thirty-six—perhaps because of his own frustrated architectural ambitions or simply because he liked and admired him. Whatever the reasons, a strong bond developed between the two men that lasted almost until the end of Rockefeller's life. Harrison, in spite of his relative success at the time, was conscious that he remained an outsider to the major group of "wealthy architects" who regularly received commissions from "the big guys." He saw Rockefeller as someone who could provide, as he said, opportunities "to work with great people and do beautiful buildings. For an architect, it was like being handed a meringue glacée; it was almost too easy."

One such opportunity was the creation of Radio City Music Hall. RCA had secured the services of the leading movie-palace expert, Samuel Lionel Rothafel, as a consultant for the enterprise. (Corbett, Harrison & MacMurray alone among the Associated Architects had actually built a theater [Fig. 19; see chap. 5].) Roxy, as he was called, was a self-made man who had tried everything from professional baseball to orchestra conducting without success, until he developed the idea of showing films surrounded with live entertainment. The formula caught on instantly throughout the United States and in Europe. Overnight Roxy became a theater personality. In 1927 he opened his own entertainment palace, the Roxy, at Fifty to Fifty-first streets between Sixth and Seventh avenues. Designed by Frederick Ahlschager of Chicago with interiors by Harold Rambusch of New York, it was perhaps the most expensive, luxurious modern theater in the world.

Roxy planned both the 6,200-seat Radio City Music Hall—which he envisioned as a cross between the Berlin Wintergarten (Wilhelm Kratz, 1928) and the Palladium Music Hall (Frank Marcham & Co., 1910) in London—and the 3,500-seat Center Movie Theater at Sixth Avenue and Forty-ninth Street. He was obsessed with the idea of unifying audience reaction by eliminating the separation between main floor and balcony, claiming the division allowed people to be crying in one and laughing in the other. He insisted that the center of the house be left open, with three shallow mezzanines replacing the usual deep balcony. Runways at both sides of the auditorium joined the stage and first mezzanine, further uniting the space. To demonstrate his theory, Roxy urged Reinhard and Harrison, along with some of the

19. Corbett, Harrison & MacMurray, Bushnell Memorial Hall, Hartford, Connecticut (1930).

Center's technical experts, to come with him to Europe to see what he called the "original ideas," meaning the sources of his concepts.

In September 1931, Roxy led O. B. Hanson, a renowned NBC radio engineer; Gerard Chatfield, his art advisor; Peter Clark, who created the fantastic Busby Berkeley-style sets for the London Hippodrome; Webster Todd; L. Andrew Reinhard; Henry Hofmeister; and Wallace and Ellen Harrison to Berlin, Moscow, and Leningrad (Fig. 20), with scheduled stops in London and Paris. In Berlin, during interludes between gargantuan meals, Max Reinhardt showed them many of the city's great theaters such as the cavelike Grosses Schauspielhaus, with its stalactite interior, that Hans Poelzig designed for Reinhardt in 1919 and Erich Mendelsohn's streamlined Universum Cinema (1929). Despite the trip's purpose, Roxy preferred socializing to visiting architecture, depriving Harrison and his colleagues of a tour of the recently completed Wintergarten, which claimed the largest stage in Europe.

When the group went on to the U.S.S.R., Ellen Harrison—the only wife on the trip—remained in Berlin. In Russia Roxy's contacts were less extensive than in Germany, but the group saw a number of theaters in Moscow, some, according to Harrison, shown to them by Constantin Stanislavsky. One left a lasting impression

20. Ellen and Wallace Harrison host a dinner for the Radio City Music Hall study group en route to Europe, 1931. Left to right: Roxy, unidentified, L. Andrew Reinhard, Henry Hofmeister, Ellen Harrison, unidentified, Frederick Goetze (treasurer), Peter Clark, Harrison.

on Harrison: the recently renovated Kamerny (Chamber), a small, experimental theater (now the A. Pushkin Drama Theater). The stage's white walls formed a concave curve that repeated the unusual, inward curve of the stage apron. Within these walls hung two additional movable straight walls that could be closed to create a field on which silhouettes were projected. Despite their ingenuity, the European techniques were not adopted for the Music Hall.[13]

Roxy's European jaunt further inflated his self-image. Provided by the Rockefeller management with luxurious accommodations everywhere the group went, he apparently saw himself in the same light as his sponsor and was running up travel expenses as if he were a Rockefeller. Less and less effort was allotted to the original purpose of the trip, and only when Harrison rejoined his wife in Berlin did he meet some of Germany's leading architects.

With her usual matter-of-fact assurance, Ellen Harrison arranged a luncheon attended by Hans Poelzig, Erich Mendelsohn, Peter Behrens, and Walter Gropius. Poelzig and Mendelsohn had been outstanding practitioners of German expressionism; Behrens sometimes, and his former apprentice Gropius regularly, were leaders of the new modernism. Harrison remembered several meetings with each architect, and Radio City Music Hall offers immediate reflections of Poelzig's and Mendelsohn's work, with which other Rockefeller Center architects and Donald Deskey, the hall's interior designer, may have been familiar, at least from photographs or drawings.[14] Berlin had a lasting influence on Harrison. Some of the most interesting small-scale work he did later was expressionistic; from the time he worked at the United Nations in the late 1940s, the sweeping, sculptural curves of his drawings were usually executed in the broad strokes of a Flo-Master pen that made a soft impact on the paper like the drawings of Erich Mendelsohn (see Figs. 109, 190).

A little over a year after the group returned from Europe, on December 27, 1932, Radio City Music Hall opened with what must have been the most gala event of the Depression (Fig. 21). Bejeweled celebrities swathed in furs arriving at the première were pictured in the *New*

York Journal alongside photographs of the needy at the Democratic Club's soup canteen. Torrential rain deterred few from attending the epic, seventeen-act opening-night production, which included performers such as Ray Bolger, Martha Graham, the Wallendas, an eighty-person corps de ballet, and fifty Roxyettes (the future Rockets). Unfortunately, "this great arena," to which the poem of dedication promised to bring "from every far-flung corner of the earth, the joyous songs and voices of mankind,"[15] failed as a business enterprise. The managers added more live stage entertainment, increasing the programs' "popularity"; but this, in turn, had a disastrous effect on the Center Movie Theater (demolished in 1954). Nevertheless, expectations for the success of Radio City Music Hall were so great that in 1933 Corbett, Harrison & MacMurray and Hood & Fouilhoux in association with the English architect C. Howard Crane, submitted an ambitious scheme for a theater complex at London's Hyde Park Corner with interiors almost identical to the Music Hall's (Fig. 22)—an unrealized project with which Roxy's name has also been associated.[16]

Meanwhile, work continued on other parts of Rockefeller Center, where the kind of art to incorporate with the architecture became a particular concern to Harrison. He had been excited by modern art from his first exposure to it as a young man in New York and Paris—an enthusiasm that continued to grow; in Europe with Roxy the previous year, he had talked with friends in Paris about the importance of including first-class art in the new complex. When the question arose who would approach the French artists, instead of employing Harrison or another person equally at home in Parisian modern art circles, the Rockefeller Center managers chose to send John Todd and Raymond Hood. They were so inept in dealing with Matisse and Picasso that Matisse turned them down immediately and Picasso never even accorded them an appointment.

It was customary at the time to display moralistic messages in public buildings. Linking this idea with the art that would decorate the Center, John D. Rockefeller, Jr., invited several well-known scholars to develop a unifying theme.[17] Among them, only Hartley Burr Alexander—a professor of philosophy—had been involved

previously with the arts, having served as advisor to Goodhue on decorations for the Nebraska State Capitol and for the Los Angeles Public Library. Alexander came up with the theme of *Homo Faber*—Man the Builder—which was accepted in January 1932. Rockefeller then proceeded to gather a second advisory group, this time composed of art historians who were to select the artists to illustrate the theme.[18] The group's conservatism was reflected in their choices: Lee Lawrie, Ezra Winter, Paul Manship, Carl Paul Jennewein, Alfred Janniot, Leo Friedlander, Barry Faulkner, Hildreth Meiere, Attilio Piccirilli, Leo Lentelli, Robert Garrison, Carl Milles, René Paul Chambellan, Frank Brangwyn, and José María Sert. Exceptions were Isamu Noguchi (who won his representation through a competition), William Zorach, Gaston Lachaise, and Diego Rivera.[19]

The art committee chose to ignore those avant-garde artists proposed by Nelson Rockefeller at the urging of his mother and of Harrison. Harrison himself did write to Léger, but the artist's strange proposal to collaborate with Walt Disney for an animated film fresco that was to move at the same rate as the RCA Building's escalator never materialized. By far the greatest dilemma of all, however, was posed by the mural commissioned from the well-known Mexican painter and loyal Trotskyite, Diego Rivera.[20]

The Museum of Modern Art had exhibited Rivera's work in 1932 (the exhibition opened December 31, 1931). Both Nelson Rockefeller and his mother owned paintings by the artist, and Abby Rockefeller had asked him to paint portraits of her grandchildren. Despite this, because of a series of misunderstandings over John Todd's invitation to Rivera to submit sketches for a mural, the artist accepted the Rockefeller Center commission only after several conciliatory interventions by Nelson Rockefeller. The title of the mural was *Man at the Crossroads Looking with Uncertainty but with Hope and High Vision to the Choosing of a Course Leading to a New and Better Future*. After Rivera's preliminary description had been approved and painting begun, his first figures made clear that the mural's main elements were very different from what was expected—especially a

21. Associated Architects and Donald Deskey, interior, Radio City
Music Hall, New York City (1932).

22. Corbett, Harrison & MacMurray, Hood & Fouilhoux, and C.
Howard Crane, project for the interior of an International Music
Hall and Opera House, Hyde Park Corner, London (c. 1933).

nightclub scene of the "debauched rich" on the left and what was unmistakably a portrait of Lenin on the right. When, on May 4, 1933, John Rockefeller requested that Lenin's face be painted over with someone else's, Rivera refused, stating that he would rather see the entire work destroyed than alter the Lenin figure. From its first inkling of the problem, the press had a field day writing headlines like the one that appeared in the *World Telegram* on April 24: "Rivera Paints Scenes of Communist Activity and John D. Rockefeller, Jr., Foots the Bill." It was all too much for the Rockefellers. The mural was eventually covered; and on February 9, 1934, it was destroyed. Rivera was paid in full and Sert—politically and artistically his polar opposite—agreed to fulfill the commission with a work entitled *American Progress: The Triumph of Man's Accomplishments through Physical and Mental Labor.*

Lachaise, Giacomo Manzù, Milles, and Sert may not have been as daring as the artists Harrison and Nelson Rockefeller preferred; but they acquitted themselves well. Overall, however, cautious conservatism obviously won out.

In his initial enthusiasm, Owen D. Young saw Radio City as the symbol of a company whose modern technology was bringing performing arts to the public. To achieve this, Young believed the RKO and RCA buildings should provide space for opera, concerts, theater, and film. To accommodate this cultural center, at a meeting of the architects and management on July 15, 1930, Hood and Corbett had suggested that the RCA skyscraper have as its focal point a grand lobby and promenade that would lead to as many as five theaters. Within a few weeks, they produced scheme F-8 for what was called the Forum, which included a grand entrance one story above ground serving as an entrance to several auditoriums and studios, and connected with shopping arcades in the buildings flanking Metropolitan Square Plaza; a smaller arcade ran to Sixth Avenue.[21] Scheme F-8 developed into one of the most complex proposals for Rockefeller Center, eventually calling for an enclosed promenade that would stretch across the entire width of the site and serve as the lobby for the RKO as well as the RCA buildings and for theaters at its north and south ends (Fig. 23).[22]

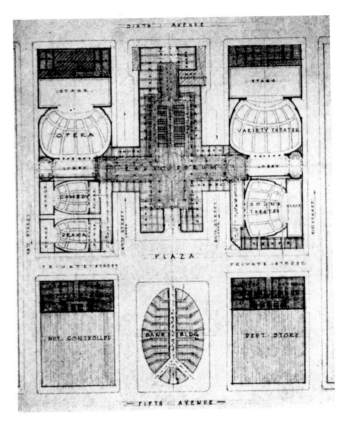

23. Associated Architects, steps in development of Forum Scheme F-8.

The Forum would have been connected with the underground concourse, which, in turn, was planned to link up with a new rail terminal at Rockefeller Center—to serve the New Jersey lines that did not have New York terminals—and with the Sixth Avenue Subway then under construction.[23] Harrison shared the general excitement about the Forum:

> We had step tiers going down, so ... you came in high up at this end, and you looked down through the whole area, and you saw these various exhibits going back into spaces all around there....
>
> But it never got going. I don't know what killed it. It was always killed. We never had enough money or people interested in it.[24]

The Forum was a costly scheme, the success of which depended on the unified composition of a number of disparate elements, including the Metropolitan Opera. The latter's failing finances seriously jeopardized the project, which was eventually abondoned.[25]

In the spring of 1934, the Rockefeller Center planners began to contemplate an expansion of the site that also incorporated the concept of a cultural center. Heydt, the Rockefeller real estate consultant, turned his attention to the area directly north of the Center's private street. By the fall, the Rockefeller Center Corporation had begun to acquire plots on Fifty-first, Fifty-second, and Fifty-third streets between the existing development and the Rockefeller properties on West Fifty-fourth Street.[26]

In January 1934, Fiorello La Guardia had become mayor of New York. He succeeded James J. Walker, forced to resign in the midst of the biggest municipal corruption scandal of the century. With one person in six unemployed, La Guardia set out to relieve the city's bleakness in ways that would be meaningful to his enthusiastic constituency. Within a year of assuming office, he proposed the establishment of a popular municipal art center and conservatory that would include halls for a symphony, grand opera, and light opera; a music library and a museum for musical materials; and space for the Museum of Modern Art and other exhibition halls. Also

suggested for inclusion were a facility for the Guggenheim art collection, a costume museum, and facilities for the Columbia Broadcasting System.[27] Harrison encouraged Nelson Rockefeller to try to ensure that the art center be located in the two blocks north of Rockefeller Center that Heydt had recently acquired. Extending the existing private street between Forty-eighth and Fifty-first streets to Fifty-third Street, the western side of the longer street could be used for the opera and for a building in which to display the Guggenheim collection. To its east could be the Columbia Broadcasting Company and a commercial building; its northern end could culminate with the new building for the Museum of Modern Art (Fig. 24).

Rockefeller, who had become a trustee of the Museum of Modern Art in 1932, suggested in December 1935 that the board consider a new building to house the growing collection. The museum had already moved once: the space limitations and other inconveniences of the Heckscher Building had prompted its relocation in May 1932 to one of the Rockefeller town houses, at 11 West Fifty-third Street. There followed several years during which the museum staff used the RCA Building's temporary gallery for special exhibitions. At a board meeting early in 1936, the trustees agreed to purchase land at 9–19 West Fifty-third Street for a new museum, and a building committee was formed that consisted of A. Conger Goodyear (the museum's president), Alfred H. Barr, Jr., and Nelson Rockefeller.

As the only architect on the museum's board, Philip L. Goodwin seemed the obvious person to design the new building. Described by a recent commentator as "an old-time New Yorker who built gentlemanly houses for people with money and time,"[28] Goodwin had received his professional training at Delano & Aldrich, an exceptionally conservative Beaux-Arts firm responsible for, among other buildings, New York's neo-Georgian Knickerbocker and Colony clubs. The trustees were understandably concerned that the architectural image projected by an institution that presented avant-garde art should be suitably avant-garde. It was agreed that Goodwin would be assisted by Edward Durell Stone, the

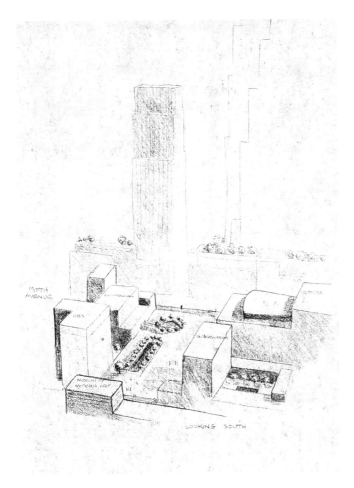

24. Harrison, plan for a northern extension of Rockefeller Center to Fifty-third Street.

25. Harrison & Fouilhoux, Morris & O'Connor, project for Municipal Art Center. Rendering by Hugh Ferriss (c. 1939).

promising young Southerner who had come to the Harrison office from Hood & Fouilhoux after Hood's death in August 1934. Stone had established himself as a modernist in 1933 with a house he designed in Mount Kisco for Richard A. Mandel. Moreover, Nelson Rockefeller liked Stone's redesign of an exhibition space at the western end of the RCA lobby (previously designated as part of the Forum) for a museum of science and industry. Harrison may have suggested that the young architect, recently established in his own office, participate in the museum design.[29]

When the museum opened in May 1939, the new building's stark functionalism was an affront to those who believed that major art institutions should use neoclassical design. Forty years later, upon the museum's announcement of a second expansion, the Goodwin/Stone façade was referred to by the press as a landmark of modern design in America,[30] which it had been from the start.

The Rockefeller Center location was endorsed by La Guardia's municipal art center committee, which asked the firms of what was then Harrison & Fouilhoux and Morris & O'Connor to collaborate on a scheme for it. The result was a stone-clad opera building designed to seat 3,500 and projected to cost about $6 million; it was to sit on a raised plaza above Fifty-second Street (Fig. 25).

As late as the summer of 1938, the possibility of an art center to the north of Rockefeller Center was still under consideration. However, the fashionable '21' Club's refusal to move from its location on West Fifty-second Street drastically complicated an already problematic real estate situation. The project was further complicated by La Guardia's appointment of Robert Moses to oversee it. Already well established within the New York power structure as president of the Long Island State Park Commission, and since 1934, as City Parks Commissioner, Moses had his own ideas about the city's art center. He favored a site to the west of the private street; and, typically, he wanted to use his own architects, particularly Aymar Embury II, instead of the Rockefeller

26. Associated Architects, International Building with La Maison
Française at left and RCA Building in background, Rockfeller
Center (1935). Not shown: RKO and British Empire buildings,
International Music Hall, Center Theater, and plaza.

Center group. In spite of the differences of opinion regarding the function and location of the arts center, an Embury scheme was drawn up for the blocks between Fifty-first and Fifty-third streets. The cost was estimated at $14.5 million for land and buildings (see Fig. 184). It was impossible to raise so great an amount at the time, and Harrison recalled that by then La Guardia had soured on the project as well; the architect quoted La Guardia's bleak opinion of the prominent socialites associated with the Metropolitan Opera: "I don't see why I should be working with these people anyway. I want an opera for *my* people."

In 1938, plans for the Eastern Airlines Building killed once and for all the idea of incorporating the opera within Rockefeller Center. The opportunity to take advantage of the construction in progress—and of John D. Rockefeller, Jr.'s, interest in donating the land he owned in the area—was missed. But almost alone among architects with an unrealized project, Harrison got a second chance, when almost a quarter of a century later John D. Rockefeller 3d asked him to build the opera house at Lincoln Center.

By the spring of 1935, seven buildings had been erected at Rockefeller Center, completing the first stage of development (Fig. 26). Critics of the day found numerous faults with the complex. Lewis Mumford labeled it a "mediocrity—seen through a magnifying glass." He particularly disapproved of the RCA Building, comparing its irregular setbacks unfavorably with the more successful step-ups of the Daily News Building and the unbroken shaft of the Empire State Building.[31] By 1939, however, Mumford had reversed his opinion—at least of the exteriors[32]—and time has proven Rockefeller Center one of the most successful urban developments of the twentieth century. (The original buildings of the Center were designated a National Historic Landmark in 1988.) As William Jordy has pointed out, it is remarkable that "a team dominated by a practical point of view should have designed a complex embracing many of the cardinal ideas of modern urbanism in the very center of Manhattan."[33] Equally remarkable is the failure of most subsequent large-scale developments to match Rockefeller Center's achievements.

For well over a year, Harrison and Fouilhoux had been the only architects at the Center besides Reinhard and Hofmeister. Illness had prevented Hood from active participation since January 1934. In 1929, Corbett, who had formed a partnership with D. Everett Waid, had accepted the Metropolitan Life Insurance commission for a mammoth building to occupy much of the block between Twenty-fourth and Twenty-fifth streets between Park Avenue South and Madison Avenue. He realized that a one-firm commission would be far more remunerative than the Rockefeller project, whose fees were divided among several firms. Together with the presidency of the 1933–34 Chicago World's Fair, Metropolitan Life began to command more and more of Corbett's attention. His new relationship with Louis Skidmore—whom he selected as head draftsman for the Fair (this enabled him to meet the major exhibitors who later became his clients)—inadvertently made Corbett the mentor of two firms that dominated architectural practice after World War II: Harrison & Abramovitz and Skidmore, Owings and Merrill. Corbett stayed on as a consultant for Rockefeller Center; but the relatively small fee he received ($5,000), compared with two-thirds of the total architect's fee to Reinhard & Hofmeister ($50,000) and one-third to Harrison ($25,000),[34] indicated the extent to which his role had diminished. Harrison's and Corbett's interests continued to diverge, and in May 1935 Harrison left to start his own firm with Fouilhoux.

Chapter 8

Harrison, Fouilhoux, Abramovitz

Even before Harrison formed his own firm, Nelson Rockefeller had asked the architect to do a job on his own. Shortly after his marriage in 1930, Rockefeller had bought an apartment on Fifth Avenue; at Rockefeller's invitation, Harrison began to redesign the space around 1934. In a pattern that would repeat itself for most of their building projects, the two men worked together intensely, impervious to the suggestions of others—including, in this case, Rockefeller's young wife, Mary Todhunter Clark. The apartment overlooks Fifth Avenue from the building's fourteenth floor, with a single room above. The way in which Harrison approached the project proves that despite his earlier endorsement of modernism in *School Buildings of Today and Tomorrow* (1931) he had by no means abandoned the vocabulary of his Beaux-Arts training.

Rockefeller had acquired a quantity of eighteenth-century French parquet, which was tailored to fit into most of the apartment's small, intimate rooms. To link those rooms that used ancient flooring with those areas laid with modern floors, Harrison chose walnut paneling, which he articulated with a flattened rococo molding; window surrounds were cut on the same motif (Fig. 27).[1] Repeating a form he had used in his own house in Huntington a few years earlier, Harrison transformed the almost twenty-foot-square dining room into a round space by cutting off the room's corners (which were made into storage areas). A window opened to the north within the wall's curve.

For the fifteenth-story observatory room, Harrison brought in Jan Ruhtenberg, a Swedish architect who had worked with Mies van der Rohe and who taught at Columbia from 1934 to 1936. Ruhtenberg designed the room in severe Bauhaus style. Harrison's introduction of Ruhtenberg may have been his way of directly acquainting Rockefeller with the International Style, which had been suggested as appropriate for the new Museum of Modern Art building.[2] Thus, we see Harrison, in 1935, using modified traditional features, juxtaposed to an essay in pure International Style.

Three to four years later, when Rockefeller acquired the floor below the fourteenth-story apartment, Harrison joined the two apartments with a gray marble spiral staircase for the outer wall of which he commissioned a mural by Fernand Léger. It was on this lower floor that Harrison created the large, much-photographed living room. Here he continued the decorative motif to outline windows and to frame murals with female figures that Matisse painted for overmantels at each end of the room. The window reveals were paneled in harewood, off-white with a satiny finish, meeting the richer walnut paneling in a razor edge.

Harrison tempered modernism with historical allusion throughout his career, making it almost impossible to guess what his solution would be for any given problem. His work reflects his personality. The large, functional public buildings belong in the mainstream of modern architecture and correspond to the public image of Harrison, the master builder. The smaller works correspond to the private Harrison, a personal, historically conscious designer of remarkable fertility; they are original and sometimes prophetic. His use of modified rococo motifs in the interiors of the Rockefeller apartment, and his later experiments with form—for example, the unusual fish-shaped plan of the Stamford, Connecticut, First Presbyterian Church (1958), the domes—imaginatively adapted to acoustical function—of two small auditoriums (1958, 1965), and the expressionistic double wing roof of a country house for Nelson Rockefeller (1965)—range far from the International Style he employed for his large projects. The same paradox was apparent in his behavior. Within the confines of his own home, Harrison, the proper architect, organized and organizer par excellence, loved nothing better than to surround himself with the messy paraphernalia of the artist and to cover large canvases with extravagant abstractions or oversize figures—in many cases copying famous art works, preferably Picasso's and Léger's. He was extraordinarily prolific and in his leisure time, when not sketching architectural ideas, he wielded the paintbrush with admirable lack of inhibition (Fig. 28). Ellen Harrison recalled that in the early years of their marriage her husband kept cans of paint beside their bed in case he woke up and wanted to work in the middle of the night.[3] She painted as well, and the couple spent many relaxed

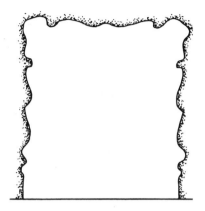

27. Reconstruction of Harrison's rococo motif used in Nelson A. Rockefeller apartment, New York City (1935).

28. Watercolor by Harrison in the style of the Purists.

hours working side by side, producing remarkable look-alikes of masterpieces of modern art. Ellen's casual appearance and reflective nature contributed to the personal side of Harrison's life.

Harrison's new partner, J. André Fouilhoux, had the kind of tall good looks that seemed more typical of an American of the Eastern establishment than of the Frenchman he was (Fig. 29). Born in Paris in 1879, he trained as a civil and mechanical engineer at the Ecole Centrale des Arts et Manufactures and, in 1904, came to the United States. From 1909 until 1917 he worked in Portland, Oregon, in partnership with Morris H. Whitehouse, leaving to serve in the United States Field Artillery in France during World War I. Upon his return, he worked for Albert Kahn and then for Raymond Hood, with whom he formed a partnership in 1927. The French engineer had helped Hood with the tricky technical problems posed by the heavy printing presses in the Chicago Tribune Building. He had also worked with Hood on the American Radiator, Daily News, and McGraw-Hill buildings—three landmarks of early modernism in New York. Fouilhoux's courteousness and consideration contrasted strongly with Hood's ebullient excitability. Charming and mild-mannered, the Frenchman was more like Harrison in personality; and because Fouilhoux was more concerned with engineering than with design, the possibilities for conflict were minimized. Despite its beginnings in one of the most economically depressed periods in the country's history, the partnership—which lasted until Fouilhoux died in 1945—seems to have worked well.[4]

The relatively small amount of construction in New York City during the doldrums of the 1930s was mostly residential, and a large percentage of this was low-cost housing. From their beginnings in the United States, the housing movement and the development of the apartment house centered in New York. In 1932 the Museum of Modern Art's *Modern Architecture* exhibition included a separate section on housing, planned by Clarence Stein, Henry Wright, and Catherine Bauer, with a special catalogue introduced by Lewis Mumford. That same year the federal government laid the foundations of its massive housing program.[5] Even before this,

New York's New School for Social Research had begun to examine slum conditions on the Lower East Side. In this endeavor, Ralph Walker—prominent designer of Art Deco skyscrapers and principal in the firm of Voorhees, Gmelin and Walker—joined Joseph Urban, Corbett, and Harrison to lead investigative teams of apprentice architects. One novice in Harrison's group was a young man named Max Abramovitz, who had recently arrived from Chicago (Fig. 30).

Abramovitz came to New York in 1931 because, in his words, "Chicago was in the dumps then."[6] New York could hardly have been much less depressed than Chicago, but it provided Abramovitz with an opportunity to teach at Columbia University's School of Architecture. When Abramovitz received his B.S. in 1929, Lemuel E. Dellenback was dean of architecture at the University of Illinois; when Dellenback became a professor of design at Columbia he invited several of his former students to join him. On the strength of a letter of introduction to Walker, Abramovitz signed up for his New School group; a clerical error landed him on Harrison's team instead. At the end of the year he had moved uptown with Harrison's other apprentices to work in the office on West Forty-second Street. Thus began the long and rich association of Harrison and Abramovitz.

In 1932 Abramovitz won second place in the Prix de Paris competition; he spent the following two years at the Ecole des Beaux-Arts on a Columbia fellowship. When he returned to the United States, he turned again to Harrison, who, still part of the Associated Architects, had started work independent of Corbett in a small office on the fifty-second floor of 45 Rockefeller Plaza. Harrison invited Abramovitz to join him there with Walter Kilham, W. K. Oltar-Jevsky, and two or three others.

The *Nation* estimated that by 1934 six out of seven of the country's architects and half its engineers were out of work. The newly formed Harrison and Fouilhoux office experienced periods of such uninterrupted unemployment that at one point Harrison put the staff to work redesigning Central Park, just to keep them busy. In 1938 the firm's continued lack of work allowed participation in more than the usual number of architectural

29. J. André Fouilhoux with Harrison (1930s).

30. Max Abramovitz (1930s).

competitions: an art center for Wheaton College in Norton, Massachusetts; a festival theater and arts center for the College of William and Mary in Williamsburg, Virginia; and a new campus and library for Goucher College in Towson, Maryland. Harrison and Fouilhoux's entry for Goucher (Fig. 31) has been called one of the first modern large-scale environmental designs in the United States.[7] The largely glazed, symmetrical elevations of the reinforced concrete library prefigure Harrison's project for a concert hall at X City (Fig. 32; see Fig. 91).

Harrison's small team was participating in design and execution of office buildings scheduled at Rockefeller Center: Time & Life; Associated Press (1938); Eastern Air Lines; and U.S. Rubber (1940; now Simon and Schuster). By now, relatively low fees initially agreed to paid only part of Harrison's office expenses and staff salaries. The firm produced a number of other projects—private houses, the Rockefeller Apartments on West Fifty-fourth Street, the Theme Center for the New York World's Fair, and the New York City Aquarium—in these some of Harrison's most innovative design ideas appeared for the first time. In a category by itself, but also significant for its inventiveness, was the African Plains for the Bronx Zoo.

Harrison realized that the houses he might design for family and friends presented ideal opportunities for experimentation. Around 1932, he enjoyed the luxury of designing a house for his wife and himself, with no one else's wishes to contend with.

The couple had been using Mrs. Milton's home on Oyster Bay for weekends. Searching for Long Island property, they looked inland to avoid the fog they both disliked. Mrs. Milton knew a Colonel Simpson who was selling eighty-five acres of wooded property near Huntington for twenty-five dollars an acre. She was going to buy the land as an investment. When at the last minute she decided not to, Harrison borrowed money to purchase it himself in 1931 (he eventually sold all but eleven acres), leaving the young architect with inadequate money to pay for construction. That April, Harrison solved this problem, too, when he visited the annual Architectural League show in Grand Central Palace: for

just over $1,000 he bought the small prefabricated Aluminaire house displayed there.

His fascination with technical innovation, his growing attraction to modernism, and his interest in prefabrication of housing drew Harrison to this simple example of the International Style (Fig. 33a,b).[8] The Tin house, as he called it, was in fact made mostly of Beschel-Duralton aluminum with non-load-bearing walls carried on a steel and aluminum frame. It had been designed by an American, A. Lawrence Kocher, then managing editor of *Architectural Record*, and a Swiss, Albert Frey, who had worked with Le Corbusier. It was an adaptation of Le Corbusier's Citrohan House (1921).

When the Aluminaire house was deposited in pieces on Harrison's property, he was faced with a major problem in reassembling it. The exterior aluminum skin had to be attached to two layers of insulation, in which wood plugs had been set to take nails from the exterior. No one had considered that once the metal sheathing was in place, these holes were almost impossible to locate![9] Instead of the eighteen days stipulated by Kocher and Frey for erection, the job took several months. And by the time the land was bought, bulldozed, a road put in, and the house assembled on a concrete base, Harrison had spent $26,000, which he could ill afford.[10]

After the birth of a daughter, Sarah, in May 1931, Ellen pleaded for more space. Harrison began to design what he thought of as an extension to the Tin house, to be connected to its north wall. He called it "an exercise in how to fit circles together";[11] the circle was becoming an important theme in his designs.

The new house's round living room is an ample thirty-two feet in diameter, with a ceiling sloping imperceptibly from sixteen feet at the entrance to sixteen feet seven inches at the window-doors opposite. Harrison made the tilt to provide drainage for the roof; the change in ceiling height, however, subtly affects the interior, directing the gaze skyward. The south wall of the living room is almost entirely glazed, with glass doors opening to the exterior. About six feet beyond the north side of the living room a second curved wall stretches approximately thirty feet; the space contained between the two walls was used as a library. Harrison later attributed the

31. Harrison & Fouilhoux, plan of Goucher College campus, competition entry (1938).

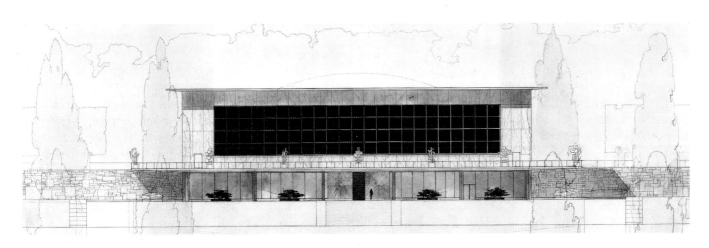

32. Library, Goucher College, competition entry (1938).

33. A. Lawrence Kocher & Albert Frey, Aluminaire House.

a) Aluminaire House shortly after its erection at Huntington, Long Island (1931).

b) Aluminaire House with its partially open ground floor made into a basement, third floor garden terrace enclosed, and a wood shed attached at one side (early 1960s).

small clerestory windows in this area to budget restrictions; but, in fact, the limited light and the dramatic drop to an eight-foot ceiling create a protected, cavelike atmosphere that invites reading and writing, and contrasts dramatically with the openness of the adjacent living room. A door on the western side of the living room leads toward a second circle, the dining room, the dimensions of which are exactly half those of the living room. Across the corridor from the dining room is a small quarter-circle bathroom the shape expressed on the exterior (Figs. 34, 35). A linear wing incorporating stables and a garage was added around the fall of 1932. To connect it with the new dining room, Harrison conceived a corridor with what he described as "a kind of Mies glass look."

In the 1930s, several architects incorporated circular rooms in houses they designed: Frank Lloyd Wright's Ralph Jester project (1938) and Stone's A. Conger Goodyear house (1940) are outstanding examples. Harrison's Huntington house seems to be an early example of round rooms in modern domestic architecture. In his entry for the Oregon State Capitol competition of 1936, Harrison adapted a circular plan to the scale of a public building.[12] Harrison again applied the circle to a domestic scheme in 1950 with the ground plan for a six-room model house for Alcoa; unbuilt, it was to be cantilevered on a slim support on an escarpment overlooking Pittsburgh (Fig. 36).

Around 1940, the Tin house was transported to another location on the property, and a second, linear wing with generous bedrooms and baths was added to the main house. The bedrooms opened onto a porch that was later widened, glazed, and used as a greenhouse. This last addition again allowed Harrison to experiment—here with materials rather than form. Instead of the cinder block covered with concrete of most of the house, he used newly developed asbestos sheathing, which for aesthetic reasons was applied inside out to the exterior of the bedroom walls (Fig. 37).

The Harrison house accommodated plaster casts of sculpture used by Janniot for La Maison Française at Rockefeller Center. Additionally, in 1942, Léger, who was living in America to escape the war in Europe, came to visit. Harrison asked him for a painting to cover a large portion of his living-room wall. Léger complied with a heroic black-and-white mural of human figures: "The Divers" (Fig. 38); within a year, he added a witty outdoor complement of animals and fish to the floor of the forty-foot circular swimming pool.

After the war, Harrison facilitated his habit of bringing office work out to Huntington—often accompanied by several draftsmen whom he would keep overnight—by converting a potato barn near the house into a small model shop. Then, around 1950, feeling the need for a proper studio, he continued his experiments with the circle in what he described as an effort to improve on the proportions of the living room.[13] The result was a room forty-two feet in diameter, with a twelve-foot-two-inch-high ceiling. A large, straight expanse of floor-to-ceiling glazing breaks the circle's curve at the south. Steel framing divides the glazing into squares, several of which, together, constitute double doors; otherwise the wall is unbroken by windows. Three skylights pierce the roof, which, like that of the living room, pitches up slightly. The enclosed studio space provides quiet privacy whereas the cross-axial living room responds to the house's traffic pattern.

The Huntington house became an important part of the Harrisons' life. Ellen Harrison preferred the country to the city; she enjoyed riding horseback and skeet shooting with her husband. Entertaining in this ample, relaxed environment was more to her liking than the formality imposed by a city apartment. Of the many friends who visited in Huntington, none were more frequent or more enthusiastic callers than Robert Moses, the New York City Parks Commissioner, and his wife, Mary. An ardent swimmer, Ellen, a month before the official opening on August 4, 1929 of the new Jones Beach, deposited a Fourth-of-July bouquet of red and white wild strawberries with dark blue larkspur at the Moses's door to say: "thank you" for Jones Beach. No sooner had she left her gift than Mrs. Moses and her two teenage daughters appeared. The two women liked one another and this strengthened the bond between Harrison and Robert Moses.[14]

34. Ellen and Wallace Harrison standing in living room door, Harrison house, Huntington, Long Island (c. 1940).

35. Dining room exterior, Harrison house (1932).

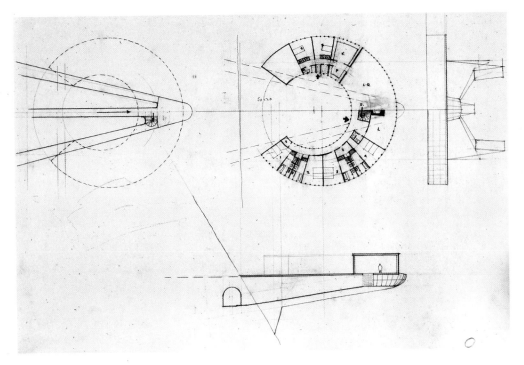

36. Harrison, Alcoa guest house (1950).

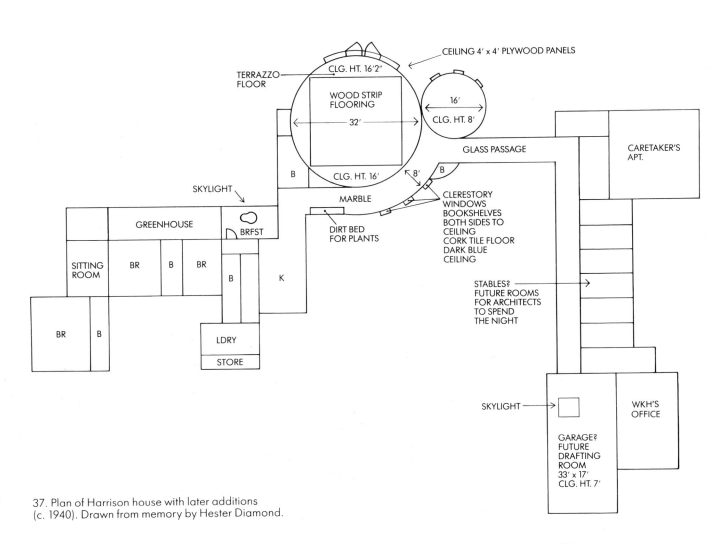

CEILING 4' x 4' PLYWOOD PANELS

CLG. HT. 16'2"

TERRAZZO
FLOOR

WOOD STRIP
FLOORING

32'

16'

CLG. HT. 8'

CLG. HT. 16'

B

SKYLIGHT

MARBLE

GLASS PASSAGE

CARETAKER'S
APT.

8'

B

GREENHOUSE

BRFST

DIRT BED
FOR PLANTS

CLERESTORY
WINDOWS
BOOKSHELVES
BOTH SIDES TO
CEILING
CORK TILE FLOOR
DARK BLUE
CEILING

SITTING
ROOM

BR

B

BR

B

K

STABLES?
FUTURE ROOMS
FOR ARCHITECTS
TO SPEND
THE NIGHT

BR

B

LDRY

STORE

SKYLIGHT

WKH'S
OFFICE

GARAGE?
FUTURE
DRAFTING
ROOM
33' x 17'
CLG. HT. 7'

37. Plan of Harrison house with later additions
(c. 1940). Drawn from memory by Hester Diamond.

39. Harrison, Albert Milton house, Washington, Connecticut (1936).

38. Living room with mural, "The Divers," by Fernand Léger, Harrison house.

In 1936 Harrison built houses for his two brothers-in-law: one in Washington, Connecticut, for Albert Milton and one in Bermuda for David Milton. At first glance, the Albert Milton house looks like two New England Greek Revival houses placed side by side. Then one sees, in reality, two two-story wings connected by a single-story corridor (Fig. 39). The siting takes advantage of the beautiful surrounding hills. Milton's wife was an exceptionally small woman, who wanted a country house to suit her size. Ellen Harrison likened the result to "a doll's house," with façades barely twenty-five feet wide, low ceilings, and small doors. Harrison simplified neoclassical grammar, eliminating capitals from the pilasters and lowering the pitch of the gable roof.

Harrison based the house for David Milton on a circular theme, as he had his own; but here the plan is a half circle with pie-shaped rooms (Figs. 40, 41). In both shape and scale, the curved plan echoes the small bay that the house overlooks. In the David Milton house, Harrison's vernacular allusions enriched his modern vocabulary. Forty years after the David Milton house was built, many of the same elements Harrison used—a stepped gable roof, prominent chimneys, upstairs portico, and dark shutters against white stucco walls—Venturi & Rauch incorporated in their Brant House in Bermuda, hailed as a significant example of the new postmodernism (Fig. 42). The resemblance between the Milton and Brant houses goes beyond the adaptation of vernacular elements. Also similar are crescent plans, circular driveways completing the crescents, and gabled entrances.

Because they had always thought of Harrison as a "skyscraper architect," his friends Julian and Narcissa Street were surprised and delighted when in 1937 he consented to design, and supervise construction of, their house in Scarborough, New York. The Street house is in the shape of an L, built in local fieldstone and steel and glass, related to the houses designed at the time by such modernists as Breuer and Gropius. Large circular windows gave the owners the feeling of "living on a boat" (Figs. 43, 44). Forty-five years later, Julian Street maintained that

40. Harrison, David Milton house, Bermuda (1936).

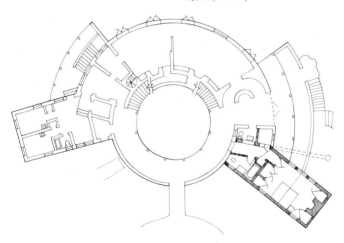

41. First floor plan, David Milton house.

42. Venturi & Rauch, in collaboration with Onions, Bouchard, McCulloch, northwest wing, Brant house, Bermuda (1975).

43. Harrison, façade, Julian and Narcissa Street house, Scarborough, New York (1938).

44. Harrison, entrance, Julian and Narcissa Street house.

building that house was one of the greatest experiences I ever had. In those days there was nothing to go by; it was a study in "how did I want to live?" After the plans were drawn up, we never changed a thing; it worked marvelously.[15]

The following year, Harrison completed another project for Nelson Rockefeller. Known as the Hawes Guest House, at Pocantico, it comprises two small fieldstone pavilions: one, rectilinear, contains two bedrooms; the other consists of a round living room, with electrically operated floor-to-ceiling windows that open on a semicircular swimming pool. Both pavilions sit firmly on a single heavy slate base flush with the lawn and are protected by a wide, flat roof over the two. Harrison asked Léger to design a cutout in the roof to provide more light for the entranceway (Figs. 45, 46). As with most of Harrison's houses, the Hawes Guest House is carefully sited to views of the surrounding landscape, in this case, the Hudson River.

The newly created firm of Harrison & Fouilhoux built its first major commission as a direct result of John D. Rockefeller, Jr.'s, decision to abandon the municipal art center for which the firm had competed earlier. Rockefeller was left with several unused plots on the blocks between Fifty-first and Fifty-fifth streets near Fifth Avenue. He decided to act on his son Nelson's suggestion to use 17 West Fifty-fourth Street for an apartment house. As a matter of course, the young Rockefeller turned to Harrison, supplying him with the first consequential project he was to execute as the head of his own firm. The Rockefeller Apartments (1936), extending north to Fifty-fifth Street, proved to be one of his distinguished designs.

To this day Fifty-fourth Street boasts many of the distinctive buildings that graced it in 1935, beginning with McKim, Mead & White's imposing Italianate palazzo for the University Club (1899) on the northwest corner of Fifth Avenue and continuing west with several elegant town houses by the same firm. All the houses on the north side of Fifty-fourth Street date approximately from the turn of the century; several have generous bay

45. Harrison, cut-out roof between the two pavilions, Hawes Guest house, Pocantico, New York (1939).

Ezra Stoller © ESTO

46. Hawes Guest house.

windows similar to those characteristic of the Boston areas Harrison frequented as a youth. To echo these neighboring bays and at the same time to provide more air, light, and a view, the architect decided to cantilever windows on the street façades of twin twelve-story wheat-colored brick buildings (with a private garden between them)—four vertical rows on Fifty-fourth Street and two on the narrower Fifty-fifth Street elevation.[16] Harrison boldly cantilevered out whole semicircular bays from the unadorned façades, because, he said: "I wanted to be able to see up and down the street." The bays were generally used as dining areas; since they were glazed he carefully set unbroken brick walls to screen the view from one bay into another. Harrison's half-cylindrical bays required complicated and costly engineering. Nelson Rockefeller, undaunted by the idea of spending extra money, wanted "to see how it would work out."[17] Harrison marveled that he had found a client sufficiently interested in architectural experiments to finance them (Figs. 47–50). To produce the final drawings he selected his firm's best designers: Max Abramovitz and Edward Durell Stone.

Since the high point of elegant Art Deco apartment houses around 1930, no important residential development had been constructed in mid-Manhattan. The Rockefeller Apartments provided the first break in this five-year hiatus; despite the depressed economy, they were an instant success. Not only were ninety percent of the 120 apartments rented on the basis of plans alone, but the completed project was acclaimed by Mumford as "the most brilliant and most successful example of modern architecture in the city."[18] The layouts of individual units were carefully conceived to include features usually found in larger, more expensive buildings—such as wood-burning fireplaces and bedrooms equipped with silent ventilators. The private interior garden was an extravagant asset. Additional attractions included views over the Museum of Modern Art garden to the south and the proximity to Rockefeller Center. Yet the apartments were rented at market prices, from eleven hundred to four thousand dollars per year. By the end of the first year it was apparent that profits would be negligible (net $11,866.34).[19] Harrison learned an important lesson: al-

though the Rockefeller Apartments were widely admired and enjoyed a high rate of occupancy, they yielded little financial benefit.

Before the end of the decade, Harrison & Fouilhoux received two more commissions thanks to the Rockefeller family. Both came from the New York Zoological Society, known as the Bronx Zoo.[20] Laurance Rockefeller, one of Nelson's brothers, was a trustee of the society, and when it received an anonymous pledge to develop the zoo's southeastern portion, he asked Harrison to study the problem.

The zoo had been built almost entirely in the late 1890s under Henry F. Osborn, father of Fairfield Osborn, the zoo's president at the time of Harrison's involvement. The architects had been Heins & LaFarge, famous for, among other things, their design (1888) for the Cathedral of Saint John the Divine. Charles Platt, also a successful establishment architect, contributed gate lodges and posts for Paul Manship's spectacular Paul J. Rainey Memorial Gate (1934). The young Harrison & Fouilhoux office thus had brilliant precedents to follow. The mysterious donor was revealed as Marshall Field III, widely known for his great wealth and philanthropic munificence.

For the addition, the zoo's trustees wanted to try a recently introduced device: instead of confining animals within cages, they were left free to roam in open spaces. The Saint Louis, Missouri, zoo had experimented with the idea after its innovation at Hamburg, but on a much smaller scale than now planned for the "Plains of Africa-In-The-Bronx," as it was referred to. Harrison assigned the project's research to Harmon Goldstone, a young draftsman who had joined the firm in September 1936, shortly after his graduation from the Columbia School of Architecture. The resulting design, worked out by Harrison with Goldstone's assistance, consisted of a dramatic juxtaposition of predator and prey. Surrounding the raised Lion Island at the site's western side is a twenty-foot-wide, thirteen-to-sixteen-foot-deep moat, landscaped so that it was soon invisible. The high wall that encircles the entire plains area below ground level was given a rustic facing and was masked by vegetation.

47. Harrison, Rockefeller Apartments, New York City (1936).
Rendering by Hugh Ferriss.

48. Fifty-fourth Street entrance, Rockefeller Apartments.

49. Fifty-fourth Street façade, view from the Museum of Modern Art, Rockefeller Apartments.

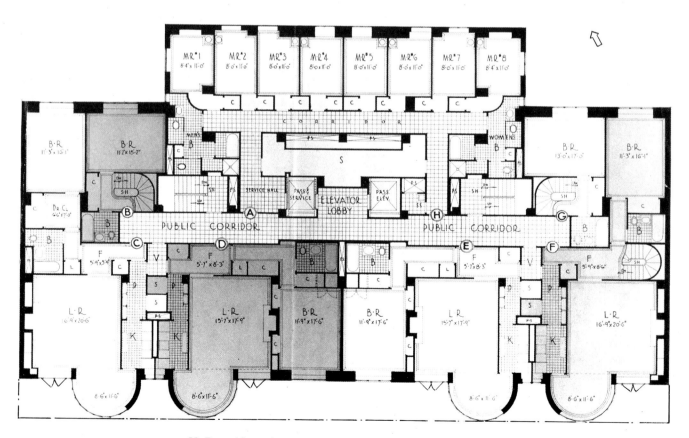

50. Typical floor plan, Rockefeller Apartments.

The treatment of both moat and wall creates so successfully the illusion of a natural habitat that the animals—ranging from lions to zebras, giraffes, antelopes, ostriches and cranes—appear to be startlingly unrestricted. The impression of verisimilitude is deepened by the absence of visible surrounding buildings and by what a contemporary article described as the "architectural feeling of the Dark Continent"[21]—accomplished by a tall stockade entrance gateway and "African huts" varying in shape from small, squat structures to forms that rise to twenty feet and consist almost entirely of thatched roofs (Fig. 51).

The African Plains, which opened to general acclaim on May 1, 1941, was realized far more successfully than the Zoological Society's second project, for a new aquarium. Since the New York Aquarium, the first institution of its kind in the United States, had been administered by the Zoological Society since the beginning of the century, it seemed logical for the new facilities to be located in the Bronx. Moses, however, did not agree; the needs of his own projects took precedence with him. In 1938 his Parks Department had taken over Coney Island's beach and boardwalk, and Moses was convinced that the new aquarium would promote development. It was pointed out that, in addition to administrative problems, there was no public for the aquarium in Coney Island; Moses is reported to have flatly asserted: "The aquarium is going to be at Coney Island or there won't be an aquarium."[22]

Sensing the aquarium's importance both to the city and to his friend's ambitious scheme for Coney Island, Harrison produced one of his most dramatic plans. He took full advantage of the magnificent twelve-acre oceanfront site, using a long, gentle curve to create a generously proportioned one-story building that hugged the beach. Two immense windows were located at either end of the façade and a curved colonnade provided an inviting main entrance. On the opposite side, a terrace restaurant offered refreshments. The building was to have been almost five city blocks long, enclosing five great circular halls dimly lit and connected by a mid-level bridge from which the visitor could enjoy a quick overview of the exhibits. Stairs to the ground level allowed a more comprehensive survey of the displays (Fig. 52).

51. Harrison, "the African Plains," Bronx Zoo, New York City (1941).

52. Harrison, project for the Coney Island Aquarium, Brooklyn, New York (c. 1940).

1. Main entrance
2. Library
3. Entrance waterfall
4. Clouds-to-earth
5. Three banks of tropical marine tanks
6. Coral reef and moray tanks
7. Shark tank
8. Ten research laboratories
9. Two banks of marine tanks
10. Eight large marine tanks
11. Oceanic tank
12. Electric eel exhibit
13. Fifty tropical freshwater tanks
14. Four large tanks (crocodiles, etc.)
15. Swamp corridor
16. Four temperate freshwater tanks
17. Eighteen temperate freshwater tanks
18. Four trout tanks
19. Crystal column
20. Sixteen small freshwater tanks
21. Seven large freshwater tanks
22. Twenty-four temperate marine tanks
23. Antarctic penguin exhibit
24. Temperate zone penguin exhibit
25. Oceanic tank
26. Auditorium

The design was barely completed before Harrison went off to serve in Washington in World War II. Abramovitz and Goldstone soon followed, and Moses's preferred architect, Aymar Embury II, took over the drawings. (By the war's end, the cost of the project was approximately five times the prewar estimate and it had to be abandoned.)[23]

The Harrison & Fouilhoux association had weathered the Depression and by 1939 was well on its way to success.[24] The young architect from Worcester was making a brilliant career for himself, and he was making it remarkably quickly; barely a dozen years had passed since his initial junior partnership with Helmle and Corbett.

While establishing himself professionally, Harrison was also making a name in education. In 1933, after teaching at Columbia and at the New School for Social Research, he was invited to join a small committee to revise the Columbia School of Architecture curriculum. The committee recommended a modern system to replace the Beaux-Arts approach and it fell to Joseph Hudnut, the school's new dean, to implement the program,[25] but the reforms took a long time to become effective. From 1939 to 1942, as associate professor of design at the Yale School of Architecture, Harrison abetted a swifter change in a school's design philosophy. By then he was committed to modernism, and became a catalyst in revolutionizing architectural education in the United States.

His last two years at Yale coincided with wartime service in Washington. Two afternoons a week, sometimes accompanied by Abramovitz, he would make the round trip to New Haven. By 1940 students were rebellious; they believed the school ignored the profession's realities and they regarded the two New Yorkers as representatives of an enlightened attitude.

In his three years as chief design critic, he was almost single-handedly responsible for transforming a curriculum that had been based strictly on the conceptual formulas of the Ecole des Beaux-Arts to a practical, modern program. Like others before him, such as Otto Wagner, Harrison presented students with real-life problems, and brought in many European modernists as visitors:

Le Corbusier; Oscar Nitzchke;[26] Josep Lluís Sert; Maurice E. H. Rotival, a French city planner; and Alvar Aalto.

Harmon Goldstone had visited Aalto's studio in Helsinki in 1935, and brought back pictures of the striking, light-colored wood furniture Aalto was producing. Harrison had been enthusiastic, and he persuaded Laurance Rockefeller and Goldstone to join him in putting up five thousand dollars each to create New Furniture, Inc., a company that for three years (until war intervened) enjoyed great success among those alert enough to appreciate Aalto's aesthetic. Harrison's office helped the Museum of Modern Art prepare an exhibition of Aalto's architecture and furniture in 1938. Harrison met Aalto on the Finn's first trip to the United States that year. When the two men finally met, there was an immediate affinity. Both were humanists in the broad sense, deeply concerned with the social implications of their work and committed to high principles of professional and personal behavior. Like Harrison, Aalto was warm and outgoing and enjoyed people. In spite of limited English, he managed to communicate. The meeting in 1938 marked the beginning of Harrison's lifelong admiration for and friendship with Aalto, who had a strong influence on his work.

Previously, Yale offered no courses on city planning and to supplement Rotival's lectures, Harrison invited speakers (many were his friends): Lewis Mumford; Robert Moses; Jasper McLevy, the elderly socialist mayor of Bridgeport, Connecticut. Buckminster Fuller and Alexander Calder also accepted his invitations to address the students. European artists included, of course, Léger and Amedée Ozenfant, who initiated a seminar on the use of color in architecture. Harrison even tried—unsuccessfully—to convince the university to let him invite Elsa Schiaparelli, when the flamboyant Parisian couturière was in New York, where he consulted her on the two-story atrium he was designing for the Eastern Airlines Building.[27]

Among Harrison's students was Porter McCray, who from 1947 to 1963 directed the Museum of Modern Art's Circulating Exhibition Department. McCray remembers that for him and his fellow students the ideas of these modernists were a revelation. The dean of the School of Fine Arts at the time was Everett V. Meeks, who had several years' experience with the traditionalist firm of Carrère & Hastings, and who was an active member of the Society of Beaux-Arts Architects. After exposure to Harrison's progressive ideas, students became so strident in their demand for reform that they asked McCray to serve as intermediary between them and the dean.[28]

Throughout the Western world diverse attitudes toward architecture were vying with one another. American popular taste favored conventional buildings derived from different combinations of historic styles, and many prominent architects continued to produce eclectic buildings according to the Beaux-Arts system. From the early 1930s, only a small minority, led by Gropius, Marcel Breuer, Philip Johnson, George Howe, William Lescaze, and Harrison practiced the stark simplicity of the International Style.

One of Harrison's chief contributions to Yale was a conference on prefabricated housing that he persuaded his client, and Yale alumnus, Henry Luce to co-sponsor early in 1939. Known as the Yale-Life Conference, it provided information on new materials and technologies, new uses of glass, steel, and synthetics, and methods of assemblage. The conference reflected Harrison's interest in innovation, and in his opening talk, he criticized those concerned with housing for focusing on social ideals while ignoring technological inventions that could lower building costs.[29]

Harrison's first working experience with low-cost housing was frustrating.[30] In 1939 a $50 million New York State Public Housing Program was financed by state bonds.[31] In 1944, during World War II, its first project, Fort Greene Houses (now Walt Whitman and Raymond V. Ingersoll Houses) in Brooklyn, was at last completed. Harrison & Fouilhoux were among nine firms designing 3,500 apartments. The Fort Greene project was designated "national defense housing," adding wartime regulations to already restrictive public-housing rules.[32] Built in the T, L, and X shapes that were common to such developments at the time,[33] uniformly bleak

thirteen-story structures are relieved only by some six-story buildings in their midst (Fig. 53).

Harrison's second such project, Clinton Hill Apartments in Brooklyn (1943), commissioned by Time-Equities Life Insurance (Fig. 54)[34] were designated as personnel housing for the nearby Brooklyn Navy Yard. Private sponsorship permitted more imaginative design: pairs of stepped back buildings are placed at angles, four buildings in each block. Harrison set linear buildings at the ends of the block, creating pleasant, self-contained spaces. There are exceptionally large windows in each living room,[35] and every apartment is well lit and well ventilated as a result of the setbacks. Blue and white nautical motifs adorn the top of each entranceway. The Clinton Hill project remains today desirable middle-income housing in its area, unlike the Fort Greene complex which soon reverted to the slum it was intended to replace.

Like other leading architects of his time, Harrison believed in the importance of building low-cost housing. While his single unit designs are noteworthy, the exigencies of this type of large building limited his expression to banality as it did that of most architects.

Despite the numerous large, low-rental apartment houses that were built with government subsidies during the Depression, the PWA's allocation of money for urban housing was relatively small compared with what it spent on roads and bridges. With the help of private industry and the press, the tremendous road infrastructure created by the government at this time encouraged the devlopment of single-family, suburban houses rather than city dwellings.[36] The *Ladies' Home Journal*, one of several magazines that took an active role in stimulating ideas for the design of moderately priced houses, sponsored two houses at the Madison Square Garden North American Exposition in May 1937. One was Harrison & Fouilhoux's "House of Tomorrow," a modern alternative to the conventional home (represented at the exposition by a Cape Cod Colonial-style house). The feature of Harrison & Fouilhoux's sleek, one-story structure was a semicircular living room with elegant plate-glass windows that dropped into the floor.

53. Harrison, Walt Whitman Houses (formerly Fort Greene Houses), Myrtle to Park avenues, Carlton Avenue to Prince Street, Brooklyn, New York (1944).

54. Harrison, Fouilhoux & Abramovitz, Clinton Hill Apartments, Section 1, Clinton to Waverly avenues, Willoughby to Myrtle avenues, Brooklyn, New York (1943).

In the mid-1940s Harrison became a member of the American Society of Planners and Architects, a progressive organization concerned with integrating aesthetics, economics, technology, and sociology with architecture. ASPA functioned for four years only, but its membership, which included Gordon Bunshaft, Gropius, Howe, Johnson, Louis Kahn, and Edgar Kaufmann, Jr., exerted an ongoing influence on urban architecture.[37]

Mass-producing houses in a factory and transporting and erecting them elsewhere had existed at least since the mid-nineteenth century, but progressive architects began to investigate the potentials of prefabricated housing. The methods of the automobile industry provided an obvious model for these experiments. Harrison's wartime experience gave him the idea of applying recently developed aircraft technology as well. With his own Tin house in mind, he approached Laurance Rockefeller about the possibility of interesting McDonnell-Douglas Aircraft in the manufacture of prefabricated metal homes. As a result George Dudley and Oscar Wiggins from the Harrison firm (after Fouilhoux's death in 1945, Harrison & Abramovitz) together with André Sire, a French designer who had worked with Auguste Perret in France, went to McDonnell headquarters in Saint Louis. There they hoped to produce two-bedroom prototypes. When Dudley telephoned to report that the aeronautics engineers had put the cost of each prototype at $2 million, Harrison exploded: "My God, I can go out into a potato field and build two aluminum houses for $2,000 each!"

Harrison tried to do better on his own land in Huntington, adapting new concrete road-building methods he had seen in Venezuela. First, concrete slabs for the floors of two houses were poured. Each house would have a living room, two bedrooms, a bath, and a kitchen. A grid of reinforcing steel rods was then erected on each slab, with all the electrical and plumbing outlets built into it. Around this, a large form of steel plates was lifted into place by a giant crane, adapted from those built during World War II to lift damaged airplanes from runways. Concrete was then poured into the form and allowed to harden into inside and outside walls. Twenty-four hours later, the crane returned to pick up the form and move it to the next house site. The same crane, equipped with a suction lifting device, picked up individual concrete roof slabs from the casting location and moved them to the appropriate shell.

The experiment proved not only that the system worked but that it had built-in efficiencies as well. The steel unit was so constructed that setting and stripping could be accomplished without disassembling the forms. The cost of the roof slabs was reduced by pouring them flat, using only edge forms. After curing, each roof slab was sprayed with an oil film to serve as a bed for the next. If the owner wished, the house could be painted as soon as the form was lifted off, and it was already fully equipped with plumbing and electrical connections. Only fixtures, doors, and windows remained to be installed (Figs. 55–57).[38] Nelson Rockefeller recognized the commercial potential of Harrison's new idea for low-cost housing in Latin America, and in 1947 he moved quickly to form the IBEC Housing Corporation—a separate subsidiary of the International Basic Economy Corporation, which he had created earlier that year. In 1948 the IBEC method was tested in Norfolk, Virginia, for a low-rent housing project of 204 duplex units sponsored by the Federal Housing Administration. Each four-room unit was meant to rent for about forty-five dollars per month. The houses were finished on time and to the full satisfaction of exacting FHA standards; they even showed a modest profit for the IBEC Housing Corporation.

An early monolithic concrete house was realized in 1909 by Thomas Edison, who used sectional cast-iron forms bolted together at the site as molds. But Edison had failed to find ways of implementing the idea for mass production.[39] Harrison became one of three men who by the early 1950s had developed adequate technology for on-site mass production in concrete. Of the two others, Edwin Wallace Neff's Airform House of concrete sprayed on an inflated balloon was probably the most ingenious, but it presented problems with construction controls and with door and window openings. R. G. LeTourneau's LeTournalayer, a mammoth machine that served both as a mold for the concrete and then as a means of carrying the house to the site, was the most elaborate, but it required an enormous capital outlay and entailed considerable transportation expenses.[40] Since the savings of all three methods applied solely to the cost of the house's concrete shell—only half the total cost—economic viability depended on constructing a large number of units. The building of 1,583 houses at Las Lomas in Puerto Rico (1953) provided the right opportunity for the IBEC Housing Corporation. Harrison's method, or derivations therefrom, was subsequently used in Chile and Iran, and in Margate, Florida, where 1,800 homes were built in 1958 in a wood adaptation.[41] By this time, Harrison & Abramovitz had become one of the biggest architectural firms in the United States. To understand the events that led to this success, we must look back to a commission of enormous significance for Harrison: the Theme Center for New York City's 1939 World's Fair.

55. Harrison, IBEC housing under construction (c. 1947).

56. IBEC housing.

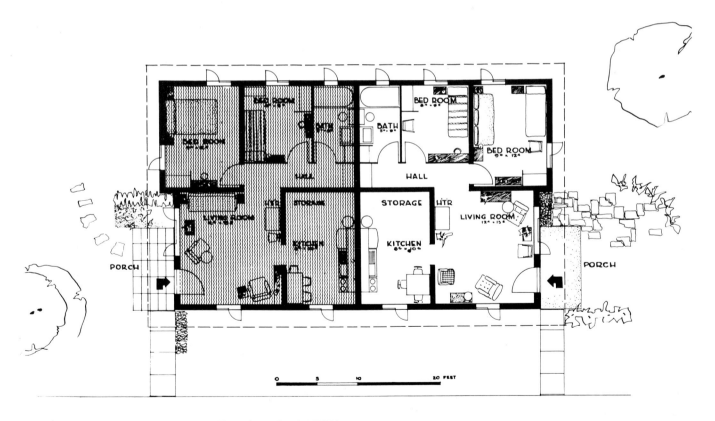

57. Plan of two-family IBEC house.

Chapter 9

1939: "The World of Tomorrow"

Even from the elevated station I could see the famous Trylon and Perisphere. They were enormous. They were white in the sun, white spire, white globe, they went together, they belonged together as some sort of partnership in my head. I didn't know what they stood for, it was all very vague in my mind, but to see them, after having seen pictures and posters and buttons of them for so long, made me incredibly happy. I felt like jumping up and down, I felt myself trembling with joy.

I thought of them as friends of mine.

E. L. Doctorow[1]

In the mid-1930s, Harrison became engaged in producing a design that came to symbolize an era: the Trylon and Perisphere for New York's World's Fair of 1939. The fair was called "Building the World of Tomorrow"; as much a product of the Depression as were the massive low-cost housing programs Harrison worked on, it was conceived in an effort to bolster the city's lagging economy.

Four years after the stock market crash, another financial panic had occurred in New York, caused by fear of a bank failure. The following year, in an attempt to control the activities of the stock market and to establish a means of economic stability, the federal government founded the Securities and Exchange Commission. In New York, for the first time, a city sales tax (two percent) was levied to provide relief for the poor. When it became clear that more help was needed, George McAneny, president of the Title Guarantee & Trust Company and head of the Regional Plan Association, proposed a world's fair.[2]

McAneny persuaded two other important businessmen, Grover A. Whalen, former New York police commissioner and president of Schenley Distilleries, and Percy Straus, head of R. H. Macy's department store, that the business community should sponsor the fair. He also struck a sympathetic chord with the all-powerful Robert Moses, by suggesting that the fair be held in a marshy area in Queens that the Parks Commissioner had long been interested in developing. After two-and-a-half centuries of producing crops of salt, hay, fish, crabs, clams, oysters, and wild water fowl, Flushing Meadows had been reduced to an enormous garbage dump.[3] The Parks Commissioner was delighted to acquire the Meadows; he wanted to extend a parkway along its edge to the Triborough Bridge. He therefore applied his considerable energies to selling the idea of the world's fair to Mayor La Guardia.[4]

Grover Whalen became president of the fair. A man of great charm and substantial skill as a negotiator, with personal access to the most influential people in the city, he was the right person for the job. By September 1935, Whalen enlisted over eighty leading business people to join the three original backers of the Fair Corporation.[5] Eventually he persuaded Winthrop W. Aldrich and Mrs. Vincent Astor to chair advisory committees soliciting nationwide participation, which they did with stunning success.[6]

On December 11, 1935, Michael Meredith Hare, a well-known theater designer and secretary of the Municipal Art League, hosted a dinner at the New York City Club. The meeting was supported by Harvey Corbett and another architect, Ian Woodner-Silverman, industrial designers Gilbert Rohde and Walter Dorwin Teague, urban planner Henry Wright, and Lewis Mumford; one hundred artists, designers, architects, and educators attended. A Fair of the Future Committee was formed[7] and Michael Hare, the committee's secretary, expressed their concept of the fair as follows:

> Mere mechanical progress is no longer an adequate or practical theme for a World's Fair. Instead we must demonstrate an American way of living. We must tell the story of the relationship between objects in their everyday use—how they may be used and when purposefully used how they may help us.[8]

To achieve these objectives, the Fair of the Future Committee called for a striking visual unity of the exhibits underlining the exposition's central theme and for the appointment of a professional group responsible for the fair's design and construction. In May 1936 the fair's directors selected a board of design under the leadership of architect Stephen F. Voorhees (of Voorhees, Walker, Foley & Smith).[9] In charge of choosing a theme for the fair were Robert D. Kohn, former president of the American Institute of Architects and an associate of the planner Clarence S. Stein, and Walter Teague. Housing dominated construction throughout the country, and Kohn fought for an exhibition devoted solely to housing, like the *Weissenhofsiedlung*, the widely discussed International Housing Exhibition that had been held in 1927 at Stuttgart, directed by Mies van der Rohe; Le Corbusier, J. J. P. Oud, and other prominent European modernists contributed. Teague, on the other hand, was convinced that the fair's theme should deal with broader issues such as economic reform and the preservation of

democratic principles, which seemed threatened by fascism and communism. The often passionate debate was resolved by a rather lopsided compromise. A conceptual theme—Building the World of Tomorrow—would be symbolized by a building, within which there would be a housing exhibit!

The fair's planners decided that their enterprise would represent the consumer rather than the producer. The fair would demonstrate that, under democracy, the salvation of The World of Tomorrow lay in the consumer society. The Theme Committee divided the fair into seven sectors to present the functional divisions of modern life—community interests, medicine and public health, science and education, production and distribution, communications and business systems, transportation, and food. Each sector would contain a central overview interpreting the social significance of separate displays. In order to integrate and dramatically summarize the fair's message, a central theme exhibit would be constructed.[10]

To find an appropriate character for the fair, on September 11, 1936, a competition was announced, open to all architects practicing in the city, "to unearth new talent and some new ideas."[11] The program called for a prototype pavilion, serving three exhibitors on a triangular plot. Three hundred and fifty-six proposals were received, among them Harrison & Fouilhoux's unusual and economical solution: tents that would emphasize the project's festive and temporary nature. One of the firm's designers, a Russian, W. K. Oltar-Jevsky, suggested this scheme, inspired by the 1896 All-Russian Exposition at Novgorod, where large tent-like structures had been lighted at night with colored lanterns (Figs. 58, 59). With few exceptions, entries showed rectangular buildings, each with a higher middle section or sometimes a straight billboard façade; most entries seemed to differ only in interior circulation.[12] It is not surprising that the Harrison & Fouilhoux project retained the Theme Committee's interest.

Harrison was awarded the contract to design the Theme Center on November 24, 1936, whereupon he immediately put aside the tent idea. He wanted to create

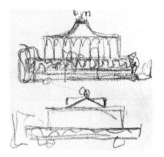

58. Harrison's sketch for a 1939 World's Fair pavilion.

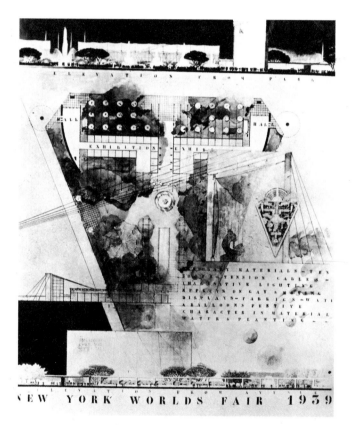

59. Harrison & Fouilhoux, project for a prototype pavilion for the 1939 World's Fair, competition entry.

a scheme that would represent a new architectural concept. For him the essence of a fair was festivity, and he tried to think of buildings of the past that had projected an air of gaiety and that could at the same time lend themselves to expressing contemporary ideals and modern methods:

> We found ourselves constantly referring to the domes and campaniles of Venice, perhaps because the flat country and water of the Fair grounds are very like that of the site of Venice and in addition the sky color of New York is practically the same.[13]

The idea of a sphere came to him early in the project. Harrison insisted that the domes of St. Mark's in Venice, combined with structural innovation, inspired the shape. Playing with this image, his designers made a number of proposals: "Giant balloons which would lift crowds in the sky; the highest tower in the world perched on top of giant balls; a hoop four hundred feet in diameter through which airplanes could fly; a crystal ball the size of a city block hung in the air on bridge trusses."[14] By itself a sphere has no scale—a ping-pong ball and the moon appear to be the same size if they are not seen in relationship to something else. The problem was therefore to project the sphere's large size.

In addition to Harrison, the group working on the theme building included Abramovitz, Joseph Huntington, Robert Carlson (a former Hood draftsman), Werner Drewes, and Goldstone. Walking home from the office one day, Goldstone noticed two enormous spherical gas storage tanks at York Avenue just north of the Fifty-ninth Street bridge. One, half full, was embedded between supporting blocks. It proved to be two hundred feet in diameter. The tank rose as emptied, and when it became a full sphere, Goldstone persuaded his boss to inspect it. Harrison agreed that the size seemed perfect, but the problem remained to create visual scale. The designers tried hanging the sphere on cables and balancing it on arches (Figs. 60, 61), but nothing seemed to do the trick until one day Harrison came into the office waving the January 4, 1937, issue of *Time* magazine. On the cover,

60. Harrison & Fouilhoux, early schemes for the 1939 World's Fair
Theme Center. Sketches by Werner Drewes.

61. Harrison & Fouilhoux, models for the 1939 World's Fair Theme Center.

next to a photograph of Wallis Simpson, whose relationship with the King of England led to his abdication, Harrison had sketched an elongated spike next to a sphere.[15] Everyone agreed that the spike was just what was needed to give the sphere magnitude.

But how should the two forms relate to one another? Harrison and Abramovitz spent long hours of research in the Museum of Modern Art's library, trying to find an idea that might help them. The drawings of the Russian constructivist and visionary architect, Jacob Tchernikhov, may well have provided the idea for a bridge between the units (Fig. 62).[16] But there were structural difficulties. Abramovitz claims that

> Waddell & Hardesty, the consulting engineers, vetoed Wally's cone-shaped tower. They produced a tiny sketch of a tower with a triangular base, arguing that 'three legs make a base: like a three-legged stool for stability' [Figs. 63, 64].[17]

In fact, the two vertical counterparts to the sphere in Tchernikhov's design were also angular. The triangular shape was accepted, but Abramovitz remembers that the complications continued:

> I had to constantly change the design team. There was one old man, MacPherson, who had worked as a draftsman for Hood. He would only work a half-day because the rest of the day he did his own watercolors; . . . he worked with pieces of string, not with instruments. Well, he was the only one who realized that when you go down in a hemisphere, the plane moves toward the center.

One of the sketches showed a dome aboveground with the lower half of the sphere underground. When this scheme was analyzed, the designers were told that a subterranean water bed on the site would make it impossible to realize. The office produced more than a thousand sketches of different versions of the design. The designers pinned sketches to the wall and discussed them in a democratic fashion, then made models of likely possibilities, subjecting them to further scrutiny.

Goldstone remembered his employer's impulsive, stimulating attitude which, he believed, Harrison maintained throughout his life:

> He doesn't have time to refine, he rather jumps from one thing to another in a series of brilliant, intuitive flashes, hoping to find a solution. Wally is a teacher, he loves to upset preconceived ideas and he himself is disconcerting in that he has no preconceptions about anything. He's absolutely unpredictable: he never knows how he'll react to the next moment of life. It's an attitude that keeps him young—he has never gotten into a rut, politically, ideologically, or architecturally—but at the same time it's very undisciplined. Max has the same kind of temperament, so they got along all right, but someone like Bob Carlson, who was systematic and thorough, was distressed by Wally's method. He [Harrison] changed things even in the working drawings. I've heard him say: 'Let's build it; if we don't like it, we'll tear it down and start over again.' He just doesn't want to be pinned down to one solution.

Abramovitz recalled that, as they sketched the different heights up to which they could move the sphere while still keeping part of it underground,

> It got uglier all the time. So I came up with the idea of having the whole thing aboveground, and standing it on legs. But then the question arose of how to get the people up to it? Someone else came up with the idea of escalators: none existed in the U.S. big enough for the job, and the firm that made the London subway escalators was brought in. So you have a big form with an escalator and the next question is, how do you get the people down? The solution seemed to be a ramp.

The ramp became the Helicline—encircling Trylon and Perisphere, it stood on supporting columns which realized Abramovitz's idea of providing a frame for the tower and ball (Fig. 65). Other members of the design team proposed to set both forms in water; finally only

62. Jacob Tchernikhov, *Construction des formes d'architecture et des machines* (Leningrad, 1931).

63. Proposal for cone-shaped Trylon and Perisphere.

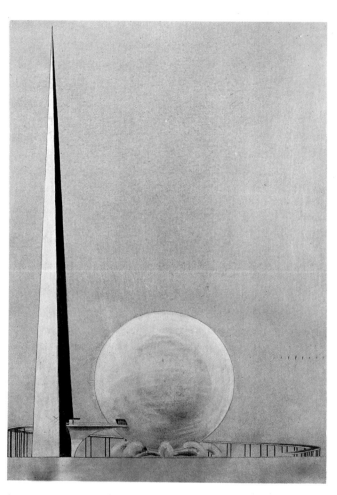

64. Final sketch of Trylon and Perisphere.

the Perisphere was placed above a reflecting pool. The final design consisted of the 200-foot Perisphere, entered by means of the world's longest escalator; the 700-foot Trylon, connected by a 65-foot-high bridge to the Perisphere; and the 18-foot-wide, 950-foot-long Helicline, down which visitors exited. Hugh Ferriss drew up the finished project for presentation to the board of design (Fig. 66).

Someone then had to find a meaning for the symbol. One of the fair's public relations men suggested that the ball represented the finite and the spike, the infinite, an idea that captured precisely the forward-looking attitude the fair sought to promote. This evoked the names of Trylon (from *tri*—three sided—and *pylon*—a gateway) and of Perisphere (from *peri*—encompassing) to designate one of the most popular architectural symbols of our time.

The Perisphere was the largest globe ever built and contained a space that was more than twice the size of Radio City Music Hall. In response to the board of design's request for a housing exhibition to fill the enormous interior, Henry Dreyfuss, the industrial designer, created "Democracity" (Figs. 67, 68). This model of the city of the future comprised a great half circle centered on a single 100-story building at the end of a grand boulevard flanked by identical subsidiary buildings. The single megatower was in turn framed by six smaller towers, the whole standing in splendid isolation in the midst of a large green space. Cumulus clouds seemed to move overhead, and the globe inside created the illusion of infinite space. To view Democracity, Harrison & Fouilhoux hung two superimposed circular platforms within the Perisphere; moving in opposite directions, they gave the visitor a feeling of floating in space. In the five-and-a-half minutes that it took to make a complete revolution, the lighting was manipulated to imitate the passage from dawn to dusk, and the excursion was accompanied by background music composed by William Grant Still and conducted by André Kostelanetz, over which the voice of H. V. Kaltenborn intoned narration. The show ended with the appearance of processions of well-regimented workers from ten equidistant points on the dome to the

65. Trylon and Perisphere seen through Helicline columns.

66. Presentation drawing of Trylon, Perisphere, and Helicline. Rendering by Hugh Ferriss.

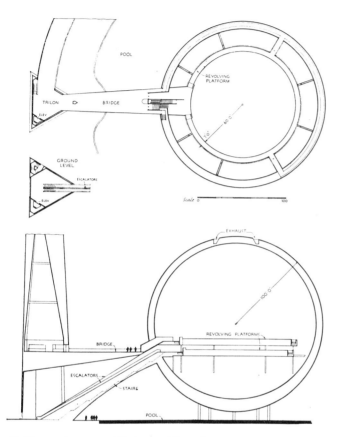

68. Henry Dreyfuss, Democracity in the Perisphere.

67. Plan and section of Trylon and Perisphere.

69. Steel framework of Perisphere, Helicline, and Trylon. Rendering by Hugh Ferriss.

crescendo of a choir singing the fair's theme song, the chorus of which was:

> We're the rising tide, come from far
> and wide
> Marching side by side on our way,
> For a brave new world,
> Tomorrow's world,
> That we shall build today.[18]

The Theme Center drawings were to be submitted to the board of design in May 1937, and tension mounted in the Harrison & Fouilhoux office as the deadline approached. Goldstone describes the situation as follows:

> We were worried because the design board consisted of establishment architects and the sphere and triangle were far out. But Wally was a consummate diplomat; he had begun to bring each member of the board to the office one at a time. In this way, he was able first of all to demonstrate the office's working method, and secondly he made each one of them feel as if they were participating in our team effort. The last man to come was William Delano; we were all scared of him. He was the height of conventionality, a gent of the old school. We were amazed how quickly he got the aesthetic of what we were trying to do. He was so sensitive to proportion and design; the lack of columns and pedestals didn't bother him at all. He gave the most solid and subtle criticism regarding the proper height of the sphere from the water, which we took into account at once. When Wally presented the design to the board, they'd already bought it one at a time.

The design was accepted with one proviso, however: in order to keep the costs of the Theme Center in line with the Fair Corporation's overall expenses, the directors insisted on a ten-percent budget cut. There was no problem in reducing the size of the sphere by ten percent—a 180-foot diameter looks the same to the human eye as a 200-foot diameter. But the reduction of the spike

from almost 700 to 610 feet threw off its relationship to the Perisphere and affected the planned contrast between the extreme height of the tower and the solidity of the ball.

Another disappointment followed. Harrison's original idea of a concrete shell was too expensive for the new budget; substituted for it was a heavy steel truss framework with a giant ring girder on eight supporting pillars for the Perisphere and a braced steel tower for the Trylon. Both structures were to be covered by one-inch cement stucco, which, in turn, was modified to "tymstone"—a less substantial magnesite compound,[19] suggested by Hugh Ferriss. Unfortunately, this solution created a bumpy surface that undermined the feeling of sleek modernity the architects had planned (Figs. 69–71). The board of design also insisted on placing a sculpture at the foot of the ramp as a kind of punctuation mark. It was not a bad idea, but the board's selection of an undistinguished figure, a male nude, entitled *The Astronomer*, by Carl Milles, was far from what the designers would have chosen. Harrison was beginning to realize how greatly working conditions could vary from the ideal—exemplified for him by the Rockefeller Apartments—when the architect is given free reign by a wealthy client. Yet, despite these compromises, the Trylon and Perisphere departed radically from the architecture of the time to create a world's fair symbol comparable to the Eiffel Tower.

In addition to the Theme Center, Harrison designed three buildings for the 1939 World's Fair. One was the Consolidated Edison Pavilion, with a sweeping concave facade placed behind a reflecting pool. Part of the façade consisted of a glass curtain wall, with the main entrance reached by a bridge over the pool. The remaining façade was made of blue glass conceived as a background for an elaborate play of fountains (Fig. 72). Harrison asked his friend Alexander Calder to adjust the play of light and of water jets to create the illusion of an aquatic ballet. Fernand Léger, also a friend of Harrison's, decorated another façade with a mural showing organic and inorganic sources of energy.[20] Inside was Con Ed's City of Light, designed by Walter Teague and Frank J. Roorder and publicized as the largest diorama ever built

70. Trylon, Perisphere, and Helicline.

71. Detail, Perisphere.

72. Harrison, Consolidated Edison Pavilion, with Trylon,
Perisphere, and Helicline in background.

73. Walter Teague and Frank J. Roorder, City of Light in
Consolidated Edison Pavilion.

74. Harrison, Electric Utilities Pavilion.

(Fig. 73). Spectators stood in a viewing gallery facing a scale replica of the New York skyline bent to make all the streets converge toward the viewer. The simulation of city life was speeded up so that a twenty-four-hour cycle was converted into twenty-four minutes. As darkness fell, the city was flooded with artificial illumination, and from overhead a voice pronounced: "This is the City of Light, where night never comes . . . a world of power at the motion of a hand."[21]

Opposite Con Ed on the Plaza of Light stood Harrison's second pavilion for the fair, the Electric Utilities Exhibit; it occupied three structures. Here, too, access was along a bridge that led the visitor over water, in this case through a round glass tunnel that passed underneath a waterfall (Fig. 74).

At the periphery of the exposition ground was Harrison's Electrified Farm, complete with cattle, horses, and chickens; a greenhouse and hotbeds; an orchard and pasture (Fig. 75). It was designed to demonstrate the latest ideas in farming, most of which were provided by the Rockefeller Institute. Harrison was particularly proud of it as an example of the uses of solar energy. The walls were brick; only the pitched roof was of glass. As Harrison remembered it, the addition of three strong electric bulbs was all that was needed to light and heat this building.[22]

The close of the fair in the fall of 1940 was a good moment for Harrison. He was the head of one of the few architectural firms to survive the Great Depression, and he had performed spectacularly at the fair. His association with the Rockefeller family—at the Museum of Modern Art (where he was elected a trustee in March 1939) and at Rockefeller Center and the Rockefeller Apartments—identified him with a small group of powerful people who controlled much of the city's cultural life.

Harrison must at last have begun to feel like an insider; he was by now well established, with men he had trained working on their own. Furthermore, the fair had brought him in touch with Sven Markelius of Sweden and Oscar Niemeyer of Brazil. Six years later they were ready to work under his direction on the United Nations headquarters, one of the most prominent architectural monuments of the modern world.

75. Harrison, Electrified Farm. Redrawn by Harrison in 1981.

Chapter 10

With Nelson Rockefeller in Latin America and Washington, D.C.

By 1939 Harrison's increasingly evident association with projects controlled by the Rockefeller family, his prominent role at the New York World's Fair, and his reputation as a teacher had placed him at the top of his profession. His office was a meeting place for some of the most interesting artists and intellectuals of the day, and his special friendship with Nelson Rockefeller introduced him to another world as well—a world centered on power and money.

Rockefeller was becoming increasingly involved with his family's various business interests. At the age of thirty, he was president of the Rockefeller Center Corporation, which he ran with a firm hand. He had also begun to study the workings of Creole Petroleum, the Venezuelan subsidiary of Standard Oil of New Jersey and the biggest oil producer in the country.[1] On his first trip to Venezuela, Rockefeller, who spoke Spanish and was keenly interested in Latin American culture, had been shocked at the attitude displayed by Creole's American employees toward the local inhabitants. The Americans isolated their compounds behind barbed wire, refused to learn the language of the country, and treated all Venezuelans with arrogance. Venezuela was a poor country, and the native population resented foreigners who flaunted their wealth. By 1940, in an effort to stimulate the Venezuelan economy, Rockefeller had created the Compañía de Fomento Venezolano (Venezuelan Basic Economy Corporation), which financed development of local industry.

During one of Rockefeller's many visits to Caracas, he talked with Eleazar Lopez Contreras, president of Venezuela, about the city's hotel problem. The capital's single tourist hotel, the Majestic, built in the late 1800s, had become dilapidated. But every group interested in building a new hotel insisted on including a casino, which Contreras adamantly opposed. The president was convinced that if he could interest the oil companies in the project, it would not have to be subsidized by gambling. Rockefeller believed that building a new hotel would allow the country to share at last in some of the enormous profits of Creole. He proposed a $1 million hotel (to be called the Avila) financed by a public stock offering, a method entirely new to Venezuela. Three hundred Venezuelan investors eventually provided more than ten percent of the capital, with several Venezuelan oil companies and the Compañía de Fomento (heavily subsidized by the Rockefeller family) putting up the rest. Rockefeller also acquired land for the hotel and provided an architect to design it. As usual, he turned to friends for these tasks.

Edward H. (Hutch) Robbins had been a Dartmouth classmate of Rockefeller's. Robbins' family connections in Venezuela facilitated his survey of Caracas, and he chose a spectacular site in the Los Cabos district for the new hotel. The site was already occupied by the old Hacienda Ybarra belonging to a Venezuelan provincial governor. Even after six months of negotiations, he refused to sell the property. But the governor and Rockefeller shared an interest in pre-Columbian art, and finally an agreement was reached.[2]

Rockefeller had repeatedly invited Harrison to accompany him on trips to Latin America; but Harrison disliked flying and without a specific reason to make the trip the architect preferred to stay close to his office. The hotel project provided such a reason. Harrison and his wife visited Caracas in April 1940. Soon after their arrival, he received an invitation to dine with one of the city's leading architects. The two men met at a restaurant, and the Venezuelan quickly came to the point: he and his colleagues were concerned about the intrusion of a foreign architect when the new oil wealth should provide local architects with their first opportunity to build. Harrison immediately assured his host that he would limit himself to the one project. He also decided to make a gesture of conciliation by incorporating into the new building as many local features as possible.[3]

To ensure against damage by earthquakes, Harrison decided that he would construct the three-hundred-guest hotel with reinforced concrete bearing walls instead of the usual masonry, as a rigid box, rather than a series of supporting posts. He adapted the local terra-cotta tile roof and broad roof overhangs, which provided protection from seasonal torrential downpours. The exterior walls were faced in cement stucco, painted the national colors—red, yellow, and blue—in the muted tones used by the peasants for their adobe huts (Figs. 76, 77).[4]

On one of their visits to the Caracas Country Club, Harrison and Rockefeller noticed that the ample facilities were used almost exclusively by the male members. Ladies maintained a permanent *paseo* in the club's entryway—strolling, standing, or sitting—to see and be seen. To accommodate this custom, Harrison placed a covered walkway with comfortable seating arrangements before the hotel's central lobby, affording an unobstructed view of the entrance.

Recently the Harrison, Fouilhoux & Abramovitz office had avoided the consequence of ignoring environmental factors in the construction of U.S. government facilities at Balboa and Coco Solo in Panama. The program issued for Panama had been used for army barracks in Maine; it was immediately apparent to Abramovitz that structures designed to withstand the rigors of a New England winter were inappropriate for the tropics. To provide sufficient ventilation, screens were used for almost all the walls specified. In Caracas, which combines a semialpine terrain with an equatorial climate, Harrison used louvered doors that open onto exterior galleries—instead of the interior corridors usual in hotels. The use of a single-loaded airy corridor was traditional in warm climates, and was quickly adopted for tropical resort facilities.[5] Each bedroom had a private balcony, some with balustrades, executed in turned wood like much vernacular architecture (Fig. 78).

The Avila's design was developed by the senior class Harrison was then teaching at Yale; it was thus the kind of real situation he found educational, and the product of a team effort—an approach that had become characteristic of his large-scale work. Caracas's environment and lifestyle also presented the practical challenges he sought for his class. Rockefeller had singled out a great array of Venezuelan problems for study and Harrison introduced them in the Yale studio: low agricultural productivity, low fishing yields, the lack of milk and other food staples, and the scarcity of housing.

Even before he decided to construct the Avila, Rockefeller had been spending a fair amount of time on the social and economic problems of Venezuela. He met regularly with seven eminent advisers he referred to as his "junta."[6] In June 1940, the group wrote a "little

76. Harrison, entrance, Avila Hotel, Caracas, Venezuela (1941).

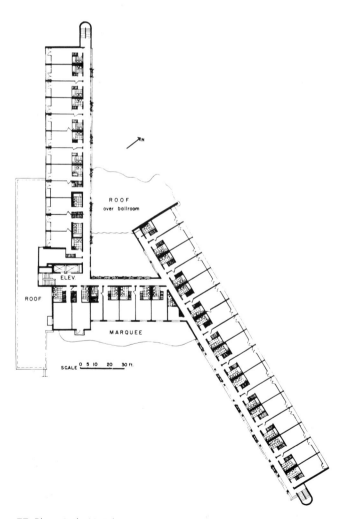

77. Plan, Avila Hotel.

78. Courtyard, Avila Hotel.

memorandum," conveyed to Harry Hopkins, President Roosevelt's advisor at the time.[7] Rockefeller's proposal for the coordination of commercial and cultural relations among the American republics fit perfectly with Roosevelt's Good Neighbor Policy, and within a week of the memo's presentation, the president and cabinet members had agreed to form a bureau for the Coordination of Inter-American Affairs (CIAA). An annual $3 million budget came, not from Congress, but from the president's own emergency fund.[8]

Nelson Rockefeller was named bureau coordinator on August 16, and Harrison remembered that "he came in with a bang." The cultural department was placed under Harrison who declared, "I'd been in an architect's office since I was fourteen years old, but I never questioned the fact that I was suddenly in a government office with Nelson: we had a job to do and we had to do it" (Fig. 79). World War II was affecting the feelings and actions of all Americans by then.

Upon his assuming full-time direction of the cultural program, Harrison and his wife moved to Washington, where they were soon as much a part of the Washington social scene as they had been of New York's. This pleasant interlude was short-lived. With no architectural commissions of consequence, Harrison's modest savings were rapidly consumed. Ellen decided that her time would be spent more profitably if she moved back to Long Island to cultivate the family's land as a working potato farm, which she did successfully until the end of the war.

In July 1941, a few months after Harrison and Fouilhoux had invited him to join the partnership, Abramovitz enlisted as a colonel in the United States Army and was shipped to China, where he designed and built military installations under the command of General Chennault. With Harrison in Washington and Abramovitz in the Far East, Fouilhoux alone was left to run the office in New York. In 1941, the firm constructed the purely utilitarian one-story Pepsi Cola bottling plant in Long Island City; in 1942, with the completion of its projects in Panama and Venezuela, its work came to a standstill.

Rockefeller's and Harrison's work together in Washington seemed to bind their friendship more strongly. When the United States entered the war, Harrison was forty-six years old, a mature man made confident by his personal and professional achievements. He had filled out physically—his face was rounder, his shoulders broader; at six feet three inches he could easily be mistaken for a former football star. By now the cigar smoking he had started at the weekly meetings to plan Rockefeller Center had become a habit: snapshots show him as a quietly assured figure with a cigar stub in the corner of his mouth, reinforcing the impression of solid toughness conveyed by his physique.

In contrast, the thirty-year-old Rockefeller, although he had proven himself equal to the complex tasks required of him, was aware that these tasks had been prescribed by his family. He was therefore enthusiastic about his new opportunity to pursue personal interests, as coordinator of Inter-American Affairs. Those who saw the two men in Washington remember Rockefeller's reliance on Harrison's judgment: the architect played an important part not only in implementing Rockefeller's projects but also in rounding out his ideas.[9]

It is not unusual for the son of a successful and powerful man to confide in a friend with whom he can share an intimacy lacking in the more complex father-son relationship. Harrison was surely such a confidant for Rockefeller, and yet the architect was always conscious of playing a subordinate role: "The things Nelson ran, he ran." Theirs was not a conventional friendship of equals, but rather an amiable relationship between artist and patron. When toward the end of his life Harrison was told about the importance attributed to his role in Washington, he looked incredulous and hastened to explain: "I was there *all* the time, the big names weren't, so I just picked up the details when things went wrong." This statement was, of course, an oversimplification, but it reveals a great deal about Harrison's success—his easy acceptance of the existing power structure, his apparently unlimited stamina, and his unwavering ability to carry out plans.

Harrison's office was assigned to replace German and Italian cultural activities in Latin America.[10] Its

79. Harrison and Nelson A. Rockefeller, accompanied by Francis
Jamieson and CIAA staffer, John McClintock (1944).

many accomplishments included a twenty-eight-week tour of South America by the American Ballet Caravan, directed by Lincoln Kirstein; an exhibition of three hundred contemporary paintings from North American museums that traveled to at least ten principal cities of Latin America; and a tour by the Yale Glee Club.[11]

One of Harrison's first moves in setting up his division in Washington was to create a "chart room" for Nelson Rockefeller. George Dudley, by this time working in Harrison's New York office, and Harmon Goldstone were assigned this task. Dudley worked out a system of weekly progress and data charts which was soon adopted by the War Department and which Rockefeller used again for the State Planning Commission when he became governor of New York.

On March 25, 1945, Harrison became director of the bureau, which was renamed the Office of Inter-American Affairs, continuing Rockefeller's efforts.[12] Despite the demands of his wartime duties, Harrison was able to travel back and forth from Maine and, helped on site by a young architect from his office, to build two private houses there. In 1941, with the completion of a spectacular house for Nelson Rockefeller at Seal Harbor on Mount Desert Island, domestic architecture took on renewed significance for him.

As a child, Rockefeller had grown to love the family's thirty-thousand-acre estate in Maine, where he spent the summers. His father's donation of 11,000 acres on Mount Desert Island between the 1920s and 1950 now makes up one-third of Acadia National Park, which to this day remains physically undisturbed. The dramatic beauty of the area's craggy, pine-covered shoreline is enriched by thousands of small islands. On their first visit to the site, Nelson Rockefeller took Harrison to the very end of the property, where bold granite boulders thrust out of the forest into the ocean. This was where he wanted the house, and he himself sank massive wooden stakes into the soil to mark the exact positioning of a large picture window he envisioned. John D. Rockefeller, Jr., was moved by Harrison's excitement about the area's similarity to a small peninsula at Corfu where he had served during World War I, and the elder Rockefeller signed over to him part of the coast adjoining Nelson's property.

Nelson Rockefeller loved to sail, and Harrison designed a conical stairwell large enough to hang sails in to dry. Rising above the roofline, this structure dominates the house's ocean side like a ship's mast. But the spiral stairway that encircles the mast's exterior and the windows piercing it transform it into a lighthouse as well (Fig. 80). (The prominence of a functional feature recalls Harrison's design for a Hall of a Country House, shown in the Metropolitan Museum of Art's 1940 Exhibition of Contemporary American Industrial Art [Fig. 81]).[13]

The Anchorage, as the Rockefeller house is called, is one of Harrison's most striking designs. Even Mr. Jr., who had expressed misgivings about the construction of a modern home in such a prominent part of a conservative community, was captivated by it and apologized to Harrison for his earlier skepticism.[14] The house is built on a plan of intersecting curves. The master bedroom occupies the second story of the outward-facing curve. On the ocean side a cantilevered porch gives the house a soaring feeling, as if it were a great boat braving the billows. On the more conventional entrance side, white pine slabs meet the ground solidly and the doorway stands within the protective inner curve (Figs. 82, 83). Interiors are bathed in natural light; and while sturdy walls protect the house's western, inland side, its eastern elevation opens to breathtaking views of the coast.[15]

Six years prior to construction of the Anchorage, the evocative Maine coast had inspired another modern architect. George Howe's Mount Desert Island house for Clara Fargo Thomas (1939) used a cantilevered deck—in this case for the living room—and local materials to relate it to its rocky site (Fig. 84). Although similar in many respects, Howe's rectilinear plan and horizontal emphasis of window panels and balcony railings convey a different feeling from that of Harrison's curved plan and various readings of the stairwell.

The Anchorage was much admired, and in 1946 William A. M. Burden, who had met Harrison during wartime service in Washington,[16] asked him to design a house in Northeast Harbor for his wife and himself. Like

80. Harrison, The Anchorage, Seal Harbor, Maine (1941).
Stairwell is visible through trees at left.

81. Harrison, hall of a country house, Exhibition of Contemporary Industrial Art, Metropolitan Museum of Art, New York City (1940).

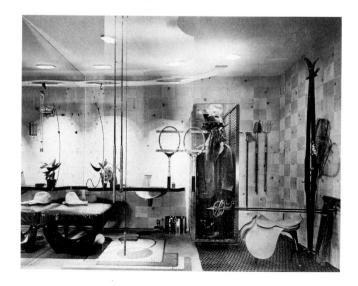

82. Cantilevered porch, The Anchorage.

83. Plan, The Anchorage.

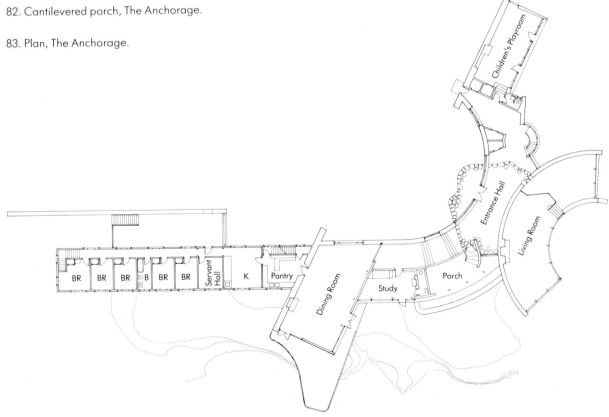

84. George Howe, Clara Fargo Thomas house, Mt. Desert Island, Maine (1939).

85. Harrison, façade, William A. M. Burden house, Northeast Harbor, Maine (1947).

86. Living, and raised dining, areas, William A. M. Burden house.

Rockefeller, Burden and his wife had summered in this part of Maine since they were infants. Their oceanfront property had been acquired from a Mrs. Corning, the mother of Erastus Corning, mayor of Albany and a pivotal figure in Harrison's later career.

The Burdens wanted a small, inconspicuous summer house (their four sons occupied a separate bungalow on the estate), to contain a large bedroom, two dressing areas, and a large living-dining room; Mrs. Burden preferred a curved shape to a straight-sided-box form. Harrison responded with a one-story, gently undulating wall, which delineates living and dining areas; hidden behind it and to one side is the bedroom area (Figs. 85, 86). The slatted ceiling of the reception area has a curve of its own, extending from a high point at the back down to the façade. Bedroom and baths are housed in a rectangular wing connected to a corridor behind the reception room. The kitchen, servants' quarters, and a playroom are in an ell defining a courtyard (Fig. 87). The Burdens wintered in Florida, and liked a local pale-gray pecky cypress commonly used there. Harrison employed the wood for the back and side walls of the living-dining area, where it blends with the white Maine pine he used for the ceiling and the interior and exterior of the façade. The exterior is firmly anchored by two massive fieldstone chimneys.

The Burdens were so pleased with the Maine house during their first summer in it that they asked Harrison to design a house in Florida. He produced an original design based on the association of free forms and regularity (Fig. 88). This unrealized project is yet another example of smaller designs in which Harrison excelled.

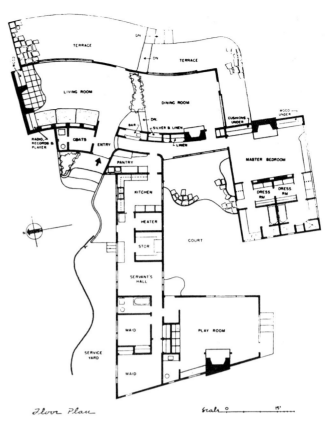

87. Plan, William A. M. Burden house.

88. Harrison, project for a house in Florida for William A. M. Burden (1948).

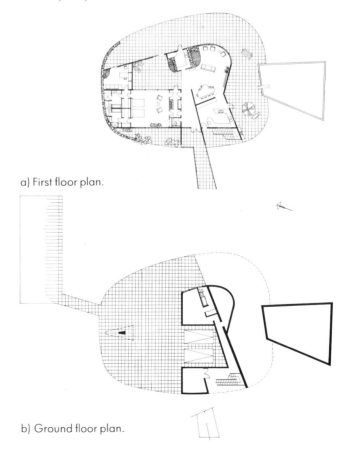

a) First floor plan.

b) Ground floor plan.

Chapter 11

Toward the United Nations

Next to Frank Lloyd Wright, who, as the father of modern American architecture and perhaps its only true genius, occupies a unique position in his field, the person commonly regarded as the most influential figure in present-day building design in this country is Wallace K. Harrison.

Herbert Warren Wind[1]

So began the second in a three-part *New Yorker* profile that appeared in the fall of 1954. Harrison was credited with $700 million worth of new buildings within the previous twenty-five years. Yet his fame outside professional circles came from a single job: that of chief architect for the United Nations headquarters.

In April 1946, after serving the government in Washington for over five years, Harrison returned to New York to resume architectural practice. As the sole partner in the office, Fouilhoux had struggled to keep the firm going through the difficult war years, but in 1945 he had died suddenly.

With Fouilhoux gone, the office was virtually without management until Harrison returned, by which time it was generating barely enough income to pay for an apartment for him and his wife. The Harrisons were hardly the only ones in New York in search of a place to live in the mid–1940s. After the relatively uncrowded living conditions of the war years, servicemen returned to find the worst housing shortage in the city's history.

While Harrison was struggling to pick up the pieces of his life in New York, William Zeckendorf, Sr., the real estate magnate, was riding the crest of a phenomenally successful career. For almost a year Zeckendorf had been negotiating the purchase of land along the East River north of Forty-second Street. Originally a swamp, known in the 1880s and 1890s as Turtle Bay, the area east of First Avenue had become the city's abattoir district. When Zeckendorf purchased the first lots late in 1945, they were the site of a string of slaughterhouses, whose stench was so dreadful that the section of Tudor City apartments backing on to First Avenue—referred to popularly as Blood Alley—was built without windows. It is hard to imagine that cattle pens, packing plants, and charnel houses existed so recently in the midst of Manhattan or that livestock was routinely hauled to the area from the West Side docks in open trucks. Because of the obnoxious use to which this midtown location had been put, it was valued at $2 to $5 per square foot, compared with $100 to $150 per square foot in other midtown locations.

The East River property was offered to Zeckendorf at the relatively high price of $17 per square foot. But the idea of investing $6.5 million in a single project did not deter him; he was convinced that once the slaughterhouses were gone the price could go as high as $100. He was equally sure that properties around the slaughterhouses would soar in value. Webb & Knapp, Zeckendorf's firm, put up $1 million against the total price for a one-year option, during which period the packing companies were to relocate. Meanwhile Zeckendorf frantically bought as much of the $2- and $5-per-square-foot surrounding property as he could get his hands on. He ultimately acquired most of the land north of the slaughterhouses to Forty-ninth Street and a great many lots to the west, between First and Second avenues—in all, about seventy-five properties, totaling seventeen acres at an average price of $9 per square foot.[2] Zeckendorf faced the question of how to use the parcel once it included the abattoir area.

In his autobiography, Zeckendorf describes the evening strolls he took with his wife, Marion, to Beekman Place, where he would stare south toward the slaughterhouses. On the fifth or sixth such visit, Zeckendorf suddenly remembered how in 1913 the open tracks to the north and south of Grand Central Terminal had been covered with a great platform to create Park Avenue—and a fortune in real estate. Why not build a similar platform, stretching east from the elevation of Tudor City to the river and north to where he was standing at Beekman Place? Zeckendorf was enormously excited by his vision:

> That night I could hardly sleep as I chased my own ideas, tied them down with facts and figures, altered them, made compromises, returned to original notions, and finally realized that I was no longer dealing with fantasy but with genuine possibility. Now I needed a top architect to help work these concepts out in concrete form, and I turned to Wallace Harrison, whose work on Rockefeller Center had brought him a deserved and estimable reputation. Harrison agreed to work on the East River, and his completed plan was designated 'X City.'[3]

For his East River property, the real estate man wanted no less than his own Rockefeller Center; to describe the idea, he picked up the same terms that had been used in the first press releases for Rockefeller Center: "A city within the city."[4] The only architects left from the original Rockefeller Center team were Harrison and Corbett. With Corbett now in his seventies, Harrison was the obvious choice.

Zeckendorf's association with Webb & Knapp was likened to "loose lightning being drawn to a lake."[5] In the eight years since he had joined the firm, Zeckendorf had transformed it from a small, conservative agency into a dealer and operator of properties in twenty states, reputedly increasing its assets by one thousand percent. The press had compared his vast appetite for real estate to Napoleon III's, and his appetite for life in general was on an equally grand scale. Good food and fine wines had already provided him with a baronial paunch that belied his forty-one years. He loved to lunch and dine at the Monte Carlo, a restaurant and night club at Madison Avenue and Forty-fourth Street he had bought for his firm. There associates and customers surrounded him at his habitual table, which was laden with telephones into which he barked dramatic decisions on seven-figure deals.[6]

The contrast between this high-living, flamboyant tycoon and the soft-spoken, eminently genteel Harrison was not so complete as appearances indicated. Beneath considerable differences in style, the two men shared a propensity to think big and the toughness and determination to achieve that bigness. Many years later Harrison said of Zeckendorf: "Bill to me was a relief because most of the people like him talked a lot and did very little, but Bill was ready to put up the money; he was like Moses, like Nelson—ready to act, to do the thing."[7]

X City was to be built on a concrete and steel platform forty feet above the existing level of First Avenue. The complex was to contain three thirty-story apartment houses with living facilities for seventy-five hundred families; five office buildings (one of fifty-seven stories and four of forty stories); a convention hall for six thousand; an opera and concert hall; a six-thousand-room hotel; a yacht landing; a heliport; and subterranean parking facilities for five thousand cars. This was Zeckendorf's chance to rival Radio City with an Aluminum City or a Television City, assuming that either Alcoa or one of the big television stations would consent to occupy the largest projected office building, as RCA had done at Rockefeller Center. Harrison saw it as an opportunity to find at last a new home for the opera, an idea which had been in germination for Rockefeller Center.[8]

Zeckendorf, still trying to round out his holdings in the East River area, was eager to keep the new project secret lest landowners raise their prices in anticipation. Therefore, he took over a number of rooms in the Marguery Hotel, 270 Park Avenue. One suite was devoted to the top-secret X City project. George Dudley from the Harrison and Abramovitz office had been selected to study the site and draw up preliminary schemes. Zeckendorf allowed only Harrison to visit this sanctum, where Dudley lived day and night for several weeks to ensure secrecy. In September 1946, Zeckendorf installed Harrison and his family next door to this suite in a small apartment, where they lived until May 1948. At the time, the Marguery had been acquired by Time, Inc., as the site for new headquarters, for which Harrison and Abramovitz proposed a design, which was rejected.

By the fall of 1946, Zeckendorf felt secure enough about land acquisition to make the X City plans public. In its October 28 issue, *Life* magazine published drawings by A. Leydenfrost, a favorite renderer of Zeckendorf's, showing two enormous curved skyscrapers on pillars flanking a wide space in which arose a domed structure. These forms—the flattened curve of the towers and the circle, developed (among other things) into domes—are recurring themes in Harrison's work.[9] Four slightly lower office slabs stood to the south (Fig. 89). A drawing dated December 12 by Hugh Ferriss displays a composition that makes the project seem even more monumental: the facilities for opera and concerts were combined in a massive structure that extended right through the bases of the curved skyscrapers. A heliport protruded into the East River (Figs. 90–92). Both the Leydenfrost and Ferriss drawings suggested cruciform apartment houses to the north. The X City site suddenly

came under consideration for the United Nations headquarters in December 1946, as described below. Harrison's Zeckendorf scheme was used to promote the idea: Dudley simply penciled in the words "General Assembly" in place of the opera, and "Security," "Economic and Social," and "Trusteeship" next to various auditoriums (Fig. 93). In this way, Harrison's design, its slab skyscrapers tempered by their curved plan and by the horizontal penetration of the auditorium structure, provided a basis for the first consideration of a United Nations headquarters on its present site.

Events that brought the U.N. to New York began at a General Assembly meeting in London early in 1946. There a Preparatory Commission decided that the international headquarters would be located in the United States; no specific site had been designated. The Preparatory Commission then established the Permanent Headquarters Committee, consisting of delegates from fifty-one countries under the chairmanship of Dr. Eduardo Zuleta Angel of Colombia. To consider the site and architecture, three groups were formed: the Headquarters Commission, consisting of delegates, architects, and other professional advisors and chaired by Sir Angus Fletcher, a British delegate; the Committee on Sites and General Questions, chaired by Juan Felipe Yriart, the Uruguayan delegate; and the Headquarters Advisory Committee (created on January 2, 1947, by the General Assembly under Trygve Lie, first Secretary-General), chaired by former Senator Warren Austin, from Vermont, Permanent Representative of the United States to the United Nations. There was immediate debate: should the headquarters be located in a city, a suburb, or a rural area?[10]

The Committee on Sites declared that the area for the project could range anywhere from six to forty square miles. Sites were proposed in New York City, Connecticut, Boston, Philadelphia, and San Francisco; each area was equally anxious to enjoy the prestige and material benefits the U.N. might bring to their communities. The mayor's New York Committee for the U.N. was chosen by Robert Moses, who envisaged an opportunity for the use of Flushing Meadows Park. True to character, according to his biographer, "other men

89. Harrison, scheme for X City. Rendering by A. Leydenfrost
(1946).

90. Harrison, scheme for X City. Rendering by Hugh Ferriss
(12 December, 1946).

91. Harrison, X City concert hall. Rendering by Hugh Ferriss.

92. Harrison, X City convention hall. Rendering by Hugh Ferriss.

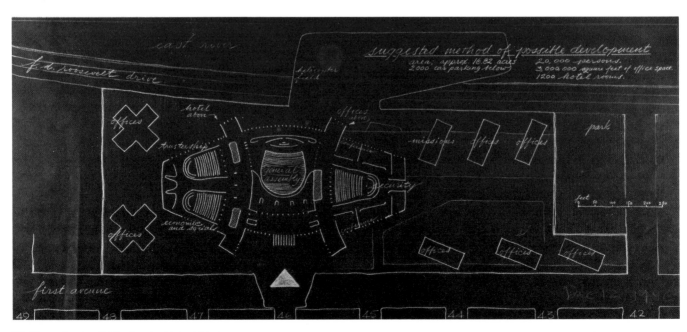

93. Plan adapting X City for the United Nations.

might see the formation of the United Nations ... as a chance for peace, he saw it as a chance for a park."[11] Moses's choice of Flushing as the site for the 1939 World's Fair had been motivated by his interest in creating a park there, and he now persuaded Trygve Lie to use what had been the fair's City Building for the U.N.'s temporary auditorium: it was converted for that purpose within a record two months. While the General Assembly met at Flushing, the Secretariat and attendant services were located in a converted war plant of the Sperry-Gyroscope Corporation at Lake Success, Long Island, a few miles northeast of Flushing.

Moses's U.N. committee was made up of eleven prominent New Yorkers, including Nelson Rockefeller and Winthrop W. Aldrich, Triborough Authority board member Charles Meyer, Grover Whalen, Arthur Hays Sulzberger of the *New York Times*, Frederick H. Ecker of Metropolitan Life, and Thomas J. Watson of IBM. There were also a number of consultants and a board of design that consisted of three engineers and three architects, including Harrison, Embury, and Louis Skidmore. In September 1946 the architects produced plans and drawings—rendered by Hugh Ferriss in his usual seductive style—presented in an elaborate brochure designed to "sell" Flushing Meadows Park to the Site Committee (Figs. 94, 95). A visitor would turn off Grand Central Parkway onto a road that passed through a row of monumental pylons sunk into a platform from which water gushed into a long moatlike reflecting pond. This imposing approach led into a large rectangular entrance court that occupied the southern end of a great terrace. Facing the court at the northern end was the domed General Assembly, one of four proposed buildings. With the exception of the General Assembly, each structure was long and low—only two stories high. The Economic-and-Social and Security Council buildings stretched parallel to the General Assembly at the west; perpendicular to these and set beside a big central lagoon, an even longer structure was to house the Trusteeship Council and various offices. A missions building was planned north of the General Assembly. To accommodate the fifteen thousand delegates and staff members then attached to the

94. United Nations project at Flushing Meadow, New York. Rendering by Hugh Ferriss (1946).

95. Walkway, United Nations project at Flushing Meadow. Rendering by Hugh Ferriss (1946).

U.N., the project was conceived on a grand scale (Fig. 96). Harrison influenced the form of the General Assembly building, which recalled the World's Fair Perisphere. It would be difficult to associate any one name with the remaining structures.

In their eagerness to convince the U.N. to choose New York, Harrison and Nelson Rockefeller resorted to one of their wartime propaganda techniques: they produced a one-reel film that showed how attractively the city could refurbish the Meadows. Their efforts were futile. During its temporary use of the area, the Permanent Headquarters Committee remained unconvinced that the malodorous swampland could be redeemed; and by December 1946, it was on the verge of selecting a ten-square-mile tract in the suburbs of Philadelphia. The Australian and other delegations from the Pacific favored a beautiful site in the Presidio section of San Francisco overlooking the Golden Gate, but the West Coast was firmly vetoed by major European delegations and by the U.S.S.R. The only other site under serious consideration was in Fairfield County, Connecticut. This too was vetoed after an inspection trip by several members of the Committee on Sites, during which they were stoned by local inhabitants protesting what they considered a foreign intrusion!

A deadline of December 31 had been set for selection of the U.N. site. On the morning of Sunday the 8th, Harrison and Frank Jamieson telephoned Rockefeller in Mexico City, where he had attended the inauguration of President Miguel Alemán. Rockefeller realized the Meadows proposal was in jeopardy and took the first plane home. He was met by Harrison and Clark Eichelberger of the U.N. Association, dedicated to promoting the U.N. They drove directly to Lake Success, though it was late on Sunday, to promote the Flushing site. The Rockefeller team then was faced with an overly suspicious guard, who delayed them for more than an hour while he doublechecked identities.[12] When finally they met with Secretary-General Lie and Warren Austin, it became apparent that only Manhattan itself, or a site very near to Manhattan, could provide an acceptable alternative to the Philadelphia site. Zeckendorf had just of-

fered to sell his X City site to Mayor William O'Dwyer, and knowledge of this proposal strengthened the delegates' insistence on Manhattan as in fact the only possible alternative.

On Monday, December 9, Rockefeller began a campaign to ensure that, if the Flushing site were rejected, the world headquarters would still remain in the state. He organized a meeting attended by John D., Jr., and Laurance Rockefeller, John Lockwood (one of the family's lawyers closest to Nelson), Francis (Frank) A. Jamieson (a Pulitzer Prize-winning newspaperman, who handled press relations for Rockefeller), and Harrison, and punctuated by telephone calls to his brothers David, Winthrop, and John D. 3d. At the meeting Nelson Rockefeller convinced his father and three brothers to give up part, or if necessary all, of their holdings in the 3–4,000-acre property they owned at Pocantico, north of Tarrytown, to create a potential site for the U.N.[13] Three members of the Headquarters Commission—Jan de Ranitz from Holland, Le Corbusier from France, and Nikolai D. Bassov from Russia—were asked to survey the site from a four-seater plane provided by the Rockefellers. If a report of this visit can be believed, Bassov showed interest only in the cost of the private plane, while the pilot never located the exact whereabouts of the site.[14] In any event, the flight seems to have confirmed the delegates' decision to consider New York only if they could be in the heart of the city.[15] On Tuesday evening, surrounded by Harrison, Jamieson, Lockwood, and his own assistant, Louise Boyer, Rockefeller broke the news to his father over the phone. "Why, Pa!" he is said to have exclaimed, then turning to the expectant group: "He wants to know how much that site along the East River would cost! He wants to *give* it to them!... Wally, how much do you think it would take to get it?"[16] When Harrison guessed $8.5 million, and the figure was accepted by John D. Rockefeller, Jr., general exultation ensued (Fig. 97).[17]

It is said that several months prior to this dramatic sequence of events, Harrison had suggested the possibility of Zeckendorf selling his X City site to New York for the U.N.; according to this report, Nelson Rockefeller had dismissed the idea as too costly.[18] Now, because of

96. Plan of United Nations project at Flushing Meadow.

Rockefeller Offers U.N. 8½ Million Gift For East River Site From 42d to 48th;

East River Site Offered to U. N. as Permanent Home

Queensboro Bridge

48th St.

Roosevelt Drive

East River

1st Avenue

42nd Street

Associated Press

Looking north at area between First Avenue and the river and Forty-second and Forty-eighth Streets

97. Announcement of John D. Rockefeller, Jr.'s, gift of a site for the United Nations.

his relationship with Zeckendorf, Harrison was chosen as the logical negotiator for an option on the site. How he accomplished this is well known: on December 10th he found the real estate man in the midst of a boisterous celebration of his own wedding anniversary and of the birthday of one of his partners, Henry Sears. Zeckendorf quickly agreed to Harrison's $8.5 million offer and confirmed a thirty-day option, signing, together with Sears, his own outline of the six blocks in question on a city property map provided by Harrison. Harrison's inability to satisfy Rockefeller's subsequent request for champagne to celebrate the multimillion-dollar deal for want of sufficient pocket money became a joke enjoyed for years.

The following day, Wednesday the 11th, the Rockefeller group swung into action: agreement had to be obtained from the city to cede its rights to the streets, river bulkheads, and various strips of land it controlled within the East River site; exemption from a gift tax had to be granted by the Internal Revenue Service (a condition of the Rockefeller gift); and the U.N. Headquarters Committee had to approve the site. Zuleta Angel, who had been recuperating from a serious illness at Columbia Presbyterian Medical Center, had himself taken by ambulance to Lake Success in order to preside over the meeting at which the site would be offered. On Saturday, December 14, basing their decision on an inspection of the land by a subcommittee and on the rendering of Harrison's modified plan for X City (see Fig. 93), the General Assembly ratified the Permanent Headquarters Committee's approval of the East River site. After a year of indecision, the site for the U.N. headquarters was decided upon within less than a week.

During the long search, many design professionals had expressed concern about the design of the headquarters. At first there was talk of an architectural competition,[19] but then it was generally assumed that several architects from different member countries would participate in the design, with an American heading the team. As early as May 22, 1946, George Howe, the noted Philadelphia architect, wrote to Eric Gugler, president of the American Institute of Architects, about a meeting of the American Society of Planners and Architects at which candidates to head the U.N. architectural staff were discussed: "The executive committee felt that a strong man with extensive experience should be proposed."[20] The committee had suggested that the man who best fit this description was Roland Wank, a Hungarian educated in Europe who had come to the U.S. in 1924; Wank had built projects in Canada and in the U.S., where he had worked most recently for the Tennessee Valley Authority. According to Howe, the rationale for this choice was a wish that "the radicals and conservatives of our profession (whoever they may be—I become more confused as to the issues involved) may stand together."[21]

By June 1946, the American Institute of Architects had formed their own Committee of Arts for the U.N. Center, which included Harrison, Eliel Saarinen, Ralph Walker, and William W. Wurster. Ten years later, David B. Vaughan, the United Nations' Secretary for General Services, who attended the committee's meetings, still remembered spending "days and days interviewing, consulting, etc.," on the same subject.[22] Despite considerable efforts, the distinguished professional organizations had little influence on the final result.

On January 2, 1947, Lie appointed Harrison director of planning for the United Nations' Permanent Headquarters. According to Harrison, ultimately he owed his appointment to the support of several powerful Washingtonians who had known him during his wartime effort in the CIAA—particularly Thomas G. Corcoran, known as "Tommy the Cork," and Benjamin V. Cohen, two lawyers who had been part of Franklin Roosevelt's famous "kitchen cabinet." He also had completely won over Lie.

When the appointment was announced, rumor had it that Nelson Rockefeller had put his own man into the job. While it would be disingenuous to think that the U.N. delegation was indifferent to the preferences of the Rockefeller family, it is also reasonably certain that men of this stature would give due weight to their own commitments and preferences. In any case, the job was Harrison's, and intricate problems lay ahead.

Chapter 12

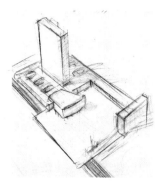

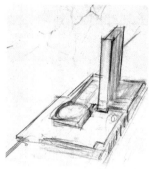

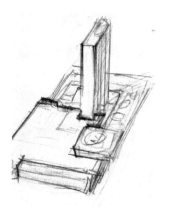

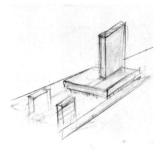

The United Nations: the battle of designs

When he was asked by the *New York Times* how he felt about his $18,000-per-year appointment as U.N. director of planning, Harrison responded:

> How do you feel when you get a job like that? It's the best job in the world almost. But it's a hell of a responsibility also. I think when I was younger, and got into Rockefeller Center fifteen years ago, I was much more elated.[1]

His experience at Rockefeller Center had taught him the realities of a project that involved several buildings and, more to the point, several architects. The first matter on his agenda was the problem of the architects—who they should be and from which and how many countries—and, like most of the decisions about the buildings, the choice was left basically to Lie and himself. A successful lawyer in Norway, Lie was a big bear of a man who had proven himself a model of executive efficiency. In Harrison's eyes, he possessed the one indispensable quality for a client: like Nelson Rockefeller, Robert Moses, and William Zeckendorf, he was "a man who could get things done."[2] The two men liked and respected each other and they soon established a pleasant working relationship.

They agreed that approximately ten political areas should be represented in developing the U.N. design: Western and Eastern Europe, Scandinavia, the British Commonwealth, South America, the Far East, and so on. Lie favored big-name architects, although some of the most famous were considered ineligible for political reasons: Alvar Aalto, one of Harrison's candidates, because Finland was not a member of the U.N.; Mies van der Rohe and Walter Gropius because they were identified with the very recent enemy, Germany.[3] Harrison's and Lie's discussions with delegates from twenty-six of the member countries produced thirty-three names, from which they chose for the primary Design Board ten well-known men who for the most part had made some contribution to modern architecture, and a secondary group of seven to serve as special consultants. In addition to the Design Board and consultants, Harrison invited three American architects who had contributed to the planning of the building complex to provide local expertise.

With a few exceptions, the list does not now seem particularly distinguished; one wonders how many were included because they held no strong convictions that might lead to conflict. The group was composed as follows:

Board of Design
G. A. Soilleux (Australia)
Gaston Brunfaut (Belgium)
Oscar Niemeyer (Brazil)
Ernest Cormier (Canada)
Ssu-ch'eng Liang (China)
Le Corbusier (France)
Sven Markelius (Sweden)
Nikolai D. Bassov (U.S.S.R.)
Howard M. Robertson (United Kingdom)
Julio Vilamajo (Uruguay)

Special Consultants
Josef Havlicek (Czechoslovakia)
Vladimir Bodiansky (France)
John Antoniades (Greece)
Matthew Nowicki (Poland)
Peter Noskov (U.S.S.R.)
Hugh Ferriss (U.S.A.)
Ernest Weissmann (Yugoslavia)

Associated U.S. Architects
Louis Skidmore (Skidmore, Owings & Merrill)
Gilmore D. Clarke (Clarke, Rapuano & Holleran)
Ralph Walker (Voorhees, Walker, Foley & Smith)

The inclusion of Le Corbusier on the Design Board was a controversial decision that was to have repercussions for years. Early in 1946 the Swiss architect had been invited to serve as France's representative to the U.N. Headquarters Commission. Le Corbusier was by then world-renowned as a leader of modern architecture and a prolific writer, with eighteen books and three volumes of his *Oeuvre Complète* already published. A few months after he joined the commission, he began to prepare a report on the U.N. headquarters, which he published at the end of the year with several last-minute updates. A typical iconoclast, the author justified the

publication of his report claiming that "an exposé of this kind isn't possible before the General Assembly, councils and commissions."[4] This statement by Le Corbusier on the U.N. contains an especially revealing section entitled "Examination of the Sites," in which he evaluated possible locations for the new headquarters:

> 1. Rockefeller Center—although Le Corbusier asserted that "New York is a terrifying city. For us it is menacing. We are not wrong in keeping at a distance!"
> 2. The New Jersey Palisades, which he dismissed as "a slope in the wrong direction [with] little promise."
> 3. Flushing Meadows, which he disqualified because it "is inescapably a suburb of New York, a dependency of New York" and would place the U.N. "in the shadow of the skyscrapers of Manhattan."
> 4. White Plains, New York; Greenwich, Connecticut; or Round Hill, Pennsylvania [he favored the latter].
> 5. Ridgefield, Connecticut; Amawalk, New York; or the Blue Mountains, Virginia, which he dismissed as being the "ends of the world."[5]

The Rockefeller donation of the East River site was announced shortly before his report went to press, in time for Le Corbusier to add several "supplements," in which he acclaimed the area, and predicted that its seventeen acres would be more appropriate than the site fifteen hundred times larger that many of the commission members had planned. Le Corbusier emphasized that the smaller site necessitated the adoption of his 1922 "Contemporary City for 3 million inhabitants" as the perfect solution for a high-density plan. The opportunity to realize his earlier scheme apparently outweighed the "terrifying" menace of New York City that he identified earlier. It was the first—and most benign—of many about-faces Le Corbusier would make concerning the U.N.

Le Corbusier, nearing sixty, remained exceptionally temperamental and difficult to work with; the French government had had a number of differences with him, on political and professional matters. Appealing to his colleagues' sense of fair play, Harrison had insisted on including Le Corbusier among the designers of the U.N.; yet, it was Harrison himself who eventually became the target of Le Corbusier's violent recriminations. Harrison had first met Le Corbusier in New York in 1933.[6] Like many colleagues Harrison believed that Le Corbusier had been the true winner of the competition for the League of Nations headquarters in Geneva in 1927, and that he had been treated unfairly in not being awarded the commission. As is often the case for public projects, political pressures had outweighed artistic values. Harrison, eager to avoid such considerations, wanted to treat the work at hand as purely architectural.

Le Corbusier, having invested six months of his time in the search for a site, was not about to miss an opportunity to realize his own ideas. On January 12, 1947, he wrote Harrison about his personal choice of architects for the job. He approved of only five: himself, Bassov, Robertson, Niemeyer, and Harrison, to be aided by a design group consisting of Weissmann, Clive Entwistle (England), Amancio Williams (Argentina), Stamo Papadaki (Greece), Matthew Nowicki, and Carlos Lazo (Mexico).[7] Architects of other nationalities could be designated as subsidiary participants if absolutely necessary. Sixteen days later, Le Corbusier flew to New York, and—before the design team had been designated officially—began to work feverishly on his own scheme for the U.N.[8]

On February 12 the Permanent Headquarters Committee confirmed the nomination of the Chinese, Brazilian, French, Russian, and English architects to the Design Board. Liang, from mainland China, was a frail-looking professor of architecture at Northeastern University at Mukden, and visiting professor of Far Eastern art at Yale; he had designed several university buildings in China. Niemeyer, a diminutive Brazilian architect, thirty-nine-years old, appeared always to be exhausted. In what for him was cold weather, he dressed in layers of oversized sweaters, which gave him a pitiful ragamuffin look. Niemeyer was reputed to be a devoted Communist; there was speculation about the political implications of his presence among the U.N. designers, but apparently he was more interested in enjoying his leisure than in political activity among his colleagues.[9] Bassov, the city planner for Leningrad, was a stocky, middle-aged Russian engineer who became famous during World War II for relocating the nation's heavy industry in the Ural Mountains. Robertson, born and trained in the United States, in 1919 went to England to complete his education and begin practice. This longtime friend of Harrison's, fifty-nine-years old, had become a polished Londoner, known for conservative work, with an occasional experiment in modernism. By March 7 Australian, Belgian, Canadian, Swedish, and Uruguayan architects also had been confirmed, as diverse a group as the others.[10]

As soon as he was named director of planning, Harrison had asked two young architects from his office—Dudley and Goldstone—to work on a program for the headquarters and plans for the operation of the project. Goldstone was to establish the U.N.'s needs in terms of facilities and space requirements, while Dudley was to refine his calculations for accommodating these needs to the site, with which he was familiar. Work began in the Marguery Hotel suite that had served for the X City studies. Office space was at a premium; Goldstone claims he worked in a butler's pantry, using drawers for files and with "my head in a sink!" At the same time, Harrison, with the help of Abramovitz and Dudley, started to organize a support staff and to assemble data for planning the site and its neighborhood.

The magnitude of the project was overwhelming. Twenty thousand people were expected to circulate daily within the U.N. buildings.[11] Goldstone refined his questions, moving from the needs of a department to those of individuals (addressing minutiae such as a request for ashtrays big enough for cigars in the men's toilet stalls—these were, in fact, included!).[12] In 1947 the General Assembly consisted of 55 member states with ten seats per delegation. The program, however, was based on a potential membership of 70 states, and planners figured that this number could grow to as many as 85, an expansion of almost fifty percent. The seating had to accommodate 700 delegates and their 240 advisors, 900 members of the general public, and 240 press representatives. The staff of the Secretariat was first tabulated at 2,300, a figure that grew within a few months to 4,400, with possible expansion projected to 5,265.[13] These figures called for 439,595 square feet of office space; 25,033 square feet of meeting rooms; and 351,483 square feet for "other services."[14] In 1987 there were 14,081 employees in the Secretariat building, which seems to have adjusted satisfactorily to the increase. Also in 1987, it was reported that 159 member countries were sending delegates to New York each year for the General Assembly, with each country's official representation reduced to six seats.

By January 23 Harrison had set up a Headquarters Planning Office on the twenty-seventh floor of the RKO Building—a location he felt was far enough from Lake Success to avoid possible political interference. The Design Board met for the first time on February 17, with only five members present: Le Corbusier, Bassov, Liang, Nowicki, and Harrison. Abramovitz, Dudley, Goldstone, and Glenn E. Bennett, secretary of the Headquarters Commission, also attended this meeting.

The architects met daily through early June for two-to-three-hour sessions in a workroom where there were a few private cubicles. They stood or sat around a table in the center of the room, talking and arguing in a mixture of French and English; only Bassov spoke neither language and had to rely on an interpreter. Next door was the drafting room, where rough concepts produced by the board were transformed into sealed designs. When the architects left for the day, designers began to work intensely, sometimes through the night, producing plans, sections, and elevations, as well as models and renderings, based on the architects' most recent ideas. Most renderings were executed by Hugh Ferriss, and plasticene models by René Paul Chambellan, both of whom, like others on the U.N. team, had worked with Harrison on Rockefeller Center. Now, fifteen years later, Harrison had exchanged his habitual cigar for an ever-present cigarette that dangled from the corner of his mouth, smoke rising into his eyes like a typical tough in French films of the day. Nevertheless press accounts

stated that Harrison "even looks like a successful architect";[15] more than ever, his appearance conveyed strength and authority (Figs. 98, 99).

In charge of the important drafting room was Michael M. Harris; born in Newark, he had graduated from Cornell University and had worked as a designer in distinguished New York firms—including that of John Russell Pope, a Beaux-Arts mogul, before he joined Harrison, Fouilhoux & Abramovitz in 1942. Harris was well informed about the U.N. and its needs. He worked with thirty to forty people, including a number of young draftsmen who became architects of some renown, among them: George Rockrise, who established his own firm in San Francisco; Arvin Shaw, later a partner of Carson, Lundin & Shaw in New York City; and B. J. Barnes, a superb drafter who married Shaw.

To assist him in his immense task, Harrison asked Abramovitz to serve as deputy director and Dudley as secretary of the Design Board. Theoretically, twenty-two people were responsible for the design, but few of the foreign architects stayed in New York for more than two to three weeks at a time and technical advisors came only when asked about specific problems. Usually no more than eight or nine men were present at the design meetings. When American consultants were asked to attend, Gordon Bunshaft often sat in for Skidmore.

The Design Board decided almost immediately that the U.N. should contain three main elements—the General Assembly, the Secretariat, and one to accommodate different councils and committees. Harrison was intrigued to find that

> nobody talked about the Assembly, the center of the whole thing; each architect wanted to do the office building because the European architects had never built a tower and they couldn't resist the opportunity!

Each architect had a distinct idea about how the elements should be situated. Liang wanted them constructed in a square layout with a Chinese garden in the center; his plan turned its back on the city, focusing inward, like a monastery. Although Liang accepted with grace the early rejection of this idea, he never budged

98. Thirtieth meeting of the Board of Design, 18 April 1947.
Among those also present at the meeting but not shown here
were Le Corbusier, Ernest Cormier, Louis Skidmore, Gordon
Bunshaft, Ralph Walker, and Hugh Ferriss.

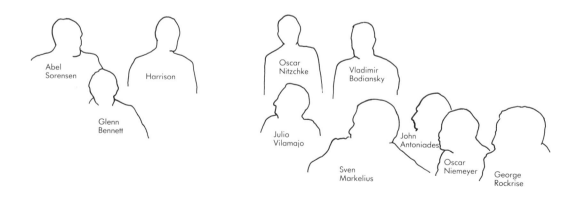

Abel
Sorensen

Harrison

Glenn
Bennett

Oscar
Nitzchke

Vladimir
Bodiansky

Julio
Vilamajo

John
Antoniades

Sven
Markelius

Oscar
Niemeyer

George
Rockrise

99. In the drafting room.

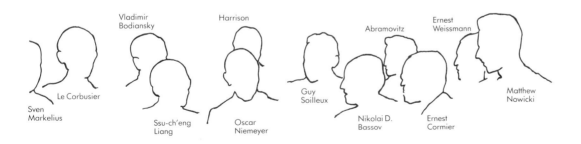

Sven Markelius
Le Corbusier
Vladimir Bodiansky
Ssu-ch'eng Liang
Harrison
Oscar Niemeyer
Guy Soilleux
Nikolai D. Bassov
Abramovitz
Ernest Cormier
Ernest Weissmann
Matthew Nowicki

from his conviction that each building should run on an east-west axis—a tradition the Chinese had followed for three thousand years. Robertson also favored inward-looking buildings, grouped around courtyards like those at Oxford and Cambridge. Markelius, city planner for Stockholm, whose appointment to the Design Board had been confirmed shortly after the original nominations, returned repeatedly to his scheme for extending the U.N. across the East River via a bridge to Roosevelt Island, where he envisioned a housing complex for its employees (Fig. 100). This issue had been raised earlier by the Headquarters Commission, but special living quarters for U.N. employees were soon ruled out. With their salaries and tax-exempt status, employees could find housing in the current market, and many of them seemed uncomfortable with the idea of living in close proximity to one another.[16]

At one of the board's first meetings, Le Corbusier presented a scheme he had developed in the fall of 1946 (Fig. 101). He had no interest in considering other designs; this became more apparent a few weeks later, when he tore every scheme except his own from the boardroom walls in an extraordinary fit of rage and frustration.[17] Then, surprisingly, in preparation for a visit to Paris, Le Corbusier wrote a letter to his colleagues with what was for him a generous conclusion: "We are an intangible group. There are no names attached to this work. As in any human enterprise, there is simply discipline, which alone is capable of bringing order."[18] Le Corbusier left New York on July 13, after the Design Board completed its assignment. But barely a month later, after seeing a publication of the board's final proposal, he decided that he alone, directing his own hand-picked team, should be in charge of the U.N. enterprise. On August 28 he wrote Harrison to this effect, enclosing a colored diagram so that there could be no mistake about the points he was making. The diagram was divided into sections of responsibility: Le Corbusier, the "studio master," was to be in charge of design, aided by Niemeyer, Entwistle, and Weissmann; Harrison, designated director of planning, was to be in charge of "administrative relations" with the city and the banks and was to have responsibility for working drawings, esti-

100. Sven Markelius, scheme for extending the United Nations complex to Roosevelt Island, with a grand boulevard to Fifth Avenue.

101. Le Corbusier, proposal for General Assembly, Council and Commission rooms (1946).

mates, construction surveillance, and accounting. The letter made amply clear that Le Corbusier regarded himself as the architect of the U.N. and Harrison as a mere administrator.

Harrison ignored Le Corbusier's attempt to restructure the hierarchy of the offices. He regarded his role as that of leading the Design Board in an effort to learn how the buildings would be used and then to come up with appropriate forms. Characteristically open-minded, he had no preconceived ideas about the forms of the different buildings or about their placement. The one thing he didn't want was the outright adoption of Le Corbusier's scheme, which had been developed before the international process began.[19]

In his account book for 1947, Hugh Ferriss recorded the receipt of $7,500 in payment for "approximately 100 presentation design studies" for the U.N.[20] A number of these studies have been preserved, and they help to illustrate the evolution of the architects' thinking. Some drawings, especially the earliest ones in which a domed structure is juxtaposed to a tall building, show obvious elements of the X City design (Fig. 102; see Fig. 89). One drawing even shows the structures seen by two people standing on a terrace in the foreground—like Zeckendorf's description of himself and his wife looking at the X City site (Fig. 103). Several of the early schemes show the Secretariat and the General Assembly locked into a massive platform (Figs. 104, 105).

Harrison began to anticipate problems with Le Corbusier when Frank Jamieson drew his attention to a scheme for the U.N. project published in the *New York Herald Tribune* on May 22, 1947, the day after the Design Board presented its scheme to the General Assembly (Fig. 106). The depth of Harrison's concern can be seen in his penciled notation on the caption the *Tribune* attached to the black-and-white glossy photograph it had used:

This is a lie, not at all scheme chosen.
                                        W. K. H.
This is a photo of Corbu's modified scheme.
How did he get a photog [sic] to take
this? [Fig. 107].

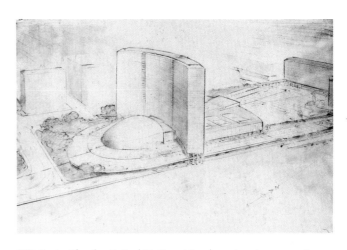

102. Project for the United Nations Headquarters incorporating ideas from X City. Rendering by Hugh Ferriss (18 April 1947).

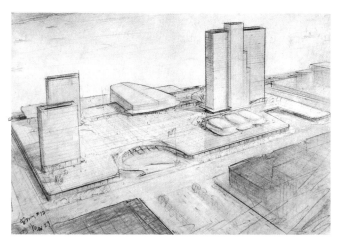

103. Project for the United Nations Headquarters. Rendering by Hugh Ferriss (18 April 1947).

104. Project for the United Nations Headquarters. Rendering by Hugh Ferriss (23 March 1947).

105. Project for the United Nations Headquarters. Rendering by Hugh Ferriss (13 April 1947).

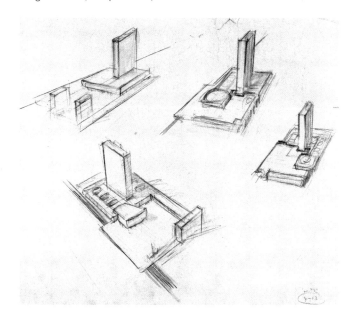

106. Project for the United Nations Headquarters published in the *New York Herald Tribune* (22 May 1947, p. 1).

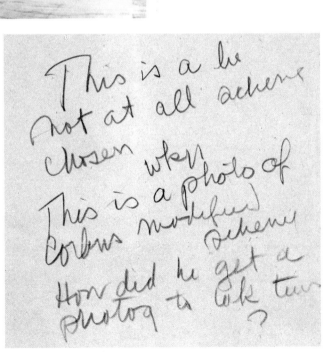

107. Harrison's notation on *Tribune* caption.

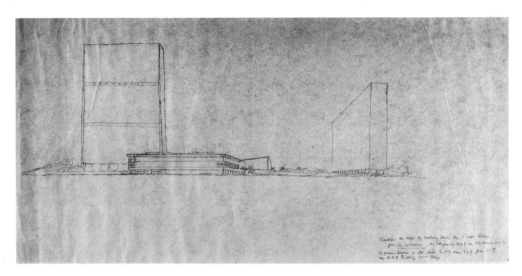

108. Le Corbusier, design for the United Nations Headquarters,
signed and dated 17 March, 1947.

109. Harrison, sketch for the United Nations.

The *Tribune* scheme closely resembles a drawing dated March 27, 1947, and signed by Le Corbusier, which the latter continually cited as proof of his authorship of the U.N.'s final design (Fig. 108). Precisely because it is signed, the drawing raises questions; members of the Design Board had scrupulously left their work unsigned to reinforce the idea of a team effort.

After Harrison's death, the photograph and Harrison's notation were discovered buried in his U.N. files; it revealed his suspicion that Le Corbusier had somehow gained unauthorized access to the drafting room to secure the rendering of his choice for the press. Harrison's consummate control of a potentially explosive situation is shown by his refraining from any public expression of misgivings about Le Corbusier's behavior. A rough sketch by Harrison, also relegated to the privacy of his files, bears the inscription in his hand: "Original sketch Ass. [Assembly] U.N. W.K.H." (Fig. 109). The undated drawing shows the complex as it was built and seems to be the architect's personal notation of the difference between Le Corbusier's scheme and the final result.

As built, the Secretariat represented the culmination of Harrison's long development of the freestanding slab that Le Corbusier had promoted. The U.N. headquarters incorporated other ideas that Le Corbusier had expressed for years. The tall Secretariat standing on its own grounds recalls his earlier concepts of a vertical city in a park. Le Corbusier had realized a solid-edged slab building in the Swiss Pavilion in Paris (1930) and in the Ministry of Education Building in Rio de Janeiro (1945). He had designed asymmetrically composed civic centers for his projects for Saint-Dié and for his second scheme for the Rio Ministry of Education.[21] Furthermore, he had used the trapezoidal form and sloping roof we see in the General Assembly Building for a number of assembly halls, beginning with one designed for the League of Nations in 1927.[22]

By the fall of 1947, Le Corbusier's change in attitude was complete. On November 7 he wrote a four-page letter to Harrison in which he traced his version of the history of the U.N. design. He gave Harrison credit only for what he described disparagingly as the "cupolas, fountains, etc." of the 1946 Flushing Meadows project,

claiming ambiguously, in the magisterial third person, that although "he wishes that his own name not be mentioned," the project in hand is "100% the architecture and urbanism of Le Corbusier"!

Harrison responded to this assault, as to the previous one, with silence, continuing to work on the task at hand. Whatever confusion may exist as to the authorship of the U.N. design, there is no doubt that Le Corbusier's Scheme No. 23A constituted an important element in the team effort. In 23A, the tall Secretariat intersects a massive, rectangular, horizontal block comprising the General Assembly and the Conference Building (Fig. 110). Pedestrian ramps extend from the Secretariat to the city streets.

But it was Oscar Niemeyer who provided the link between the French architect's design and what was ultimately realized at the U.N.[23] Everyone admired Niemeyer's accomplished schemes, but he was so intimidated by Le Corbusier, his former teacher and employer, that he seldom dared to present the projects to the board. One day, according to an associate architect, he produced a sketch on a used envelope that was too good not to show, and it was drawn up. The scheme separated the General Assembly from the Secretariat, moving it to the Secretariat's north; the mass of the General Assembly was reduced by taking away the conference and council rooms which were incorporated into a third structure at the river's edge. Niemeyer's solution (32) opened up the space into what seemed like a vast park with buildings in it (Fig. 111).[24] Even Le Corbusier eventually had to admit it was good, although he did so only after a day-long filibuster during which he called for committees to make the final design decision.[25] Harrison encouraged breaking apart Le Corbusier's buildings and making the other changes called for in Niemeyer's scheme; on May 1, 1947, at the thirty-ninth meeting of the advisory architects, Harrison made the following announcement:

> I propose we think in terms of those schemes on the walls now [Numbers 13 (Abramovitz, Niemeyer), 17 (Niemeyer, Bassov), 23 (Le Corbusier), 25 (Antoniades), 29 (Markelius), 31 (Soilleux, Niemeyer), 32 (Niemeyer), 33, 36 (Weissmann),

110. Le Corbusier, Scheme 23A.

111. Oscar Niemeyer, Scheme 32.

34 (Soilleux)]. These are similar in arrangements of rooms and relations; they agree on the Secretariat. There are still questions about one story or two [for the Conference Building]. In the early days there were many plans. One of them was Le Corbusier's. The only scheme that gets complete satisfaction is an early idea of Le Corbusier as carried out [i.e., presented] by Niemeyer. To develop this from here on out we should all concentrate on going to the users with that scheme.

　　　This seems a good compromise to me. That is my way of approach. Any objections?[26]

Le Corbusier, Niemeyer, Weissmann, and Bodiansky agreed to the proposed solution in a joint statement they issued on May 7, but in spite of this there was almost immediately a confrontation between Le Corbusier and Harrison. For practical reasons, Harrison was convinced that the required area in a Conference Building should be reduced in horizontal size, arranging it in two floors instead of one. Le Corbusier was adamant that it should be spread out on a single floor. Harrison decided to avoid a vote, which he felt would strain the relationship between opposing factions, and made the decision himself in favor of the two-level plan.

In later years Harrison, in his gentlemanly fashion, referred to this issue as the only obstacle Le Corbusier had posed. But an equally heated debate with Le Corbusier developed over his insistence that the Secretariat's façades be protected from the sun. Given that the Secretariat was to be a tall building, it was logical for the architects to think of it in terms of a typical American office tower, with daily, year-round use of the offices as opposed to the periodic use to be made of the meeting halls.[27] They agreed that the structure of each of the U.N. buildings would be in steel and reinforced concrete, but they still had to select the material for the skin to cover this framework. In one of his earliest statements about the buildings, Le Corbusier had referred to stone façades.[28] But for a maximum amount of sun and natural light in the Secretariat—as opposed to the artificial lighting of the meeting halls—overall glazing seemed to offer a better solution. The Design Board therefore decided that the building's major east and west elevations would consist of glass curtain walls with the narrow (seventy-two-foot) north and south ends solidly faced with marble (carried across the long sides as a thin cornice). Lie apparently suggested the unbroken stone sheathing for the Secretariat's narrow north and south sides.[29]

In 1947 there was only one glass-and-aluminum-skin skyscraper in the United States: Pietro Belluschi's nearly completed Equitable Building in Portland, Oregon (Fig. 112). Continuous glazing was therefore still an unfamiliar solution to the problem of the skyscraper wall. But even in those energy-rich days, the use of this much glass raised the question of heat gain and loss. Harrison knew, of course, that the Secretariat's orientation was not due north-south, as was widely supposed, but twenty-nine degrees east of north, in alignment with New York City's grid; accordingly the building's west wall would not be as directly exposed to the sun as was generally feared. Harrison initiated several studies to determine just how many hours of sun the building might expect each year and what measures could be taken to minimize unwanted solar effects. Four basic solutions were considered (each one in conjunction with the use of venetian blinds): plate glass; double plate glass; Thermopane (tinted double-glazing); and a double window of Thermopane and plate glass. As usual, Le Corbusier had his own solution—the *brise-soleil* (fixed exterior overhangs) that he had projected for his buildings in Algiers (1933) and employed later in Rio de Janeiro. Preliminary investigations revealed that the extra steel and other materials required for *brise-soleils* would add considerably to construction costs. It was also pointed out that in the harsh New York winters, they would be natural collecting places for snow and ice that could fall and create a dangerous hazard. Only the embedding of steam or hot water pipes in the *brise-soleils* could have prevented such a hazard—a precaution that would, in turn, have increased heating costs so drastically as to cancel out any possible savings they might have afforded in climate control.[30]

As a result of Le Corbusier's obstinacy, the debate about the Secretariat skin assumed monumental proportions. Again, Harrison acted decisively and diplomati-

112. Pietro Belluschi, Equitable Building, Portland, Oregon (1948).

cally. He turned the problem over to Syska & Hennessy, the then relatively small firm of young mechanical engineers that he had selected for the project. The engineers solved the matter by administering a simple heat test: they placed two twenty-four-hour thermometers that recorded temperatures on an ink graph two feet away from two different windows oriented as they would be in the U.N. building. One window was made of thermal glass (Thermopane); the other was not. Readings were recorded for two weeks, at the end of which the thermometer in front of the thermal glass window had consistently registered a temperature of ten to fifteen degrees less than its mate. The test proved that Thermopane alone, without *brise-soleils*, could moderate heat and cold, thereby justifying its price of fifty percent more than plate glass.

Thermopane was functionally necessary only on the west side of the Secretariat, but the architects were concerned about the psychological and aesthetic effects of using blue-green, heat-resistant Thermopane on one side of the building and clear glass on the other. To avoid such a dichotomy, they used Thermopane for both the east and west elevations, doubling their glass costs but extending the green tonality to all the building's windows.[31] The color refinement was continued in the lobbies, where walls and columns parallel to the green east and west façades are faced with green marble; those that parallel the white north and south façades are faced with white marble. Years after the Secretariat was completed, Le Corbusier still had not accepted this solution, bitterly criticizing the tinted glass (by then common in tall buildings) for casting what he called a "cadaverous light."[32]

For the General Assembly and the Conference Building the delegates requested that their spaces be kept separate from those of the press and public. Harrison ensured that this was achieved in both buildings by placing the two groups on different levels. The Conference Building rises to five stories on the river side and to four on the west side. The Security, Economic and Social, and Trusteeship council rooms are housed in the easternmost section, each with a large glass wall facing the river, similar to Harrison's design for a concert hall for X City (see Fig. 91). Below the council rooms, the conference rooms have the same structural frame, with full-height windows at each side of a blank middle section.

The General Assembly was considered the heart of the new "World Capitol," and as such it occupied the plan's focal point; in preparation for the design of its interior, Harrison covered the drafting room walls with as many plans for parliamentary assemblies as his researchers could find. Ranging from the U.S. Congress to the British, French, and Italian parliaments and a number of those in South American capitals, he found that the individual arrangements showed only minor differences—with the exception of the British Parliament, where opposing parties sit facing each other. Originally, the U.N. Assembly was designed as two funnel-shaped auditoriums that met at their narrow ends, and the resulting hourglass plan was a direct expression of this functional arrangement. A major budget cut (to be described in chapter 13) eventually necessitated reduction of the Assembly to a single auditorium with open-well lobbies at either end, thereby rendering meaningless the building's pinched-middle plan. But like every other aspect of the headquarters design, the external shape of the General Assembly had been arrived at through a rigorous exchange of ideas among the members of the by then dispersed Design Board. Reluctant to reopen this exchange by questioning the relationship of the General Assembly's exterior to its new interior, Harrison simply pulled the building together with flattened curves (Figs. 113, 114).[33] The decision ignored the connection between form and function and was widely criticized on this score.[34] At the time, the structure was a startling new example of a building treated as a free sculptural shape. New York City was unprepared for such a radical departure from the rectilinear norms of the prevalent International Style.[35]

In 1952, the year the General Assembly Building was completed, Harrison also completed a small auditorium for Oberlin College in Ohio, designed on the hourglass plan he had been unable to realize at the U.N.[36] To accommodate the wavy shell recommended by the acousticians Bolt, Beranek & Newman, he designed the interior walls and the ceiling as a series of cubic

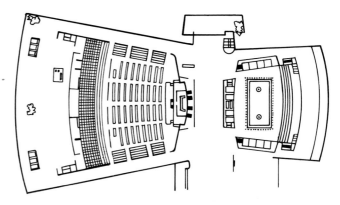

113. Original plan of General Assembly.

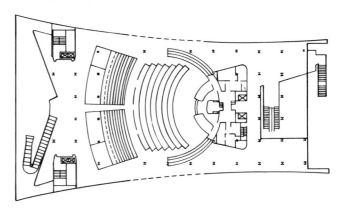

114. Modified plan of General Assembly, as built.

forms—with a hung, angled plaster ceiling. For the façade, he used one of the curvilinear motifs of which he was so fond. Public reaction to the design was even stronger in Ohio than in New York, as witnessed by the local press's calling Oberlin's new auditorium "The Most Controversial Building in Ohio" (Figs. 115, 116).[37]

The Design Board had intended that the curve of the General Assembly's roof and side wall would differentiate it from the rest of the complex and thereby emphasize its importance. (Originally, the Assembly's south façade was to curve forward slightly.) But juxtaposed against the strong, tall lines of the Secretariat, the concave west wall and roof made the Assembly building seem weak and uncertain by comparison (Fig. 117).[38] Harrison had approved the General Assembly roof as an uninterrupted curve with minor enclosures for machinery. But the plan changed when Lie ran into funding difficulties and had to appeal for a government loan. Harrison is reported to have said to his colleagues, "According to Senator Austin, if you're going to get this loan request through Congress, the building should have a dome."[39] The subsequent addition of a dome—the typical American symbol of government—over the curved roof of the Assembly Hall may have helped to gain congressional approval, but even more important to the approval were a number of cost-saving alterations. One of these changes necessitated lowering the Assembly roof which made the dome more unfortunately prominent (Figs. 118, 119). The steeply angled low dome is neither dominating nor decorative, and behind it at the north, the boxes enclosing elevator machinery appear clumsy and unrelated.[40]

Plans to use the same marble as the north and south ends of the Secretariat for the Assembly's flanks were also sacrificed to economy, and only a border in marble now surrounds the English Portland stone that was employed instead (Fig. 120). Neither the color nor the texture of this pinkish stone, it was soon pointed out, blends with the marble used elsewhere.[41] Other aspects of the building were also criticized: the rigidity of the ramps, the overbearing canopy of the delegates' entrance on the First Avenue façade, the discordance between the north, public entrance—composed of marble piers alternating with

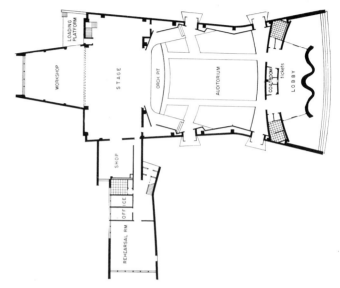

115. Harrison, plan of auditorium, Oberlin College, Oberlin, Ohio (1952).

116. Harrison, façade of auditorium, Oberlin College.

130

117. General Assembly (1952) and Secretariat (1950), seen from west.

118. United Nations Headquarters, seen from south. Harrison's
library (1963) is in the foreground, Abramovitz's twin tower
apartment building (1966) is in the background.

119. United Nations Headquarters, seen from east.

120. Detail of north entrance to General Assembly building.

vertical bands of photosensitive glass—and the south elevation, whose glazing was similar to the other U.N. buildings. Harrison himself regretted the awkwardness of the narrow, rectangular passageway that connects the eastern elevation of the General Assembly with the Conference Building (see Fig. 118).[42]

The Assembly Hall itself has worked well. Technologically ahead of its time, it was the first auditorium in the world to take advantage of all the (then) new mechanical and electrical aids.[43] The gilded wood sheathing of its slanted walls hides irregular surfaces that assure effective acoustical functioning. Reminiscent of Aalto's tilted wood walls at the New York World's Fair, the room focuses on the dramatic light slot behind the speaker's podium (Fig. 121). The majestic space of the main, delegates' entrance is also appropriate to its function. What might have been a cold, cavernous area is humanized by the gentle angle of the balconies that open onto it—an angle recalled in the parabolic arches that support the ramp (Fig. 122). Unfortunately, the ceremonial front entrance quickly took a second place to the more accessible western entrance.[44]

In the last years of his life, Harrison said simply of the U.N.: "I and the others expressed the Assembly with the slope of the roof and walls. Does it go with the office building? Perhaps not, but how do you do it better?"

Harrison's tolerance for pressure and controversy would be tested again as the prospect of the U.N. became a dynamic ingredient in the political and business life of New York City. For if designing the U.N. buildings was one problem, the question of their relationship to the existing fabric of the city presented a whole set of other problems, which could be solved only with the cooperation of several major figures in the city's administration. One of these was the mayor, and another, the Parks Commissioner, who was also chairman of the Triborough Authority.

Harrison recalled that "no one had any use for Bill O'Dwyer, but he turned out to be great—he was determined to do the U.N."[45] The brawny, blue-eyed mayor of New York was one of eleven children of impoverished Irish parents. A Jesuit education in Spain served him well during his arduous climb up the political ladder in the

United States. Unfortunately, neither his training nor his subsequent status as a lawyer, magistrate, county court judge, and district attorney were sufficient to clear his name of its associations with organized crime. Whatever these associations may have been, O'Dwyer sincerely loved New York and was highly ambitious for the role he could play in its improvement. The U.N. provided him with a golden opportunity.

Robert Moses was another powerful figure to be contended with. Earlier, Moses had fought against a midtown location for the U.N. headquarters. For him Flushing Meadows was "The Natural and Proper Home of the Capitol of the World."[46] But even the mighty Moses was overruled by the combination of Rockefeller, O'Dwyer, and Trygve Lie. Once it was apparent that the U.N. delegates would come to New York only if their headquarters could be situated in Manhattan, the Parks Commissioner was quick to accept the East River location; and with his usual talent for coming out on top of what might seem to be defeat, he was made U.N. construction coordinator for the city and granted complete control of those spheres that affected the city, such as roads and fences.[47]

On May 21, 1947, the mayor made a public statement that outlined the city's responsibility in the overall planning of the U.N. To facilitate nonlocal traffic through the site, a six-lane tunnel was to be excavated under First Avenue between Forty-first and Forty-eighth streets, with all private and public utilities in the tunnel area to be rerouted. To accommodate the twenty thousand people who would be coming daily to the site, Forty-seventh Street was to be widened between Second and First avenues. Several buildings between Forty-first and Forty-third streets on the west side of First Avenue were to be torn down to make two small formal parks. The narrow forty-foot tunnel on Forty-second Street between First and Second avenues was to be reconstructed to the full one-hundred-foot width of the street and the Forty-second-Street trolley line was to be eliminated eventually. The city agreed to sell to the U.N. for a nominal $1.5 million its Housing Authority Building, which had been completed recently on the site at Forty-second Street. An aerial easement would be granted over FDR

121. Assembly Hall with murals by Fernand Léger, General Assembly.

122. Delegates' entrance, General Assembly.

135

Drive so that between Thirty-seventh and Fifty-first streets the drive could be reconstructed under an esplanade to be built by the U.N., with access/egress ramps at Forty-second and Forty-eighth streets. Work on the drive was to be paid for by the U.N.; the remaining cost of $15 million was to be covered by the city.[48]

By the time the international headquarters was completed, New York City had spent $25,806,300, two-thirds as much again as its original estimate. Additional expenses involved the costs of renovating the temporary headquarters in Flushing for use during the design and construction of the new buildings; condemning the remaining strips of private land in the area; resettling the building materials yard and freight barge terminal of the Lehigh Valley Railroad; and removing and relocating 270 residential tenants who had been living on the site. In addition, as a result of the federal tax dispensation for the U.N., the city rezoned and restricted advertising in the surrounding neighborhood.[49]

The city reaped extraordinary benefits from these concessions. Before the complex was finished, property values in the U.N. neighborhood had appreciated to sixty-five dollars per square foot, and in the 1950s and 1960s several institutions and a major corporation asked Harrison & Abramovitz to design buildings near the U.N. Harrison built a twelve-story building, clad laterally in limestone with a glazed façade, to house the Carnegie Endowment for International Peace (1953) at the northwest corner of Forty-sixth Street and First Avenue.[50] He constructed a similar building clad entirely in limestone for IBM World Trade (1958) on the opposite, southwest, corner of the avenue. Abramovitz designed the Institute of International Education (1964) on First Avenue between Forty-fifth and Forty-sixth streets with the Edgar J. Kaufmann Conference Rooms by Aalto. This was followed by a pair of large steel and glass apartment towers for Alcoa (1966) between Forty-eighth and Forty-ninth streets facing the northern border of the U.N. site. More recently, Roche & Dinkeloo's U.N. Plaza Hotel (1976) and office complex (1984) have joined the Harrison & Abramovitz buildings. Without the U.N., the city would have had to provide slum clearance for most of the neighborhood. The private capital that ac-

tively began to seek investment there might have been attracted only if the city had resorted to lowering property values. In the long run, savings and increased tax income to the city far outweighed its immediate expenditure.[51]

O'Dwyer and Moses were willing to make almost unlimited concessions to accommodate the new international headquarters within its site and in relation to the areas immediately adjacent to it. They were less receptive to proposals for its relation to the rest of the city, including a grand axial approach which might stretch as far as Grand Central Terminal.[52] Moses maintained the city's resistance to this scheme and encouraged the City Planning Commission, chaired at the time by the future mayor, Robert F. Wagner, Jr., to try to resolve the problem by simply widening the south side of Forty-seventh Street between First and Second avenues—opposite the preliminary site for the Secretariat—by one hundred feet. Protesting a solution it considered inadequate, a special committee of the New York chapter of the American Institute of Architects confirmed the insufficiency of the City Planning Commission's proposal and in its stead suggested a six-part plan focused on redeveloping the blocks between Forty-fifth and Forty-eighth streets between Lexington and First avenues and creating a wide boulevard and an underground pass with parking facilities.[53]

No one was more eager to apply this grand approach to New York than William Zeckendorf, who waged a futile, year-long campaign to try and persuade Moses to change his mind (Fig. 123; see Appendix B). Throughout these impassioned proceedings Harrison maintained a dignified aloofness. Considering his Beaux-Arts training, there is little doubt that he favored the grand approach. But unlike Zeckendorf, who tended to forget the practical implications of his ideas, Harrison was a realist. He knew that time and money were essential to the building of the U.N. He realized that the cost both in lost tax revenues and in the construction and maintenance of an important boulevard would be more than the city would be willing to undertake. By wisely refusing to take sides, the architect avoided a possible complication of the project at hand and at the same time kept the good will of a former client and of the city's most

123. William Zeckendorf's proposed concourse to the United Nations Headquarters (spring 1947).

powerful official, with whom he also succeeded in maintaining his personal friendship.

As usual, Moses moved quickly on his decision, ordering Forty-seventh Street widened from First to Second avenues. Within a short time the Design Board repositioned the Secretariat at Forty-second Street, but it was too late: Moses's orders had already been executed, leaving the existing stub of broadened street that inexplicably dramatizes the neon advertisement for Pepsi-Cola across the East River.[54] It is ironic that the building the sign crowns had been designed by Harrison & Fouilhoux.

Chapter 13

The United Nations: the critics

On May 21, 1947, the Headquarters Advisory Committee of the General Assembly unanimously approved the Design Board's final plan.[1] The estimated cost was $85 million; it was now up to Trygve Lie to secure the necessary funds. Turned down by the International Bank and advised that the amount was too high for Congress to approve, he decided that the request would have to be pared down.[2]

Harrison greeted the news that the design had to be altered for economy's sake with stoic equanimity and immediately mustered the draftsmen under Harris's direction to make the necessary changes. The Secretariat building was reduced by six floors (from forty-five to thirty-nine); the General Assembly, as already noted, was reduced from two halls to one; four of the Conference Building's conference and committee rooms were eliminated (leaving eighteen instead of twenty-two), and in place of one of the largest (Conference Room Number 4) a smaller room was placed directly under the General Assembly hall; the generous circulation areas were cut back—in the Conference Building, for example, interior corridors were eliminated entirely; parking facilities were reduced from two thousand to fifteen hundred; and the installation of certain communication equipment was deferred. In addition, Harrison decided that an enclosing fence that seemed of particular interest to Moses would be paid for by the city.[3] In short, the project's materials and details were simplified and the plan was tightened, but the general scheme remained essentially the same.

The report that was presented to the General Assembly and then submitted to Congress for funding in the summer of 1947 relied on visual means of presentation similar to the techniques used in Nelson Rockefeller's wartime chart room in Washington. Through numerous charts, diagrams, plans, and sections by Robert Pontabry (from the Harrison & Abramovitz office), accompanied by brief explanatory texts, the report described the three U.N. buildings, and suggested constructing a tower at the north end of the site for specialized agencies and missions.[4] On August 11, 1947, Congress granted an interest-free loan of $65 million.

The Secretary-General had been growing increasingly impatient with the international architects' complex discussions concerning the headquarters, and he was obviously relieved at the prospect of their ending. As Harrison said: "He wanted to get it built."[5] Their task completed, each foreign architect received a $5,000 fee and returned to his country. Le Corbusier was reluctant to leave, insisting that without him the project could not be realized properly. He finally departed only when Lie made it clear that he would not tolerate his continued participation.[6]

Having just completed the design process for the U.N., Harrison turned his attention to an even larger project. It, too, involved the coordination of buildings on a single site; in this case, about 80 acres in old St. Louis. The project was to commemorate Thomas Jefferson's Louisiana Purchase, with the design to be selected by means of an open competition: the Jefferson National Expansion Memorial Competition. Announced June 1, 1947, the program was unusually indeterminate: in effect competitors were asked to create their own program for land use and development of the unoccupied, government-owned site; plans were to include landscape design and sketches of sculpture and painting.

Harrison based his plan on facilities for what must have been one of the most compelling issues of the time: the constructive development of atomic energy. The linear plan included two historical museums, buildings which would provide meeting and working space for the Atomic Development Authority, and spaces for public contacts such as exhibitions and libraries. The focal building of the Authority was a tiered, circular conference center. Additional buildings would house non-Authority offices and commercial premises together with recreation areas (Fig. 124).[7] The practicality of the concept was at polar opposites from Eero Saarinen's prize-winning, abstract design for a monumental parabolic arch. Like the calm arrangement of diverse units at the United Nations, Harrison's plan for the Jefferson National Expansion Memorial Competition is in sharp contrast with the more agitated manipulation of uniform units in his earlier design for X City.

In September, the U.N. draftsmen under Harris relinquished their cramped quarters in the RKO Building to the Harrison & Abramovitz office and moved to the site, establishing themselves on the second floor of the inherited Housing Authority building. Located at the northeast corner of Forty-second Street, it was near completion at the time of the Rockefeller gift. The ugly structure was an embarrassment to the U.N. architects, but the cutback ruled out its demolition. (It was finally torn down in 1960, when Harrison designed a new building to serve as the U.N. Library [1963].)[8]

The fall of 1947 saw Harrison dividing his time between his office at Rockefeller Center and the U.N. design rooms, a pattern that lasted for several years. Lie had engaged Harrison & Abramovitz to make working drawings for the structures. As director of planning, Harrison was therefore in the ambiguous position of hiring his own firm. "He was very tough on himself," said H. L. McLeod, the head of finance for the Headquarters Planning Office. "An architectural firm doing a job such as Harrison & Abramovitz did for the U.N. buildings would ordinarily charge a fee of several million dollars. Harrison & Abramovitz insisted on doing the job for just cost plus the actual overhead. They didn't make a cent of profit."[9] The U.N. proved to be the first in a series of large urban facilities, including Lincoln Center and the Albany Mall, for which the firm in large part waived a profit. While the publicity value of these major monuments is undeniable, Harrison's deep civic consciousness also must have played a role.

Now began the arduous tasks of preparing working drawings and making crucial choices of contractors and experts in engineering, air-conditioning, landscaping, and the like. Two hundred fifty draftsmen worked at the Housing Authority building, where Michael Harris was spending his days and a good part of his nights. He remembered Harrison's relentlessness, driving everyone to meet stiff deadlines he had set:

> His enormous capacity of getting work done at all times, by people of all ages, but particularly young people, from whom he seemed to have a knack of drawing out the most possible. But he could be infuriating, and sometimes I felt he didn't care if I lived or died as long as the job got done.[10]

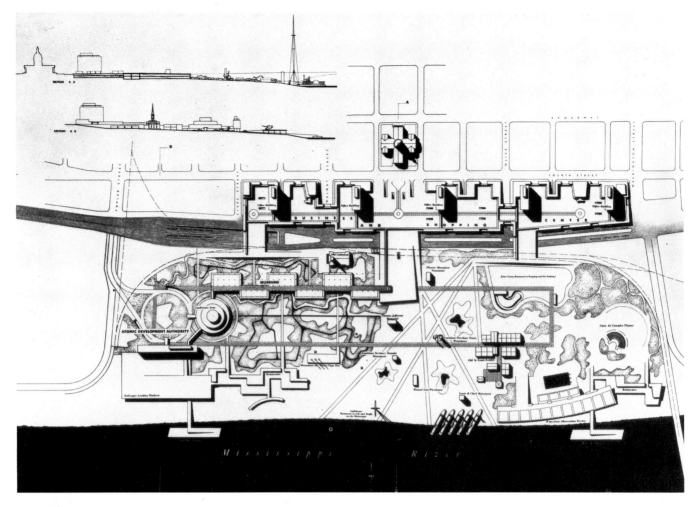

124. Harrison & Abramovitz competition entry for Jefferson
National Expansion Memorial (September 1947).

When in 1950 the Secretariat was almost ready for occupancy, the draftsmen moved to the second floor of the
headquarters' skyscraper. By then major problems had
been resolved and, according to Harris, "everyone was
working together like one big happy family."

The Secretariat had been scheduled for completion
by June 1949, and the Conference and General Assembly
buildings for early 1951. The Secretariat was, in fact,
ready for occupancy on August 21, 1950,[11] and the Conference Building was completed in July 1951, followed
by the General Assembly, in October 1952. Miracu-
lously, the $65 million budget was exceeded by only $2
million. The relative rapidity of construction and the remarkable adherence to budget were due to a great extent
to the widespread idealism and enthusiasm generated by
the idea of a United Nations. From representatives of
participating countries to architects, negotiators, and
even unskilled construction workers, most of those con-

nected with the project were convinced that the organization represented a step toward world peace. Like
Rockefeller Center during the Depression, the U.N. was
the most important construction project in post–World
War II New York; in a city harassed by myriad new problems, the U.N. represented hope for making New York
the political capital of the world. But efficient realization
of the international headquarters was also accomplished
thanks to Harrison's expertise. It had taken him barely
three months to obtain a workable project from a group
of architects including some of the most temperamental
men in the profession. He himself said there was "no
time for architectural politics, feuds and quarrels."[12] In a
talk he gave in April 1947, Harrison noted his concern to
avoid problems like those that had arisen at the 1933–34
Chicago World's Fair, where a voting committee of architects became embroiled in "a battle royal, with one
clique working against another," and at the League of

Nations, which took eleven years to complete. He claimed to have used as a model Stephen F. Voorhees's direction of the 1939 New York World's Fair: "He had *authority*, though he hardly ever used it, and never insisted on his own ideas—but, having the authority, he eliminated the clique."[13] Harrison followed his model well, and once the design was established, he implemented it in masterly fashion.

At the start of the design discussions, Harrison went to Washington to discuss a no-strike agreement with William Green of the American Federation of Labor. With the exception of a two-week work stoppage in September 1947, the agreement held.[14] Early in 1948 major U.S. steel producers raised the price of semifinished steel. Forewarned by this increase, Harrison moved to protect the project from future surprises. When all the bids were in, he called Benjamin F. Fairless, president of U.S. Steel, and told him that his company had made the lowest bid, and it would get the contract only if Fairless guaranteed the price and availability of the steel. Fairless agreed, and the $2.5 million contract was signed on December 10, 1948. When the Korean War began in June 1950, steel became scarce, and with outstanding deliveries still to be made for the General Assembly and Conference Building, Harrison reminded Fairless of his promise. The steel was delivered on time.[15] Harrison ended his retrospective account of this incident with the observation: "Fairless was an old-fashioned entrepreneur, he kept the steel company going at a tremendous rate—he honored his word, and delivered—it wouldn't be the same today."

When Harrison served as director of planning for the U.N., he was at the peak of his prestige as founder and head of a large architectural office. At that time an architect in his position controlled many aspects of construction. Moreover, Harrison knew exactly who wielded power in a supremely power-conscious city, and he made sure he maintained access to that power in order to construct the buildings he was entrusted with in a manner commensurate with that trust.

Two special areas of the U.N. construction proved to be particularly successful. Harrison engaged Bolt, Beranek, & Newman, a firm of young men who had just completed their acoustical training in Los Angeles with Vern O. Knudson, then considered one of the greatest experts in the field. The exceptionally good acoustics in the different public rooms at the U.N. launched the firm on its rapid path to success. Harrison's innovative solutions to the problems of air-conditioning the U.N. buildings also resulted in a remarkable quality of environmental control. Because many people of different nationalities would be working in the Secretariat, with a great variety of habitual response to climate, it was requested that the design provide individual temperature control and operable windows. This, combined with the continuous glazing of the Secretariat's east and west elevations and its northwest orientation, challenged climatological skill.

To carry wind loads and to create efficient interior space, the building had a steel frame of two exterior and two interior column lines, with girder frames between columns rigidly connected to them. Floors consisted of short-span reinforced concrete slabs. Normally, the façade would show deep floor structures and suspended ceilings required for duct work carrying the extremely heavy loads. In fact, the floor slab was cantilevered approximately thirty inches beyond the structural columns and the ceiling in that area was tilted up to meet the floor slab at the glass skin. This showed only a thin line on the exterior and left enough space for the ducts.[16]

Services and mechanical systems were placed in three of the Secretariat's floors (6, 16, 28), and in the top floor, and the basement. The exteriors of these floors were covered with grillwork, interrupted by a narrow, horizontal glazed band (see Fig. 117). The arrangement saved one foot in height per service floor and kept the rest of the building free of most machinery. Elevator machinery was located at the center of the floors, leaving office space at each end. A clear ceiling height of nine feet six inches was normal throughout the building. Grills and diffusers provided low-velocity air, while high-velocity air issued at regular intervals from units under the windows with water coils for heating and cooling, every other one of which was adjustable.[17] The provision of six air-conditioning units for every seven window bays and the integration of air-diffusers into standard fluorescent light fixtures provided unusual flexibility.[18]

In the General Assembly building, Harrison created a small scandal by making fully visible on the ceiling of the delegates' entrance the massive and complicated duct work of the air-handling system (see Fig. 120). This preference for bulky, nonrectangular forms to smooth, streamlined surfaces may reflect Markelius's influence. It can also be perceived as part of the postwar period's general movement toward greater freedom of architectural expression.[19]

At the U.N. (as he had at Rockefeller Center), Harrison played an important role in the acquisition of artworks. When the organization began to receive gifts from every participating country, he persuaded Lie that a review committee was needed to control the quality of works accepted. This did not, however, solve the question of funding art he wanted to buy for the new buildings. The large, lateral walls of the General Assembly's hall were of particular concern to Harrison, and he asked his friend Fernand Léger to provide rough sketches for murals. Harris was sent to Paris to describe the project to Léger, who agreed to make the drawings for $5,000. Harrison showed the scheme to Nelson Rockefeller, who immediately donated the artist's fee. Because of Léger's association with the Communist party at the time, he was not permitted to enter the United States to execute the works, but his sketches allowed a young art student to paint the murals according to the master's specifications (see Fig. 121). Their execution by another hand perhaps partially explains the disappointing quality of these murals. Harrison also was responsible for obtaining for the U.N. sculpture by Henry Moore and Barbara Hepworth.

In widespread coverage of the design for the U.N. buildings, the press repeatedly compared them to Rockefeller Center. To understand the implications of this comparison, it must be remembered that, as Rockefeller Center had neared completion, it had been criticized as the "tombstone of capitalism . . . with windows."[20] Even a decade later, in the late 1940s, in a general assessment of the city's architecture Mumford condemned the whole concept of Rockefeller Center as "the end of a period, not the beginning of one."[21]

From the first unveiling of the Design Board's model and plans in 1947 until its completion in 1953, the U.N. was the object of high praise and sharp criticism. Reporting on a preview of the design at Flushing, George Barrett wrote of the Secretariat in the New York Times: "The massive vitreous structure . . . is probably the most radical building design ever attempted on a huge scale."[22] Philip Johnson declared the project to be "the best modern piece of planning" he had ever seen.[23] On the other hand, Mumford devoted six of his influential Sky Line columns in the New Yorker exclusively to the headquarters; most of them were devastatingly critical. He condemned, among other things, the inadequate site—"a fleabite of land," with no "provision for growth"[24]—and the buildings' design, which he charged with failing to create a cohesive whole and found "far from being an admirable expression of the idea of the U.N."[25] For Mumford, the prominence of the Secretariat in relation to the General Assembly destroyed the expressive possibilities of the complex; they were woefully wanting in what he felt "should be as beloved a symbol as the Statue of Liberty, as powerful a spectacle as St. Peter's in Rome."[26]

In retrospect, Harrison noted, with a hint of annoyance, that from its beginnings everyone had seemed to want Rockefeller Center to be something other than what it was, and that the same had been true of the U.N. From the day he was appointed director of planning, he demonstrated his pragmatic attitude toward the project: "The basic problem . . . is not to try to symbolize the U.N. in some highly imaginative design, but to construct a capitol where the world representatives can work efficiently and in comfort."[27] In an interview in the New York Times Magazine, he explained his perspective:

> The best building in Rockefeller Center is the big one. Why? Not because we decided to raise the best and biggest building in the world to symbolize something. It's because we decided how deep in from the window an office could be and still make a place for a person working away from the light. That building grew out of our problems, not out of a philosophical concept.[28]

Harrison wanted the same kind of practical solution for the U.N., which he thought of as a workshop—rather than a symbol—for peace.[29]

"Not since Lord Carnarvon discovered King Tut's tomb in 1922 had a building caused such a stir," *Architectural Forum* declared of the Secretariat in 1950.[30] And there were well-publicized interviews with a variety of architectural personalities. Upon completion of the Secretariat, Frank Lloyd Wright stated with characteristic authoritarianism: "The building for the U.N. is a glorification of negation. A deadpan box with no expression of the nature of what transpires within the building."[31] William Delano declared that "buildings of glass look neither stable nor dignified. And they certainly do not have a monumental appearance."[32] While Mumford, in a burst of praise, wrote of the Secretariat:

> No building in the city is more responsive to the constant play of light and shadow in the world beyond it; none varies more subtly with the time of day and the way the light strikes, now emphasizing the vertical metal window bars, now emphasizing the dark green of the spandrels and underlining the horizontality of the composition. No one had ever conceived of building a mirror on this scale before, and perhaps no one guessed what an endless series of pictures that mirror would reveal.[33]

Although he grudgingly maintained some of his earlier criticisms, his statements—which included an accolade in the same article that referred to the Secretariat as "a snow Queen's palace, exhaling by night a green moonlight splendor"—give the impression that he admired the buildings or at least the Secretariat, in spite of himself. Upon completion of the complex in 1953, the architect and critic Henry Stern Churchill made this judgment in his cover story on the U.N. headquarters in *Architectural Record*:

> The planning of the U.N. group is a triumph of clarity and ingenuity, a putting together and sorting out of an almost incredible variety of elements and functions. It is also a triumph of technical skill, of structural ability, of mechanical engineering. Almost every possible device of a mechanical nature has been used to further the comfort of the users of the buildings, to speed up communication, to disseminate information quickly and accurately. It is, in other words, a very fine example of American architectural skill.[34]

The U.N. buildings are what Harrison had hoped they would be—functional solutions to the ways in which they are used. Contrary to the predictions, the architecture has proved surprisingly adaptable to the enormous increases in membership, and the people who use the buildings are unanimous in their praises of them. If it were not for the marble framing of the Secretariat's northern and southern flanks, the building would be recognized as the first glass-wall skyscraper, a building type probably more widely imitated than any other in the history of architecture. As it is, Harrison's Secretariat provides an essential link between Belluschi's Equitable Building and the all-glass-wall skyscraper. Unlike Belluschi's building, where the glass and aluminum skin is locked onto the supporting structure, the Secretariat's glazed façades are truly independent free-hanging screens. The combination of the glass's blue-green color with the black masonry behind wire-glass spandrels[35] gave it an extraordinary reflective capacity, which was recognized immediately by architects who replicated and elaborated on it to produce what has become today's ubiquitous mirror façade. Placement of the elevator banks in the core of the building made possible the unadorned, slim rectangular form Harrison had fought for in vain for the RCA Building.

A year after the Secretariat was completed, Gordon Bunshaft produced the all-glass-walled Lever House on Park Avenue and Fifty-fourth Street. Within five years glass towers were rising across the United States and around the world. The building that may have lacked eloquence as a symbol of world peace became one of the most influential progenitors of American technology at the service of bureaucratic efficiency, and a true symbol of Western civilization at mid-century.[36]

143

Chapter 14

Big Buildings

While the U.N. was being completed, Harrison's wide-ranging contacts and reputation had brought to the firm a number of other large projects, which were well under way. By the early 1950s, Harrison's name was virtually synonymous with the tall office tower. His preeminence in the area was confirmed when noted historian Talbot Hamlin asked him to contribute the authoritative entry on office buildings for his encyclopedic survey of contemporary architecture, *Forms and Functions of Modern Architecture* (1952).

Creating a tall office building required the carefully orchestrated collaboration of a number of specialists. Three architectural firms had worked together to realize Rockefeller Center, but by now a variety of experts in many different fields contributed to large and costly projects which had to be completed rapidly so that they could begin to pay for themselves.[1] They required a vast amount of drafting that needed no particular design ability and could be accomplished competently by a number of associates working in what came to be known contemptuously as "plan factories."

The origin of the large-scale architectural office can be traced to the last decade of the nineteenth century. Daniel H. Burnham in Chicago was one of the first architects to organize a large firm that employed numerous people and to limit his own activities strictly to those of executive head. Soon most large architectural firms adopted this specialized assignment of responsibilities. About 1905 Albert Kahn developed a method of work in his Detroit architectural office that resembled the new techniques of mass production in the automobile factories he was designing.[2] By 1950, nine-tenths of the 19,000 registered architects in the United States were working in large offices. At mid-century, the firms of Harrison & Abramovitz and Skidmore, Owings & Merrill were the foremost examples of the system.

While the large, systematized architectural office offered important advantages, it had clear enough weaknesses. No single, characteristic expression could survive the process of consensual enterprise, and the best analyses and technologies often merged to create products so similar that it became difficult to know which office had designed which building. Rockefeller Center was correctly categorized as the last of its kind, where artistic sensibility could still predominate, by and large, as long as rentability was unharmed. But twenty years later, the use of any kind of external ornamentation—let alone costly artwork—had become taboo. The cool, mechanical impersonality of the clamorously welcomed International Style, together with escalating construction costs and the virtual disappearance of artisans capable of producing architectural ornamentation, made anonymity almost inevitable.

By mid-century, between sixty and seventy people of widely different ages and functions worked in the Harrison & Abramovitz office. Listed under Harrison's name on the company letterhead were Max Abramovitz, Charles Abbe, Oscar Wiggins, Michael M. Harris, Harmon Goldstone, and George Dudley. Unlike most architectural offices, the list of head people changed every few years; only Abramovitz participated as a partner (from 1941) with Harrison in the firm's profit-sharing. Harrison, referred to with a mixture of respect and affection as The Boss, maintained solid control of the office's activities, and in this sense the firm resembled the more traditional, highly personalized offices of individual architects, such as Goodhue or Hood.

Harrison was masterful at finding and dealing with clients, but at the same time he remained the creative head of Harrison & Abramovitz, producing his own designs, synthesizing the ideas of others, and making the final decisions on those projects for which he took design responsibility.[3] Central to his extraordinarily wide range of contacts was his association with the Rockefeller family. At the same time that he emerged as a major twentieth-century architect, Harrison's relationship with Nelson Rockefeller was more like the one that was maintained within the princely patronage system of the past. Like many such past relationships, it had liabilities as well as assets.

Beginning with his friendship with Nelson Rockefeller in the late 1920s, the Rockefeller connection was consolidated in a number of ways. In addition to his role in several of Nelson Rockefeller's Latin American enterprises and to his election in 1939 to the Museum of Modern Art's Board of Trustees, by the early 1950s Harrison was also a trustee of the Rockefellers' Government Research Foundation, Colonial Williamsburg, the Rockefeller Brothers' Fund, the Rockefeller Foundation, and the Museum of Primitive Art (the collection now permanently exhibited in the Michael Rockefeller Wing of the Metropolitan Museum). As well, he participated in Nelson Rockefeller's Point IV Program, "Partners in Progress," and in the Rockefeller Brothers Fund Special Studies Group, headed by Henry Kissinger. And he served as consultant to Rockefeller Center.

From the beginning of his career, Harrison donated time to a wide range of educational and cultural endeavors.[4] Many of these provided him with ample opportunities to meet potential clients—opportunities that were facilitated even further by his membership (from 1933) in two of New York's most exclusive private clubs, the Century and the Knickerbocker.

Harrison's professional success and his solid position at the heart of New York's power structure had little effect on his lifestyle. In 1948 Laurance Rockefeller gave the Harrisons the use of a two-bedroom apartment in a building he owned at 834 Fifth Avenue. But even after the couple moved to this elegant address, just a few blocks away from the Nelson Rockefeller apartment, their home looked more like a bohemian painter's garret than the residence of a successful architect. (Ellen's marked disrespect for conventionalities undoubtedly played a part in this.) Besides, the Harrisons preferred the relative informality of country entertaining, and their Long Island house replaced the prewar office as an international meeting place for architects and artists. Shortly before Harrison died, Harmon Goldstone analyzed his old friend: "Wally never resolved what he wanted: to have the freedom of being poor and an artist, or to pursue his ambition for power, money, and social prestige. He never seems happier than when he's making a mess, painting in old clutter; but of course he lives in a very proper world."[5]

Harrison's "proper" world included the world of big business and big building projects. The Alcoa Building in Pittsburgh (1953) provides a good example of how a project came to the firm and how it was handled within the office. In the late 1940s, Fritz Close, who had been with Alcoa for twenty years, was working in the company's architectural sales division. Close had met Harrison in the early 1930s when he was just starting his career with Alcoa; the company had supplied aluminum spandrels for the Empire State Building, and Arthur Vining Davis, the self-made chairman of Alcoa, was determined to win a similar contract for the proposed Rockefeller Center. Davis was a go-getter, who, from the time he joined his first and only employer in 1888, devoted his life to making aluminum a household word in America. Having himself received a negative response from John D. Rockefeller, Jr.'s, personal staff, Davis refused to take no for an answer and ordered Close to pursue the project. He was convinced that if Close could get to one of the project's principal architects, he would obtain the aluminum order. As an unknown, it was hopeless for Close to ask for an appointment, so Davis instructed the young man to spend every morning in the reception area of Corbett, Harrison & MacMurray, where the receptionist could point out the top men. Day after day from 9:00 to 11:00 a.m. Close obediently posted himself in the architects' waiting room, watching people rush in and out. No one seemed to notice his existence, until one morning Harrison stopped in his tracks:

> "What the hell are you doing here again?" he asked.
> "I want to see a principal," replied Close.
> Harrison responded, "Well, I'm a principal, come on in."[6]

Close got the contract, and in the process Harrison made yet another lifelong friend.

Close continued his climb up the corporate ladder. In 1946 the eighty-year-old Davis suddenly decided to move his office from Pittsburgh to New York. When, to indulge this whim, he suggested that the company build an aluminum-faced office tower on Park Avenue and Fifty-eighth Street, Close brought in Harrison. The architect proposed an irregular, U-shaped building, its slightly setback north wing rising to ten stories, a back section of thirteen stories, and a south wing of twenty stories; the U's interior was built up to the second story, on which there was an open terrace. The large, glazed street-level façade allowed passersby to see a commodious display area.[7] The scheme provides one of the first examples of Harrison's skillful arrangement of large building masses. The project remained unrealized because the company's directors objected to relocating their corporate headquarters in New York, but it may have influenced their decision three years later to build a comparable building in Pittsburgh.

Alcoa wanted an office tower that would accommodate its 1,160 employees (then working at several different locations in downtown Pittsburgh) and at the same time be a showplace for all possible uses of aluminum. As Close described the job to Harrison, the commission would be offered to him on the condition that "everything in metal be in aluminum except the building's structural steel."[8] This versatile application of an industrial product to a showpiece building for that product continued the practice begun by early twentieth-century modernists. Bruno Taut engaged in a similar exercise with his Steel Pavilion for the Leipzig Fair in 1913 and with his Glass House, the German glass industry's pavilion for the Werkbund Exposition in Cologne in 1914. Harrison's interest in experimenting with new materials and new forms was provoked by the challenge.[9]

Unless the caulking between bricks or stones is restored periodically, masonry construction will develop leaks; the same problem exists for glass and steel, with the additional danger of cracks in freezing weather. An all-metal skin that would be weather-tight without caulking seemed therefore to offer a perfect solution to the problem. Harrison asserted that for a number of years he had been toying with a modular system for a metal curtain wall, but that the exact shape of the panel had remained unresolved until it was turned over, in his words, "to one man from Paris." The man was Oscar Nitzchke, the Swiss architect whom Harrison had invited to teach at Yale in the winter of 1938.

Nitzchke recalled that the diamond design he developed for the Alcoa Building came from a drawing he had done while he was enrolled as a student at the Ecole des Beaux-Arts in the 1920s.[10] It was to be executed in panels roughly six feet wide and twelve feet high (one floor), stamped from aluminum sheets one-eighth of an inch thick. Each aluminum panel incorporates in its upper half a relatively small, round-cornered window—four feet two inches by four feet seven inches, framed with inflated rubber gaskets that are deflated to allow them to pivot so they can be cleaned from inside. The eight-inch-deep metal pattern is self-cleaning, and the unwelded interlocking joints that replace caulking create a four-way labyrinth that excludes rain penetration (Figs. 125, 126).

As the first aluminum-skin skyscraper, the thirty-story Alcoa Building succeeded in providing a dramatic showplace for the aluminum industry. Its aluminum curtain wall is only one of many technical innovations and refinements. Electric wiring was mounted on aluminum bars that weighed just over half as much as their copper counterparts. Sixty percent of the building's water pipes were aluminum, a solution that represented a twenty-five percent economy compared with traditional plumbing.[11] Heating and cooling air were transmitted through aluminum pipes suspended from the ceilings. The system eliminated radiators and reduced piping, thereby retaining fifteen thousand square feet (the equivalent of one-and-a-half floors) of what would otherwise have been unusable space. Additional savings were made because aluminum, being so much lighter than the materials for which it was substituted, could be supported by a structural steel frame that was thirty to fifty percent lighter than normal.

Also innovative was the way in which the building's design influenced its method of construction. In only one month two teams of five men stamped out the required story-high aluminum panels at the Pullman Standard Car Manufacturing Company in Hammond, Indiana. Panels were bolted to metal clip angles attached to the spandrel beams: three teams of twelve men could install the prefabricated panels at a rate of two-and-a-half floors per week.[12] Because all the work was done from the inside, weather problems—as well as scaffolding—were eliminated, thereby further accelerating installation.[13]

Within Alcoa's L shape, a four-and-a-half-story aluminum and glass structure, referred to as the "bird-cage," provides the building's entrance area (Fig. 127). It hangs from two beams cantilevered from the tower's fifth floor. From the bright, airy lobby, visitors move through a passageway sheathed in extruded aluminum[14] into the elevator hall, where the eighteen-foot-high ceiling, made of a woven mesh of aluminum bars with translucent plastic panels, is supported by Norwegian rose marble walls. The floor consists of straight wide bands of alternating black and white marble. Even the elevator cabs were custom designed with elegant interiors of rolled wire mesh. Aluminum was used wherever possible for details throughout the offices. Additionally, rich wooden panelling, marble, and carpeting appear on the two top executive floors, connected by a five-foot-wide semicircular aluminum staircase, reminiscent of the one descending from the Eastern Airlines Building lobby. In a recent interview, Fritz Close recalled his amazement at Harrison's interest in details—from individual toilet facilities for each executive office to proper lighting for the typing pools. No aspect of the design was too modest for the architect's attention.[15]

Upon its completion, *Architectural Forum* hailed the Alcoa headquarters as "America's most daring experiment in modern office building," its skin, "the beginning of true industrial design in architecture."[16] In fact, Alcoa's skin was one of the few uses of aluminum, among the many tried at the headquarters, that were widely adopted and are still prevalent.

When Harrison received the Alcoa commission, the only high-rise building bordering the open space intended as a park in Pittsburgh's downtown area—the so-called Golden Triangle—was the William Penn Hotel (1916; now the Westin William Penn Hotel). Around the time he began work on the Alcoa project, Harrison received a request from the Mellon family to build a headquarters for The Mellon Bank and U.S. Steel across the park from where Alcoa would stand. Richard Mellon, who was president of the Mellon Bank, was also a majority stockholder of the Alcoa Corporation; furthermore, Harrison & Abramovitz were highly recommended by Webster Todd, who had worked with Mellon.[17]

125. Harrison, Alcoa Building, Pittsburgh, Pennsylvania (1953).

126. Detail, Alcoa Building.

127. Entrance, Alcoa Building.

The forty-one story tower, named 525 William Penn Place (1951; Fig. 128) and now Three Mellon Bank Center, was as conservative as Alcoa was daring, and as costly as Alcoa was economical: the verticality of its limestone ribbon piers flanked by stainless steel fins recalls the RCA and Empire State buildings.[18] Despite its shortcomings, 525 William Penn Place marked the beginning of a productive relationship between Harrison & Abramovitz and the developer, John Galbreath.

In 1950, Galbreath was still struggling to establish himself in real estate. He had been introduced to Harrison by Benjamin Fairless of U.S. Steel, and the Mellon Bank–U.S. Steel project had offered him a perfect opportunity to build a tall building. Shortly after Galbreath executed this first job for Harrison & Abramovitz, in partnership with Peter Ruffin he opened a New York office, which would serve as the developer for many of the firm's future buildings. Galbreath got along particularly well with Abramovitz, who found himself working more and more on Galbreath-Ruffin projects, while Harrison worked on projects for Nelson Rockefeller.

One exception to this pattern was Harrison's later Marine National Exchange Building in Milwaukee (1962), intended by the bank's president to resemble the Alcoa headquarters. The Milwaukee building is sited on an attractive two-block downtown riverfront, but its meager budget limited the architects' possibilities. The result is an anonymous high-rise distinguished only by the attractive glass-enclosed pavilion, similar to Alcoa's, that serves as the bank's entrance.

A year after signing the contract with Alcoa, Harrison agreed to design an eighteen-story aluminum-skin office building in Dallas for the Republic National Bank (1954). He had met Karl Hoblitzelle, chairman of the bank's board, in New York, and later saw him socially at Hoblitzelle's summer home on Cape Cod, where the design concept was developed. As construction progressed through the first year, the price of land in downtown Dallas began to skyrocket, and Hoblitzelle began to talk about amortizing its value to better advantage by adding floors to the building. Harrison made the necessary engineering studies and reluctantly agreed to double the building's height—to thirty-six stories. The design called for a rectangular office tower juxtaposed on its wider side with a deep eight-story pavilion housing the bank and the tower's main entrance. With its alternating vertical strips of white marble and glass, the pavilion's façade is reminiscent of the General Assembly's main entrance façade. The pavilion's Ervay Street elevation is windowless, as are the tower's narrower elevations, while its broader elevations are articulated by horizontal window bands (Fig. 129).

Even more disturbing than the last-minute height change was the client's insistence on topping the building with an emblem to emphasize its then unprecedented height (in Dallas). Hoblitzelle's idea was to replicate the Statue of Liberty, with an illuminated torch that would be visible for several miles across the plains. "Now," asked Harrison in retrospect, "what do you do in a case like that? Tell him he can't have it? If he wants it, he'll have one put up anyway. All you can do is present what you consider superior designs as forcefully as you can, and hope your arguments will sink in." To his immense relief, his suggestion for a simple spikelike form was finally agreed upon in principle.[19]

The Republic National Bank Building has long been surpassed in height by the steel and glass boxes, reflecting glass towers, and mansarded skyscrapers of succeeding decades. But it is by no means dwarfed by the more recent buildings. Its contrast of verticals—in the bank entrance façade—and horizontals—in the tower fenestration—together with its boldly patterned surfaces, make a strong statement that typifies office building design of the period.[20]

In 1956, Harrison & Abramovitz tried to duplicate the Alcoa concept in stainless steel for the Socony-Mobil Building in New York (between Forty-first and Forty-second streets and Third and Lexington avenues). The mammoth building was not designed by Harrison; only the bold, curved architraves of the main entranceways bear his unmistakable touch (Fig. 130). The slackened curves are emphasized by their solid metal sheathings, which stand out against the building's glazed base. In contrast to the practical and economic advantages of aluminum, for Socony-Mobil stainless-steel cladding was impractical (many panels cracked) and expensive.

128. Harrison & Abramovitz, Three Mellon Bank Center, Pittsburgh, Pennsylvania (1951).

129. Harrison, Republic National Bank, Dallas, Texas (1954).

130. Harrison's ''eyebrow curve,'' entrance, Socony-Mobil Building, New York City (1956).

After the war, American architects had not been receptive to changes; in large part, they continued to use concepts that dated from the early 1940s. By mid-century the International Style, shorn of its social idealism, had become commonplace. Without new building types to engage them, designers looked increasingly to new materials as a means of innovation, and Harrison's metal skins represented an important breakthrough that spawned innumerable imitations and variations during the late 1950s and early 1960s. More recent uses of metal sheathing such as Hugh Stubbins's Federal Reserve Bank in Boston (1978), which eliminates the aluminum's surface pattern, have been more successful in combining technical advantages with a satisfactory aesthetic. Harrison's claim that Alcoa's aluminum and glass entrance hall inspired large, glazed public areas in office buildings such as Roche and Dinkeloo's Ford Foundation Building in New York (1967) may have had some validity.

Another personal contact—the architect Frederick King, Harrison's old friend from the time they had worked together at McKim, Mead & White—played a role in securing several other large commissions he received after the war. The first of these were for the U.S. Embassy office buildings in Havana and Rio de Janeiro, both completed in 1952, at a time when Harrison was too occupied with the U.N. headquarters to give either assignment much attention other than a rough preliminary design. In the late 1950s, King again approached Harrison about the possibility of working on the mammoth Central Intelligence Agency headquarters in Langley, Virginia. King was a college classmate of then–CIA Director Allen Dulles, who relied on him to suggest a large architectural office to build the new Agency building (1961). Harrison accepted the commission with some reluctance because of the complicated working conditions imposed by the need to protect CIA security. Harrison, Abramovitz, and King collaborated on the building's design, a colossally long eight stories containing one million square feet of usable space. Its forbidding concrete grid elevations are tempered slightly on the front and sides by a wide, undulating, single-story pavilion (Fig. 131). A freestanding, dome-shaped pavilion is connected to the main building by an underground passageway.

When the Korean War ended in July 1953, government limitations on materials were lifted and a tremendous spurt of office construction ensued in New York. The city was in the midst of a rapid transformation: between 1950 and 1956 New York lost 64,000 garment industry workers while it gained 15,000 jobs in service industries and construction. This change from a manufacturing to a service economy created an urgent need for more office space. Additionally, amenities such as air-conditioning, which many people now considered indispensable, were available only in new buildings.

Because there had been so little office construction during and immediately after World War II, New York's better office buildings, including Rockefeller Center, had been assured of one-hundred-percent occupancy and had waiting lists of would-be tenants. But the sudden availability of space in the mid–1950s encouraged several of Rockefeller Center's most important tenants to consider moving elsewhere. In an attempt to meet the competition, the Rockefeller Center management decided in 1953 to build an addition to its U.S. Rubber Building. In notes for an autobiography he began toward the end of his life, Harrison stated: "It gave me great satisfaction to have been one of the original six architects and the only architect having worked from start to finish on Rockefeller Center."[21] He did indeed serve as a paid consultant for Rockefeller Center from 1933 until 1976—except between 1941 and 1946, when he was serving the government, and between 1946 and 1949, when he was devoting most of his time to the U.N.

To make way for the first postwar building at Rockefeller Center, the Center Movie Theater at Sixth Avenue and Forty-ninth Street was demolished. In its place Harrison designed a nineteen-story air-conditioned addition (1955) to the west side of U.S. Rubber's original building. The extension consists of a limestone-clad slab tower with a two-story exhibition space at street level (Fig. 132); it resembles the Eastern Airlines Building to the east.

The success of Harrison's Corning Glass Center in upstate New York (see next chapter) made it logical that Arthur A. Houghton, Jr., president of Steuben Glass, would choose him to design a new New York office

131. Harrison & Abramovitz, Central Intelligence Agency
Headquarters, Langley, Virginia (1961).

132. Harrison & Abramovitz, addition to U.S. Rubber Co.
Building, New York City (1955); at west (far left), Associated
Architects, U.S. Rubber Co. Building (1940; now Simon &
Schuster Building).

building (1959) in place of the company's 1937 five-story structure by William and Geoffrey Platt. The problematic, L-shaped site on Fifth Avenue and Fifty-sixth Street, already narrow on the avenue, extended more than halfway down the block and narrowed even further at the east. Despite his complaint that the site presented "a dreadful form to work with," Harrison collaborated with Houghton and Rushmore H. Mariner, vice-president in charge of construction, to produce one of his most distinguished office buildings. Using only a little more than two-thirds of the Fifth Avenue frontage for the main twenty-six-story tower, he left the remainder of the frontage free to a depth of about sixty-five feet, where a long, narrow seven-story wing rises along the northeastern part of the site. The office building's entrance is located here. Set back from this base, a small, intermediary twelve-story tower rises above it. Massing the low, narrow building next to the tall, wider tower, with the twelve-story tower almost completely hidden behind the two, was an ingenious solution to maximizing use of a difficult site. Setting back the smaller wing gives additional prominence to the Steuben display room at street level in the Fifth Avenue tower. This small corner of the city is pleasantly enhanced by the reflecting pools in front of both areas (Fig. 133).

Spandrelite backed with enamel was commonly used at this time for glass curtain walls such as Harrison had proposed for the Corning Glass Building. Inserted between the head of the window on one floor and the window spandrel of the floor above, Spandrelite produces an opaque effect that hides rough construction behind the glass. To avoid the appearance of horizontal ribbons on the exterior curtain wall that Spandrelite would produce, for the Corning Glass Building Harrison insisted on clear glass for the spandrel areas, continuing the translucency of the windows. To conceal the rough concrete block behind the clear glass in the spandrels, a painted metal panel would be placed approximately six inches behind the glass.[22] When Mariner told Harrison the additional cost would be about two hundred fifty thousand dollars, the architect—recently frustrated by his dealings with several Metropolitan Opera committees—exploded: "Goddamn it Rush, if you want to louse

up the building, do it. I resigned from Lincoln Center this morning!"[23] Because Mariner sympathized with Harrison he relented, and clear glass was used. It was a fortuitous decision that almost certainly would not have been made by a committee client. The same personal relationship accounted for the spectacular Josef Albers mural that decorates the Corning Glass lobby. Harrison felt so strongly about having the painting in the ground-floor area that he offered to pay for it himself should there be a funding problem. Once again Mariner bowed to such resoluteness and made the necessary funds available.[24]

One of the most dramatic changes in midtown Manhattan brought about by the altered real estate conditions of the 1950s was the Rockefeller Center management's extension of its ownership to Sixth Avenue. At the time the decision was made to enlarge the U.S. Rubber Building, Laurance Rockefeller and Gustav Eyssell, chairman of the board and president of Rockefeller Center, Inc., respectively, enlarged John D. Rockefeller, Jr.'s, initial holdings on the west side of Sixth Avenue between Fiftieth and Fifty-first streets. Since demolition of the Sixth Avenue elevated railway in 1939, businesses located on or near Sixth Avenue had hoped for the area's improvement. In an attempt to expedite this improvement, in 1945 the thoroughfare was renamed the Avenue of the Americas and in 1950 an architects' advisory committee was established for it, chaired by Corbett, then seventy-seven years old.[25] Neither the renaming nor the committee affected the avenue's development. Not until 1956 did the combined prestige of Rockefeller Center and Time, Inc. overcome prejudice against the area: the new Time and Life Building (1960) was the first important building in thirty years to go up on the western side of the Avenue of the Americas.

Time, Inc. was one of several original Rockefeller Center tenants that needed more space. Already in 1946, Harrison & Abramovitz had been asked to study the possibility of a new headquarters for the company on the site of the Marguery Hotel (Madison to Park avenues, between Forty-seventh and Forty-eighth streets). The architects worked with Perry Prentice, at that time editor and publisher of the company's magazine *Architectural*

133. Harrison, Corning Glass Building, New York City (1959).

155

Forum, to develop an intricate project for a thirty-five-story office tower: its supporting piers would be spaced at irregular intervals between the tracks of the New York Central and New Haven railroads, which lay directly below the site. The building's main slab was to have been bracketed by wings of approximately eighteen stories, flexing away from it at about a 45-degree angle at the front and back (Fig. 134).[26] The unusual configuration provided an interesting break with the traditional alignment of façade and street, but at $30 million, Time, Inc. president Henry Luce dismissed the proposal as too expensive.[27]

It took over ten years—including the rejection of one urban and several suburban sites and of proposals made by both Eero Saarinen and Gordon Bunshaft—before Time, Inc. began construction of a new building on the Avenue of the Americas. Time, Inc.'s partnership with the Rockefeller Center Corporation, Rock-Time, gave Time a forty-five-percent interest in the new building, thereby allowing the publishers to participate in the income from outside tenants and also to take an active interest in the headquarters' design.[28] The Time and Life Building was to be the first and northernmost in a series of four new Rockefeller Center structures on the avenue. Harrison proposed a broad forty-eight-story slab with a seven-story L-shaped wing wrapped around the north and west sides that would serve as a boundary between the tower and its uptown neighbors. He envisioned broad piers sheathed in limestone that would recall the earlier Rockefeller Center buildings, but the design had to be modified to comply with the requirements of the Rockefellers' new business partner.

Time, Inc. made two specific requests: that the building's supporting columns not intrude into office space; and that in-sloping windows and out-sloping spandrels create full visibility with minimal glare. Although the second requirement was vetoed, the needs that led to it helped produce the final design. The first requirement prompted Harrison to place the building's steel supporting columns outside the floor area, creating the largest tower floors built in the city since World War II: thirty-two thousand five hundred square feet of broad free span from core to exterior wall on each floor. The limestone columns are twenty-eight feet apart, and between each pair of columns are two aluminum-encased air-conditioning risers, with water risers at the column corners. An aluminum and glass grid based on the building's basic module completes the exterior, which expresses perfectly the building's structure (Figs. 135, 136).[29]

Both interior and exterior of the new Time and Life Building were a radical departure from earlier Rockefeller Center architecture. A group of Time executives, the Rockefeller Center officers, and Michael M. Harris spent sixteen months studying the plans and agreed on a four-foot-eight-inch-square building module that regulated the overall design and interior partitioning. Designs for Business, a firm specializing in offices, used the module to create a new concept for the space. Until then, most office towers had contained two ring corridors; beside the public corridor for elevator banks and service areas, another corridor usually ran through the middle of the office areas. The "bay plan," as it was called, eliminates this second corridor, substituting for it short transverse passages that run out from the central corridor to the building's perimeter, with offices opening directly from the passages. Almost all the partitions are movable, attached to floor and ceiling by receptacles placed four feet eight inches apart in one direction, four feet in the other. The four-foot modules fit into the twenty-four-foot-deep space available along the north and south walls; the building's modules on the east and west vary a few inches so that not all partitions on these sides match the windows exactly.[30] The resulting offices may seem crowded, but the system proved to be exceptionally flexible and gained space equivalent to an entire floor. Harrison later claimed that the client's participation had been excessive: "They took the idea and carried it to the bitter end. Everything was efficient, but there was no space. They took the space and divided it so you were cramped; their system produced a factory."

The Time and Life Building was designed before the 1961 amendment to the Zoning Resolution extended previous New York City regulations regarding bulk and ground coverage to new, larger-scale buildings and offered a trade-off for open plazas. To achieve its actual

134. Harrison, project for a new Time and Life Building (1946).

135. Harrison, new Time and Life Building, New York City (1960).

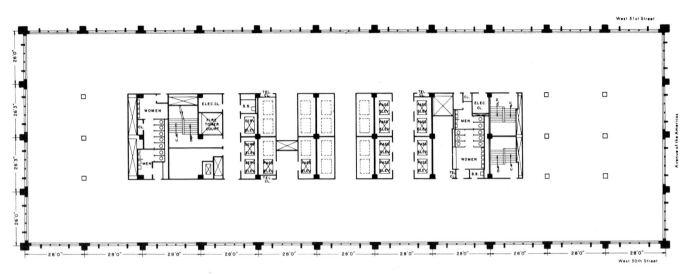

136. Typical floor plan, new Time and Life Building.

height, Rockefeller Center had to buy the Roxy Theater, immediately to the west of the new building, in order to acquire its air rights. This acquisition allowed the planned forty-eight stories to occupy only three-quarters of the lot, leaving ample plaza space on both Sixth Avenue and on Fiftieth Street. Whenever possible, Harrison tried to provide open, green areas near his large buildings, and for the space around the Time and Life Building he designed a long reflecting pool at the building's base, bordered by trees to the north and south. For the sidewalk he repeated the wave pattern he had introduced in the forecourt of the U.N. and had used for the sidewalk at Alcoa in Pittsburgh. Here the pattern continues inside, and, together with large murals by Fritz Glarner and Josef Albers, which he suggested, it helps to animate the enormous and otherwise impersonal elevator lobby.

The new Time building signaled an important change in Harrison's career. By the time it was projected, Nelson Rockefeller was concentrating more and more of his efforts on politics and fewer on building. Rockefeller's success as Coordinator of Inter-American Affairs had encouraged him to pursue his political interests: several years as Assistant Secretary of State for American Republic Affairs (1944–50) were followed by his appointment by Harry S. Truman to the chairmanship of

the International Development Advisory Board (1950–52), and then by his chairmanship of President Eisenhower's Advisory Committee on Government Reorganization (1952–53) and a post as special assistant to the President for foreign affairs (1954).[31] Four years later Rockefeller was elected governor of New York State, in the first of what many believed to be a series of maneuvers calculated to win him a future presidential nomination. Looking back on his friend's all-consuming commitment to politics, Harrison mused: "A taste of power gets you, apparently."

The Time and Life Building was the first large Rockefeller commission on which Harrison worked directly with a member of the family other than Nelson. Laurance Rockefeller represented the family, and he and Harrison were joined by Gustav Eyssell and by members of a Time, Inc. committee. That Harrison found himself in the late 1950s designing for a client comprising several groups of people was symptomatic of the times. It was increasingly common for the architect to be responsible to a committee, and often that committee was made up of individuals with widely divergent interests and tastes. For a man, now in his sixties, who regarded his relationship with the client as a crucial factor in the creation of a building—"The amount of beauty an architect can achieve in his design is always limited by the amount of imagination and feeling for beauty the client has in his system"[32]—he found it difficult to accept a new approach to his profession. But it was the approach with which he would have to contend for subsequent additions to Rockefeller Center and for Lincoln Center, which, together with the Albany Mall, constitute the three monumental achievements of the last part of his life.

When three additional large towers for Rockefeller Center were first proposed in 1963 for the west side of Sixth Avenue,[33] Harrison drew up some interesting plans for the project: The buildings—for Exxon (1973), McGraw-Hill (1973), and Celanese (1974), which he worked on with Abramovitz and Harris—were each to be placed at a different distance from the Avenue of the Americas, with the new McGraw-Hill Building oriented north-south instead of east-west and sited at midblock between the Avenue of the Americas and Seventh Avenue, with a private street cutting through the block. The remaining half-block between the McGraw-Hill Building and the Avenue of the Americas was to be used for a sunken landscaped plaza, conceived originally by Abramovitz to extend in front of all three sites, interrupted only by walkways under the adjacent streets. This long, open plaza would have connected with the continuous underground shopping areas of the other Rockefeller Center buildings.[34] It took the new zoning requirements for additional open space into account in a logical continuation of the formula that had worked so well for the original Rockefeller Center.[35] A plan of this project bears Harrison's handwritten comment: "My scheme for west side turned down by . . . " (Fig. 137). The name of the person who rejected the scheme has been crossed out and is illegible, but whoever it was must be held in part responsible for the bleak arrangement that was adopted in its stead: all four towers are lined up parallel to each other, with small, identical setbacks from the Avenue of the Americas for the two middle towers and a partial setback for the southernmost tower; McGraw-Hill's sunken plaza is realized in a reduced scale (Fig. 138).[36]

As built, the three most recent Rockefeller Center buildings have none of the structural expressiveness of the Time and Life Building. The narrow strips of limestone that sheath the Celanese and McGraw-Hill buildings make only a half-hearted attempt to relate them to the older buildings in the complex. They are identical in form to one another, and the monotony of their exteriors is emphasized by their overbearing size and tediously similar relationship to each other, to the Time and Life Building, and to the avenue. In fact, the area's overall architectural aridity is relieved only by a small, block-wide park at the western end of the McGraw-Hill Building, which extends, across Forty-ninth Street, to a landscaped passageway west of the Exxon Building. Behind the McGraw-Hill Building Harrison managed to create a delightfully unexpected vest-pocket park, spanned by a walk-through waterfall that recalls the one he placed in front of the Electric Utilities Exhibit at the 1939 World's Fair (Fig. 139; see Fig. 74).

Soon after its completion, the new Time and Life Building spawned a series of poor imitations on the Avenue of the Americas between Fifty-first and Fifty-fourth streets: the Equitable Life (SOM, 1961), J. C. Penney (Shreve, Lamb & Harmon, 1965), Hilton Hotel (William B. Tabler, 1963), Sperry-Rand (Emery Roth, 1962), and ABC (Emery Roth, 1965) buildings. Eero Saarinen's black granite CBS Building (1965) is alone in its architectural distinction. There are no shops at street level, nor are there benches or any other concession to human usage in what the critic Peter Blake called in 1965 a "chaotic conglomeration of piazzas, piazzettas, piazzetines, arcades and courts."[37] Despite the project's unquestioned commercial success, by the time the McGraw-Hill and Exxon buildings were occupied in 1973, critical opinion unanimously condemned the new Rockefeller Center buildings as milestones in Sixth Avenue's relentless progression toward monumental sterility.

Now, more than a decade later, even the dullness of the avenue's new architecture seems preferable to the tawdriness south of Forty-seventh Street. Paradoxically, like the much-criticized South Mall at Albany, the redeveloped section of Sixth Avenue works well for people. The absence of formal seating does not deter picknickers

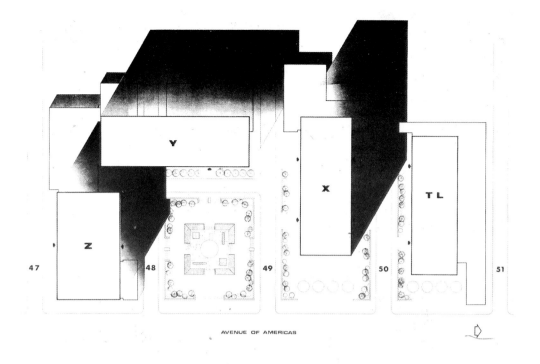

AVENUE OF AMERICAS

MY SCHEME FOR WEST SIDE TURNED DOWN BY ~~███████████~~

137. Harrison's scheme for the western extension of Rockefeller Center to the Avenue of the Americas (TL = Time and Life Building; X = Exxon Building, now Standard Oil Building; Y = McGraw-Hill; Z = Celanese Building).

138. Harrison, plan of western extension of Rockefeller Center as built.

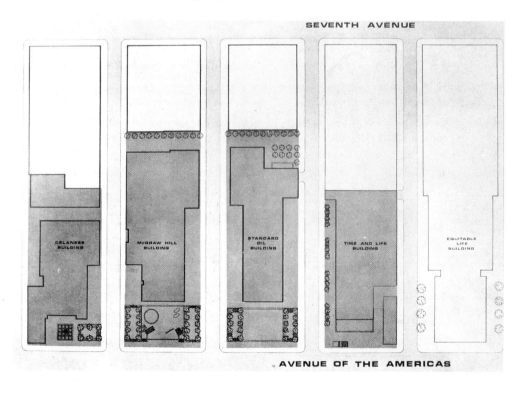

SEVENTH AVENUE

CELANESE BUILDING

McGRAW HILL BUILDING

STANDARD OIL BUILDING

TIME AND LIFE BUILDING

EQUITABLE LIFE BUILDING

AVENUE OF THE AMERICAS

139. Vest-pocket park behind the McGraw-Hill Building (1973).

140. Harrison, Rockefeller Center buildings on the Avenue of the Americas (1974).

162

and sunbathers, who use fountain ledges and every other available perching place in clement weather, giving the area an appealing sense of vitality. Compared with the dark, congested canyons to which many midtown Manhattan thoroughfares have been reduced by recent over-scaled development, Sixth Avenue has a pleasantly airy, light-bathed quality (Fig. 140).

During the years that Harrison designed highly visible luxury office buildings and institutions, he also worked on several housing developments. Throughout the post–World War II period of regulated building activities, priority for materials such as structural steel and copper for pipes went in general to low-income housing and particularly to housing for returning veterans. In the 1940s, the New York City Housing Authority was thus able to continue work it had started in the previous decade with a growing number of projects, mainly in Harlem, Queens, and Brooklyn. Among these was a state-subsidized $12-million low-cost housing complex for five thousand people that Harrison built at Astoria, in Queens (1951). Although it consists of low-rise buildings, Astoria belongs among Harrison's large projects because of the massiveness of the development.

Harrison's commission for Astoria probably came through Robert Moses, who, after 1949, as chairman of the mayor's commission on slum clearance, controlled New York City's housing development. The twenty-two buildings that Harrison constructed for Astoria are identical seven-story brick cruciforms with relatively small aluminum sash windows. At first glance they appear to follow the usual dreary formula for this kind of program, but the project has several distinctive features (Fig. 141). Commonly used in the housing projects built immediately after the war, the cruciform plan consolidated circulation by cutting down excess corridor areas and promoted maximum light and ventilation to apartments in the protruding wings. But because of its relatively high cost, by 1949 the cross plan was being discarded in favor of rectilinear slabs.[38] Astoria, which was started in 1948, was one of the last developments to profit from the advantages of this type of plan. It was also one of the few projects that did not take the form of high-rise towers,

which were increasingly displacing lower buildings for housing at the time.[39]

In both plan and height, therefore, Astoria was a cut above comparable projects of the period; but equally important was the way in which Harrison took maximum advantage of the spectacular site. The area runs almost flush to the river with only a low rise inland. The architect placed the westernmost buildings almost at the water's edge and left an unusually large amount of space open to ensure spectacular views of the river and, beyond it, Manhattan's towers. In this respect, also, the Astoria project differs from the clogged vistas of the superblocks contemporaneous with it.

Harrison's next housing projects—only one of which was realized—were provided by the Rockefeller family. In an effort to arrest the thirty-year deterioration of the area on upper Broadway known as Morningside Heights, in 1947 nine of the educational, religious, and medical institutions located between West 108th and 125th streets formed a nonprofit rehabilitation agency called Morningside Heights, Inc.[40] David Rockefeller, who had actively encouraged the agency's formation, became its first president. One of the corporation's initial plans was to construct a cluster of six twenty-story middle-income cooperative apartment houses on two large blocks (ten acres) at Amsterdam Avenue between 123d and LaSalle streets. The buildings, which were estimated to cost $16 million, were to be racially integrated. Ready for occupancy in 1957, 970 Morningside Gardens (Fig. 142), as it was called, was one of six New York City Title 1 housing projects made possible by the 1949 Housing Act. Except for its more sensitive window treatment and its pleasantly landscaped site, the development is physically similar to other such projects built at the time. Its exceptional success is due in large part to considerable government assistance and long-term, low-interest mortgages that facilitated real tenant ownership.[41]

The other housing project was initiated by Nelson Rockefeller in 1966, after he became governor, and was part of his enormous, statewide middle-income housing program, to which Starrett City and Co-op City belonged. Harrison was asked to design Battery Park City,

163

141. Harrison, housing, Astoria, Queens (1951).

142. Harrison, 970 Morningside Gardens, New York City (1957).

a community for more than 63,000 people that was to be built in a landfill area of approximately ninety-eight acres between Battery Park and Chamber streets. In addition to housing for low-, middle-, and upper-income families, the project was to include a 2,200-room hotel, two large office buildings, public services, recreation and shopping facilities, as well as space for light manufacturing and for parking. Its riverfront location and ambitious scale resembled Harrison's earlier X City project; but while his design for X City had included a number of imaginatively shaped large and smaller structures, the scheme for Battery Park City shows the buildings as all more or less alike, except for a pair of larger towers at the northern and southern ends of the site. As well, the bulk of the project consisted of twelve linear high-rise buildings placed in monotonous parallel rows in what, had it been built, would have been a visually arid arrangement (Fig. 143).

Perhaps their disappointing quality can be explained partly by the fact that Harrison worked on these plans while he was trying to complete the Metropolitan Opera House and was designing the Albany Mall. Rockefeller's timing on Battery Park City was also problematic: his proposal for the country's largest urban development was made almost simultaneously with the city's own Lower Manhattan Plan. The battle that ensued between Governor Rockefeller and Mayor John Lindsay at the time resulted in two other designs, one for an East River site and one for the original Hudson River site.[42] Neither of these proposals were any more practical than Harrison's. It would take almost twenty years and a whole new cast of characters before Battery Park City became a reality.

143. Harrison, project for Battery Park City, New York City (1966).

Chapter 15

Small Buildings

It is not always in his world-famous commissions that Harrison's design ability appears to best advantage. Many of his smaller achievements testify to a more intriguing, more complex talent, and he himself readily admitted his preference for small-scale work. When asked in the midst of his enormous undertaking at Lincoln Center whether he enjoyed coordinating big projects, he responded with his usual frankness:

> I hate it. But I've had to do it because I've had to make a living. Poor old Bach had to walk behind the hearse once a week; otherwise, he didn't get his organist's pay. I get more fun out of designing a small thing than a big one. Architecture is something small—something you can touch with your fingers.[1]

Before the end of World War II, Harrison's Long Island home, the Rockefeller Apartments, and the Northeast Harbor house for Nelson Rockefeller exemplified this special sensitivity. After 1950 the size and number of Harrison's commissions allowed him less time for such projects. There are, however, a few noteworthy exceptions that embody his personal style: among these are the First Presbyterian Church at Stamford, Connecticut, two auditoriums, one for Rockefeller University in New York and another for the National Academy of Sciences in Washington, D.C., and a small lodge for Nelson Rockefeller at Pocantico.

In 1848, completion of the New Haven Railroad line connecting Stamford with New York City brought to Stamford a large influx of new residents, among them one Alexander Milne and his wife. Milne was a Scot by birth, a stonecutter by profession, and a Presbyterian by faith. It took him only a few years to organize his Presbyterian brethren and to found a house of worship in Stamford: in 1854 they erected a white frame colonial church at the intersection of Atlantic and Broad streets. This was replaced in 1884 by a stone building to accommodate its 295 members; by 1952, the one-hundredth anniversary of the church's founding, the congregation had multiplied more than five-fold and needed greatly expanded facilities that would include such contemporary amenities as parking space, a playground, a nursery, classrooms, and meeting rooms.

In the early 1940s First Presbyterian's foresighted pastor had bought 10.8 acres of hilly woodland on centrally located Bedford Street. The church's building committee now proposed to use this land for the new facilities, but the committee's interest in a modern design by what its members described as a "top-drawer architect"[2] was opposed by members of the congregation who favored a traditional colonial building. A compromise solution was adopted: Sherwood, Mills & Smith, a local firm of young architects, would be asked to study the project in collaboration with an outside architect, to be decided upon. Thorme Sherwood had met Harrison the previous year, and, impressed by him "as an architect and as a man," he urged that Harrison be chosen as the outside participant.

Harrison was following with great interest Abramovitz's design for three chapels of different faiths at Brandeis University (1955). In addition, his training with Goodhue, one of America's foremost church architects, had helped make the design of a religious building a particularly appealing challenge to him. Donald F. Campbell, First Presbyterian's pastor, remembers that at his first meeting with Sherwood, members of the congregation, and Harrison, the latter "expressed his interest in getting to know me and our theology. He wanted to go to Europe to look at churches there. Wally didn't know what he would do, but he was honest about it. He was the only one without preconceived ideas for the project." As a result of this meeting, Harrison, in association with the firm of Sherwood, Mills & Smith, was asked to design the church complex: he would be responsible for the sanctuary (and a bell tower added in 1968); Willis N. Mills would take on the remainder of the project, consisting of a small chapel and an educational complex.

Harrison's task was not an easy one. The basic spiritual order of Presbyterianism consists of ministers and ruling elders, who are elected by the congregation. Presbyterian policy is determined ultimately by each member of the congregation, who must approve every decision made by a parish. This democratic system applies even to the design of a church. The first member with whom the architect had to deal was Walter N. Maguire, chairman of the building committee. Among the youngest ever to graduate from Yale Law School, Maguire had built one of the most successful law practices in Stamford in the 1930s. His expert financial advice was primarily responsible for the success of the church's investment record. Maguire came to his first meeting with Harrison under the impression that the new church was to be in the New England colonial style recommended by his subcommittee. This design was a far cry from what Harrison had in mind, and he had some explaining to do; nothing could have contrasted more with his own artistic temperament than the crusty parishioner's facts-and-figures approach, attuned to the complexities of high finance. Nevertheless, in a short time the two men came to like and respect one another.

Harrison was neither a revivalist nor an eclectic. He had in mind combining aspects of the Gothic tradition with modern technology to produce what he described as a new kind of sacred building. He was particularly intrigued by the medieval use of stained glass, an interest he returned to in a question that he posed to both clients and colleagues: "Have you ever thought what it would be like to live inside a giant sapphire?"[3] Early in 1953, soon after he received the commission for the sanctuary, Harrison took a two-month vacation, during which he visited churches and cathedrals in England, France, and Italy. As a student he had been fascinated by Gothic architecture, and he was eager to return to Chartres and to visit the cathedral at Beauvais—of which only the choir survives, but where stained glass is used even more extensively than at Chartres.

The first idea he sketched for the sanctuary was, according to Dr. Campbell, "startlingly beautiful: it was made entirely of glass and steel, in the shape of a modified megaphone [for acoustical purposes]; he knew it wasn't practical, but he wanted to show the possibilities of what might be accomplished"[4] (Fig. 144). The design was altered, and it passed the hurdle presented by Maguire's conservatism. Harrison's obvious sincerity and his evident dedication to the task finally won over every member of the congregation, and his design was approved.[5]

144. Harrison working on sketches of the First Presbyterian
Church, Stamford, Connecticut (1958).

In his discussions with Harrison, Campbell explained his conviction that neither a Gothic nor a Byzantine church would properly express Christian theology as it was interpreted by American Presbyterians. Both styles appealed to the purely transcendental, while, as Campbell explained, his religion addressed a God who was as much a part of everyday life as he was a transcendental being—a concept that the new sanctuary should somehow convey. Harrison carefully noted Campbell's ideas and even asked for reading references to scholars of the early church and of the Reformation. So seriously did he take the commission that in 1956 he went to Europe again, this time to Sweden to look at Lutheran churches and back to France to see the stained-glass windows designed by Léger for the church of Sacré-Coeur at Audincourt.[6] Léger told Harrison about Gabriel Loire, an artist in stained glass who worked in the town of Chartres, using techniques based on early Christian art; his method was to insert thick, brightly colored chunks of pot-metal glass into wood, stone, and concrete. Harrison went to the small town of Visp, near Zermatt, in Switzerland, to see examples of the abstract designs Loire had produced.

In his recently completed aluminum-skin office buildings for Alcoa and Republic National Bank, Harrison had successfully invented a new use for a relatively new metal. He now turned his attention to Loire's *béton-glas*, to see if this material of medieval origin could be used with a structural system of folded concrete that would span a space without supports. On the grounds of his Long Island home, in the same area where he had worked out the problems of prefabricated housing, Harrison spent painstaking hours tilting heavy concrete panels to test the angles at which they would stand and hold weight. The result was the use of 152 similar precast concrete panels for the sanctuary, rising to a height of sixty feet to support the structure. Each concrete element is reinforced with rows of protruding steel rods that are fastened to the rods of adjoining concrete sections and then reinforced with larger rods and a layer of cement. For almost the entire width of the side walls, the panels are inlaid with thick chunks of faceted, multicolored glass. At either end, where the church is made of concrete

unrelieved by glass, the exterior walls are covered with slate shingles, as is most of the roof. Able to hold almost eight hundred people, the church is 234 feet long, 54 feet wide, and covers an area of 11,500 square feet. The plan's possible interpretation as fishshaped, and associations of the fish with early Christian symbolism, quickly gave rise to the popular name of the Fish Church, even though such an image was not part of Harrison's intent (Fig. 145).[7]

Upon entering the narthex, the visitor is surprised momentarily by its darkness: only a small amount of light filters through the stained glass at the rear. A few steps to the left lead into the soaring, bright space of the nave, where the side walls break into five great folds, each twenty feet wide, made of intricately fitted triangles filled with patterns of jewel-colored glass. The soaring concrete frames recall the ribs of a Gothic vault, an effect that is completed by the meeting at the apex of the stained-glass side walls in the Gothic symbol of hands touching in prayer (Figs. 146, 147). The inward tilt of the lateral walls satisfied Dr. Campbell's ideas about his religion's earthly orientation.

With Dr. Campbell's help, Harrison chose themes for the three large areas of stained glass: the two-hundred-foot-wide windows of the sanctuary would represent the Crucifixion on the north wall and the Resurrection on the south wall, with the rear wall of the narthex devoted to the smaller symbols of Christ's teachings. Harrison made abstract designs with color indications, for which templates were then cut and sent to Loire in Chartres. Only the narthex window was designed by Loire. The French glassworker eventually provided twenty thousand one-inch-thick chunks of amber, emerald, ruby, amethyst, and sapphire glass, each one faceted like a precious stone. These glass chunks were then imbedded in matrices of concrete according to the design specifications.

The technicalities of the sanctuary's acoustics were worked out with the help of Bolt, Beranek & Newman, who had advised Harrison at the U.N. Although the acoustics were nearly perfect when the sanctuary was full, some corrections were necessary to eliminate reverberation when the space was partially empty. Because

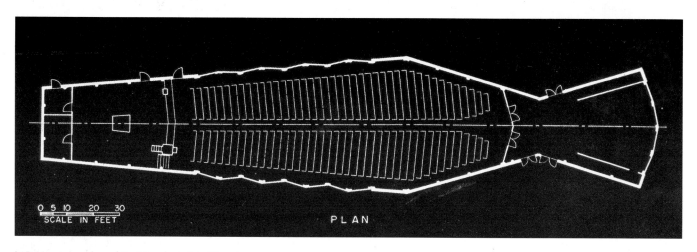

PLAN

O 5 10 20 30
SCALE IN FEET

PLAN

145. Harrison, plan of First Presbyterian Church.

146. First Presbyterian Church.

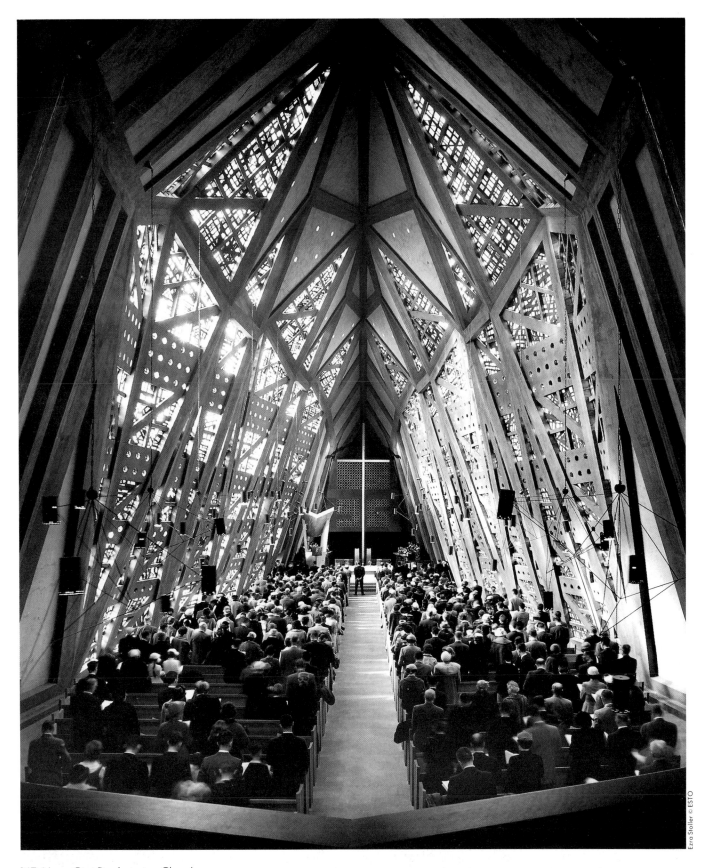

147. Nave, First Presbyterian Church.

Presbyterians hold the Bible to be a rule of government and discipline as well as of faith, Harrison designed a marble sounding board suspended over the pulpit in the shape of an open Bible: the preacher stands literally under the Book. Pulpit, communion table, and lectern are all easily visible from every area of the church.

During the first two years of preliminary design work, Harrison met with Campbell at least once a month. During the three following years, in which final designs were made and implemented, Harrison was assisted by Yen Liang, a Chinese architect who had worked with him at the U.N. Campbell was touched by Harrison's concern with detail—such as the form, placement, and kind of wood to be used for the pews, choir benches, and other church furniture. Harrison was apparently ready to take infinite pains with every aspect of the project, no matter how minor, telling Campbell simply "I'm not an artistic genius: what we've done in the past has been through trial and error."

When it was finally completed in 1958, Harrison declared that "the church was the most satisfying job I ever worked on."[8] Twenty-five years later, Michael Harris marveled at the senior partner's willingness to devote so much time and effort to so relatively small a project: "He was dedicated to the profession. He knocked himself out for a client like the Stamford church. He received very little pay, but that didn't make him work any less hard on it. He was one of a kind."

Harrison's commitment to the First Presbyterian Church went beyond completion of the sanctuary.[9] In the course of planning, Campbell had described to Harrison the magnificent thirty-six-bell carillon presented to the congregation in 1947 by the Nestlé Company as a gesture of appreciation to the community for its hospitality. The carillon had been dismantled when the property was sold, and the congregation was now eager to have a permanent bell tower.

After the sanctuary was completed, Harrison continued to think about the belfry. For him, thinking about architecture meant designing, and the walls of his office were soon covered with hundreds of drawings for the bell tower (Fig. 148). At first he thought he would build the belfry in the same materials as the sanctuary, but in

the fall of 1962, Maguire sent him a page from the Whitney Museum catalogue, *The First Five Years*, showing Richard Lippold's brass and copper wire sculpture, *Primordial Figure* (Fig. 149). Lippold's sculpture convinced Harrison to eliminate the enclosing glass to make an airier, more open structure, which he believed would recall the medieval *flèche* and thereby share the Gothic sensibility of the sanctuary. Not until the mid-1960s, when Maguire and his family provided the funds, could the parish afford to construct the tower. As built, four reinforced concrete posts rise two hundred fifty-five feet from a twenty-five-foot-square base. When the time came to erect the stainless steel spire—which was thirty feet high and weighed eighteen thousand pounds—Harrison decided to put it in place by helicopter. The operation was completed in under an hour and afforded considerable savings when compared with what scaffolding would have cost. The Carillon Tower was dedicated on June 16, 1968, almost a year after Walter Maguire's death (Fig. 150).

Some of the twentieth century's most significant modern places of worship were built in the 1950s. Le Corbusier's Chapel of Notre-Dame-du-Haut at Ronchamp was outstanding among several distinguished churches and chapels erected in Europe after the Second World War. In the United States, Eero Saarinen's Kresge Chapel at the Massachusetts Institute of Technology; Philip Johnson's Kneses Tifereth Israel Synagogue at Port Chester, New York; and Frank Lloyd Wright's Beth Sholom Synagogue at Elkins Park, Pennsylvania, all date from this decade. Harrison's Stamford church holds an important place among these landmarks.

Two small country houses that Harrison worked on in the 1960s continued the fanciful mode of the First Presbyterian Church. One was his renovation of an old pinewood barn Nelson Rockefeller had had transported ten years before from the top of a nearby hill to the oceanside property his father had given Harrison in Seal Harbor, Maine (about 1960). The architect had rarely visited the place; now, encouraged by his wife, he accepted the need to escape his heavy workload occasionally. He enlarged the barn and opened up half the wall facing the ocean to make a huge picture window. A front

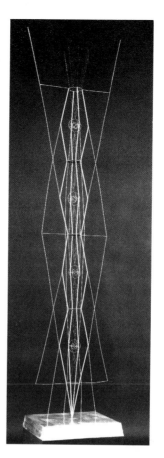

149. Richard Lippold, "Primordial Figure" (1947–48). Brass and copper wire, 96 × 241 × 18 inches. Collection of Whitney Museum of American Art. Gift of the Friends of the Whitney Museum, Charles Simon (and purchase). Acq. 62.27.

148. Harrison, sketch of First Presbyterian bell tower (1968).

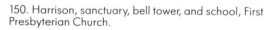

150. Harrison, sanctuary, bell tower, and school, First Presbyterian Church.

door was cut into the barn's side at a point just high enough for it to fit under the roof's longer western slope, which ends at ground level. In the small triangle remaining between roof and door is a porthole window, remindful of the water's proximity. Harrison was sensitive to the oriental flavor of this part of the Maine coast, and the house's wood construction, openness, and floor-to-ceiling sliding window that looks onto an infinitude of ocean and islands are Japanese in feeling. He further emphasized this influence by creating a Japanese dry rock garden on the house's ocean side. On the carefully raked sand, a string of large flat stones ends with three boulders stepping up to the front door in the manner of a Japanese tea house. The result is a serene oasis within the murmuring pine forest overlooking the bay (Figs. 151, 152). It provides yet another example of the architect's remarkable design freedom and versatility.

It was also as a retreat that Nelson Rockefeller had built at Pocantico the so-called Lodge, which proved to be one of Harrison's most lyrical works (1965). Rockefeller was first attracted to the site's small pond, which he regarded as a possible setting for a sculpture; a work by Jacques Lipchitz was set on a small island in the water, and the new house, to be constructed at the pond's edge, was to provide an ideal place from which to see it.[10] In view of his increasing estrangement from his wife of thirty years, the Lodge would provide a quiet, contemplative place, isolated as it was in a heavily wooded area, where Rockefeller, who was by then governor of New York State, could be on home ground and at the same time maintain his privacy.

The Lodge's outstanding feature is a saucer-shaped, thin concrete roof that seems to hover weightlessly among the trees, gently protecting the glazed façade (Fig. 153). Harrison compared the roof with an airplane wing: only two-and-a-half to three inches thick, its down-sloping silhouette complements the hull shape of the house's platform, which is cut away to clear the flow of a small stream. Harrison had worked with the Hungarian-born engineer Paul Weidlinger on a new kind of concrete shell roof for the Hopkins Center at Dartmouth College (see chapter 17). He now asked Weidlinger to help him apply the same technology to this small

151. Harrison's converted barn, Seal Harbor, Maine (c. 1960).

152. Interior, Harrison's converted barn.

174

153. Harrison, the Lodge, Pocantico (1965).

154. Plan, the Lodge.

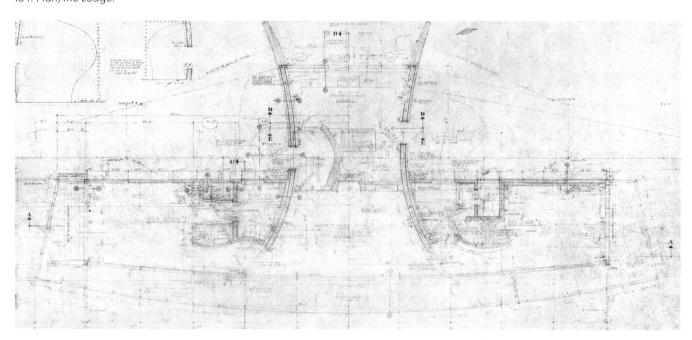

house. It was an extravagant decision, since this kind of construction, while economical for covering long spans, represented a costly tour de force when applied to a smaller area. The engineer complied, however, and Harrison was thrilled to discover that while the roof was under construction, a slight pressure exerted on one side of it made the other side see-saw up! This flexibility was controlled by a small fieldstone segment that projected beyond the center of the north (back) elevation and allowed for a play of one-half inch up and one inch down.

The house has only two slightly convex central supporting walls; approximately sixteen-and-a-half feet apart, these bend toward each other in the flattened curve Harrison often used (Fig. 154). The northern part of the space between the walls is occupied by the kitchen, the southern part by the living room. A large fireplace dominates the living room's north wall, while sliding glass doors suspended in slender metal frames form the house's entire southern elevation. At the southern half of this central space, at either side of the living room, two bedroom areas of approximately twenty-eight-and-a-half feet each extend to the east and to the west. Each bedroom is enclosed at the north by a masonry wall with sliding horizontal windows, and each contains a spacious bath and dressing area, which is, in turn, enclosed by a curvilinear wall at its south (front) side. In this way, the sensuous curve of the roof is repeated by the two interior supporting walls, by the front part of the porch, and by the platform. (The south walls of the bath facilities are a more insistent variation of the curve motif.) This fragile-looking structure, barely fourteen feet wide and eighty feet long, sits by the pond in front of a six-foot-high granite formation, like some ethereal, momentarily alighted flying creature.

At mid-century, Harrison was not alone in his interest in expressionism. Le Corbusier in France, and Eero Saarinen in America, are among those who strayed from the early tenets of modernism to which they had adhered until then. This phase of Harrison's design development is very much in character with his keen awareness and receptiveness to new ideas. During the years that Harrison began to produce some of his most expressive buildings, he also designed several small, pared-down modern structures. Among these are additions to Rockefeller University's fifteen-acre site between Sixty-fourth and Sixty-eighth streets on New York City's East River.

Founded in 1901 by John D. Rockefeller as a unique biological and biomedical facility, within fifty years the Rockefeller Institute had become one of many similar research centers in the United States. In 1954, a restructuring of the institute began. The Rockefeller Institute became Rockefeller University, requiring new buildings to house a graduate students' residence hall, executive offices and rooms for visiting professors, a lecture hall, a residence for the president, and a new laboratory building. Harrison was by now so closely associated with the Rockefellers' building program that it was a matter of course for David Rockefeller to ask him to study the project.

The alignment of the older buildings along the river left enough space between them and York Avenue to allow what Harrison called "a little city planning out of nothing." He designed this space in a conservative Beaux-Arts manner: an axial entrance road leads to the centrally located Founder's Hall and divides the campus into a northern and a slightly larger southern section, in each of which he placed one of two similar modern buildings. These sober three-story structures sit on rough fieldstone bases: they are faced according to a framing module in northwest limestone and glass on the western, York Avenue, side and in steel and glass on the eastern, campus, side. The hall to the north (1958) contains luxurious executive offices in the southern part and visitors' rooms and dining facilities in the northern part, called the Abby Aldrich Rockefeller Hall. The hall to the south (1959) houses graduate students. Floor-to-ceiling windows on the east side of both buildings provide ample views of the beautifully landscaped grounds (Fig. 155).[11]

Placement of the halls at the site's westernmost part and the more closed nature of the western elevations form a protected area, bounded at the north by the handsome, tall buildings of New York Hospital (Coolidge, Shepley, Bullfinch & Abbott, 1933). The result is a distinctive place, a serene and bucolic academic enclave in the midst of the city.

Harrison once said that "without the other arts architecture is like a bald baby or a bald old man."[12] For this scholarly environment, he was eager to provide space for as much contemporary art as possible. David Rockefeller shared this concern, and by 1957 he had contributed sufficient funds to begin a small collection for the new halls. The task of selecting the artworks was entrusted to Dorothy Miller, Alfred Barr's assistant at the Museum of Modern Art, who by this time had established a reputation for a good eye and discerning judgment. For only a few thousand dollars each, she acquired work by such artists as Franz Kline and Bradley Walker Tomlin, now considered masterpieces of the period. In addition, a small area for loan exhibitions was provided in the entrance to the Alfred H. Caspary Auditorium, another structure Harrison designed for the complex.

Harrison did not restrict his interest in combining art and architecture to his prestigious commissions. When he encountered opposition to the idea of incorporating sculpture and painting in the facilities he designed for Public School 34 (1956) on Twelfth Street between Avenues C and D, he fought intensely for them. Thus, in the midst of one of Manhattan's toughest neighborhoods, Harrison's three-part International Style building is graced unexpectedly by a sculptural bronze grill by Mary Callery, set within the northern boundary wall. He also succeeded in having the young artist who executed Léger's murals in the U.N. General Assembly paint a mural for the school.[13]

Given complete freedom of design at Rockefeller University, Harrison adopted a more adventuresome style for its Caspary Auditorium. The auditorium was to provide a new kind of hall, primarily for lectures but flexible enough to accommodate other events such as concerts, films, projection television, and relatively small scientific conventions. Harrison used one of his favorite forms, the circle, for a large dome whose hemispheric interior was intended to create a feeling of intimacy between the audience and the speakers or performers. He cited the Greek amphitheater as the basis of his design, but there was another source as well. In the fall of 1954 Harrison had visited Iran to study plans for an IBEC housing project there. The original exterior of Caspary Auditorium, a mosaic of Italian tiles in various hues of blue with highlights of green, yellow, and white, reflected the influence of the tile-covered mosques he had seen while in the Middle East (Fig. 156). It was a stunning design, but to everyone's consternation, within less than eight months of its completion (1958), the tiles started to fall off. It was the only technical failure on Harrison's part for which no satisfactory remedy was found: the dome was stripped of its colorful cladding, exposing the concrete shell, which remains unadorned to this day. Typically, Harrison blamed only himself, citing his insufficient allowance for the wide variations in temperature to which the exterior would be subjected.

More successful than its exterior, the auditorium's interior is approached through a funnel-like passageway that contains a curved double stairway at either side. The compressed space of the passageway releases the visitor into the generous, open hemisphere of the auditorium, where the circular motif is developed. Semicircular rows of seats descend at a sharp angle to the proscenium stage, backed by a sound baffle in the form of a three-quarter circle in which separate rectangular sections can be moved to different angles. The dome, articulated by convex circles of different sizes, encompasses stage and audience. Harrison worked effectively with Bolt, Beranek & Newman to develop the different dimensions of the dome's circular protrusions (Fig. 157).

Harrison used the same dome shape for the auditorium he completed in 1970 for the National Academy of Sciences in Washington, D.C. By this time he had finished the Metropolitan Opera House at Lincoln Center, and as a result of his experience there he worked whenever possible with Cyril Harris as his acoustical advisor. This collaboration produced an interior treatment of the dome that is quite different from the Caspary's. In place of the New York structure's convex circles, the interior of the Washington shell is covered with adjoining, plaster-covered, triangular projections reminiscent in shape of the church interior at Stamford. The triangles' base points are placed along cycloids, curves traced by a point on the circumference of a circular disc as the disc rolls along a straight line, with a changing center of curvature that encourages optimum distribution of sound.

155. Harrison, east elevation, Abby Aldrich Rockefeller Hall,
Rockefeller University, New York City (1958).

156. Harrison, tiled exterior, Caspary Auditorium, Rockefeller
University. At east (far right), Abby Aldrich Rockefeller Hall.

157. Interior, Caspary Auditorium.

The enclosing shell formed by these triangles touches neither the auditorium's exterior walls nor its floor, but is suspended by metal-coil springs attached to fixed trusses above the ceiling. These structural features insulate against exterior noise and provide excellent acoustics (Fig. 158).[14]

By 1958 the house for the president of Rockefeller University had also been completed, tucked into the only free riverfront site, at the northeast corner of the property. Harrison appears to have taken special pleasure in designing this basically single story, suburban-type house in Manhattan. The visitor enters across a rectangular covered terrace with a curvilinear cutout in its concrete ceiling that recalls the Hawes Guest House at Pocantico Hills (see Fig. 45). The main part of the thirteen-room house is divided into three equal rectangles, aligned longitudinally, with the shorter sides facing the river: a dining room large enough to seat fifty people, an open atrium with a rectangular pool, and a spacious living room. A long wing with three bedrooms, a kitchen, and servants' quarters extends west at the north side of the house. A partial second story in a meandering shape that echoes the terrace roof cutout provides two additional bedrooms.[15] The architect took full advantage of the unusual, parklike site to open up the house's exterior with uninterrupted floor-to-ceiling sliding glass panels and the interior with the atrium and terrace (Fig. 159). The president's residence carries to a handsome conclusion the institute's pastoral campus atmosphere.

Harrison was pleased with his work for Rockefeller University, and a few years after its completion he was delighted at the opportunity to design the building that now faces its entrance across York Avenue: the nurses' residence for the Memorial Sloan-Kettering Cancer Center (1962). At the time it was built, the twenty-story tower, in glazed white brick, gray glass, and aluminum, provided 150 modest apartments for 225 nurses. The impossibility of building medium- or low-rental housing in this area made the accommodations (at monthly rentals of seventy-one dollars for a studio and fifty-eight dollars per person for the apartments) exceptionally attractive. In what appears to be an attempt to relate the building to the nearby university, Harrison placed the tower on a

158. Harrison, auditorium, National Academy of Sciences, Washington, D.C. (1965).

159. Harrison, atrium, President's house, Rockefeller University.

planted terrace raised above sidewalk level, with floor-to-ceiling windows in the reception rooms that run the entire length of both sides of the residence. The effect is pleasant from the interior, but the landscaped area is too small to affect the building's rather bland presence within the city block.

It was within another academic context, in this case at Princeton University, that Harrison designed a small library at the invitation of J. Robert Oppenheimer. Of the many remarkable individuals Harrison knew, perhaps the most intriguing was the charismatic atomic physicist. Named chairman of the General Advisory Committee of the Atomic Energy Commission in 1947, Oppenheimer fell prey to Senator McCarthy's anti-Communist inquisition and to years of surveillance. In 1953 Oppenheimer was suspended from the commission as an alleged security risk. Although his name was eventually cleared, the gentle, frail-looking Oppenheimer suffered tremendously from the episode. It was shortly after this troubled time that the Harrisons met the physicist and his wife. Oppenheimer's brilliant intellect and wide-ranging interests, which, like Harrison's, included a love of classical music, made him exactly the kind of person the architect was drawn to. The two couples enjoyed a close friendship for a number of years.[16]

Oppenheimer was affiliated with Princeton's Institute for Advanced Studies, which he headed from 1947 to 1966. Two years after he became head of the Institute, the possibility arose of building a new library for history, social science, and mathematics; but, partly because the idea was opposed by the mathematics department, the building committee did not approach an architect about the project until 1959. First a proposal by Marcel Breuer and then one by Kenneth Stone Kassler were rejected.[17] At this point Oppenheimer turned to Harrison, who, true to form, succeeded in getting the project built. Nevertheless, it was not accomplished easily: the building committee took two years to accept his design, and three more years were needed to construct the relatively small structure that now houses the Historical Studies and Social Science Library. It was completed in 1965, just two years before Oppenheimer died.

Harrison's design consists of a two-story building, only one floor of which is aboveground. This main floor (sixty-eight by eighty feet), which sits on an elevated concrete platform, is divided by a ten-foot-wide central corridor into a reading and service area at the north and into stacks at the south. A relatively large amount of space was left open for the display of specialized periodicals, an important feature of the library's holdings. The simplicity of the structure itself, the careful detailing of its interior, and the sensitive choice of materials—such as the terrazo floors with inlaid beige wool carpets—create a serene, low-keyed elegance.

On the exterior, between the columns that support the heavy concrete roof slab, one-by-four teakwood boards with rabbeted, shiplap joints are arranged in a variety of panels. This finish provides an unexpectedly delicate note between the heavy concrete roof and platform. A separate mathematics wing is connected to the library by a glass-enclosed corridor.

The Princeton library's most distinctive feature is the roof, where Harrison experimented with combining structure, skylighting, air-conditioning, and artificial lighting in a single overhead system that serves the entire building. The system comprises glazed, shaped concrete beams, each with a forty-foot span and supported by fifteen-inch concrete girders, five feet deep, with a duct running through the bottom of each beam.[18] The girders rest on concrete columns twenty feet apart. The curved soffit and haunch of each beam picks up daylight from the north-facing glass panels and reflects it downward. The unusual, wavy ceiling is apparent only from the interior, where the glazed uprights provide uniformly good lighting and allow flexibility in placing the partitions (Figs. 160–162).

The Corning Glass Center in upstate New York was one of Harrison's most straightforwardly modern designs for a small project. In 1851 Amory Houghton Sr. (a great-great grandfather of then board chairman Amory Houghton) began his career in the glass industry. By 1864 Houghton and others had laid the foundations of what was to become a flourishing family business, which moved in 1868 from Brooklyn to Corning, New York. Like the Presbyterian congregation at Stamford,

160. Harrison, Library for History and Social Sciences, Institute for Advanced Study, Princeton, New Jersey (1965).

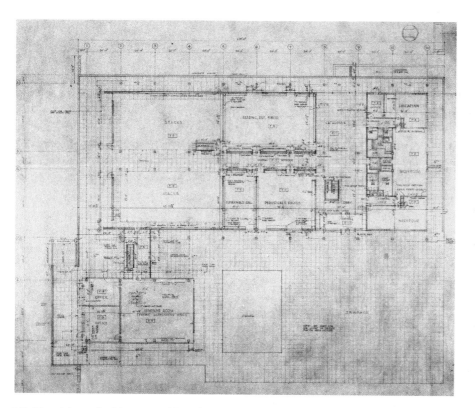

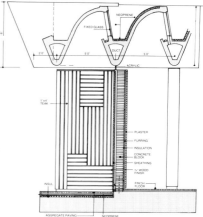

161. Plan, Library for History and Social Sciences.

162. Detail of beams, Library for History and Social Sciences.

Corning Glass had decided to celebrate its centenary with a new building. It was to consist of three separate parts: a glass museum, a library, and an auditorium with recreation areas. From the beginning, the Corning factory had consistently attracted large numbers of visitors; it was also the town's biggest employer. The new buildings, therefore, were envisioned as a focal point for the community as well as a public relations center for the firm.

Unlike the Presbyterians, who did not require a specific deadline, Corning's directors decided to construct the new buildings barely twelve months before they were determined to have them completed, in time for the anniversary. Within twenty-four hours of their decision, Rushmore H. Mariner, the Corning executive, who (as noted in the previous chapter) later worked with Harrison on the Corning Building in New York, presented a random list of possible architects—headed by Harrison & Abramovitz, who at the time were associated with Charles Abbe—to Amory Houghton, chairman of the board of Corning, and his cousin Arthur Amory Houghton, Jr., president. The latter had known Harrison for some time, and he immediately designated his preference for his old friend.

Within days Harrison was at Corning to visit the site near the riverfront. During this first visit, he decided that the program should be contained within a single building rather than three.[19] Shortly thereafter, a factory for the manufacture of glass and an executive dining room were added to the program. Just three weeks after money was appropriated for the project, Corning's tight schedule was further complicated by the outbreak of the Korean War; suddenly, certain building components were scarce, and more expensive materials had to replace them—such as steel windows substituted for the aluminum windows that had been specified. Nevertheless, the Corning Glass Center was completed on time and with flying colors, receiving the Architectural League's silver medal in 1954. It was the kind of project at which Harrison excelled. His no-nonsense solution to the functional program integrated the right amount of imagination without unnecessary complexity; and his efficiency and expertise served him well under the special limitations of materials and time.

Harrison's Corning Glass Center is based on twenty-by-twenty-foot bays articulated by naked steel frames (Figs. 163, 164). Within these frames, different types of glass are used in much the same way that different types of aluminum were later used for Alcoa. Photosensitive glass similar to that employed at the U.N. Secretariat, but in elongated panels over concrete blocks, produced a marblelike effect for the right side of the façade, with clear glass at the left. Glass brick alternates with clear glass at the back of the long rectangular structure and with photosensitive glass at the building's intersection with a bridge that leads to a metal-enclosed glass-blowing area. This connecting bridge is in itself a showpiece. It is made entirely of Pyrex tubing separated by rubber gaskets, the same tubing that Corning had produced for Frank Lloyd Wright's Johnson Wax laboratory office building, where it was used horizontally (with some leakage problems) instead of vertically.

The building sits on a 300-foot-long plinth of Vermont marble and rises one story, with a second story sunken below ground. Access to the entrance door is across a short elevated walkway that abuts the raised semicircular driveway in a drawbridge-and-moat effect. (Harrison's original scheme had called for a reflecting pool the entire length of the façade, but it was eliminated for budgetary reasons.) On this first floor were the historical museum, exhibition gallery, library, and administrative offices, all of which were organized in relation to two inner courtyards. The auditorium and recreation areas were located on the lower floor. After passing through the museum, the visitor entered the science and industry gallery, laid out around a circular courtyard thirty feet in diameter that was enclosed by curved, butt-jointed glass panels set on lead shims. At one side of the courtyard was a glass-bottomed pool, through which watery, greenish light penetrated to the auditorium foyer below. The second courtyard, rectangular in shape and removed from the visitor's path, provided daylight to the administrative facilities.

163. Harrison, Corning Glass Center, Corning, New York (1951).

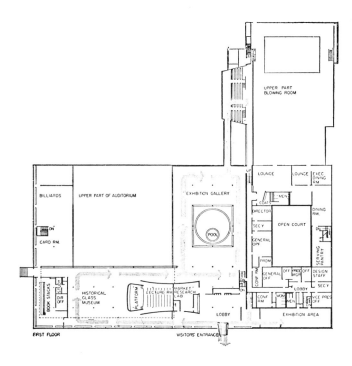

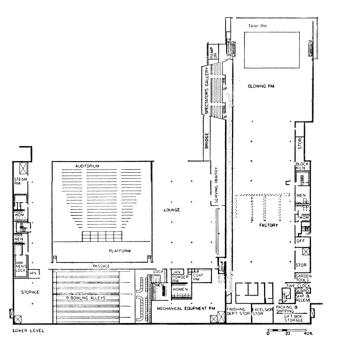

164. Plans, Corning Glass Center.

The circular courtyard was one of several devices Harrison used to achieve a variety of light effects that were modeled after his experience of Egyptian architecture. The brightness of the areas close to the glass enclosure fades as one moves away from it toward the museum's mysterious darkness, broken only by the pinpoint spotlighting of precious objects displayed on glass shelves.

Within three decades of its completion, the Corning collection grew from 2,206 objects and 1,493 books to 19,177 objects and a library of 24,260 volumes. Talk of expansion had been going on for some time when, in June 1972, an unusually strong flooding of the nearby Chemung River inundated the center and helped convince Amory Houghton, Jr., who had taken over his father's chairmanship of Corning, that a new museum should be built.[20] The commission went to Gunnar Birkerts, a Michigan architect. His Museum of Glass now wraps around one corner of Harrison's Center; the contents of the original museum have been moved into the new building, and a cafeteria now occupies the space. Even before the flood, the courtyard pool had been removed.

Shortly before his death, Harrison was asked how he felt about his work being superseded by that of another architect. He answered thoughtfully:

My little building turned out to be very useful. It had a great big square room, big enough for an orchestra. It was wonderful because the acoustics were good. It had game rooms and all that. But then along comes Amory Houghton's son, and he's persuaded to build a museum around it. You never know what's going to happen. After you leave a building it's somebody's else's. It's a responsibility you have to leave the day the owner takes over. . . .

And then he added, with a smile: "Unless you happen to be Frank Lloyd Wright."

Chapter 16

Lincoln Center

The U.N. headquarters had been completed for only two years when Harrison received the second monumental commission of his middle years. His role at Lincoln Center for the Performing Arts represents a peak in his career, equal in importance to the contributions he had made to Rockefeller Center and to the United Nations. The project was built, however, in the face of enormous difficulties with the collaborating architects, with the intervention of innumerable Lincoln Center committees, and at the expense of Harrison's design integrity.

Once again, the commission came to Harrison through friends. Arthur Houghton, Jr., president of Corning Glass, was an influential director (and chairman of the board) of the New York Philharmonic Society. The Society had performed at Carnegie Hall since it was built in 1891, but early in 1955 the hall's owners decided to replace the ten-story complex of two auditoriums, artists' studios, and apartments with a more remunerative office building; they notified the Philharmonic that when its lease expired in 1959, it would not be renewed.[1] Faced with the possibility of having to construct a new concert hall for the Philharmonic, Houghton consulted Harrison. Houghton recalls the architect standing up, pacing back and forth, and then saying, "I was asked yesterday by the Metropolitan Opera to explore the possibility of a new opera house. Why not think of putting the two halls together in some fashion?"[2] The notion of a music center that would contain facilities for opera, symphony, and other types of performance had been discussed since the 1920s, but it was Harrison's ability to adapt an existing idea to a specific situation that made it a reality. The concept of a cultural center for the performing arts would be imitated in cities around the country.

Another friend had involved Harrison with the Metropolitan Opera project. Early in 1955, Robert and Mary Moses were guests of the Harrisons at a midday Sunday dinner at their house in Huntington. The architect's extensive work in New York had brought him into frequent contact with Moses, and for over twenty years the two men had known each other professionally and socially.

Moses was well past the midpoint of a long civic career during which he had enjoyed unusual power under the administrations of six New York governors and five New York City mayors. In the 1920s and the 1930s he had built state parks and parkways. From 1945 until 1957 he had focused on the city, drastically altering the lower east side of Manhattan. By the end of his career, Moses had been directly responsible for $27 billion worth of public works construction.

Moses was the kind of achiever Harrison admired; the scale of his accomplishments surpassed even such giant builders as William Zeckendorf or Nelson Rockefeller. There is no doubt that Moses was the ruthless power broker described by his biographer, Robert Caro, but he was also a highly literate, cultivated, and charming man of exceptional intelligence, with whom Harrison shared a great many mutual interests.

In the course of their long friendship, Moses discussed many of his current projects with Harrison but it was characteristic of him that he almost always preferred to use his own team of architects to execute them; in that way, he could exercise complete control.[3] While enjoying his Sunday dinner, Moses surprised Harrison by asking if he would be interested in building an opera house on a parcel of land located west of Columbus Avenue between Sixty-third and Sixty-fourth streets. He was offering a city block within a twenty-five-acre site that he had chosen for development from the City Planning Commission's master plan—an area that was situated around what was then known as Lincoln Square.

In 1949 Congress had passed the Federal Housing Act to encourage rebuilding the country's blighted inner cities. Title I authorized $1 billion in loans and $500 million in capital grants over a five-year period to help localities clear slums and provide low-cost housing. It stipulated that a municipality could acquire slum sites and make them available for private redevelopment; any loss incurred in the resale of the site, plus any cost of community facilities accessory to the project, would be shared two-thirds by the federal government and one-third by the city. The law's new concept of urban renewal provided Moses with an exceptional opportunity for large-scale real estate development. He saw Title I as the means for a "reborn West Side, marching north from Columbus Circle, and eventually spreading over the entire dismal and decayed West Side."[4] Two institutions, both in need of midtown sites on which to build, provided Moses with an attractive rationale for razing eighteen square blocks of slums and building a cultural center in their stead: Fordham University and the Metropolitan Opera Association. The president of Fordham, Father Laurence J. McGinley, had for years hoped to establish a midtown campus and was delighted with the Lincoln Square site. But Moses had been unable to interest George Sloane, chairman of the Opera Association board, in a location so far north of Broadway's Great White Way. The commissioner realized the success of his project would require the financial and moral support not only of Sloane but also of the entire Metropolitan Opera board and its wealthy patrons. No one had better entrée to this group than Harrison, who, in fact, sat on the Metropolitan's so-called New House Committee, created in 1949 for the specific purpose of replacing the opera's home. Moses also knew that Harrison had been making drawings for a new opera house for over twenty-five years, from the time it had been planned as the focal point of Rockefeller Center. Harrison was a strong man to whom people turned naturally as someone who could be trusted no matter what the complexities or temptations of a situation. Personally and professionally his comportment was as strictly prescribed as that of a Henry James character.

True to form, Moses showed an uncanny instinct for getting what he wanted. Harrison described the offer to a fellow member of the New House Committee, Charles M. Spofford, a New York lawyer who succeeded Sloane in 1955 as chairman of the Opera Association's executive committee. Spofford immediately recognized both the viability of the site and the need to have as head of the project a well-known figure who would inspire potential donors. Nelson Rockefeller was an obvious choice, but his candidacy for governor of New York State left him no time for such a demanding job. Instead Spofford approached John D. Rockefeller 3d. John Rockefeller neither shared his brother Nelson's interest in building nor was particularly interested in the performing arts, so it surprised many—including Harrison—when the reserved, laconic, elder brother accepted.[5]

165. Lincoln Square area, looking southeast, New York City (1957).

Robert Moses, in providing the land, and John D. 3d, in creating the incentive for funding, implemented the creation of Lincoln Center. Curiously, these founders also imposed upon the project its most severe limitations. Moses's insistence on the incorporation of a public park within the complex cramped the plan and handicapped the architects before they could even begin to design the constituent buildings, and Rockefeller's indecisiveness and reliance on committee decisions hopelessly confused the client-architect relationship.[6]

The Lincoln Square area had first been developed in the 1870s as tenements and low-grade apartments for white-collar workers.[7] In the 1920s it began to show signs of the west side's general deterioration, and by the 1950s it had sunk so low that it was used as the seamy setting for the film *West Side Story*. Most of the middle class had long since fled to the suburbs, leaving a new, increasingly Puerto Rican population of over 5,000 poor families. Ninety-seven percent of the apartments in the Lincoln Square neighborhood and all its rooming houses were located in pre-1901 buildings, less than half of which contained private baths. In addition, much of the area was occupied by business establishments, whose heavy truck traffic helped to blight the neighborhood still further (Fig. 165).[8]

In the fall of 1955 a Lincoln Square exploratory committee was formed: Charles M. Spofford and Anthony Addison Bliss represented the Metropolitan Opera; Floyd Blair and Arthur Houghton, Jr., represented the Philharmonic-Symphony Society; Wallace Harrison served as architectural advisor; and John D. Rockefeller 3d as chairman. Others were soon added, including Lincoln Kirstein, co-founder and managing director of the New York City Ballet. When the enlarged committee met on December 13, it chose as its official name the Exploratory Committee for a Musical Arts Center.[9]

While the Exploratory Committee was meeting every other Monday over lunch at one or another of the exclusive clubs to which its members belonged, Moses was exerting pressure on Harrison to produce a preliminary site plan for a brochure the commissioner planned to publish in February 1956. From the beginning the opera house was the focal point of Lincoln Center, with

Harrison as its architect. As such, he was regarded as the orchestrator of the whole Lincoln Center project—no easy task, considering that the participating organizations had not yet been decided upon. But even the tentative plans convinced Harrison that what had by then become two blocks—four acres—were inadequate for the number of potential institutions slated for the complex. With John Rockefeller's help, he persuaded Moses to provide another block, extending the site from Sixty-second to Sixty-fifth streets. A major problem with the availability of this three-block site was the existence of a working twelve-story office building at the eastern end of the block between Sixty-second and Sixty-third streets; it belonged to Joseph P. Kennedy. At John Rockefeller's behest, in March 1956, Kennedy finally agreed to sell the building for $2.5 million (about seven times the price paid for the adjoining slum properties), $1.5 million of which was paid by Lincoln Center and the remainder by the city and federal governments.[10] (Because of the delay in settling on a price, the concert hall was switched from this southeast location to its present, northeast location.)[11]

When Moses's Slum Clearance Committee issued its plan for the Lincoln Center Renewal Area early in 1956, voices of opposition were soon heard. The plan included the Metropolitan Opera, the Philharmonic, and possibly the New York City Center of Music and Drama. To the south would be a campus for Fordham University and nearby a fashion center, a skyscraper hotel, and the mandatory housing for four thousand middle-income families. The Council on Housing Relocation, representing the slum tenants who would be forced out, and a local committee representing the area's businesses both filed petitions. Politicians and private citizens harangued city hall about the inhuman practice of removing slum dwellers before adequate housing was provided. There were also protests against the use of public money to subsidize the purchase of land for sectarian use—for Fordham, a Roman Catholic university. Moses remained undeterred; characteristically, he ignored the opposition, and, in fact, only ten percent of Lincoln Square's local residents were relocated in public housing.[12]

On February 17 and 18, at the invitation of the Exploratory Committee, twenty-two individuals, including Harrison and several of its other members as well as members of the Metropolitan and Philharmonic boards, participated in a two-day meeting to determine which performing arts in addition to the opera and symphony should be housed at Lincoln Center.[13] The vote was for ballet and theater, with strong interest expressed in providing advanced training for young professionals in drama and music. With the inclusion of these constituents, the Exploratory Committee renamed itself and was incorporated as Lincoln Center for the Performing Arts, Inc. on June 22, 1956; John Rockefeller was elected its president.[14] It was agreed that the corporation would be a beneficent landlord to its constituent tenants and serve as artistic coordinator for their activities. Each constituent was to be managed by its own autonomous board of directors; and the constituents' role in governing Lincoln Center, Inc. was specified in a by-law that provided for three directors from the Met, two from the Philharmonic, and an appropriate number from subsequent member organizations to be determined by the Lincoln Center board.[15] Lincoln Center, Inc. thus served as an umbrella organization for several constituents, only two of which—the opera and the Philharmonic—were established at the time of incorporation.

The Exploratory Committee had decided that different architects should design the constituent buildings, and Harrison suggested Abramovitz for the Philharmonic. John Rockefeller had assumed that Harrison would choose the architects for the remaining buildings and would coordinate their designs, as he had for the international team at the U.N. Having completed that difficult project only three years before, and recalling his earlier experience with cooperative architecture at Rockefeller Center, Harrison was unwilling to face the trying business of another group effort. Instead, he asked the Lincoln Center directors to select the architects from an advisory group that he would designate; he would serve as host and chair their meetings. (He had served in this capacity for an unbuilt opera house and auditorium project in Los Angeles in the late 1940s.)[16] His group included Alvar Aalto, his much-admired friend from

Finland; Sven Markelius, the Swedish town planner who had participated in the design of the U.N.; Pietro Belluschi, whose Equitable Building in Portland, Oregon, provided a step in the development of the U.N. Secretariat's glass wall; Marcel Breuer, the Hungarian-born International Style architect of Bauhaus background; and Henry R. Shepley, Harrison's former mentor at the Boston Architectural Club and the only conservative architect among this group of modernists. Three other invitees, Edward Durell Stone, Ieoh Ming Pei, and the office of Skidmore, Owings & Merrill, did not respond.[17]

A conference of the advisory architects, acousticians, and stage designers was held from October 2 to 12, 1956, to discuss the site plan, the shape of the opera house auditorium, and the acoustics of all the auditoriums. John Rockefeller and representatives of the Metropolitan, the Philharmonic, and spokespersons for a possible dance theater attended the sessions relevant to their interests. Day after day, in a conference room at Harrison & Abramovitz, the architects moved chunks of plasticine and hastily constructed cardboard models around a three-block site representing Sixty-second to Sixty-fifth streets between Amsterdam and Columbus avenues. The models roughly represented the opera house (3,800 seats), the concert hall (2,800 seats), a multi-use theater (2,200 seats), and a recital hall and/or theater (1,000 seats). In addition there were a music school (the Juilliard), and a performing arts library and museum of indeterminate sizes. The architects wrestled first with the problem of axis. Should Lincoln Center open to the south and the north, as Moses's Slum Clearance Committee had assumed in its own plan, which made the complex part of a mall linking Fordham University with four to eight legitimate theaters to the north (to be under the direction of Broadway producer and real estate magnate Roger L. Stevens)? Or should the cultural center be designed on an east-west axis that would acknowledge the active Broadway area and its juncture north of the site with Columbus Avenue, where it forms the small triangle, Dante Square?

Led by Breuer, several of the advisory architects expressed their disapproval of the south-north axis's isolation of the plaza and recommended that the axis be changed to east-west (Fig. 166).[18] Gradually, the group shifted toward an axial access at the east; only Markelius held out for an off-axis entrance at the northeast (Fig. 167). The orientation of the axis affected the plan, giving rise to two basic concepts. One was an enclosed plan that turned its back on the intrusive city to focus on the arts within—Venice's Piazza San Marco was the frequently cited example. The other was an open plan, proposed in the hope that one day the complex would be connected to Central Park by a broad allée—like those leading to the Paris Opera or to St. Peter's in Rome (Fig. 168). In response to this second concept, Markelius developed a proposal similar to the one he had made for a grand approach to the U.N.: Lincoln Center would be built on a plaza five meters above street level, connected to Central Park by a grand artery bridging Broadway and terminating at the unexpected northern entrance.

It was soon discovered that the greensward scheme could never be realized because the Ethical Culture Society and the YMCA were located in the area that would have to be demolished for it, between Lincoln Center and the park. Not even Nelson Rockefeller's alleged wish for a clear sight line to Lincoln Center from his Fifth Avenue apartment was sufficient to overcome the obstacles presented by these two powerful institutions.[19]

Toward the end of the conference, Aalto sketched a casbah, an enclosed area isolated from the hubbub of New York City and pierced only by narrow entries.[20] Breuer produced a variation of this idea: a narrow, flat-roofed building on stilts, its underside surfaced with acoustical tile to keep out the city noises, with a monumental opening to the east. The architects unanimously endorsed the idea of an inward-looking, walled center. Because this scheme was feasible only if Moses relinquished his park, they subsequently drew up alternatives to it, always with the opera house placed at the center of the plaza's western side facing east, the concert hall at the southeast corner facing north, and the Juilliard School building at the plaza's northern perimeter (Fig. 169). On the eve of the last day of the conference, Moses's reluctant concession to trade part of the park he wanted at the southwest corner of the site for comparable land elsewhere sparked several proposals that placed one of the smaller halls in the park area (see Fig. 166).

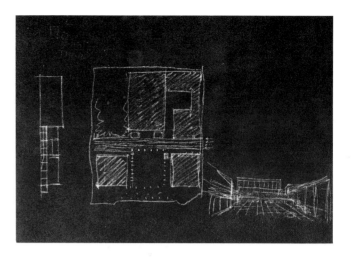

167. Sven Markelius, preliminary site plan for Lincoln Center. Entrance at northeast, with Robert Moses's park area respected (30 October 1956).

166. Philip Johnson and Pietro Belluschi, preliminary site plan for Lincoln Center, New York City. Axial entrance at east, and a building projected at southwest where Robert Moses wanted a park (12 October 1956).

168. Scheme for a grand approach to Lincoln Center from Central Park, shown in relationship to Lincoln Center, as it was built. Rendering by William F. R. Ballard (1966).

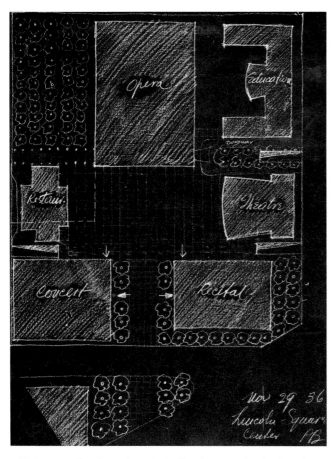

169. Pietro Belluschi and Henry R. Shepley, site plan for Lincoln Center. Axial entrance at east, with Moses's park respected (29 November 1956).

Six weeks later, when some of the advisory architects returned for a meeting on November 30, they were told that Moses had changed his mind about relinquishing part of the park in exchange for another space,[21] so Harrison & Abramovitz drew up a plan respecting the park (Fig. 170). It centered the opera house and placed the concert hall and dance theater to the southeast and northeast respectively; facilities for the Juilliard School, a library, a museum and a theater were crowded against the northwest periphery. Two years later, in March 1958, when Lincoln Center, Inc. made an offer to purchase the block between Sixty-fifth and Sixty-sixth streets, the Harrison & Abramovitz office drew up a new plan (Fig. 171). Enlargement of the site must have been a factor in the remarkable freeing up of the plan.

A year prior to the advisory architects' first conference, the Exploratory Committee had requested a preliminary feasibility report from Day & Zimmerman, a Philadelphia engineering firm that had to its recommendation only a study for a civic center in Baltimore. In instructing Day & Zimmerman, the Exploratory Committee relied to a great extent on the outdated estimates compiled in the 1940s by the Met's first New House Committee. On November 5, 1956, based on tentative design suggestions and conjectural costs, Lincoln Center, Inc. established a budget of $55.4 million for land and buildings, allocating $23.6 million for the opera, $4 million for the concert hall, and $5 million for the dance theater. An additional $19.6 million was reserved to support "the educational and artistic plans of the new center and for contingencies."[22]

Within a year, only $13.8 million had been raised,[23] and a growing number of questions were being asked about the design and construction of Lincoln Center's buildings. To address these questions and to make the ultimate decisions, the Lincoln Center, Inc. Building Committee was created in October 1957, also chaired by John Rockefeller.[24] The establishment of building committees for each constituent soon followed, with the result that each constituent architect had to contend with a minimum of four different groups: the constituent's board of directors and its building committee, along with Lincoln Center's board and its building committee. There would

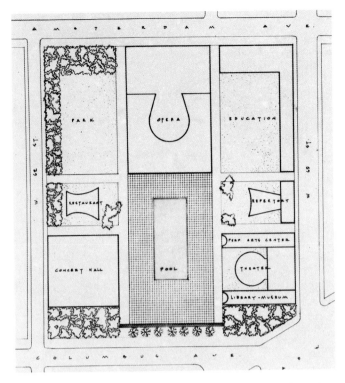

170. Harrison & Abramovitz, site plan for Lincoln Center based on same principles as Fig. 169 (31 December 1956).

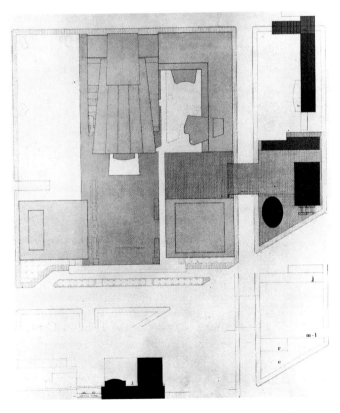

171. Harrison & Abramovitz, revised site plan for Lincoln Center, including the block between Sixty-fifth and Sixty-sixth streets (10 March 1958).

also be a number of subcommittees, which held the purse strings for art, furnishings, and other essentials.

In 1958 the Lincoln Center constituents designated the architects for their respective buildings. From the advisory group, Abramovitz had already been chosen to design Philharmonic Hall (the name was changed to Avery Fisher Hall in 1973); Belluschi was now selected for the Juilliard School. The two Europeans, Aalto and Markelius, were vetoed by board members who favored using only American-based architects; Breuer, who seemed rigid in his opinions, was generally unpopular; and Shepley was considered too conservative. At Harrison's suggestion, Eero Saarinen was chosen for the Vivian Beaumont and what became the Mitzi E. Newhouse theaters and Gordon Bunshaft for the museum-library. (The theater and museum were eventually housed in one building, designed as a joint venture by Saarinen and Bunshaft.) In the absence of an institutional constituency for the dance theater, no one questioned Lincoln Kirstein's choice of Philip Johnson (Fig. 172).

At the time of their commissions for Lincoln Center, all of the architects already had achieved particular distinction. Bunshaft's Lever House had been standing for six years, and Mies van der Rohe and Philip Johnson's Seagram Building had just been completed. Both buildings were almost immediately acclaimed modern landmarks. Eero Saarinen, son of the world-famous Finnish architect Eliel Saarinen, had emulated his father, achieving at the age of thirty international recognition as a designer in his own right. By the 1950s, the young Saarinen was the darling of the architectural profession, earning a *Time* cover story on July 2, 1956 (Harrison had had his *Time* cover story four years earlier in the September 22, 1952, issue). Older than these three architects, Pietro Belluschi had immigrated to the U.S. from Italy and had settled in Portland, Oregon; he had built extensively in the American northwest, including numerous school and college buildings and a small concert hall for the University of California at Berkeley. When he received the Juilliard commission, he was dean of MIT's School of Architecture. The situation was best described by Harold C. Schonberg, the music critic for the *New York Times*,

172. Lincoln Center architects and advisors, from left to right:
Sven Markelius, Harrison, René d'Harnoncourt, and Philip Johnson
(early 1958).

in an article entitled "Six Architects in Search of a Center":

> Suppose six great pianists—Horowitz, Rubinstein, Novaes, Serkin, Richter and Backhaus, say—were locked in a room and ordered not to come out until they had decided on the correct interpretation of Beethoven's 'Hammerklavier Sonata.' How many eons would pass? How many wounds would be inflicted? Yet in another field, much the same thing is actually going on at the same moment.[25]

With the exception of Harrison, the architects displayed the kind of self-confidence and authoritarianism that might be expected in artists of their accomplishment. It was widely acknowledged that Harrison's accomplishments equalled those of his colleagues; in the *Time* story on Saarinen he was referred to as a "twentieth-century form giver" in the same league as Wright, Le Corbusier, Gropius, Mies, Breuer, and Neutra.[26] His chairmanship of the group should have allowed him to impose the sort of strong leadership he had exercised at the U.N., but for reasons never fully explained, at Lincoln Center he chose to exert his authority so cautiously that his opinions were consistently disregarded.

The consulting architects for the U.N. had been as strong willed and difficult as the Lincoln Center group. But at the U.N., Harrison, the only American working on home ground, was director of planning while the other architects served officially only as consultants; his every decision had been backed strongly by Trygve Lie, who had the power to carry them out. At Lincoln Center, Harrison was, by choice, one of several collaborators, all of whom had had American experience and whose educational backgrounds may have been intimidating to one with a modest apprenticeship. In addition, Harrison never got real support from John Rockefeller; in fact, before the project was completed, Rockefeller would become a threat to his authority. Grief over the recent mental illness of his brilliant only child and his own sudden hospitalization for prostate surgery just before the

U.N. complex was completed undoubtedly compounded Harrison's uncertainties at this time of his life.

No sooner had the collaborating architects been designated and new meetings held as of November 1958 than bitter disagreement about the site plan broke out more strongly than ever. Six more months of meetings every other week would be required before the plan was again set. Looking back at the experience, Philip Johnson remarked that "John Rockefeller thought architects were like doctors who could collaborate to make better medicine."[27] Nothing was further from the truth. Bunshaft and Saarinen, both stubborn individualists who shared a habit of declaiming their opinions with no tolerance for criticism, were furious at being squeezed into left field, so to speak. In response to what he described as "a lousy site plan," Bunshaft, seconded by Saarinen, returned to the concept proposed earlier by Aalto and Breuer—that of incorporating all the Lincoln Center components into one continuous building with penetrations.[28] But this raised the thorny issue of which architect would design the megastructure. In agreeing that the opera should be at the center's focal point and that the next two most important halls, of almost equal size, should flank its vista, the architects kept returning to a formal, axial solution for the main complex. Once again they began to petition against Moses's park, and until early in 1959 John Rockefeller was still trying to persuade Moses to compromise. About the park the commissioner remained inflexible; he did, however, eventually accept the idea of expanding Lincoln Center another block north between Sixty-fifth and Sixty-sixth streets, with a pedestrian bridge linking the two areas. On October 1, 1958, the southeastern half of the block was purchased. (The remaining portion was acquired in 1965.)

The ultimate authority to approve the overall design rested with Rockefeller's board, but Rockefeller chose to plead ignorance of architectural aesthetics and asked René d'Harnoncourt, the courtly, Austrian-born director of the Museum of Modern Art, to serve as artistic advisor to his committee.[29] D'Harnoncourt's name figures in the minutes of a number of the architects' meetings from the fall of 1958 until mid-January 1959.[30] As

173. Model of Lincoln Center with peripheral arcade and a building placed in Moses's park area (1958).

174. Model of Lincoln Center with modified arcade and including Moses's park (19 January 1959).

the meetings went on, Harrison seemed increasingly reluctant to participate. Associating his role as director of planning for the U.N. with his relatively long hospitalization, he reminded his colleagues again and again that he could serve only in the capacity of chairman and that they "had to make up their own minds." Perhaps by this time he already sensed that the prolonged debates of the different Lincoln Center groups were counterproductive. While the others circled the conference-room table, effectively destroying the latest product of the Harrison & Abramovitz office, he sat silently absorbed in making design doodles.[31]

Bunshaft and Saarinen's megastructure proposal met with a counterproposal for a "fence" enclosing the whole complex,[32] and Johnson, who admits to behaving in his usual "Peck's bad boy" fashion, suggested a tall arcade of fine steel piers that would surround it on three sides, providing a unifying element for the otherwise unarticulated side walls of the two halls on Columbus Avenue.[33] Despite the tricky question of who would design such an arcade, schemes with arcades and colonnades kept appearing through the early months of 1959 (Figs. 173, 174).

In May a site plan was finally agreed upon. Although later modified in terms of the opera's relative pro-

portions, it established the basic relationships between the six Lincoln Center constituents (Fig. 175).

While they worked through various alternatives, the architects made decisions regarding the raised platform on which Lincoln Center would be set, access to the garage below, and the pedestrian bridge that would link the Juilliard School to the main complex. By August they had decided that the height and mass of the Philharmonic Hall and of the dance theater opposite should be the same; the buildings would differ only in the design of their façades. To relate the three largest halls that would face the common plaza, the architects specified that their exterior balconies at the promenade level were to be at uniform height. The concrete structures were to be sheathed in either quartz, marble, or granite,[34] and agreement was later reached upon Italian travertine. Despite these basic specifications, each building was eventually subjected to so many design modifications that Lincoln Center today only approximates what was then decided upon.[35]

Harrison's own struggle to design the opera house is a case in point. While working on the site plan, the collaborating architects had from time to time conceded to him that the opera could be the one sculptural entity among Lincoln Center's otherwise rectilinear components. It was not to be.

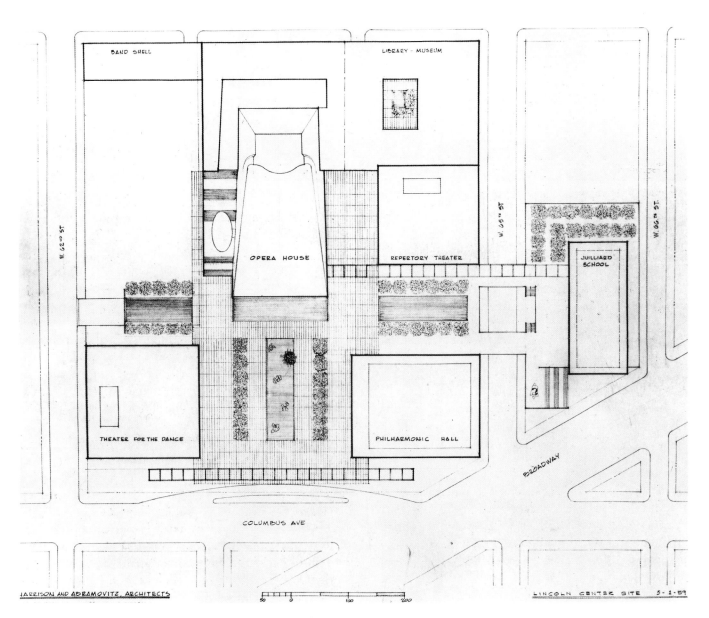

BAND SHELL

LIBRARY - MUSEUM

W. 62ND ST.

OPERA HOUSE

REPERTORY THEATER

W. 65TH ST.

W. 66TH ST.

JUILLIARD SCHOOL

THEATER FOR THE DANCE

PHILHARMONIC HALL

BROADWAY

COLUMBUS AVE

HARRISON AND ABRAMOVITZ, ARCHITECTS

50 0 100 200

LINCOLN CENTER SITE   5-1-59

175. Harrison & Abramovitz, site plan for Lincoln Center with
altered repertory theater and museum-library (1 May 1959).

197

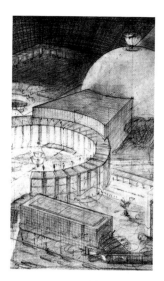

Chapter 17

The Metropolitan Opera House: beginnings

In his colorful history of lyric drama in New York, Henry Edward Krehbiel dates the city's first operatic performance, an English ballad opera presented at the Nassau Street Theater, to 1750.[1] Seventy-five years passed before New York experienced Italian opera and eight more until a proper opera house opened its doors—the first of four auditoriums in which Italian opera was performed regularly in New York for almost six decades. Lorenzo da Ponte, Mozart's librettist, and the so-called Palmo, a restaurateur, were the partial owners and managers of the first two houses. Not until the founding of the Astor Place Opera House (1847–50) and the Academy of Music (1853–86) did the fate of opera in New York come to depend on the city's social elite.

As a gesture of revolt against the Academy's tight control by members of the city's more firmly established society, New York's new rich, headed by Mrs. William Kissam Vanderbilt, decided to build an opera house of their own with a new company. It was called the Metropolitan Opera Company, and it opened in 1883 at Thirty-ninth Street and Broadway in an eight-story twin-towered building designed by Josiah Cleveland Cady, who had won a limited competition for the project. Cady was a respectable architect who had built several Presbyterian churches, but had no previous experience with theater design; indeed, at the time he was invited to enter the competition, he had never attended an opera performance, nor had he ever visited a European opera house. His success in the competition was due to the single fact of his having provided more boxes than any of the other entries. It was an all-important consideration for an institution financed in large part by the stockholders' ownership of these boxes, but the jury's emphasis on the economic rather than the functional merits of the design produced a house with poor sight lines, crowded lobbies, inadequate storage space for scenery, and a firetrap balcony (Figs. 176,177).[2]

From the start, Cady's opera house was criticized, aesthetically as the "new yellow brick brewery on Broadway," and on practical grounds for its lack of rehearsal space and storage areas; worst of all, it was said that no less than seven hundred of its seats had obstructed sight lines.[3] Serious efforts to replace the building were not discussed until 1918, when Otto Kahn was elected president of the Metropolitan Opera Company. The hope was that a new building could be completed within two or three years.

Two years later the new house had still not materialized, and Philip Berolzheimer, a wealthy businessman, came up with the idea of a center for the performing arts. The proposal coincided with interest in a peace memorial to celebrate the end of the war. Mayor Hylan liked the idea and went so far as to obtain the state's authorization to acquire a site for the arts center at Fifty-seventh to Fifty-ninth streets between Sixth and Seventh avenues. Arnold Brunner, a Beaux-Arts architect known for his public buildings, presented a scheme for it that connected the neoclassical opera house's large terrace with the park by means of a bridge spanning Fifty-ninth Street. Berolzheimer announced the project publicly on June 14, 1922; but the site was too expensive, and construction estimates rose from $15 million to $30 million. When Hylan failed to win reelection in 1925, the arts center idea was dropped.[4] Not so the project for a new opera house.

Kahn's purchase of a midblock site on West Fifty-seventh Street has been referred to (see chapter 6); Kahn proposed the site for a new opera house with commercial development to subsidize it. Early in 1926 the directors of the Metropolitan Opera and Real Estate Company endorsed the idea, and Kahn asked Viennese architect and stage designer Joseph Urban to submit a scheme for the project.[5] Urban designed a great oval buttressed by four corner towers with a tall, slender tower rising over the Fifty-seventh Street elevation; the low plinthlike mass of the base was to accommodate the opera with offices above (Fig. 178).[6] Despite the merits of this proposal, in February 1927 Kahn named the more prominent Benjamin Wistar Morris 3d architect, with Urban working with him as his associate. The collaboration lasted only three months, until May 1927, when the two men began their own separate schemes.

Morris worked on a traditional horseshoe-shaped theater, while Urban developed a shallow, wedge-shaped auditorium derived from the design for Richard Wagner's Festspielhaus (begun by Gottfried Semper, executed

176. Josiah Cleveland Cady, the first Metropolitan Opera House, New York City (1883). Photographed in the 1890s.

177. Plan, the first Metropolitan Opera House.

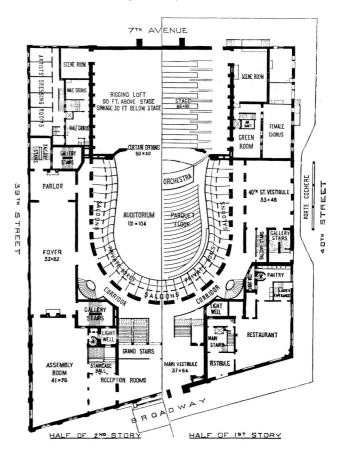

178. Joseph Urban, scheme for Metropolitan Opera House at West Fifty-seventh Street (1926).

by Carl Brandt and Otto Brückwald, 1876) in Bayreuth, Germany. In June the architects presented their schemes (Figs. 179 –182) to Kahn, who presented them to the opera's stockholders in October. By then Urban had resigned when it became apparent that the stockholders preferred Morris's diamond horseshoe. Morris's scheme was also rejected: the boxholders objected to the location and to the association of a commercial tower with the opera. It was Morris's subsequent design that inspired the plan for Rockefeller Center, for which Corbett, Harrison & MacMurray also had submitted a proposal for the opera house (see Figs. 12, 15).

Shortly after the opera withdrew from the Rockefeller Center project, declining attendance and dwindling revenues prompted the stockholders to reincorporate as the Metropolitan Opera Association (which retained the system of box ownership until 1940). Around the same time, the New York Philharmonic was being threatened with eviction from Carnegie Hall, and once again the idea arose of combining the facilities. In 1935 newly elected Mayor La Guardia tried to do just this with his project for a municipal arts center. Benjamin Wistar Morris and his partner, Robert O'Connor, proposed a stylized deco scheme for a double auditorium building to be constructed at Columbus Circle (Fig. 183). We have noted the attempts to incorporate a municipal arts center into the proposed northern extension of Rockefeller Center, to which Harrison contributed (see Figs. 24, 25). Submissions for this project also included a scheme by Aymar Embury II (Fig. 184). Again in 1946 the possibility of a music center was discussed, and the following year William Zeckendorf's plan for a monumental extension of the U.N. included an arts center (see Fig. 123). None of these projects were realized.

In 1949 the Metropolitan Opera Association appointed two committees to study the problem of the opera house: an Old House, or Rehabilitation, Committee, which favored renovation,[7] and a New House Committee, which pressed for a new building. Harrison sat on the New House Committee,[8] and on June 1, 1949, he agreed to the other members' request that he submit proposals for several possible sites, incorporating specific improvements.[9] One of these was for an opera house,

179. Benjamin Wistar Morris, Scheme C for Metropolitan Opera
House at West Fifty-seventh Street (1927).

180. Plan, Scheme C, Metropolitan Opera House.

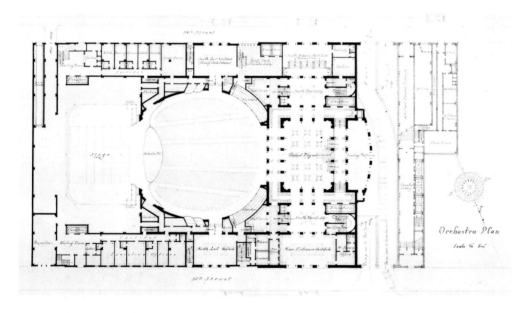

181. Joseph Urban, Scheme IX, Metropolitan Opera House at
West Fifty-seventh Street (1927).

182. Plan, Scheme IX, Metropolitan Opera House.

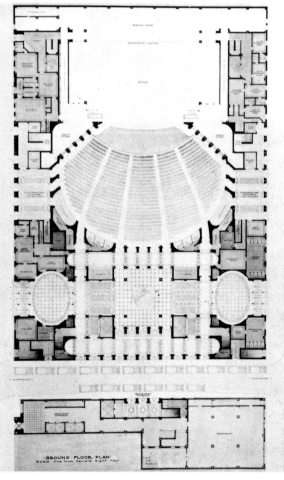

concert hall, and underground garage between Washington Square and West Third Street (Fig. 185).[10] Within less than a year, the New House Committee formally recommended construction of a multiauditorium music center rather than an opera house alone, stating that such a center would be self-supporting, with an excess annual income of $650,000.[11] Public opinion also favored the concept of a music center. Despite these encouraging prognoses, nothing happened.[12]

When Lincoln Square became a potential home for a new opera house in the mid-1950s, it presented a solution to a search that had lasted a half-century. But the legacy of wrangling and delay was to continue and even to intensify. The correspondence and records of meetings reveal constant disagreement, frustration, and anger about practically every aspect of the building. Those connected with the opera regarded it as Lincoln Center's greatest attraction, superior not only to the other constituents but to the center as a whole; and this attitude would sour financial and all other arrangements between the Met and Lincoln Center—including, to Harrison's dismay, the design.[13]

From its inception, the role of the opera as a fiercely exclusive bastion of social conservatism had equalled—if not overshadowed—that of its artistic accomplishments. But times had changed: the city's power structure had been altered, with a corresponding change of the people who controlled that structure. Furthermore, stunning new buildings such as the U.N. and Lever House had ushered in modernism. Neither the professionals at the Metropolitan Opera nor the board of directors had kept pace with these developments. Given their general conservatism, most of the directors had little understanding of—or even interest in—the aesthetics of modern architecture. Yet, for reasons totally unrelated to either style or working methods, this inflexibly traditional client had chosen a modernist architect who was passionately committed to innovation and experimentation. The ensuing confrontation was an unequal battle: no individual could have withstood the power of the Met establishment. The battle was between modernism and traditionalism, but it was also—perhaps to a greater extent—between imaginative creativity and pedestrian

183. Benjamin Wistar Morris and Robert O'Connor, isometric, Municipal Arts Center for Columbus Circle, New York City (1 October 1935).

184. Aymar Embury II, Municipal Arts Center for northern extension of Rockefeller Center (1938).

cautiousness. The outcome was bleak: it is difficult to think of a building that has been worked on for a longer period of time, that has embodied more ambitious goals or greater flights of fantasy than Harrison's Metropolitan Opera House, yet has been realized so unsatisfactorily. Many ambitious architectural designs have been compromised seriously, but none perhaps more radically.

For a quarter of a century Harrison had dreamed of designing the finest modern opera house in the world, and when Moses first asked him for sketches he could use to "sell" the idea of the new cultural center, he responded with a series of spectacular visionary fantasies (1955–56). One scheme depicts a circular double colonnade—reminiscent of Bernini's square for Saint Peter's in Rome—which opens toward Broadway at the east and provides a spectacular entranceway to the opera (Fig. 186). The opera house itself rises west of the colonnade, first in a barrel-vaulted structure before the higher, mammoth dome of the auditorium. The roofs of both structures are covered with tiles forming bold zigzag patterns; like the original tiled dome of Rockefeller University's Caspary Hall, they reflect the influence of Harrison's recent visit to Iran. A tower rises at the westernmost part of the site, while a wedge-shaped concert hall opens from the southern side of the colonnade. Other schemes provided variations on this theme, with a wedge eventually replacing the opera's dome (Figs. 187–189).

These early schemes for Lincoln Center are ample proof that at the age of sixty Harrison, like many architects in their later years, was still producing some of his most imaginative ideas. But he also had to address the practical problems of the opera's interior, especially the backstage areas. To do this, he worked closely with the Metropolitan Opera Building Committee, in particular, with Anthony Bliss and Herman Krawitz.[14]

Bliss's family connection with the Met dated to 1893, when his grandfather joined the board. Bliss's father, Cornelius, became a board member in 1932. He was a passionate opera buff, and his son recalls endless discussions at home on opera-related subjects. Upon the death of the elder Bliss in 1949, George Sloane and Charles Spofford asked Mrs. Bliss if there was a member

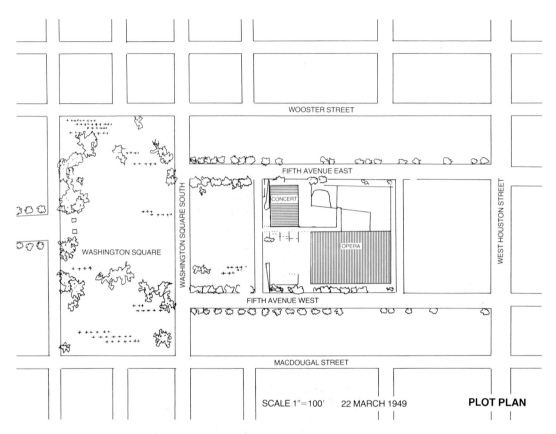

WOOSTER STREET

WASHINGTON SQUARE

WASHINGTON SQUARE SOUTH

FIFTH AVENUE EAST

CONCERT

OPERA

WEST HOUSTON STREET

FIFTH AVENUE WEST

MACDOUGAL STREET

SCALE 1"=100'   22 MARCH 1949   **PLOT PLAN**

185. Harrison & Abramovitz, plan for opera house and concert
hall south of Washington Square, New York City (1949).

186. Harrison, scheme for Metropolitan Opera House at Lincoln Center (fall 1955). Rendering by Hugh Ferriss.

187. Harrison, scheme for Metropolitan Opera House at Lincoln Center: lobby is wedge-shaped, like the concert hall (18 October 1955). Rendering by Hugh Ferriss.

188. Harrison, scheme for Metropolitan Opera House at Lincoln Center: façade modified (fall, 1956). Rendering by Hugh Ferriss.

189. Harrison, scheme for Metropolitan Opera House at Lincoln Center: lobby and auditorium are contained within an angular, funnel-shaped structure, with parts of double colonnade enclosed (fall 1955). Rendering by Hugh Ferriss.

of the family who would like to take her husband's place on the board. She recommended her son.

By January 1956 debate over a new house for the Met had become sufficiently heated to cause a number of administrative changes: Lauder Greenway took Sloane's place as chairman of the Metropolitan Opera Association and Bliss became president of its board of directors. Bliss had been trained as a conservative lawyer and his priority was the opera's financing. His approach did not facilitate the design process; he himself described his meetings with the architects as "a murderous experience,"[15] and the usually imperturbable Harrison is reported to have regularly emerged from private sessions with Bliss so angered that "he was red in the face."[16]

Herman Krawitz had come to the Met in 1953 after founding and managing the Falmouth Playhouse in Massachusetts. He began his nineteen-year career with the opera as a production analyst and consultant. In 1955 he was awarded a New York Community Trust fellowship that enabled him to spend the summer visiting every European city with an opera house or theater of interest. While no major theater had been built in the United States for almost thirty years, in Europe the devastation of World War II had necessitated the construction and restoration of dozens of theaters and opera houses. Nowhere was there more building activity than in Germany, where even relatively small municipalities had their own opera houses.

Krawitz combined brash aggressiveness with intelligence and professional expertise. He moved rapidly from responsibility for stage construction to being "in charge of all aspects of the operation." As he describes it:

> [Rudolph] Bing [the Met's director] was fundamentally against change; he pooh-poohed the idea of a new house, he lived from week to week, he had no long-range view. Bliss and I were the ones who advocated looking ten, twenty years ahead. Everybody was terrified it wouldn't work.[17]

Krawitz approached the project with exuberant optimism. For his tour of Europe he had developed a technical questionnaire that he conscientiously put to the managers of the theaters and opera houses he visited. He maintained that the answers alerted him about what *not* to do; the Metropolitan Opera was unique, requiring what amounted to custom-built facilities. To ascertain the requirements for these facilities Krawitz consulted with the technicians who used them. Additionally, Krawitz cited Franco Zeffirelli and Tyrone Guthrie as influences on his thinking about stagecraft, and Dimitri Mitropoulos, Thomas Schippers, and Erich Leinsdorf as musical advisors.

On April 7, 1956, Krawitz (who in 1954 had been promoted to Administrator of Stage Departments)[18] returned to Europe, this time accompanied by the Harrisons, the Blisses, John D. Rockefeller 3d, Allen I. Fowler of Day & Zimmerman, Herbert Graf, and Walther Unruh, stage designer for the new opera house in Cologne and for the reconstructed opera houses in Hamburg and Vienna. It was a fourteen-day trip to auditoriums in England, France, Germany, Austria, and Italy, reminiscent of Harrison's 1931 trip for Radio City Music Hall. The group's predominantly traditional taste is revealed in its preference for François Cuvilliés's elaborate rococo theater in the Munich royal residence as an aesthetic ideal for the new opera house.

Bliss and Krawitz were bound by the wishes of the Met's director, Rudolph Bing, who took an increasingly active part in the project as it progressed. Born in 1902, Bing was the only son of a well-to-do Viennese family. After a modest career in Vienna, he went to England; there he became interested in contract management and was asked in 1936 to serve as general manager of Glyndebourne, the summer opera festival he reputedly made the English equivalent of the Salzburg Festival. Ten years later he conceived the Edinburgh Festival. In 1949 Bing came to New York to raise financial support for Glyndebourne. He met with Edward Johnson, the Met's director from 1935 to 1950, and it was Johnson himself who offered Bing his job. The tall, stately Viennese impresario was duly introduced to the board, whose members were put off by his imperious manner. Nevertheless, a month later he was summoned back from Europe and given the position. The directors' first impression of Bing was not inaccurate: he was, in fact, an arrogant, difficult man who never missed the opportunity to assert the cultural superiority of Europe. The directorship of the Met provided him with the chance to produce grand opera in the only manner he believed was suitable. He was quick to adopt all the old criticisms of the existing opera house, referring to it as "a relic of an earlier age."[19] However, when Harrison broached the possibility of new ways of presenting opera—in the round, for example—Bing summarily dismissed the suggestion, asserting that opera had always been presented on a proscenium stage and always would be.[20] During the Austrian director's second season in New York, Moses announced that a large site at Columbus Circle—running west between Fifty-ninth and Sixtieth streets—could be made available to the Metropolitan Opera as part of the city's condemnation proceedings for a housing development. Almost the entire $1.2 million required to pay for the site had been pledged when the federal government put an end to the project on the grounds that it did not conform to current housing laws.[21] This disappointment made Bing skeptical: from then on he refused to believe that a new opera house would be built, and he was reluctant to be associated with the project until it became a certainty.

Bliss, Krawitz, and, later, Bing, together with various Metropolitan Opera and Lincoln Center committees, were Harrison's client for the new opera house. Bliss was a lawyer and businessman, concerned above all with the project's practical aspects; Krawitz was basically a technician interested in stagecraft; Bing was a European impresario rooted in nineteenth-century tradition, who, in his own words, insisted that "The Met is a museum, not an avant-garde theater or a place for tryouts."[22] All in all, they were very different clients from the likes of John D. Rockefeller, Jr., Nelson Rockefeller, or Trygve Lie—practical, decisive men with the means and the power to implement their every decision quickly.

By the time the advisory architects held their first meeting in October 1956, Harrison had worked for over a year on the Lincoln Center plans in general and the plans for the opera in particular. As a long-standing member of the opera's New House Committee, he was well aware of the project's requirements. For advice on the building's theatrical engineering he had chosen George C. Izenour, a professor of theater design and technology and director of the Electro-Mechanical Laboratory at the Yale School of Drama, and Jo Mielziner, the stage designer. For acoustics, he had brought in Hugh Bagenal, a British expert who had just completed work on the London Festival Hall; Bagenal was to collaborate with Bolt, Beranek & Newman. Because of the lack of recent theater construction in America, there had been little opportunity for Americans to prove themselves in a situation comparable to the one at Lincoln Center.

Izenour was known for his revolutionary ideas about theater technology; his innovations were designed to mechanize many chores previously performed manually and to make the effects they produced more impressive.[23] For the new opera house, Izenour recommended not only the latest technology but also a wedge-shaped, as opposed to the traditional horseshoe-shaped, auditorium[24] (related to the shape proposed by Urban). Krawitz and Bing were more conventional in their thinking, and by September 1956, Krawitz had rejected Harrison's request to hire Izenour and Mielziner.[25] In their stead the Met Building Committee invited Walther Unruh, the German theater specialist, to attend the advisory architects' first meetings. Dogged in his preference for everything European, Bing was more comfortable dealing with Unruh, who was eventually engaged to advise on stage technology.[26]

Bagenal was eliminated as a possible acoustical advisor early in the discussions. Despite general mistrust on the part of the opera people toward Bolt, Beranek & Newman (perhaps well founded in view of the disappointing results of their work at Philharmonic Hall), the firm continued to advise on acoustics until Cyril M. Harris appeared on the scene in 1962.

These disagreements about technical consultants were disturbing to Harrison, but more so were the widely differing conceptions of the opera house itself with which the management presented him. References were made to the suggestion of Francis Robinson, an assistant manager, that, among others, the Beaux-Arts San Francisco War Memorial Opera House (1932) might be taken as a model.[27] The 3,252-seat, multipurpose San Francisco auditorium had twenty-five boxes with excellent

190. Harrison, scheme for Metropolitan Opera House at Lincoln Center (fall 1956). "My sketches for the opera house started with a bird, like Sidney" (Harrison's statement to author, 8 April 1982).

sight lines, but no other semicircular tiers. Even less acceptable to Harrison were examples suggested by Robinson later with conductor Max Rudolph: the Elliott Hall of Music at Purdue University (1940), the Indiana University Auditorium (1941), and the Fox Theater in Atlanta (1929). The architect was amazed by these preferences for what seemed to him outmoded, provincial theaters. He protested to Bliss that such suggestions were "like comparing an autobus and a Rolls Royce," and that they should be thinking instead on the grand scale of La Scala or the Vienna Opera.[28] Harrison continued to think along precisely these lines; using a form that was to appear later in Jörn Utzon's prize-winning design for the Sydney Opera House in Australia (published 1957), he made hundreds of sketches of evocative sail-like shapes that are echoed in one of Hugh Ferriss's later renderings of Lincoln Center (Figs. 190, 191). In this same expressionistic mode, Harrison produced a design for a boldly faceted crystalline structure similar to the First Presbyterian Church in Stamford (Fig. 192; see Fig. 146).[29]

In the fall of 1955, about the time Harrison had started to work on the Met design, he received a commission for the Hopkins Center, a performing arts complex at Dartmouth College. Nelson Rockefeller, an alumnus of the college, was chairman of the building committee, and he proposed Harrison. The college had been raising money for this badly needed facility for over thirty years, and those in charge of the project responded with a warm expression of appreciation to the architect's care and sensitivity. That Harrison's design for the center broke with the college's two-hundred-year tradition of architectural conservatism reflects the trust placed in him. The small Dartmouth building committee, which included members of the center's faculty, worked out the program with Harrison, who designed and built the facility on schedule and within the allotted budget of $7 million.

The Hopkins Center includes a 450-seat theater, student and alumni halls, numerous studios and workshops, and a 900-seat auditorium. The center is set prominently on a green surrounded by brick Colonial buildings, and Harrison looked for a solution that would

do justice to this prominent location. With his usual interest in experimentation, he asked the structural engineers Paul Weidlinger and Mario Salvadori to develop a system of hanging cables from the stage area to supports at the building's façade (Fig. 193). Harrison hoped that this structural concept would allow a tall enclosure for the stage area with a gentle roof curve projecting toward the façade. When the engineer's calculations showed that this curve would be too low for the auditorium, the scheme was abandoned.

It was inconceivable that Harrison work in the traditional historic mode used for the campus; but, at the same time, alumni protest about the modernity of his first scheme led him to a solution that he felt would be compatible with the existing neo-Georgian architecture. According to his own account, his second scheme combined structural innovation with historic precedent in its allusion to the form of Florence's fourteenth-century Loggia dei Lanzi (Fig. 194a, b).[30] The arches were intended to echo the windows of the neo-Georgian library across the green, using thin, concrete shells, structurally similar to arches erected by Felix Candela in Mexico and by Pier Luigi Nervi in Italy, but with few precedents in the United States. To test the soundness of the three-inch-thick arches, Weidlinger and Salvadori used the design first for a five-car garage. Convinced that the method was viable, Harrison made the arch the module for the Hopkins Center. From its obligatory use, as the location of the post office, the Hopkins became an active cultural center for Dartmouth College and the surrounding area. Whatever the building's aesthetic shortcomings, it has served its purpose well.

By the spring of 1958, a design featuring a variation of the staid arches of the Hopkins Center had replaced Harrison's earlier schemes for the Metropolitan Opera House.[31] The roof was removed to expose the barrel vaults of a double arcade enclosing structurally independent stage and seating; the two parts of the arcaded shell were to be separated by an insulating space.[32] The Met façade was to have five glazed arches, each more than eight stories high in front; a vaulted ceiling, 228 feet wide and 225 feet long, hung on a cantilever principle, extended over the lobby and auditorium to meet a

191. Harrison, scheme for Lincoln Center. Rendering by Hugh Ferriss.

192. Harrison, scheme for Metropolitan Opera House at Lincoln Center (28 October 1957). Rendering by Hugh Ferriss.

193. Harrison, early scheme for Hopkins Center, Dartmouth College, Hanover, New Hampshire (1957). Rendering by Paul Sample.

194. Harrison, Hopkins Center (1962).
a) Façade.

b) Plan.

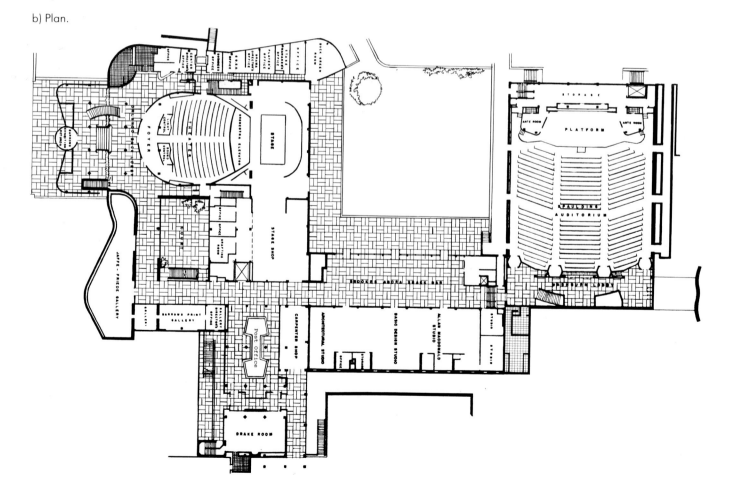

195. Harrison, model, Metropolitan Opera House (spring 1958).

fourteen-story stage loft. The north and south sides of the building were to be flanked by recessed, lower wings (Fig. 195).

Harrison's early drawings, made before the participating architects were chosen, had included all the Lincoln Center buildings. Certainly, the introduction of distinct designs for the constituents became a major element in his subsequent thinking. And, of course, the schematic, promotional concepts he had first presented required adjustments to the program's practicalities. But what had become of his fanciful reinterpretation of Bernini? His dramatic, tile-covered domes? The shimmering facets of his crystalline design? Compared with any one of these early projects, the arcaded design of 1958 is hard to imagine as the product of the same hand. During the three years Harrison had worked on the Lincoln Center opera house design, he had suffered conflicting instructions, changes in programs, and differences of opinion with the client and the other Lincoln Center architects.[33] Were these pressures so debilitating that they discouraged him completely from pursuing his more ambitious ideas?

In May 1958 John Rockefeller released Harrison's arcaded design to the press.[34] Nowhere was the wide divergence of attitudes among the Lincoln Center architects demonstrated more clearly than in their reactions to this design for the Met's exterior: for Breuer it was "dignified," for Johnson it was "flamboyant."[35] But the estimated cost of realizing the design came to $30 million—$7 million more than Harrison's original estimate; consequently, although the necessary committees and the other Lincoln Center architects eventually approved the plan, cost cuts were called for.

By November 1958 the architects estimated that total costs for the complex would be $79.4 million, sixty-four percent over the $48.5 million construction budget,[36] and John Rockefeller asked all the Lincoln Center architects—regardless of the various stages of completion and approval of their designs—to alter their plans in order to reduce costs by twenty-five percent. By this time, Krawitz was so dissatisfied with the project's development that he was calling for the dismissal of both Harrison and Abramovitz.[37]

Harrison had already made major changes for economy; confronted with this new call for reductions, he further squeezed the opera's cubic volume, sacrificing the Opera Guild offices, the Opera Club, the ballet school, two rehearsal stages, four rehearsal rooms, a museum and exhibition area, an archival area, two passenger elevators, all double-deck elevators (which were reduced to single-deck), and ten percent of the lobby space and auditorium circulation. These changes lowered the estimated cost to $26 million.[38] Krawitz called the new house "adequate," whereupon Bing declared that "to build only an adequate and not the best opera house possible today in New York City would make the country the laughing stock of the world, and the opera a subject of Russian propaganda."[39]

There ensued a painful round of new designs, new estimates, and redesign, which lasted more than a year (Fig. 196). Harrison had to his credit several successful auditoriums and his part in Radio City Music Hall, one of the most spectacular theaters of all time, but he was unwilling to fight for any one particular solution. He had become convinced that nothing he came up with could please everyone in this clash of opposing interests. In desperation, at a meeting on October 28, 1959, attended by the architects, John Rockefeller, Rockefeller's assistant, Edgar Young, and C. D. Jackson, Harrison presented two different designs and threw the choice open for the others to make. The first design was the earlier, barrel-vaulted scheme, while the second enclosed the vaults in a stiff rectangular frame; both included the slab-shaped office building behind the opera that Harrison had proposed for services in early schemes (Fig. 197; see also Figs. 186, 189). Except for Abramovitz, who favored the contrast of the first project's sculptural form with the overall rectilinearity of Lincoln Center, the architects preferred the classical design of the second project.[40] The Rockefeller group went along with this solution, which approximates what we see today.[41]

Thinking back to the long sessions at Lincoln Center, Harrison recalled similar disagreements among the architects at Rockefeller Center. But there were important differences between the two situations. At Rockefeller Center the Associated Architects had worked

214

196. Harrison, schemes for Metropolitan Opera House (1958–
59). Note seven-bay scheme at lower left.

197. Harrison, model, Metropolitan Opera House (28 October
1959).

together on all the buildings; it was therefore imperative that they eventually reach agreement. At Lincoln Center each architect was responsible only for his own part of the complex; each jealously guarded his autonomy, yet wanted a say in his neighbor's work. The situation encouraged the most negative kind of competitiveness, as Harrison said:

> So we . . . worked with models and that made it easier to get along with each other. Well, on Lincoln Center I don't believe Eero [liked] the Opera. I know Bunshaft didn't. I know Johnson didn't. But nobody ever came up with anything any better that we could see, because back in the very beginning, when we had Breuer and Markelius and Aalto, people like that on it, we never could agree with them either. So I don't think it was just me. It was just that people don't necessarily see things the same way.[42]

At the meeting in October 1959, a practical question arose that would also dramatically affect Harrison's design. It was pointed out that the additional heating and air-conditioning necessitated by the large areas of glass in the three main Lincoln Center buildings would entail expensive maintenance costs. Harrison and Abramovitz had advocated glass façades for these buildings to create an interplay of movement between the people inside and those outside, and, with the exception of Johnson, the other architects liked this solution. Bliss, however, insisted that extensive glazing was impractical; throughout the winter of 1959–60 he sat in on the architects' meetings and repeated his objection until Harrison proposed another design with less glass. It was roundly rejected by the other Lincoln Center architects.[43]

By this time, expense had become the overriding criterion for everything connected with the building of Lincoln Center. The astronomic escalation of costs was due to a number of factors—among them, misleading preliminary estimates, rising prices, and changes in the program. The New York State Theater provided the single exception to the general pattern of deficit-induced design changes. Soon after the Metropolitan Opera and the New York Philharmonic were established

as the nucleus of Lincoln Center, the dance theater was included and the New York City Ballet designated as its most likely occupant. The New York City Ballet was a part of the City Center of Music and Drama, with no independent institutional existence of its own; but Lincoln Kirstein, its co-founder in 1948 with George Balanchine, and a passionate devotee of dance, was a member of the Lincoln Center Exploratory Committee and was determined to bring the ballet there.[44] Kirstein, the brilliant, autocratic impresario, poet, critic, and editor, had already chosen Philip Johnson in the fall of 1957 as the architect for the Lincoln Center dance theater. Johnson seems simply to have carried out Kirstein's instructions as to what George Balanchine, the director of the New York City Ballet, wanted the new theater to be.[45]

The dance theater was also financed more easily than the other constituents, in large part through the efforts of Nelson Rockefeller, who had been elected governor of New York in November 1958. Lincoln Center's combination of culture and monumental building was irresistible to the new governor; and he suggested to the city a relationship between Lincoln Center's dance theater and the 1964–65 New York World's Fair that provided an excuse for state funding to match the city's. (The agreement was signed April 6, 1961.) With financing spoken for, there was little interference from the Lincoln Center committees; with no official constituent for the building, there could be no active constituent committees. The dance theater was consequently built on schedule, with few design revisions, and within one percent of its authorized budget.[46]

By April 1960, estimates for Lincoln Center were still well over budget, with a total estimate of $142.5 million, almost twice the fund-raising goal of $75 million established in 1956. By this time Harrison was projecting a cost of $40 million for the opera house, and he became the target of intense pressure to again redesign the opera for economy.[47] Taking this as an opportunity to better accommodate their own designs, several of the collaborating architects called for the incorporation of their own radical changes in the opera.

It was the last blow for Harrison, who interrupted Bliss's vacation to inform him of his exasperation. At the time Bliss was staying in a Rocky Mountain camp with which all telephone communications had been severed by an electric storm. He actually had to climb a telephone pole to take Harrison's call. According to Bliss, the architect was in an uncharacteristically agitated state, and told him:

> Tony, they want the south side of the Opera to line up with the State Theater façade and the north side with the Philharmonic façade; the façade of the opera pulled back and more space between the buildings, which means the opera house will have to be shorter and narrower.[48]

Just about every aspect of Harrison's design had been subjected to modification, and these new demands threatened the very essence of his concept. To make the opera house shorter and narrower, he would have to eliminate the two recessed bays at either side, which already had been squeezed. He would have to place some of the rooms that were to have occupied these bays over the auditorium, thereby altering the structural principles and organization on which he had based his design.[49] Furthermore, the entrance would have to be cut back so substantially that what he had planned as a large, elegant lobby would be reduced to a skimpy envelope for the main stairway. Harrison explained this to Bliss in a last-ditch effort to save what remained of his design. Bliss was horrified to find himself forced to make a momentous decision without the help of the opera board, most of whose members were already scattered for their vacations. By his own admission, he was ill qualified to make such a decision; with no strong convictions of his own, he chose to go along with the other architects' wishes.

The changes were accepted, with devastating results. Harrison's original plan had called for structurally independent stage and seating areas enclosed within a double shell. Reduction of the lateral bays affected the areas for the Met's administrative offices, the opera club, and the opera guild's Belmont Room, and for the ample lobbies between them and the auditorium. These offices and private rooms were relocated between the auditorium and the outer shell, narrowing the lobbies and mak-

ing it difficult for the audience to get in and out of the orchestra. The shortening affected the grand tier, where very little space was left for the audience to circulate between the main stairwell and the glass façade (Figs. 198, 199). Although Harrison was still nominally the architect for the Met, essentially his design had been obliterated.

The summer of 1960 dealt a decisive blow to Harrison's opera house; it also marked the first serious questioning of the twenty-story office tower he had planned behind it, having envisioned that the taller building's windowless east façade would serve as a backdrop for the opera (Fig. 200). In addition to housing the opera's administrative facilities the tower was to provide extra revenue for the Metropolitan. It was the same idea that Morris had proposed thirty-three years earlier for Otto Kahn's new opera house, that Corbett and Harrison had used soon afterward for the Riverside (Roerich) Museum and Master Apartments, and that recently has been adopted widely as a means to bolster the finances of a number of nonprofit institutions.

Gordon Braislin, the real estate specialist, claimed that it would be impossible to rent windowless space,[50] even though it was to be occupied exclusively by conference and utility rooms, which were often constructed without windows. In response to this objection Harrison made a few halfhearted attempts to design a window pattern for the tower's east façade (Fig. 201); but by June 1961 the Lincoln Center building subcommittee decided to suppress the tower, claiming that there was an insufficient market for office space in the Lincoln Center neighborhood to justify construction costs. As questionable as the tower may have been aesthetically, the practical grounds on which it was rejected could not have been more ill founded. Its elimination forced even more service facilities into the opera house's already crowded peripheries.

Every summer seemed to bring a new crisis to the opera project. Early in 1961 the Lincoln Center directors became convinced that Harrison was incapable of producing a design within their budget, and they began seriously to consider a change of architect. They

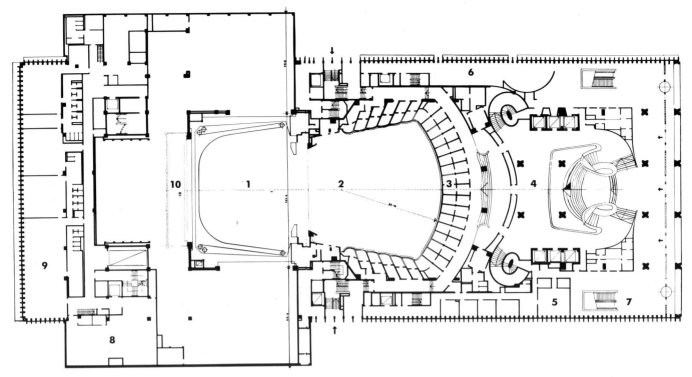

198. Box level plan, Metropolitan Opera House. Drawing by
E. M. Feher.

1. Main stage
2. Auditorium
3. Boxes
4. Public areas
5. Executive offices
6. Bar
7. Escalators
8. Storage area (wardrobe)
9. Costume shops
10. Paint frame area (next level above)

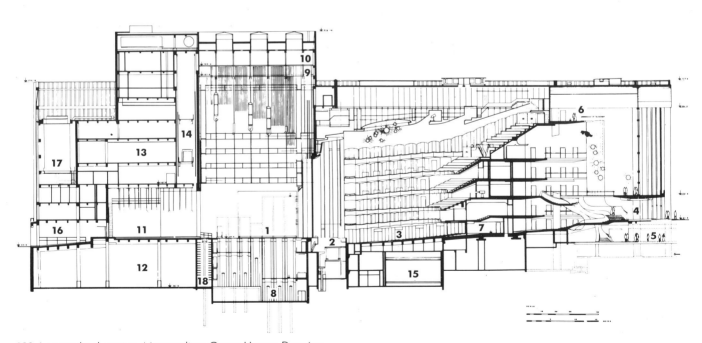

199. Longitudinal section, Metropolitan Opera House. Drawing
by E. M. Feher.

1. Main stage
2. Orchestra space
3. Auditorium
4. Main lobby (entrance Plaza Level)
5. Lower lobby (entrance Garage Level)
6. Restaurant
7. Control (lighting-sound)
8. Mechanical area (sub-stage)
9. First grid (working level)
10. Second grid (motor drives-107 stage pipes)
11. Back stage
12. Scenery storage
13. Shops
14. Paint frame area
15. Rehearsal area
16. Loading platform
17. Air-conditioning cooling towers (supplying all facilities of Lincoln Center)
18. Drop cut

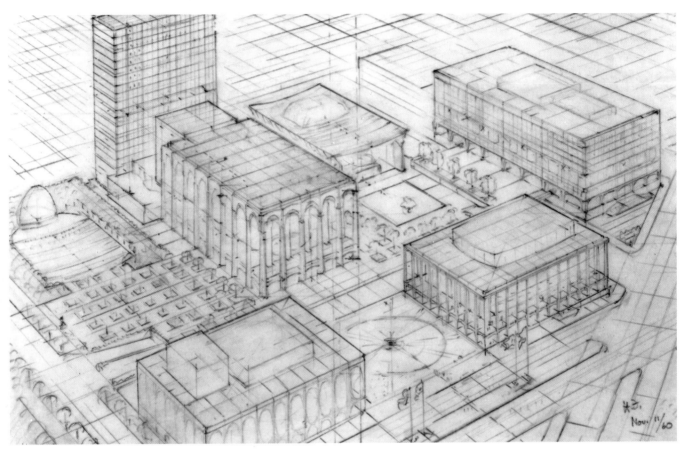

200. Lincoln Center. The Metropolitan Opera House is shown with its office tower (11 November 1960). Rendering by Hugh Ferriss.

201. Harrison, alternate proposals for the tower façade behind the Metropolitan Opera House (3 November 1960).

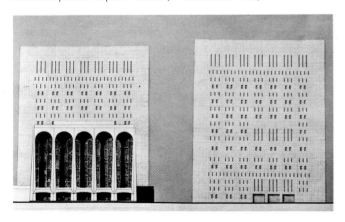

202. Harrison, Metropolitan Opera House, with louvered sides (December 1961). At right is the Vivian Beaumont Theater.

acknowledged some of the arguments he might be expected to use in his own defense, among them the "unreasonable demands of the opera, weak Lincoln Center management in making decisions, impossible working arrangements and interference from the panel of architects and the evils of 'committee design.' "[51] In June a meeting was held between Bliss, John Rockefeller, and Harrison, at which the architect later claimed he was "fired."[52] Harrison had threatened to leave the job a number of times in the past, and this might have been another such occasion; but in view of the board's misgivings, Rockefeller and Bliss now accepted his threat. Whatever happened at this confrontation (Bliss left it in such a disturbed state that he failed to see an oncoming taxi and was knocked down by it),[53] Harrison referred to it with bitterness to the end of his life. As it turned out, the architect was not fired, but given six weeks in which

to draw up new plans within the allotted budget,[54] and on July 7 he presented to the executive committee of the Metropolitan Opera Association plans that conformed with their financial restrictions. To achieve this, he had eliminated the stage elevators and a turntable, as well as the Opera Club (withdrawn and reinstated on several previous occasions) and two blocks of stage workshops, and had relocated dressing-room and rehearsal spaces. In the course of these alterations, Harrison had also pared down what he regarded as Bing's extravagant technological demands. Estimates for stage equipment had varied from $2,648,000 (Gallagher & Speck, Chicago) to $8,882,000 (Wiener Bruckenbau, Austria);[55] Harrison understandably opted for the lower bidder. Bing immediately pronounced the plans unacceptable on the grounds that the stage equipment was inadequate.[56]

203. Some of the men who made Lincoln Center. From left to right: Edward Mathews (SOM), Philip Johnson, Joseph Mielziner, Harrison, John D. Rockefeller 3d, Eero Saarinen, Gordon Bunshaft, Max Abramovitz, Pietro Belluschi.

In December Harrison presented "another new model," described in the minutes of an executive committee meeting as "acceptable to the other Lincoln Center architects."[57] The Building Committee and the directors of Lincoln Center also approved this design, which retained Harrison's façade but at Bliss's insistence substituted modified louvers at three-feet-four-inch intervals for the arches on the sides (Fig. 202). Minor compared with the conceptual design changes of the previous year, this alteration nevertheless concluded the transformation of Harrison's ideas.

The very nature of an architectural commission, with its attendant restrictions, makes purity of design a rarity; the larger the commission the less pure it is likely to be.[58] The Metropolitan Opera House is a case study of the extent to which an architect can compromise, and the price that is paid for such compromise. Some architects have refused any compromise; more numerous are those who have refused to compromise beyond a certain point. When Lincoln Center was still in its planning stage, Ralph Walker turned down the commission for a band shelter in what was to become Damrosch Park because he was convinced that the park's proximity to heavily trafficked streets rendered the program impossible to execute. More recently, I. M. Pei preferred to sacrifice the time he had spent on remodeling the Vivian Beaumont Theater rather than accept the restrictions imposed by Cyril Harris's acoustical requirements. Had Harrison known beforehand the extent of his design compromises, he would perhaps not have accepted the Lincoln Center commission. As it was, only his strict sense of obligation can explain his ability to have persevered (Fig. 203).

Chapter 18

The Metropolitan Opera House: completion

Harrison's difficulties were far from over when at last construction began of what by then was his forty-third set of plans for the opera house. For one thing, the Metropolitan Opera Building Committee, advised on technology by Walther Unruh, complained of a lack of cooperation on the part of Harrison and the engineers.[1] Encouraged by Bing, Unruh pushed for complex and costly stage equipment; Harrison's questioning of whether this expensive gadgetry might be less indispensable to the Met's next director than it was to Bing provoked Unruh's complaint of "deviations and deterioration" regarding his plans.[2] Having had to make so many changes himself in the interests of economy, Harrison could sympathize with Unruh on this score, even though he knew that as the architect he alone would bear responsibility for all aspects of the opera house. Indeed, Unruh quoted Harrison as saying: "In the end nobody will blame the general contractor (who remains anonymous), the architect is the one they'll hang."[3]

According to an American tradition, the client for a large public project is expected to employ a person with military background to supervise construction. The practice is based on the assumption that a former officer accustomed to dealing with the mammoth organization of the military has the know-how to cope with the intricacies of any large building project. Accordingly, in April 1957 retired Major General Otto L. Nelson, Jr., then a vice-president in charge of housing for the New York Life Insurance Company, was asked to head a special Lincoln Center, Inc. staff for building. Nelson's work related mainly to the acquisition of land and the eviction of tenants—a job he dispatched with maximum efficiency. Additionally, he authorized the formation of a joint venture of four contractors who were to construct the center. It proved to be an impractical arrangement.[4]

In the spring of 1959, with construction scheduled to begin, the directors of Lincoln Center appointed Colonel William F. Powers Nelson's deputy. Powers, a retired officer of the Army Corps of Engineers with a long list of major construction projects to his name, soon found that dealing with New York contractors and their construction unions was a different proposition from working with military men bound to obey strict orders. The revised estimates Powers received upon coming to the job were described by C. D. Jackson as the "first trip together to the cold shower."[5] As we have seen, within a year these estimates had again risen dramatically, and the alarmed Lincoln Center directors decided that someone besides John Rockefeller was needed to coordinate and control the architects and the respective committees. This time General Maxwell D. Taylor, an even more prestigious military man, was chosen to exert the authority that was needed to check the increasingly chaotic situation. In January 1961, Taylor replaced Rockefeller as president of Lincoln Center, and Rockefeller became chairman of the board. Soon after, the architects began to express their concern at the degree to which they were being asked to change their designs for the sake of economy. They unanimously recommended to Taylor that he cut back the building programs rather than allow costs to further influence the designs.[6] Taylor, however, never had the chance to act on this, or any other, aspect of the project—after four months in New York, President Kennedy summoned him to Washington to conduct a special assignment in the aftermath of the Bay of Pigs.

Three years of construction problems ensued before the Lincoln Center, Inc. committee finally turned for help to a man with experience in large-scale commercial development: Carl Morse, chairman of Morse-Diesel, one of the country's most successful construction companies. Morse cultivated his image as a tough guy who had made it on his own the hard way and, among his other oddities, delighted in referring to himself as "Mr. S.O.B."[7]

Once he came to Lincoln Center (to which he donated his consulting services free of charge), Morse's first move was to dissolve the joint venture of contractors, to which he referred with his usual bluntness as "a corporate structure for stupidity."[8] He also short-circuited the roundabout system of committees that the architects had contended with until then. At first the architects had consulted with the constituent building committees and reported to the constituents' boards, but as cost became an increasingly important factor in the design of each building, direct contact between the architects and their constituents' boards had been denied on the grounds that the

architects were too persuasive![9] They were asked to report to the constituents' building committees, which reported to their constituent boards, which reported to the Lincoln Center directors. Morse insisted on personally reporting the contractors' prices to the constituents' boards. He proved to be the only person with sufficient knowledge, self-confidence, and toughness to enforce decisions. In fact, Morse assumed the position that had been held by John D. Rockefeller, Jr., at Rockefeller Center and by Trygve Lie at the U.N.—and that should have been held by John D. Rockefeller 3d at Lincoln Center.[10]

The size and complexity of the opera house project magnified many of the problems suffered by each one of the constituents. Harrison had had to modify the exterior to satisfy the other Lincoln Center architects and Bliss; for the stage and the auditorium spaces he had been subject to the wishes of the Metropolitan Opera Building Committee. But there remained the opera house's interior décor; and in the spring of 1961, at a luncheon session at Sardi's attended by the architects, Bliss, Richard Bolt, Leo Beranek, and Robert Newman, the long-standing incompatibility between the acousticians and the others present was brought to a head.[11] When they were engaged for the Met's acoustics, Bolt, Beranek & Newman had proposed a movable ceiling area of approximately 175 by 200 feet; Harrison commented in retrospect:

> The idea of having that over your head, moving up and down with sixteen men who maintained the lighting system on that thing—with the problem of noise and squeaks and all the mechanics involved—was so great that I knew we weren't getting any place.[12]

Nevertheless, despite his initial reservations, Harrison suffered through five years of fruitless discussion before he replaced Bolt, Beranek & Newman with Vilhelm L. Jordan and Cyril M. Harris in 1961.

Jordan was a Danish acoustician, who was commuting to New York to work on the State Theater with Philip Johnson and to Australia to work on the opera house in Sydney. Harris, the holder of a Ph.D. in physics, was both a professor of architecture and a professor of electrical engineering at Columbia University. He had established himself as an authority on acoustics with the publication in 1950 of *Acoustical Designing in Architecture*, a book he had written in collaboration with Vern Knudsen, who had trained Bolt, Beranek, and Newman. As early as 1959 Krawitz had tried to engage Harris as an acoustical consultant to the Met, but at the time Harris was embarking on a year's sabbatical in Japan.[13] Two years later Harrison asked Vilhelm Jordan to consult for the Met on acoustics. On September 27, 1961, Jordan wrote Harris telling him of Harrison's offer and the practical reasons why he needed an American collaborator: Jordan intended to apply the same procedure to the opera house that he was using at the State Theater—a relatively new method of acoustical analysis based on models through which are generated ultrasonic wavelengths (sound waves above the audible range of frequencies) scaled down in the same proportion as the linear dimensions of the model.[14] Given such large auditoriums as the New York State Theater and the Metropolitan Opera, the one-tenth-scale models Jordan proposed were big, cumbersome structures. A model of the State Theater already occupied Jordan's entire work space in New York, and the Met project presented him with the logistical problem of coordinating the research he wanted to pursue in his Copenhagen studio with the actual building of two auditoriums in New York. Jordan hoped to solve the problem with Harris's collaboration on an equal basis.

The men had previously met once, approximately ten years earlier, in London. A genius who was obsessively committed to perfection and a loner par excellence, Harris was at first skeptical about working with another acoustician (something he claimed he had done only once before). But he was intrigued by the challenging opera house project, and in the spring of 1962 he consented to join Jordan in signing a contract with the Met. At the outset the two men were so concerned about presenting a unified front that they had a joint letterhead printed to reinforce the image of their partnership. This period of harmony was short-lived. From the beginning Harris had misgivings about Jordan's use of acoustical models, and he made several trips to Jordan's thatch-roofed studio on the outskirts of Copenhagen to elicit further explanations of his associate's application of the method to the State Theater. After a year's study Harris concluded that the ultrasonic frequency range models did not accurately reflect conditions in a real auditorium, because Jordan was not properly taking into account the nature of the materials used and the degree of humidity that might be present. There was also continuous friction between the acousticians regarding public statements about their work: while Jordan constantly tried to publicize his use of models, Harris insisted that models had in no way affected the design.[15] Fearing that his name would be connected with a technique that he adamantly repudiated, Harris became alarmed about his association with Jordan. He went to considerable lengths to dispel the connection, even insisting that Jordan destroy their joint letterhead stationery.[16]

Harris's refusal to work with Jordan's acoustical models ruled out any possible agreement on how best to assure the acoustics of the opera house. There were other disagreements as well: Jordan wanted to hang vertically suspended acoustical clouds, approximately ten feet by ten feet, over the orchestra pit and to affix horizontal reflector banks above the backs of each chair in the auditorium. Harris was convinced that neither measure would significantly affect the acoustics of the house.[17] The practical outcome of these conflicting opinions was that Harris, who was on the spot, decided to ignore Jordan and work directly with the architect. As Harris himself said matter-of-factly: "Jordan was over there with his models and I was here day by day."[18] Harris's "day-by-day" contact with Harrison was as pleasant and productive as his dealings with Jordan had been problematic. He later claimed that Harrison was the only architect he had ever known whom, out of respect, he addressed only by his surname: "You shook hands with Mr. Harrison, you didn't need a contract with him. He was a gentleman of the old school."

When Harris came to the opera project, he had advised on the acoustics of about fifty relatively minor auditoriums and theaters across the country and one in Havana, participating in decisions about size, shape, and number of seats for each hall. Before he was engaged by the Metropolitan Opera, plans for a seating total of 3,800 seats already had been established, calling for five levels of horseshoe-shaped tiers above the orchestra level. In fact, serious doubts had been raised about the size of the hall in relation to the quality of sound that could be achieved in it. According to Harrison:

> We had been told by all the people we had visited in Europe that a good hall should not be more than 3,000 seats. When you get beyond that you lose the resonance to some extent. But we had to have 3,800 to satisfy the Opera's need for income. So torn between the two we built the hall to 3,800 [in reality, 3,765] seats and we asked the acoustical man to do the best job he could for that number.[19]

There remained for the "acoustical man" all-important questions regarding the detailed shape of the house, balcony depths, and materials to be used. These decisions were made almost solely on the basis of their acoustical implications.

Sound reaches a listener directly from the stage and indirectly from reflections bounced off an auditorium's inner surfaces. The elaborate plaster and wood ornament favored in the nineteenth century was ideal for acoustics because it broke up sound to a maximum degree; unadorned, rectilinear, modern interiors do just the opposite. The reconciliation of acoustical requirements with modern lines and the increased seating capacities necessitated by present-day economics remains one of the most troublesome and challenging problems of contemporary design. Harrison had dealt with acoustical problems in the meeting halls at the U.N., at the Stamford church, and at the auditoriums at Oberlin College and Rockefeller University. He was therefore keenly aware of the complexities of acoustical engineering and eager for dependable guidance in this crucial area.

Harris explained that sound dies if its waves hit too many flat, vertical surfaces, and so the front of each balcony was made convex with a central slice inward to deflect sound down toward the orchestra level. The size of each balcony was also subject to acoustical considerations: if the balcony is too big, sound remains trapped

underneath it. (A full-scale model of one box was made to try out the seating Harris proposed.) Because a fixed number of spectators had to be accommodated in the balconies to achieve the total required capacity, the height of the box area was reduced so that the balconies immediately above them could be expanded. This alteration affected the uniformity Harrison had intended for the different levels of horizontal seating.[20] Additionally, two boxes on each tier were sacrificed to allow for the installation surrounding the proscenium of a large "mix" panel which Harrison topped with a Mary Callery sculpture; the panel would blend the sound of the orchestra as it rose from the pit.[21]

Harris made equally drastic changes for the auditorium ceiling, which he insisted must have an irregular surface to scatter sound. He also asked that the ceiling be suspended on springs to isolate it from energy released by the tremendous amount of mechanical equipment needed for the stage and for temperature control. (The floor sits on a cushion of lead and cork, thereby completely isolating the auditorium from its enclosing shell.)

Harrison wanted a spectacular central chandelier to be the focal point for the interior when the curtain was down. With these technical and aesthetic requirements in mind, he designed the ceiling's stepped circular forms (Fig. 204), selecting the irregular, claret-colored wood sheathing (of West African Kewazinga) on the side and rear walls for its acoustical properties.[22] Only the gold fluting on the balcony cuts and the waffle pattern on the proscenium mix are without acoustical significance.

A number of other decorative details, such as the color of the seats and the satin swags and light clusters adorning the balcony fronts, were imposed, against Harrison's repeated protests, by yet another committee—a decorating committee that included Mrs. J. B. Ryan (chairman), Lucrezia Bori, Mrs. Francis Gibbs, and Mr. Robert Lehman (Figs. 205, 206).[23] No record of a decision to create this committee, no complete list of its members, no minutes of its meetings have been found. Yet the demands imposed on Harrison by this group were the hardest for him to swallow. Perhaps because they were made by predominantly non-professionals who relied on the techniques of interior decoration

204. Harrison with model of Metropolitan Opera House interior.

205. Interior, Metropolitan Opera House, with balconies as
Harrison designed them (spring 1966).

206. Interior, Metropolitan Opera House, with swags added to
the balconies (fall 1966). Sculpture above proscenium by Mary
Callery.

rather than on those of architecture (as they were used, for example, at Radio City Music Hall),[24] they irritated him more intensely than some of the most extreme alterations required of his design. Later in his life he referred more often to the absurdity of permanently draping the opera's balconies with satin swags than he did to any other modification of his ideas for the Met.

A few weeks before the opera house was completed, an orchestra and singers were brought in for trial runs. On one such occasion Harrison heard parts of *Don Giovanni*, which to him "sounded more beautiful than you'd ever hear again." But just days later, during another tryout, the architect sat in the same seat and could hear almost nothing. He changed seats and heard perfectly. Returning to the original seat in Row J, he could again hear almost nothing. Upon investigation, Harrison discovered that the removal of a single absorbent board to fix a light had been sufficient to upset the acoustical relationship with one seat. This detail troubled him, and he walked around the auditorium worrying about other details that might have been overlooked. Years later he remembered his anguish:

> Imagine what you would do! You sit there and think: "I've spent about twenty-five years working on this Opera. I've spent some forty odd millions of other people's money on the Opera. And I can't hear anything!" Well, you ask yourself: where do you go? I mean it's almost worse than killing someone.[25]

The final test came on April 11, 1966, when a full-scale opera rehearsal of Puccini's *La fanciulla del West* was scheduled, the last of the yearly Opera Guild–sponsored afternoon performances for students. Architect and acoustician sat together, waiting for what Harrison later referred to as the "$45 million aria." They watched some three thousand children file to their seats, and Harrison mumbled with a smile, "I wonder if the balcony is going to hold up when it's filled with people." It was a revealing quip from this accomplished designer, who, despite his achievements, never ceased to question his own work. Not only did the balcony hold up, but five minutes after the curtain rose it was apparent to techni-

cians and critics alike that the opera's acoustics were excellent.[26] Harris, who had climbed to the last row of the balcony, could hear the slap of every discarded card during the miners' game of faro. The Metropolitan Opera House remains to this day the only large auditorium at Lincoln Center that has not been redesigned because of faulty acoustics.

As for the outer lobby, the filling of what had been planned as soaring, open areas facing the glass façade created two huge walls at either side.[27] The Metropolitan Opera Art Committee decided, against Harrison's wishes, to adorn these walls with two large paintings they wanted to be visible from the plaza (Fig. 207). Harrison was opposed to the placement of paintings in this location—he had suggested that they be hung on the north and south walls rather than the west walls—as well as to the choice of Marc Chagall, whose work of the last forty years he regarded as a conservative cliché. But Chagall was a name familiar to the public at large. Besides, Chagall's wife was a close friend of Bing's wife, and so Chagall it was who received the commission and produced *Les Sources de la Musique* and *Le Triomphe de la Musique* (the latter incorporating portraits of Bing and ballerina Maya Plisetskaya). A rare note of bitterness tinged Harrison's reminiscence of the incident:

> I failed in not getting the paintings in the proper places. I picked Lehmbruck sculpture and I would have picked world-class artists like Léger but Bing was the boss, he ran the show. Bing didn't understand me and I didn't understand him. I remember his strutting out of one of the meetings on the Opera's décor like a toy soldier one day.

The opera's generous double staircase, which Harrison conceived in the grand manner of the Paris Opera, stands as he planned it before the elimination of the preceding entrance hall (Fig. 208). He had wanted to use white marble to sheathe the concrete balustrade and stairs. In its present circumstances, the stair appears cramped, and it is further impoverished by the crude texture of the balustrade. The lobby floor was to be in off-white terrazzo with inserted squares of dark marble; the east wall of the box offices and the stair parapets were

207. Harrison, façade, Metropolitan Opera House.

208. Harrison, grand staircases, entrance level, Metropolitan Opera House.

also to be faced with rich, dark marble. The cost of all these finishes was estimated at $450,000.[28] Not only was this considered excessive, and the special materials eliminated, but four months before opening night, Harrison was paying out of his own pocket for a design change in the rails of the main lobby.[29]

In three areas within the new house Harrison was able to execute his own ideas with relatively little interference, although two of these, ironically, no longer serve their original purpose. He designed an elegantly spacious restaurant, the Top of the Met, where a continuous glass façade provided the diner with a dazzling view of the Lincoln Center plaza below (Fig. 209). The restaurant's back wall was covered with three large canvases by Raoul Dufy, which had been painted in 1950 as scenery drops for Gilbert Miller's production of Jean Anouilh's *Ring Round the Moon*; at Harrison's request, they were donated to the opera by the producer.[30] Composed of charming scenes of people riding, eating, dancing, talking, and generally enjoying themselves, they gave a feeling of gaiety to what was designed as a fitting update of Sherry's, its legendary predecessor at the old Met. Shortly after the new opera house opened, however, the restaurant was discontinued on the grounds that it was not financially viable. The space is now occupied by ticketing computers.

For simple refreshments, Harrison also created a small Opera Café situated at the north side of the opera's ground floor (Fig. 210). This inward-looking area, decorated by designer Garth Huxtable, offered the operagoer an intimate alternative to the more formal restaurant above. In 1979 it was converted into a store for books on the performing arts, records, and memorabilia, which has proved more profitable than the sale of food and drink. Controlled by Harrison, the clear, straightforward design of both eating areas contrasts dramatically with the frumpiness of the neo-Georgian and Empire décors of the opera clubs, chosen by the Met's decorating committee.

Harrison was later able to alleviate at least one of the design losses he suffered at the Met. The Arnold and Marie Schwartz Atrium, inaugurated in 1979, helped to

209. Top of the Met restaurant, Metropolitan Opera House.

210. Garth Huxtable, Opera Café, Metropolitan Opera House.

230

solve the problem created by the elimination of his proposed office tower. The makeshift manner in which offices were crammed into the building's peripheries was highly impractical, not the least because of the long distances separating people who had to work together. (It was precisely the problem Harrison had managed to avoid—over Le Corbusier's objections—for the conference areas at the U.N.) One of the most pressing requests after the building's occupation was for improved space for the house manager and his staff of sixteen to twenty people, who deal with business and the media. Asked to study the problem, Harrison created a cheerful, light-filled office space in a former stairwell between the lobby and concourse levels at the building's southeast side.

The opera's official grand opening on September 16, 1966, was sold out; its least expensive family circle seats were priced for the occasion at $200 apiece. Lady Bird Johnson, representing the President of the United States and accompanying President and Mrs. Ferdinand Marcos of the Philippines, as well as the Mayor of New York City, John Lindsay, and his wife were among the numerous celebrities attending the event. The next day's *New York Times* described the evening as having provided "the kind of glamour the nation has come to associate with New York on a good day" (Figs. 211, 212).[31] At the gala white-tie dinner following the opera at the Top of the Met Restaurant, Harrison, who had made the opening possible, was seated neither at the presidential table nor with John D. Rockefeller 3d and his party. Apparently unruffled, however, he sat through dinner looking very much the handsome, distinguished elder statesman. Always fiercely supportive of her husband, Ellen Harrison remembers that "Wallace in his modest way just looked happy."[32]

Harrison loved classical music. Since his first exposure to opera as a young man in Manhattan he had looked for occasions to hear good music. The architect certainly derived satisfaction from the knowledge that he had created an acoustically perfect hall, with excellent sight lines and a workable stage area in a building that he was confident would function for many generations to come. Nevertheless, he had been deprived of many of the aesthetic decisions, and he must have had mixed feelings

211. Harrison at opening night, Metropolitan Opera House (16 September 1966).

212. Auditorium, Metropolitan Opera House, opening night.

on this evening, when at age seventy-one he found himself at the end of ten years' work. William Schuman, president of the Juilliard School, also present, remembers that Harrison all but repudiated his responsibility for the opera's design, remarking: "The Metropolitan Opera House will represent what the people wanted who supported opera in the middle of the twentieth century in New York."[33]

With 3,765 seats, the Metropolitan is the world's largest repertory opera house.[34] It was also the first opera house to be completely air-conditioned, and unlike La Scala and the Vienna opera, it uses no electronic amplification. Final costs have been estimated between $45 and $47.5 million. During its first season, the Met employed a staff of one thousand, controlled by fourteen different unions. The General Motors of Opera, as it was referred to, operated that year on a budget of $10 million, with a $2 million annual deficit.[35] By the 1985–86 season total expenses had risen to just under $74 million with a deficit of almost 24 million.[36]

Bing and his people had gotten what they wanted: for all its increased seating capacity, the new auditorium occupied only one-third of the building's structure, as opposed to two-thirds in the old Met. The enormously increased stage area included the main, cruciform stage with its three slip stages (right, left, and up center)— served by seven hydraulic stage lifts, two orchestra lifts, and two scenery lifts, motorized stage wagons, turntable and rigging—plus twenty-one rehearsal rooms.

The auditorium demonstrated a new kind of seating arrangement, which the music critic Irving Kolodin aptly named "Opera House on the American Plan."[37] By widening the arc of the horseshoe plan and flattening its curve, Harrison managed to combine the newer, fan shape he had considered originally with the traditional horseshoe plan. This solution pulled the first rise closer to the stage than in any previous large opera house. As these proportions reoccur in each rising tier, the viewer in any given seat is brought some ten feet nearer the stage. The heavily criticized "partial-view" seats so prevalent in the old opera house are reduced to only a handful in limited side boxes. The sight lines are also treated in a new way: instead of converging at midpoint of the

rear stage in the conventional manner, they meet at the front of the orchestra pit, providing a more comprehensive view of the stage and of the conductor. The "Americanization," or democratization, of the opera included the means of entrance and exit, which are the same for all ticket holders (see Figs. 198, 199).

Functionally, the new Metropolitan Opera House fulfilled almost to the letter the goals established by the New House Committee in 1950. The only substantial difference from the original program was that acoustical considerations had necessitated fewer seats (3,765 instead of 4,500). The opera's technical accomplishments, its consideration for audience, performer, and employee, were hailed, but not its architecture. Writing in the *New York Times*, Ada Louise Huxtable voiced the consensus of informed opinion when she called the opera "average, rather than adventurous or avant-garde,"[38] and referred to the "*retardataire* fussiness and esthetic indecision of the rest [of Lincoln Center, excluding the Beaumont Theater and the Juilliard School]."[39] It is revealing that when Harrison received the American Institute of Architects' coveted gold medal award the year after the opera's completion, an article in the Institute's journal began with a discussion of his lodge for Nelson Rockefeller rather than the new opera house.

Despite the disappointments, Lincoln Center stands as the first manifestation of a national cultural movement of almost fanatical proportions: over three thousand facilities for the performing arts were built in the United States during the 1960s.[40] Its successes and its failures served as a model for cultural centers around the country.

New York's center for the performing arts was conceived at a time of naïve optimism and self-confident ambition in the United States, before the doubts and defeats of the Vietnam War changed the national mood. Having been involved with the project from the beginning, Abramovitz recently noted the inordinate expectations Lincoln Center had inspired:

> Lincoln Center was to be the biggest and best of its kind in America. In addition, the association of John Rockefeller's name with such an undertaking

213. Lincoln Center, New York City. From left to right: State Theater (1964); Metropolitan Opera House (1966); Avery Fisher Hall (1962).

created a feeling of unlimited possibilities. The staff of each Lincoln Center constituent threw in every technical and design innovation they could think of. The sky was the limit. Then realistic estimates came in.[41]

In 1955, approximately at the time Lincoln Center was first discussed, President Eisenhower appointed a commission to study the possibility of building a national cultural center in the nation's capital. As at Lincoln Center, a committee served as client for the Washington complex, and, like Lincoln Center, its costs escalated and its design problems multiplied as the project progressed. In the 1950s Congress was still reluctant to spend public money for the arts, and three years passed before enactment of the National Cultural Center Act allowed the appointment of a board of trustees, who engaged an architect for the multitheater complex. The architect of their choice was Harrison's former draftsman Edward

Durell Stone, now nearing sixty and well established in his profession. The Washington project seemed to bring out the best in Stone. Adopting a format that had been discussed in the earliest planning sessions for Lincoln Center—a single building that would incorporate all the complex's different elements —he created what the critic Brendan Gill described as "an elaborate many-sided pavilion with several auditoriums unfolding like the petals of some enormous flower from a central gathering place and fanning out onto a terrace that, among fountains and gardens, dropped gracefully down to water's edge."[42] The $75 million estimate for the execution of this design was accepted by the board, but by 1961, when President Kennedy appointed Roger Stevens board chairman, costs had risen. Stevens's estimate came nearer to $100 million, and, perhaps remembering his brief involvement with Lincoln Center, he called for a new, less ambitious design, which is what we see today. It is a rectangular structure 630 feet long, 300 feet wide, and 100 feet high, veneered in white marble and surrounded by thin, fluted and gilded columns. The three major auditoriums (two theaters and an opera house) open off an immense sixty-foot-high promenade that runs the entire length of the building; a second, identical lobby extends at right angles from the promenade to the entrance. What is now called the John F. Kennedy Cultural Center has been variously described as a "Brobdingnagian shoebox, a beached whale, and the world's largest Kleenex box."[43]

Before the building was completed, the $30 million estimate for construction of this scaled-down version of the Kennedy Cultural Center had increased by more than one hundred percent (to $66.4 million).[44] Even with the lessons of Lincoln Center close at hand, Washington's cultural center suffered some of the same problems as its New York predecessor, as did many later cultural centers across the country.

The symmetrical arrangement of Lincoln Center's neoclassical buildings around a central plaza, distantly related to the classical scheme of Michelangelo's Campidoglio in Rome, also brings to mind Chicago's summation of Beaux-Arts principles in the Court of Honor at the 1893 World's Columbian Exposition, the so-called White City. In 1924 Louis Sullivan had accused the fair's revivalism of setting back the course of modern architecture by fifty years.[45] By the same token, critics in the mid-1960s judged retrograde Lincoln Center's return to an axial Beaux-Arts plan and the neoclassical façades of its main buildings (Fig. 213). In fact, there is a striking similarity between Lincoln Center's plan and arcade motif and the Gothenburg, Sweden, Götaplatsen, built from 1923 to 1934, in part by Sven Markelius (Fig. 214).

In retrospect, the 1960s have emerged as a time of extraordinary design complexity. The International Style that had dominated most of the century was suddenly the subject of increasing criticism, and the brutalist style, which was hailed for its flamboyant modernism in such buildings as Paul Rudolph's Art and Architecture Building at Yale (1962) and Kallmann, McKinnell & Knowles's Boston City Hall (1968) failed the test of time.[46] The way was opened for new ideas, many of

214. Götaplatsen, Gothenburg, Sweden. From left to right: City Theater (Carl Bergstein, 1934); Art Gallery (A.L. Rondahl, 1925); Concert Hall (Sven Markelius, 1939).

which were based on premodern forms and concepts. Lincoln Center was among the first—and admittedly tentative—examples of this renewed interest in a classical vocabulary.[47] Although it was not to be his last word, Lincoln Center brought Harrison's career full circle from his Beaux-Arts beginnings. Upon its completion, he was already hard at work on another colossal project, Nelson Rockefeller's massive state government complex at Albany. In the meantime, he had been given the opportunity to indulge his fertile imagination again with a second world's fair in New York and to redesign completely the city's second largest airport.

Chapter 19

Whence, oh whence,
did the Fair appear?
Out of the nowhere into
the here.
Did it just spring up in a
flash when bidden?
No, you can bet your
life it didden.
How was the marsh
grass changed to
roses?
By a crusty magician,
name of Moses.
He'll make you, while
turning a somersault,
Good bricks without
straw, good beer
without malt,
He'll build you a
mansion out of knot
holes,
Or a garden out of a
mess of pot holes.
He looked at a waste of
mud and sand,
And Moses envisioned
a Promised Land.

"The Promised Land of
Mr. Moses"
by Ogden Nash[1]

Commissions of the 1960s: the World's Fair and New York City's airports

It was Governor Nelson Rockefeller who had first suggested a relationship between New York's 1964–65 World's Fair and Lincoln Center and offered the potential for state financing that it implied. Obviously it was in the best interest of Robert Moses, the newly appointed president of the fair, to encourage such a relationship. At a meeting of the Lincoln Center architects in the summer of 1960, Moses therefore announced that Lincoln Center's dance theater would be used during the fair for a "music festival for performances by great nations."[2]

For forty years, Moses had dreamed of making Flushing Meadows into a park. This was what he had hoped for when he chose the Meadows as the site of the 1939 World's Fair, Building the World of Tomorrow. But once the fair was over, the area had reverted to its former desolation. In 1945 he had tried again to salvage the Meadows, this time as a home for the U.N. headquarters. Again, he had failed. By 1960, at the age of seventy, Moses saw the forthcoming world's fair as his last chance to transform Flushing Meadows.

There were also practical reasons for Moses's concern with the fair. At this stage in his career, his image as a devoted civil servant had become seriously tarnished. In 1959 the efforts of the Citizens Union, a respected group of New York civic reformers with whom Moses had begun his career in public service, had uncovered a connection between the commissioner's Slum Clearance Committee and organized crime. The subsequent *New York Post* headline on June 30, 1959—"Costello Pal got Title I Deal"—was the first in a barrage of unsavory attacks on the Moses committee, culminating in the disclosure that its vice-president, Thomas J. Shanahan, was at the heart of the corruption. Any other public official implicated in such a scandal would have been ruined, but Moses's power by this time was so great that Mayor Robert Wagner was afraid to dismiss him. Nevertheless, the commissioner was understandably eager to take on a job that would put him in a more favorable light. The fair seemed to provide just such an opportunity.[3]

By the time Moses became president of the fair, the Fair Corporation had appointed a design committee to develop a theme and a central plan. Harrison was its chairman, and Gordon Bunshaft, Henry Dreyfuss, Emil H. Praeger, and Edward Durell Stone were the committee members. Harking back to his experience of the 1939 fair and relying on his usual good sense, Harrison suggested that each member of the committee work with their own designers to come up with new ideas.

The architects began with the premise that the new fair had to achieve a better sense of unity and cohesion than the 1939 fair had managed to attain. The earlier fair's popular amusement area, for example, had been so far away from the commercial and national pavilions that once there, visitors simply stayed until they were ready to leave, without returning to the exhibitions. Bunshaft strongly opposed the custom of allowing the exhibitors to build their own pavilions. Using the same concept he had proposed for Lincoln Center, he argued for a single building that would house all the exhibitions. Bunshaft recalled that Harrison liked his doughnut-shaped project and wanted to present it to Moses in the most favorable light:

> Wally said, "Let's put the scheme we like in a corner so we're not emphasizing it." Moses walked in and went straight to that design. He wanted to talk about it. He loved that design. I've never seen a client more sold than he was.[4]

Moses's enthusiasm was short-lived.[5] He knew that if the Fair Corporation was to be burdened with the responsibility and expense of building individual exhibits, it would compromise his goal to use the fair as a means to establish a park, as had been the case in 1939. When Moses rejected the designers' proposals and insisted that each exhibitor be responsible for building and demolishing its own pavilion, Bunshaft resigned, making the following statement to the press:

> We were trying to design a plan that would be an expression of our times. Mr. Moses and the board wanted a repeat of the old World's Fair plan of 1939. Why should architects hang around four years beating an old cat?[6]

Two months later, the other designers followed suit. Alone among them, Harrison remained involved with the fair's direction by agreeing to serve on its executive committee. Without any of his colleagues' anger or bitterness, his own comments on the Moses decision showed the wisdom of experience:

> I didn't agree with their [i.e., Moses and his assistants] decision, but they had their reasons and prevailed, as clients often do against architects.[7]

Individual responsibility for each pavilion seemed to rule out visual unity, and Moses suggested only that the architects follow the fair's theme: Man's Achievements on a Shrinking Globe in an Expanding Universe and his Desire for Peace through Understanding. The result hardly lived up to what the commissioner claimed would be "the single greatest event in history."[8] Absorbed completely in his personal aims, Moses failed to project either the fair's theme or its stated goal: Peace through Understanding.[9] In fact, the pop artist Andy Warhol's "Ten Most Wanted Men" paintings, exhibited at the New York State pavilion, conveyed a far more powerful image than anything designed for the fair, which was soon referred to as the "Pop Art Fair."[10] Of the nearly two hundred exhibition pavilions that were eventually built, only three were the responsibility of the Fair Corporation, one of which was Harrison's Hall of Science.[11]

Ever since the Russians had launched Sputnik in 1957, the popular imagination had conceived of science in terms of outer space, and Harrison tried to create an environment that would evoke the stratosphere. (Actually, the most significant scientific development, first publicly exhibited at the fair, was displayed in a demonstration of nuclear fusion at the General Electric pavilion.) Harrison believed that the structure of a twentieth-century building devoted to exhibiting science should be clearly visible. Consequently, his design bent a single, relatively thin (one-and-one-quarter feet) eighty-foot-high wall into ten gentle undulations, the first two and last two overlapping with enough space between them to

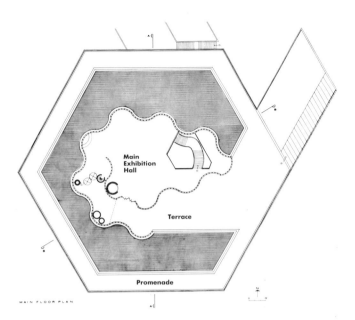

215. Harrison, plan of Hall of Science, 1964 World's Fair, New York City.

216. Entrance, Hall of Science, 1964 World's Fair.

form an entranceway. At the time, Harrison stated simply that the structure resulted from his search for a fresh approach to building a wall;[12] later he pointed out that in this instance "a thin wall did the work of a thick wall,"[13] on the same principle that makes a curved piece of paper stand more firmly than a straight piece of paper. It was a principle that had been used in eighteenth-century garden walls, and had been adopted by Thomas Jefferson at the University of Virginia. The museum stood in a pool of water animated by gushing fountains. The pool was in turn delineated by a hexagonal walkway that spanned the water only at the hall's entrance (Figs. 215–217). The sight and sound of strong water jets playing before the Hall of Science's undulating walls created exactly the feeling of excitement and festivity that Harrison associated with a fair. Like the prospect of the Theme Center for the 1939 World's Fair, the commission for the Hall of Science touched a responsive chord in him.

Thinking of the interior effect, Harrison decided to use a variation of the *béton-glas* technique he had employed so successfully in the First Presbyterian Church at Stamford.[14] He took for his palette the rich colors of the stained-glass windows in Paris's thirteenth-century Sainte-Chapelle, choosing blue alone to evoke the heavens' infinity. Alluding again to the dramatic light effects that he had discovered in Egypt, he plunged the visitor into a darkened eighty-foot-high, free-form space barely illuminated by the small amount of blue-tinted daylight that penetrated the structure. The result was a child's wonderland, which uncannily created the excitement of a space-age experience by means of one of the world's oldest crafts.

As foundation conditions were marshy, the soil had to be excavated until it was equal in weight to the proposed building; this left enough space for a large underground exhibition area within the supporting structure. The somber intricacy of the substructure provided an interesting contrast to the ethereal atmosphere of the huge hall above. Described by Ada Louise Huxtable at the time of its completion as "worthy of the cabinet of Dr. Caligari,"[15] this massive network of reticulated and faceted reinforced concrete columns and spans created a dramatic science-fiction setting for the displays (Fig. 218).

217. Aerial view, Hall of Science, 1964 World's Fair.

218. Underground exhibition space, Hall of Science, 1964 World's Fair.

Ezra Stoller © ESTO

The fair got off to a bad start with its opening on April 22, 1964, marked by major civil rights demonstrations against several state pavilions. By the end of July, attendance was forty percent less than expected, and by the end of its first season, in October, the fair showed a deficit of $17,540,000.[16] In January 1965 Moses refused to provide George C. Moore, chairman of the fair's finance committee, with the detailed figures Moore had requested, and five of the nine bankers on the committee (including David Rockefeller) resigned.[17] After further investigations and probing by the press, the shocking facts of Moses's padded contracts with unions, contractors, engineers, and suppliers began to be revealed, as well as the escrow account he had set up to ensure payment of his own high salary.[18] The 1964–65 World's Fair, possibly the largest array of exhibits ever assembled at one time in one place, was visited by 51.6 million people.[19] Yet revenues to New York City and State were less than $2 million, making the fair both a financial and a critical disaster. Ironically, it was Moses's presidency of the fair project, which he had assumed as a means of clearing his name, that definitively revealed his unprincipled methods to the public. A lifetime of exposure to the temptations of money and power had been too strong for him to resist.

But Moses had gotten his park: on June 3, 1967, Flushing Meadows–Corona Park was officially dedicated. He had envisioned the Hall of Science as the first in a series of buildings that would become New York's equivalent of the Smithsonian Institution in Washington and the Museum of Science and Industry in Chicago. Yet because the cost of the Hall of Science had been almost twice the original estimate ($7.6 million),[20] Moses understandably refused to put Harrison in charge of the building's projected alteration into a permanent museum. Stoically, Harrison remembered that "the minute I finished it, Moses gave it to Max O. Urbahn. He was no good as a designer, but he was practical; he was going to change the whole approach to the project."

The New York World's Fair Corporation published a brochure that pictured an ambitious three-building arrangement for the projected new museum: in addition to the Hall of Science, there was to be a second serpentine building similar to Harrison's, and an enormous, low, circular structure.[21] City officials protested the cost of this scheme and subsequent pared-down versions of it; consequently Harrison's hall stands as he built it, a far more evocative reminder of the fair than U.S. Steel's nearby Unisphere: supported by the piles and foundations that had been set originally for the Trylon and Perisphere, the skeletal world globe that served as the fair's symbol is something few remember.

Flushing Meadows is well known as the site occupied by New York City's two world's fairs, but less familiar is the relationship of both fairs to the existence of nearby La Guardia Airport. Mayor La Guardia had planned the airport named after him to supplement Floyd Bennett Field in Brooklyn, before then the city's only municipal airport. Completion of the airport was expedited to coincide with the opening of the 1939 fair, and indeed, as the fair ended its first season, La Guardia Field, as it was then called, began to function, heralded as the largest airport in the world. By the time William O'Dwyer had replaced La Guardia as mayor in 1945—only a few years after its much-publicized opening—the airport's runways were drastically in need of repair. The main terminal was also soon hopelessly inadequate for the enormous increase in air traffic after World War II. Several years passed before the New York Port Authority assumed responsibility for La Guardia, when it became leasor of the city's three major metropolitan airports—La Guardia, Idlewild, and Newark. Even then, La Guardia was neglected because interest was focussed on the spectacular new field at Idlewild (now John F. Kennedy International) Airport.

Work on Idlewild was begun by the city of New York in 1942 to help alleviate the congestion at La Guardia Field. Intended primarily for international flights, Idlewild was to be constructed on landfill in Jamaica Bay, a few miles west of La Guardia on Long Island. The project crawled along for five years until it came under the jurisdiction of the Port Authority, which, within a year—by July 1948—had opened the first part of a planned $250 million facility and had scheduled final completion for 1960. Occupying 5,070 acres, with an uprecedented

219. Harrison, early scheme for Idlewild Airport (1946).
Rendering by Hugh Ferriss.

140 separate gates, Idlewild was nine times the size of La Guardia and two to three times that of Newark. From December 15, 1954, through the end of 1960, Harrison served as a consultant for Idlewild, with the title of Co-ordinator of Exterior Architecture. He helped Thomas Sullivan of the Port Authority to establish an overall plan for the growing terminus; he also advised on roadway and building locations, and helped coordinate exteriors of the different buildings and landscaping of the 160-acre central plaza (Fig. 219).

When Harrison began to work on the Idlewild plan, the idea of separate terminals for different airlines was anachronistic; the current tendency was to consolidate most air facilities. The more traditional plan was adopted because of the unprecedented size of the operation, which would have made centralization prohibitively expensive. Apparently Harrison eventually found it impossible to work within the strict limitations imposed by the Port Authority and with the massive group of participants that included the Port Authority's own planners, architects, engineers, and highway experts as well as the firm of Skidmore, Owings & Merrill. It is difficult to determine the extent of his influence on the appearance of Kennedy International Airport today.

Once the master plan for Idlewild had been completed, the problems at LaGuardia once again claimed attention. After years of neglect, the prospect of the 1964–65 World's Fair finally provided the impetus to execute the necessary improvements. The two stages of La Guardia Airport admirably illustrate the design evolution of the first two generations of this new building type, now in its third generation. The first La Guardia Airport, with its sober, neoclassical main terminal and hangars designed by Delano & Aldrich, belonged to the pioneer airport generation, built from approximately 1930 to 1950 and consisting of a simple building from which passengers had direct access to the planes.[22] Harrison's La Guardia renovation, completed in 1964, was typical of the second airport generation, which began to appear in the late 1950s in response to the demand for more aircraft positions and gates; it was at this time that concourses with additional gates were added to existing terminals. The third and most recent generation of airport design tries to add even more gates, often by means of satellite configurations, sometimes by moving passengers mechanically to the aircrafts because of the great distances involved.

At La Guardia, Harrison decided to replace completely the earlier semicircular terminal with a six-block

220. Harrison, main terminal, La Guardia Airport, New York City (1964).

221. Harrison, plan, La Guardia Airport.

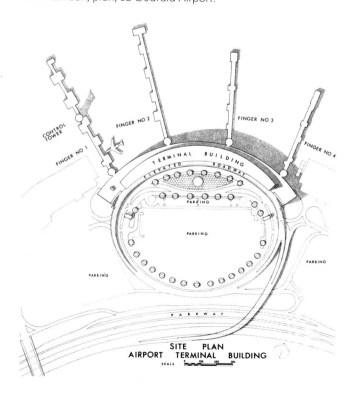

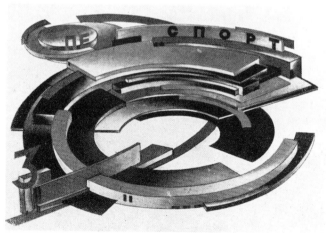

222. Jacob Tchernikhov, *Les Bases de l'architecture contemporaine,* (Leningrad, 1931), Fig. 212.

aluminum and glass arc from which five concourses or fingers projected, each with its own gates (Figs. 220, 221). The terminal's long façade hugs two levels of access roads in a welcoming curve, with useful protection provided by the second-floor overhang. The building's curved shape was determined in part by the functional requirements of automobile access, but also in deference to the earlier Delano & Aldrich hangars that remained on the site: it was generally agreed that a curved façade would interfere least with the older buildings.[23] The gently tilted parasol roof, supported by piers at either side, is meant to symbolize flight, and it successfully gives an airy, light feeling to the structure. The resulting configuration, consisting of overlapping circular layers crowned by a tilted plane, resembles a design by Jacob Tchernikhov in Harrison's library (Fig. 222; another was referred to earlier in connection with the Trylon and Perisphere, see chapter 9).[24]

In sharp contrast with the sober, modern terminal is the airport's control tower, a 150-foot reinforced concrete hyperbola punctured with porthole windows (Fig. 223). The tower's functional material and form produce an expressionist image and a striking reminder of the various modes in which Harrison worked.

Parking facilities are a crucial factor in airport design, and it is unfortunate that this part of Harrison's La Guardia program proved to be inadequate. By the mid-1970s, when it became apparent that growing air-commuter traffic necessitated additional parking facilities, the Port Authority erected an unsightly steel grillage garage (1976) directly in front of Harrison's terminal; it almost obliterates the terminal's façade. Only Harrison's control tower remains clearly visible, its strange shape beckoning determinedly despite all obstacles.

Harrison's ability to win these giant commissions was particularly noteworthy at Idlewild and La Guardia airports since his client, the Port Authority, had been for many years the avowed antagonist of his friend Robert Moses. Whatever disappointments Harrison experienced in his work for the airports once again he left his mark on two of the city's major facilities.

223. Harrison, control tower, La Guardia Airport.

Chapter 20

The Albany Mall: beginning

The story of Harrison's last monumental commission began on November 4, 1958, when Nelson Rockefeller became governor of New York State. Less than halfway through his first term, Rockefeller enlisted Harrison's help to build, in Albany, the colossal group of office, legislative, administrative, and cultural buildings that embodied the governor's idea of what the state capitol complex should be. The South Mall, now called the Nelson A. Rockefeller Empire State Plaza, took eighteen years and almost a billion dollars to realize. It was the largest building project ever undertaken by the state of New York. It was also the most criticized.

Rockefeller came to his first elective office with a margin of over half a million votes, the first of four equally spectacular gubernatorial campaign victories. A month before the election, the cover of *Time* magazine showed Rockefeller, with the caption: *Full of a desire to do big things.* No description could have been more prophetic. By the time he had resigned the governorship on December 19, 1973, Rockefeller had not only passed a vast amount of legislation and instigated innumerable programs, but also "changed the physical face of the state more than any other governor since De Witt Clinton built the Erie Canal."[1]

From the beginning of Rockefeller's career, Harrison was part of the small circle of intimate associates on whom the politician relied for advice. Harrison was often referred to as the "idea man,"[2] a role he had first played for Rockefeller in Washington during World War II. At that time the young Rockefeller, grappling with his first government job, began to seek the older man's judgment on subjects other than architecture. He also came to rely on Harrison to get things done, and to win the architect's approbation he was often willing to moderate some of his more willful behavior. On many occasions, Harrison's rare combination of intelligence, ethical behavior, and warm human understanding tempered the millionaire's hard-nosed impetuosity.[3]

Rockefeller had been in office a year when he began to involve Harrison in his building program. In response to the great increase in college enrollment that was taking place throughout the country during the 1950s,

Rockefeller established a major initiative to improve both the quality of education and the physical facilities of the state university system. At his request, in 1960 Harrison had formed a committee to study the problem; he had also begun to design a new campus for the state university at Albany. Harrison envisaged a picturesque solution—"Goodhueesque," in his own words[4]—that would have left the hilly site intact. The scheme was a far more sensitive response to the new awareness of student needs than the strict, rectilinear plan by Edward Durell Stone that eventually was substituted for it.[5]

Even a century ago, when the state capital had been an active commercial center, Stanford White, the famous New York City architect and dashing man-about-town, had described an evening there as "misery, wretchedness, ennui and the devil."[6] In the middle of the twentieth century, Albany's downtown suffered from the same problems of depopulation, devitalization, and serious degeneration as many other American cities at the time. By the fall of 1960, Albany's eleven-term (1942–83) Democratic mayor, Erastus Corning 2d, realized that drastic measures were needed to save the city's core from total abandonment. A group of prominent citizens and concerned business people had formed the Downtown Albany Development Committee; the mayor joined the group, and on October 11 he requested a $25,000 appropriation from the Albany Common Council (to be matched equally by local businesses) for a survey of the downtown's possible improvement by the Newark firm of Candeub, Fleissig & Associates. Rumors persisted that Governor Rockefeller intended to centralize state agencies in the downtown area, and Corning was worried that the governor might bypass the city—and himself—in developing such a project. Indeed, only a few months after the mayor's request for a survey, Rockefeller began to put his own plans into motion; on April 6, 1961, a law was enacted that created the Temporary State Commission on the Capital City.[7] In a concession to regional political pressures, the governor announced that Albany's renewal would be part of a tri-city plan for Albany, Schenectady, and Troy.[8]

The commission held its first meeting on July 6, 1961, and upon the advice of Rockefeller's appointee,

George Dudley, retained the services of three planning firms, referred to subsequently as the Associated Planners: Rogers, Taliaferro, Kostritsky & Lamb of Baltimore had worked on the Golden Triangle in Pittsburgh and Constitution Plaza in Hartford, Connecticut; Maurice E. H. Rotival, the French planner whom Harrison had introduced to his classes at Yale in the late 1930s, now had an office in New York City and had played a large part in the replanning of Caracas and of New Haven; John Calbreath Burdis, an Englishman, presided over a small Albany firm and served as head of the planning department at the Rensselaer Polytechnic Institute in Troy.

Much has been made of Rockefeller's alleged determination to clean up the seedy downtown area southeast of the state capitol known as the Gut. Again and again the story is told of the new governor's embarrassment that Princess Beatrix of the Netherlands, who made a state visit to Albany in 1959, and the king and queen of Denmark, who visited in 1960, had to drive through the bawdy neighborhood in order to reach the governor's mansion. The story ends with the governor's triumphant transformation of this unsightly slum into the pristine monumentality of the South Mall. The truth of the matter is that Rockefeller had decided to situate his visionary government complex between the capitol and the executive mansion in a lower-middle-class Italian neighborhood known as "The Pastures," which consisted mostly of federal and Victorian houses (Fig. 224). To disguise the fact that his vision would require the brutal displacement of approximately 6,000 people from a stable neighborhood—to the outrage of its inhabitants—Rockefeller used the Gut's proximity east of this area to promote the new project as slum clearance.

As usual when he was considering a new building project, Rockefeller turned to Harrison, who recalled the governor's obsession with the image he had retained of the Dalai Lama's palace at Lhasa in Tibet:

> he showed me how he wanted to stop the valley with a great wall going north and south . . . he wanted the feeling of separating the Mall into a

224. "The Pastures" site chosen by Nelson A. Rockefeller for the
South Mall, Albany (now Nelson A. Rockefeller Empire State
Plaza).

localized community, up on top of the hill, so that he could not only get the vista of the wall but of the whole capital adjunct at the top.

He had seen a wall similar to that stopping a valley in Tibet when he had traveled there not so long before and that was one of the main things he kept asking for, as it developed.[9]

But because Harrison was currently at work on the state university, Rockefeller ruled out the possibility of his also working on the Mall. Harrison remembered the conversation ending abruptly, with Rockefeller saying, "I can't give it to you because I've already given you a job."

Rockefeller soon changed his mind. A few days later he called Harrison and asked if he would be interested in designing the Mall instead of the state campus. The architect's immediate response was a boyishly enthusiastic, "You bet."[10] Many years later, Harrison commented on this sequence of events with the indulgence he often showed where Rockefeller was concerned:

In those days when Nelson talked about something, I had it one day and lost it the next. I didn't mind. I didn't take it too seriously. It was stimulating.

In this case, for better or for worse, Harrison was to be saddled with the Mall. In the midst of his exasperation with frustrating and inconclusive meetings with the Metropolitan Opera House committees, he must have relished the possibility of renewing his old one-to-one architect-client relationship with Rockefeller.

Candeub, Fleissig, the planners engaged by the city, designated a badly deteriorated area north of the capitol (largely by H. H. Richardson, 1881) for the new state offices. The mayor's group determined that it was here, rather than in the district to the south chosen by Rockefeller, that the new complex could best be integrated with plans to rehabilitate the retail center to the east. With the Candeub, Fleissig recommendations in hand, Dudley worked with the Associated Planners to determine the best location for the new state capitol. Periodically, enormous presentation drawings based on elaborate analyses

were shown to the governor.[11] Five sites were considered (Fig. 225), including the downtown core designated by Rockefeller that was, in fact, chosen by the Associated Planners. Candeub, Fleissig's recommendations were taken into consideration only with respect to integrating some of the highway system with the new plan. Given the governor's well-known preference, Dudley said later that the Associated Planners' research had been only an academic exercise, and that the choice had been made with the feeling of "Now that we know it's where we wanted it in the first place, how do we get on with building it?"[12]

Rockefeller's concept was brilliant theoretically: a ravine directly south of the capitol would be spanned by a monumental superstructure on which the government complex would rise. Under the platform, roads would connect the complex with the intricate network of highways that the governor was in the process of having built throughout the state (Figs. 226, 227). But, in fact, the plan for the superstructure left a good deal to be desired. Its formal rigidity and its complete failure to relate to the existing city were in diametrical opposition to the best qualities of Rockefeller Center, which both Rockefeller and Harrison invoked as their model. Instead, the plan's Beaux-Arts symmetry, with its long axes and contrasting high and low buildings, suggested the traditional influence of Rotival, who approached the project, according to Dudley, "as if Albany were the crossroads of the Western hemisphere."[13]

Following a mandate to study the surrounding region as well as Albany, the Associated Planners made a number of other recommendations. Like the earlier Candeub, Fleissig proposal, the Associated Planners' project for the new state buildings was only one part of the plan to revitalize the state capital. Equally important, in their opinion, was the massive renewal of Albany's business center; development of both sides of the Hudson waterfront, including construction of a new bridge across the river (the Albany-Capital Harbour Project); creation of a new convention hall, an art center, and a transportation center; development of housing; and construction of major arterial routes to the center of the city. In their report of February 1, 1963, the Associated Planners presented statistics about the natural wealth and growth

225. Possible sites for South Mall:

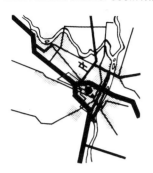  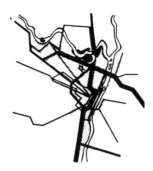 

a) south of the present Mall, rejected because state buildings would be dispersed;

b) the city's downtown core, directly south of the state capitol;

c) overlooking the Mohawk River, rejected, with the Thatcher Park site, as too isolated;

d) Thatcher Park, on top of the Helderberg Mountain range;

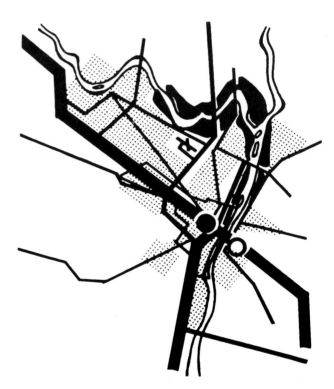

e) undeveloped area across the Hudson River from Albany, rejected because too far away from Albany's core.

226. Harrison, South Mall and arterial system as planned.

227. Harrison, South Mall under construction and arterial
system, seen from the east.

potential of the tri-city area in order to substantiate their proposal for a program that would include roads to connect Albany, Schenectady, and Troy, housing and community renewal, a nuclear research center, and general economic development.[14]

The new government complex interested the governor most, and of course, that is what was built. Of the other proposals made by the Temporary State Commission for the Capital City, only the bridge, Riverfront Arterial I-787, and some downtown rehabilitation were executed. The convention hall was incorporated into the Mall, and the connector under the Mall, which was to join the Riverfront Arterial with Route I–90 to the north and the New York Thruway to the south, was built only from the arterial through the South Mall, where it ends with a U–turn.

Surprisingly, the South Mall's first major opponent was the mayor of Albany himself. Despite his patrician background and demeanor—the Groton- and Yale-educated Corning was the great grandson of an Albany mayor (and a childhood friend of Nelson Rockefeller)—he was not loath to rub elbows with some of the city's most questionable Democratic-party bosses, and he did not hide his anger at the state's intervention in matters that he considered strictly municipal. For seven months he successfully blocked the Temporary State Commission's appropriation of land and money, which he described as "hasty and ruthless...what might be expected in a dictatorship."[15] Finally the Great Compromiser, as the mayor was called, came up with a plan to finance the South Mall that he felt would sufficiently maintain his balance of power with the state. Corning proposed that Albany County sell a series of forty-year bonds to build the Mall and then turn the money over to the state, which would take on construction as the county's "agent." The rental fees the state paid the county over forty years would be sufficient to cover the debt incurred by the sale of the county's bonds. With the debtor paid off by the year 2004, the state would become sole owner. Additionally, the mayor wanted—and got—Rockefeller to agree to pay the city and county an indemnity of approximately $13 million for the supposed loss of real estate taxes that the city would suffer.

Corning's method of financing the Mall provided an astute way of circumventing New York State law, which specifically prohibits the state's contraction of a debt unless the debt is authorized by law, and which further prohibits such a law from taking effect until it receives a majority of the votes at a general election.[16] The bill presenting the scheme was passed on April 16, 1963, by a vote of 55 to 1 in the senate and 141 to 4 in the assembly. Because state law does permit a local government unit to sell bonds to finance self-supporting projects without calling a local election, Albany County could legally float the bonds needed for financing. But to ensure the success for his financial maneuvering, Rockefeller persuaded the legislature to enact yet another law, authorizing the commissioner of the Office of General Services (OGS)—a department created by the governor in 1960 specifically to oversee the South Mall—to contract on behalf of the state with cities and counties for the construction of state buildings and their lease to the state. The Mall bonds imposed on the state an irrevocable contract to pay Albany County rent regardless of any legislative objection.[17] The scheme eventually provided the necessary cash to build the South Mall, but its deliberate bypassing of normal democratic procedures became one of the most roundly censured aspects of the project.

As for the amount of money to be raised, by the time the Mall was completed in 1978, a total of $985 million worth of bonds had been authorized (the last $25 million of which were issued in 1982 to pay for "claims and improvements").[18] John Byron, the state's director of construction at the South Mall from 1970 until its completion in 1976, describes the first estimates for the mall as follows:

> Someone asked what it would cost and somebody said $250 million. That stuck, unfortunately. It seemed like a lot of money then, but when the designs came in on paper the cost estimates were $480 million.[19]

At no time was the much-quoted $250 million an official estimate, and repeated references to this figure in statements and articles about the Mall are misleading.

In his first term as governor, Rockefeller successfully filed for the state to appropriate the 98.5 acres he wanted for the Mall site, ordered the site cleared, and came to an agreement in principle with Corning on a means of financing the project. Having got this far, Rockefeller became obsessed with getting the work well under way—in fact, beyond a point of no return—during his second term; and he was relentless in exerting pressure to achieve this end.

Rockefeller had made up his mind that he was going to bring about what he described as "Albany's transformation into one of the most brilliant, beautiful, efficient, and electrifying capitals in all the world."[20] He treated the enterprise as his own personal project, going over every line in every architectural drawing and blueprint, giving his opinion on building materials, the color of cladding marble, and the location of every building and tree.[21] Though nominally Harrison was the governor's chosen architect for the South Mall from its inception, he was consulted neither on the choice of site nor on the plan. He was merely informed of the evolution of the site-selection process, and eventually he was presented with the plan that had been worked out by the Associated Planners in accordance with Rockefeller's concept.

Harrison remembered a flight from Washington to New York with Rockefeller, who:

> . . . drew out on the back of an envelope a sketch plan as it had been recommended by this land planning commission, and the locations and everything, and asked me what I thought of it. I said I didn't know much about it but it looked pretty good to me.[22]

The plan called for five relatively low buildings: a nine-story legislative building and an eight-story justice building, a long, five-story motor vehicles building, and two cultural buildings that were to flank a memorial arch. It also called for a large, forty-four-story office tower and six twenty-story agency buildings, all sitting on a five-story landscaped platform with three large reflecting pools and playing fountains (Figs. 228, 229).

With the exception of the southernmost end of the platform, where a library was substituted for the memorial arch and two of the six proposed agency buildings were eliminated, the plan was adhered to exactly. Rockefeller dictated the Mall's basic concept; he also controlled the actual design of each building to an extraordinary degree. Robert Klein, one of Harrison's chief draftsmen from 1958 to 1978, recalls the architect's assertion that, of all the Mall buildings, he had had some freedom only with the library and the meeting center.[23] Harrison had also said with resignation of his role at Albany: "I had a lot to do with everything Nelson didn't do with the design of the thing."[24]

Rockefeller's interest in an unrealized project he had seen in Harrison's office suggested the keystone shape of the Mall's tower, which was echoed in part in the four agency buildings (Figs. 230, 231).[25] In designing the tower and agency buildings, Harrison looked to several precedents. The tower's shape combined the lozenges of the Pan American Building in New York, of Abramovitz's Phoenix Building in Hartford (1964), and of Gio Ponti's Pirelli Building in Milan (1959).[26] The tower's plan seemed to accommodate ideally the requirements for large conference spaces and a number of uniform offices on each floor. The agency buildings repeated this plan, but approximately by half, substituting a triangular marble-clad elevator stack in each building for the lozenge mass of the tower. The agencies were cantilevered six stories above the platform's lowest level (two stories above the plaza) to leave the plaza open and to allow for maximum flexibility in the office layouts. Structurally, it was an economical system for relatively small buildings, where the levels below grade had to be kept free for the concourse and for parking.[27] Unfortunately, the buildings' similar forms and rigid alignment recall the aridity of urban renewal in the 1960s, against which there was already a strong reaction in the mid-1970s when these buildings were completed. Furthermore, seen from the west, in conjunction with the massive windowless platform elevation, the solid marble elevator stacks present a grim view (see Figs. 228, 229).

228. South Mall, seen from the west.

229. South Mall, seen from the north. Counterclockwise from
State Capitol in foreground: Justice Building (1972); Performing
Arts Center, "The Egg" (1975); Erastus Corning Tower (1973);
Cultural Education Center (1974); four Agency buildings (1977);
behind them, Motor Vehicles Building (1972); Legislative Office
Building (1972).

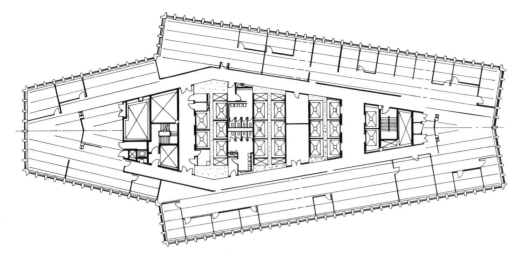

230. Harrison, plan of Erastus Corning Tower.

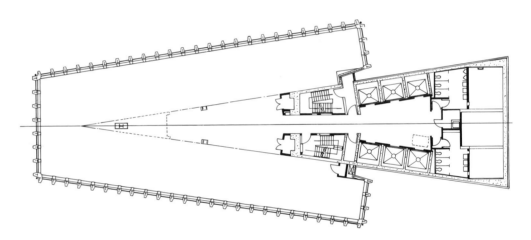

231. Harrison, plan of an Agency Building.

254

As for the meeting center, known as the Egg, again it was the governor rather than his architect who determined the building's form. A much-repeated story has it that in discussing the planned meeting center with Harrison at lunch one day, the governor took a plastic container of cream, held a grapefruit over it, and declared that the capital needed "something like that."[28] Harrison welcomed the ovoid shape proposed by Rockefeller, for he thought it would blend into the complex more easily than another angular building; moreover, the shape provided him with an opportunity to eliminate the rectangular envelope that usually encloses the cylindrical theater shape and thus to expose the theater's structure.[29] The result was the 983-seat main theater and the smaller, 500-seat recital hall, expressed together on the exterior as an ellipsoidal, inverted shell varying in thickness from five feet at the base to a little more than a foot and a half at the top. The Egg sits on a tripod pedestal that emerges thirty feet above the plaza level and has its own substructure and foundation at the platform's lower level (Figs. 232–235).[30]

From his first talks with Harrison about the Mall, Rockefeller was candid about the political need to include other architects. Harrison remembered that the governor spoke with his usual blunt practicality:

> I have got to have a group of people working on Albany, because it's a very big job, and we need to give work to a lot of people. It's got to be spread around the state. You cannot have it all coming from New York City.[31]

Harrison's experience with large public projects had made him all too familiar with this kind of consideration. While the planners of the Mall had failed to include him—the Mall's chief architect—in their meetings, they were careful to invite a local architect, Henry Blatner, known primarily for the schools he had produced. Soon thereafter, the question arose of including an architect from Buffalo because it was the home of Walter J. Mahoney, the powerful state senate majority leader. Several upstate architects were suggested, but to spread the goodwill even further, a firm composed entirely of architects from Buffalo—James & Meadows & Howard—

was created solely to design the legislative building. A Syracuse office, in this case the preexisting firm of Sargent, Webster, Crenshaw & Folley, was selected for the justice building (see Fig. 229).

Harrison himself probably suggested the inclusion of Carson, Lundin & Shaw of New York City for the motor vehicles building, as all three architects had worked with him before. Harrison had encouraged the choice of what was then the firm of Carson & Lundin to design the Esso Building at Rockefeller Center during his own wartime absence from New York. Arvin Shaw had worked with him at the United Nations.

The two local firms and Carson, Lundin & Shaw were responsible for the interiors and structures of the three peripheral buildings—legislative, justice, and motor vehicles—to which Harrison accommodated his design for the exteriors. Because of steel shortages at the time, he wanted to use as much concrete and as little steel as possible. He envisioned the Mall as being the first group of important concrete buildings in the United States, in the spirit of some of the more interesting modern developments by European architects. Unhappily, he was eventually to admit that his use of concrete at the Mall had not been cost efficient.

The heavy overhangs of the legislative and justice buildings' top floors were designed to accommodate the large spaces that had been requested. The gracelessness of the forms, which have been criticized as trite Le Corbusian, is accentuated by their prominent placement near the old capitol. Here, too, the governor's intervention was in large part responsible for the resulting design. Harrison remembered that

> Nelson was determined the buildings shouldn't be separated, as they were at the Hartford Mall, where he felt there was no unity between the separate buildings. To achieve unity, the legislative building was expanded at the top and the justice building cut back.

Harrison was well aware of the need to relate visually the disparate elements of this enormous complex. He had insisted on a uniform sheathing for all the buildings, choosing a limestone that would be compatible

232. Harrison's sketches for Performing Arts Center.

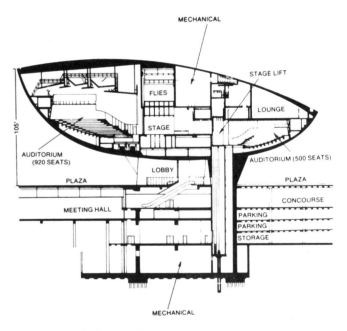

233. Section, Performing Arts Center.

234. Lounge, Performing Arts Center.

235. Performing Arts Center.

with the exterior of the nineteenth-century capitol build-ing, which serves as the Mall's focal point. (In fact, a re-minder of the architect's intention survives in the limestone cladding that was added to the exterior of the Bell Telephone Company annex before a final decision was made on materials for the Mall.) But the governor decided that only marble could achieve the grandeur to which he aspired, and he chose Vermont Pearl White and Georgia Cherokee marbles—two forbiddingly cold and characterless white stones that intensify the stiffness of the South Mall buildings and that are particularly incon-gruous juxtaposed with the handsome, rustic Fingerlake stone of the platform's east wall (see Fig. 235).

In the choice of materials, as in so many of the de-sign decisions at Albany, Harrison proposed and Rock-efeller disposed, following a predictable pattern that applied to the recommendations of others besides Har-rison, on technical as well as aesthetic questions. One such case was Rockefeller's insistence on including high-security medical research laboratories within the Mall platform despite the technical arguments against such an inclusion.

Before the first drawing was made or the first dollar appropriated, Rockefeller had formed a definite concept of the new government complex. It was his baby, and his dominance of the project surpassed the behavior of the most possessive parent. The depth of Rockefeller's emo-tional involvement with the Mall was demonstrated dra-matically at a meeting—before the Mall model was unveiled in December 1962—between Rockefeller, Har-rison, Dudley and his assistants, and Blatner to discuss housing for some of the people who had been displaced by the development. Situated prominently in a zigzag layout on the architects' model, in the area directly south of the Mall, were several low-rise buildings planned as housing for the elderly (see Fig. 226). But for Rockefeller these structures represented an aesthetic intrusion, and upon seeing them he became visibly agitated. "These buildings are too big, don't you think so, Wally?" he growled tensely, as he strode across the room and grabbed one of the offending replicas with both hands in a frenzied effort to pry it off the model.[32] Neither the housing for the elderly nor the 900-unit low-income

236. Nelson Rockefeller and Wallace Harrison at the South Mall.

housing that had been promised as part of the South Mall rehabilitation was included in the project.[33]

Shortly after Harrison's death, Abramovitz recalled that "the wonderful thing about Wallace was that he would say no to Nelson. But that changed. Toward the end Wallace did what Nelson wanted."[34] Since the early Rockefeller Center days, when Harrison had introduced him to architecture's complexities, Rockefeller had become aware that he had only to say the word to see realized even his most impractical architectural ambitions. At Albany he decided to put this awareness into practice: the former acolyte reversed his role with that of the older man. While Rockefeller made himself the designer as well as the client, Harrison stopped saying no and simply took orders. The architect had come full circle, simply coordinating and administering the job in much the same way as he had at the beginning of his career, at Rockefeller Center.

When Harrison decided to participate in the large Rockefeller Center project, he had done so with the full awareness that it would affect the subsequent direction of his work. By his own admission, he had had to fight throughout his life to maintain his identity: "At Rockefeller Center I worked with the other architects, at the Mall it was with Nelson." Even as a junior architect at Rockefeller Center, Harrison questioned many of his colleagues' design decisions. Harrison's reluctance to fight committee constraints at Lincoln Center is partly understandable, since the committees themselves were severely constrained by financial and bureaucratic considerations. More surprising is his reluctance to question Rockefeller's decisions at Albany (Fig. 236).

In the last decade of Rockefeller's life a subtle change occurred in his friendship with Harrison. Abramovitz has described the professional effects of this change, but there seems to have been a profound, underlying cause for the altered quality of the dialogue between architect and client. Rockefeller's political disillusionment in the 1970s provided ample cause for some of his altered behavior;[35] but even before he had retired from the vice-presidency, his conduct had profoundly disappointed Harrison in several respects.

The architect's life was in every way a testimony to the Puritan ethic that had molded his character from an early age. In contrast with his tolerance for compromise in design, he had no comparable tolerance for moral compromise: a kind and compassionate man, he was unbending as far as his own ethical standards were concerned. Rockefeller's failure to live up to these standards in his personal dealings with Harrison, especially at the end of his governorship, was a source of considerable sorrow to the architect. He never understood, for example, why Rockefeller sold, for a relatively small amount of money and without prior consultation with him, a painting by Fernand Léger that he had given the governor a few years before.[36] And he was shocked and hurt by Rockefeller's withdrawal of the fund he had provided for many years to pay for the institutionalization of Harrison's daughter.[37] After a number of such incidents, Harrison may simply have lost faith in Rockefeller.

Perhaps it is precisely the existence of faith—in a common goal or in each other—that enriches the collaboration between an architect and a client; without it, there is an unidentifiable lack in the work. Certainly this is true in the case of Harrison's last Rockefeller commission. Harrison could not reconcile with his own beliefs the motives and means of self-aggrandizement that underlay Rockefeller's interest in the Albany Mall, and perhaps he was quietly expressing his change of heart when he observed later that the greatest problem with Albany was that "nobody knew what they were building the Mall for."

259

Chapter 21

The Albany Mall: construction and completion

The problems that dogged construction of the Mall reveal a great deal about American public building practices at mid-century and provide a measure of Nelson Rockefeller's political power at the time.

When New York State awards a construction contract for more than fifty thousand dollars, the contract must conform to Section 135 of the State Finance Law, commonly known as Wicks Law. Dating from the 1920s, when it was passed in response to pressure from trade contractors, the law requires separate contracts for plumbing, electrical, heating, and ventilation work; it also requires that the contract be awarded to the lowest responsible bidder, who must be established in the trade and able to post a bond guaranteeing completion of the work. For the Mall, in addition to respecting these basic requirements, separate contracts were also let for the erection of all structural steel, and for construction of the main platform, of the elevators, and of the power-operated platforms used to wash the windows of the high-rise buildings.

The state system differs from the one that governs commercial construction, under which the client engages one general contractor who is solely responsible for the project and therefore has a vested interest in assigning specialized jobs to the most efficient and economical subcontractors. The state's so-called multiple contract system—unless it is controlled by one of several sophisticated methods of planning that did not exist when the Mall was begun—complicates the painstaking coordination between prime contractors' and prime- and subcontractors' work that is essential for efficient operations on any large construction site. Often the state system favors low cost to the detriment of quality and promotes what are normally subcontractors to the status of prime contractors. Consequently the client loses control of the work.

The expeditious construction of the first phase of Rockefeller Center was at least partly attributable to Harrison's application to each building, one after the other, of the same construction methods, executed smoothly by a single general contractor. At the Mall, frenzied efforts to satisfy the governor's demand for speedy execution led to the decision that all the buildings be constructed simultaneously. With the exception of the four agency buildings, each structure at the Mall was treated as a separate project with its own set of prime- and subcontractors, all scrambling to work at the same time. The simultaneous construction of so many large and complex buildings made coordination of the numerous contractors almost impossible.

After a session with the governor, Harrison would turn over two or three sketches to draftsmen in his office for preliminary drawings. Usually at this stage, the client must either accept or reject a design so that the architect can proceed to develop working drawings, on the basis of which construction contracts are negotiated. At Albany, the Office of General Services was the client, and as such theoretically responsible for design approval. But just as Rockefeller sidestepped Harrison when it suited him, so he often chose to ignore the OGS. Consequently, he would frequently relay a design decision directly to Harrison, without informing those who were officially responsible for its implementation.[1]

Once a design was accepted, approximately twenty people in the Harrison & Abramovitz office produced working drawings for it. Because of the state's insistence on dealing with every office on an equal basis, three separate sets of drawings—architectural, engineering, and foundations—were produced for each building, which then had to be coordinated by the OGS. (In private enterprise the mechanical and foundation engineers are normally subordinate to the architect, who is responsible for these aspects of the project.) For on-site supervision, Harrison & Abramovitz maintained a permanent construction chief at Albany with a staff of two or three assistants, as well as an engineering consultant who visited the site every week. Harrison himself spent several days every month at Albany.

The OGS let the contracts and put its own series of supervisors in charge: as commissioner of the OGS, General Cortlandt Van Rensselaer Schuyler—succeeded by Major General A. C. O'Hara—worked with Brigadier General William W. Wanamaker, who served as on-site coordinator from 1962 to 1971. Schuyler was a four-star general who had been part of General Eisenhower's staff at the invasion of Normandy and had gone on to serve as

chief of staff of the NATO forces. At the end of World War II, the Pentagon had assigned him to Rockefeller's staff in Washington; there the two men became friendly, and Rockefeller suggested the possibility of employing him after his retirement. Schuyler's appointment was an arrangement for military supervision of construction similar to the one at Lincoln Center, with the difference that Schuyler had no construction experience. Schuyler tried to remedy this lack by calling in Wanamaker, a West Point graduate with a degree in engineering and a long line of distinguished government and industrial projects to his name. Wanamaker quickly realized that the Mall was on a different scale from anything he had experienced to date, and in December 1966 he engaged the George A. Fuller Company in an attempt to provide the kind of commercial savvy that Carl Morse had brought to Lincoln Center.

One of the first contracts to be awarded was for the platform, in effect a gigantic concrete building five stories high, one-quarter mile long, and one-third mile wide. It was to house three levels of parking as well as a small four-story parking area in the northwest corner, together with loading and service zones, mechanical and support facilities, and a grand concourse connecting every part of the Mall. Harrison compared the substructure's projected uses with those of the underground mall at Rockefeller Center. The contract for the platform foundation went to Fehlhaber-Horn in June 1966 and specified a completion date of September 1968 (mechanical work was to be finished by December 1969). No other work could take place until the platform foundation was completed, and problems developed almost as soon as excavation began.

In December 1963, long before contract drawings were made, a firm of foundation specialists, Moran, Proctor, Mueser & Rutledge, had worked from the architects' preliminary sketches to produce an extensive subsoil analysis. The firm made strong recommendations regarding the kind of foundations that were needed for the different buildings. A large part of the report was devoted to construction difficulties presented by the site, which lay on top of a glacial gully that had been filled with gelatinous blue clay in the mid-nineteenth century in an attempt to create more space for the city's growing population. Because of the clay, the piles for the massive Alfred E. Smith Building had already sunk several inches since its construction thirty-some years before. As a result, serious measures to stabilize ground conditions had to be taken before work could begin. These measures surpassed in difficulty even the most dire prediction: about 3 million cubic yards of earth were eventually excavated and disposed of, and 22,000 steel H-piles driven into the clay under what John Byron has described as impossible circumstances—"when one pile was driven in, the pile next to it would come back up!"[2] The difficulties of this operation were further complicated by the problems it produced in transporting the enormous volume of excavated material through the city streets, the rapid decline in labor productivity, the city's quick move to forbid pile-driving at night, and other work restrictions imposed by the state.

Despite these complications and the consequent delays, the state continued to let major contracts, and by the summer of 1968 thousands of construction workers were swarming over the site. At the peak, there were 63 prime contractors and over 1,300 subcontractors and suppliers (about equally divided), producing a total of approximately 2,500 workers at the Mall at the same time.[3] Fuller's inspection team grew from 75 to 180 people. Given the density and diversity of workers in the area, confrontations soon arose among different construction groups vying unsuccessfully to work in the same locations. The harsh upstate climate added to the already difficult working conditions. In desperation, the state paid some crews overtime to work on weekends and at night to expedite the job.

Labor was a constant problem. In the early 1960s, when urban improvements had first been considered, Albany was a stagnant city of approximately 129,726. There was so little development that the city's construction workers regularly accepted lower wages for the same jobs that other crews performed for higher pay in nearby areas. The enormous labor requirements of the Mall drastically changed all this. As Byron explained: "The need for skilled and even unskilled labor put labor in the driver's seat for demands. Contracts were reviewed every two to three years amidst tremendous negotiations." Soon after work began in the summer of 1965, a series of jurisdictional disputes and a subsequent lockout by the contractors shut down the Mall for thirteen weeks and raised wages to the same level as in the surrounding areas; it also produced a thirty-five-hour week. In 1970 alone the employers' association was faced with 217 labor disputes—about ten times as many as before construction of the Mall—together with innumerable wildcat strikes. As a result, the project was forced to absorb a median annual increase of twenty percent in wages and fringe benefits over three years.[4]

Increased wages were only part of the problem. Many of the union trades required at the Mall had no local practitioners. Steam fitters, among the highest paid skilled laborers in the industry, had to be flown in from out of state; structural steel workers, traditionally American Indians, came from reservations in the northern part of the state, with some from Canada who were accepted with reluctance by the union; numerous other trades, such as lathers, plasterers, and carpenters, had to be imported from New York City. The project's immensity also created a variety of freak labor situations—for example, timber decking that was so big it had to be entrusted to members of the one existing dock workers' union in the state, brought in from New York City, rather than to the local carpenters who would normally handle such a job.

Because of the many restrictions, the best contractors were rarely anxious to accept contracts for state construction. The period's nationwide building boom, which provided plenty of commercial work, along with the enormous financial commitment required by these multimillion dollar contracts, further alienated most potential contenders for the Albany jobs. Consequently, more than a third of the contracts were let on the basis of a single bid. Every contract stipulated an expected completion date, the period of time the work would require, or both; but from early in the construction process, the eighteen months' delay in finishing the platform foundation pushed every other job behind schedule. Contractors were forced to keep teams in the field for months— sometimes years—longer than planned, while the costs of material and labor escalated faster than ever as the United States became increasingly involved in the war in Vietnam. Faced with bankruptcy if they held to their original agreements, the companies working at the Mall asked to renegotiate their contracts, failing which they threatened to leave the half-finished site after exhausting their original fee, and to sue for delay damages. Having had prior experience only with road, bridge, and sewer construction, the Attorney General's office was totally unprepared to contend with the situation. The only way it could cope was to adhere to the letter of the law, rejecting out of hand any possibility of renegotiation.

The state attorneys realized that the "contractors were spending more time planning their lawsuits than fulfilling their contracts,"[5] and they knew that if the contractors walked off the job the state would be faced with endless litigation, and with a new series of time-consuming and expensive competition bidding. To circumvent the New York law that allows change orders for state projects only if an order does not alter the scope of the work first contracted for or the original estimates for the work, on April 30, 1969, a special law known as the Equitable Adjustment Act was pushed through the state legislature, due to its strong union backing. Based on federal precedent, it permitted the adjustment of contract fees and deadlines if the contractor could prove the state responsible for delays and increased costs. It empowered the OGS eventually to award $146 million of work adjustments, unlocking the deadly impasse, but at the same time providing grounds for a new barrage of criticism.[6]

Harrison distanced himself from the project's agonizing day-to-day practical problems. He could excercise no control over its finances, and he dealt with the contractors as best he could given the limitations of the situation. It was not easy. Being unable to select and retain contractors on the basis of their quality took a great toll, and he believed that the state suffered considerably from the restrictions placed upon it:

> We always knew that we would need some of them [i.e., the best contractors] on a great job like this, and that if we didn't get them we would be out of luck.[7]

In his haste to erect the South Mall, Rockefeller had created a situation with unique difficulties. Once it became apparent that the state had lost control over both its management of the site and its adherence to the original terms of its contracts, there developed what was commonly called "the Albany factor," a phenomenon whereby every problem was magnified and every building cost increased fifteen percent over what it would have been for a comparable project elsewhere in the state.[8] A few years after the Mall's completion, when he was asked about its enormous cost overruns, Harrison looked perplexed:

> I don't know why costs went up so much. It's easy to blame inflation, the war, and so forth, but when people hear someone else is earning more money, they add more to their prices. It's typically American. No one worries about costs going up, but about whether they're going to get *their share* of the costs—the unions, the entrepreneur are all out for the almighty dollar. You can keep it down by competition, but great contractors don't want to build state buildings, they don't earn enough.

After a short pause he added:

> The difference with the United Nations was a couple of wars. It was another world in terms of costs.

It was another world in many ways. In the two decades since the architect's work at the U.N., many changes had taken place. The United States's unsuccessful involvements in Korea and in Vietnam had dispelled the euphoric idealism that had followed World War II. The political climate was different; labor conditions were different; and, finally, Harrison's relationship with his client was different. Not only did the governor dictate what he wanted, but his demands were no less imperious when he changed his mind, despite the havoc wrought with schedules and with budgets. Rockefeller was oblivious to the enormously complex ramifications of building decisions and to the way in which they affected coordination of the architects, engineers, and contractors; and he was apparently unconcerned about how his behavior affected his long-time association with Harrison.

Rockefeller's changes of mind are well known to those who worked on the Mall's construction. To balance the imposing presence of the French Renaissance-style state capitol building, Rockefeller had suggested that a memorial arch, to be called the Arch of Freedom, be placed at the end of the axis that runs south from the capitol. In response, Harrison designed a slightly flattened, 336-foot version of Eero Saarinen's Saint Louis archway, to sit on a rise of land between Madison Avenue and Lincoln Park, flanked by two low structures that would house the state library and archives. A new state museum was to occupy the arch's plinth; the arch would stand in an outdoor amphitheater with one of New York's most important historical documents, the Emancipation Proclamation, enshrined in its stage (Fig. 237). By the spring of 1965 the scheme for the arch and its two relatively modest accompanying buildings had been replaced by plans for a much larger structure. The new solution would be more costly than the original concept, but the governor chose to ignore this in order to satisfy the library administration's increasingly aggressive demands for more space. Harrison was amenable to the change, judging that the area at the Mall's south axis would be better contained by an important building mass than by an open arch (Fig. 238). When it became apparent, however, that the library administrators were demanding an even larger structure than the one proposed in the revised plan, he was understandably upset: "The library . . . developed into an enormous building, and developed as it progressed, which is a hell of a hard thing."[9]

Despite these difficulties, Harrison created a potentially magnificent display area for the as yet undesigned museum. In 1977 the temporary exhibition, "New York School, Painting and Sculpture," installed by architect Richard Meier, provided a stunning demonstration of the area's adaptability to one of a number of possible uses (Fig. 239). Unfortunately, the way in which the state later decided to use this part of the building, for a Museum of the State of New York, in which highlighted tableaus stand in near darkness, obliterates the space.

The addition to the Mall of the Cultural Education Center, as the library-museum is now called, was per-

haps justified by the community's needs. More difficult to justify was the inclusion of the state's Department of Health laboratories, a move that was opposed by almost everyone who worked in the laboratories. When talk of the new government complex began, the Department of Health's research and diagnostic divisions were located in Albany near the Medical School and the Albany Medical Center on New Scotland Avenue. The facilities were badly outdated, and Dr. Hollis Ingraham, the commissioner of the department, had started to explore the possibility of renovating them. A plan had actually been drawn up when Ingraham was approached by Governor Rockefeller's right-hand man, William Ronan, who explained that the governor felt strongly about including the Department of Health in the Mall platform at the base of the Erastus Corning 2d Office Tower, where it was already budgeted. Should the department's existing facilities simply be renovated, the governor would have to go back to the Legislature for funding. Ronan made it clear that if Ingraham cooperated with the governor's wishes, he could have anything he asked for, but that if he went along with those of his colleagues who preferred to stay in their present location, his department would get no financial help from the state.[10]

It was a difficult offer for Ingraham to refuse, despite the researchers' repeated reminders that they worked closely with the Medical School, from which they would be separated at the Mall. Furthermore, it would be infinitely more complicated to incorporate the isolated facilities required by their study of highly contagious diseases into a building complex than to maintain them as discrete entities. Inclusion at the Mall of research facilities, whose very nature entailed changes of program and consequent changes in equipment, also led eventually to redesign and structural alterations. Later inclusion of a kidney-disease center and enlargement of the microscopy department were two examples of such changes.[11] In addition, to placate the large number of doctors and scientists who objected to working in the windowless rooms assigned to them within the platform, measures had to be taken to allow natural light from the Department of Health's three-story atrium to penetrate additional areas.[12]

237. Harrison, project for a Memorial Arch (1964), South Mall.
Artist's rendering.

238. Harrison, Cultural Education Center, at south end of the
Mall.

239. "New York School, Painting and Sculpture," exhibition
installed in South Mall museum space by Richard Meier (1977).

The platform structure itself was subject to major changes. When by the end of 1967 the city was unable to raise the funds necessary to realize its projected convention center at a site east of the Mall, Mayor Corning once again exerted his apparently irresistible powers of persuasion. At the state's expense, the 2,500-seat hall, together with dining facilities to service it, was included in the South Mall. The consequences were formidable: a considerable area of the platform that had been designated for parking, services, and the concourse and that was to be supported by conventionally spaced columns, suddenly had to be restructured to create a large area of columnless open space (Fig. 240).

240. Interior, Convention Hall (1975).

One of Rockefeller's changes came about inadvertently. In a celebration speech made shortly after his triumphant election to an unprecedented fourth term, the governor promised the legislators they would be in their new building for the next session. No sooner was the statement made than Rockefeller's aides pointed out to him that while the justice building was indeed almost ready for occupancy, the legislative building was still at least a year away from completion. Undaunted, the governor, to retain his credibility, allocated an additional $300,000 to accelerate work on the legislature.[13]

Program changes made by the governor—including the often arbitrary changes that tenants requested and that Rockefeller approved—are referred to in the profession as change orders. Change orders alter the approved contract cost and extend the time stipulated to complete work; they are costly and time-consuming in terms of materials, labor, and the architect's and consultants' fees. It is the responsibility of the architect and consultants to approve these changes, which in large projects are often difficult to review and monitor accurately. Under these circumstances, instead of charging the usual percentage, the architect and consultants generally charge directly for their services, based on the time spent plus overhead and profit—relatively small additional amounts when compared with the actual costs of the changes and the disruptive effect they have on construction schedules. At Albany, the many millions of dollars' worth of change orders became a major factor in the delays and the escalation of costs.[14]

Rockefeller stated repeatedly that the South Mall was being built to last for at least a hundred years. Everything about the Mall had a larger-than-life quality, and criticism of it was on an equally grand scale. Photographs of the first models were published in the September 1963 issue of *Progressive Architecture*, under the headline: "Cacophony of Forms in New York Capitol." Equally damning was the same magazine's coverage of the completed Mall in the May 1979 issue in an article entitled "Halicarnassus on the Hudson."[15]

And this was only one aspect of the criticism. Shortly after construction of the Mall had started, Arthur Levitt, the state comptroller, launched a relentless attack on the project's finances, beginning with the state's method of raising money and continuing, year after year, with the Mall's rising costs. Levitt was the only Democrat who held a major office during the predominantly Republican administration from 1959 to 1974, and the Mall provided his most visible means of attacking the administration. In the spring of 1971 Levitt began to publicize the audit he had completed on March 31, in which he claimed that the new South Mall buildings would cost three-and-one-half times more than the most recently completed state office buildings at the so-called state campus—a complex Governor Thomas E. Dewey had begun to develop in the late 1940s—while providing almost fifty percent less "usable" space. Levitt concluded that the Mall's functional space had cost between $127.93 and $239.48 per square foot.[16] Compounding Levitt's attack, in January 1971 the press began to publish the additional fees to contractors provided for by the Equitable Adjustment Act, dubbing the South Mall "Rocky's Vietnam."[17] Around the same time, the rise in fees for the Mall's architects, engineers, and supervisors from $36 million to $55 million came under widespread attack. Meanwhile, in November 1970 a federal grand jury was impaneled in Albany to investigate allegations that materials for the South Mall were being diverted to build houses for several labor leaders.

Completion of the Mall did not put an end to hostile articles by the local press, which featured at least two lawsuits filed in connection with the project: one against the state by Foster-Lipkins, the office tower's original contractor, with which the state had terminated its agreement for failure to meet deadlines; the other by the state against Carson, Lundin & Thorson (successors to Carson, Lundin & Shaw), architects of the motor vehicles building, from which, the state charged, slabs of marble weighing up to fifteen-hundred pounds were in danger of falling.

There was more. Even the handling of the remarkable art collection that was assembled for the Mall—admittedly "a collection that any museum in the Western World specializing in contemporary art would be proud to have"— was criticized on the grounds that the art was disadvantaged by the "inhumanity" of the concourse exhibition space.[18] At Harrison's urging, $2,653,000 of the state's South Mall funds had been set aside for the acquisition of art.[19] Like his father before him at Rockefeller Center, Nelson Rockefeller enthusiastically backed the architect's wish to enrich the complex with painting and sculpture. Harrison chaired a commission that included Seymour Knox, the patron of the Albright-Knox Art Gallery in Buffalo; Robert Doty, an art administrator from Rochester; and René d'Harnoncourt, who was succeeded after his death in 1968 by Dorothy Miller. It was a knowledgeable group, and its members were conscientious in their selection of some of the best painting and sculpture then available by artists who had worked in New York State. Robert Motherwell, Clyfford Still, Mark Rothko, Morris Louis, Claes Oldenburg, and David Smith were among those whose work was included (Fig. 241).

The problems of the South Mall followed an illustrious precedent: it took two controversial competitions (the first in 1863, the second in 1866) to name Thomas Fuller, a Canadian, the architect for the state capitol; his neo-Renaissance design was to cost $4 million. When, by 1875, $7 million had been spent and completion was nowhere in sight, a new capitol commission appointed an architectural advisory board, consisting of Leopold Eidlitz, H. H. Richardson, and Frederick Law Olmsted. Upon their proposal for an entirely new project in Romanesque style, they were asked to take over Fuller's job. So complicated were the problems presented by the controversy over the building's style that it was not finished

241. Harrison standing in front of a painting by Al Held in the
Concourse.

until 1898, twelve years after Richardson's death.[20] By that time the $25 million spent on the capitol had made it the most expensive building on the North American continent.[21]

Nor are the particular architectural and financial problems of the Mall unique in our time. Within the past twenty-odd years a number of public buildings have incurred long delays and enormous cost overruns; the design of almost all these buildings is disappointing. The question arises repeatedly why, when compared with buildings in the private sector, so many large government buildings are often longer in the making, more costly than planned, and aesthetically unsatisfactory. The federal government has provided particularly conspicuous examples in the nation's capital: the FBI Building by C. F. Murphy & Associates of Chicago (1975) was ten years late in its completion and cost more than twice its estimated $60 million; the new Library of Congress by DeWitt, Poor & Shelton (1980) was sixteen years in the making and cost $48 million over its estimated $75 million; the Philip A. Hart Senate Office Building by John Carl Warnecke & Associates (1982) took ten years to complete and rose $50 million over its projected $87 million. Earlier, the great expense and impoverished design of Harbeson, Hough, Livingston & Larsen's Rayburn Building (1965) were such that Ada Louise Huxtable referred to it as a "National Disaster."[22]

Harrison had been acutely sensitive to Rockefeller's criticism of his Sixth Avenue buildings, and he had agonized over every decision at the Metropolitan Opera House, but he seemed singularly untouched by the widespread criticism of the Mall. Could his apparent indifference confirm indications that the design was in large part not his to answer for?[23]

The project's cost became even more notorious than its disappointing design. The Mall was one of the largest and most ambitious building programs in recent U.S. history, and Levitt subjected it to a particularly harsh brand of public criticism.

"Usable" space is generally defined as the area outside a building's core, including circulation space, that is available for the tenants' use. To suit his purposes, Levitt applied the term only to the actual offices, excluding such conventionally included areas as corridors. Levitt's damning comparisons of the Mall's costs with those of the state office campus also were disingenuous: the campus's low-grade, five-story reinforced concrete structures were not equivalent to the Mall's luxurious facilities. Finally, the comptroller resorted to the unusual measure of adding interest charges for long-term financing to the Mall's overall construction costs, thereby further prejudicing comparisons with projects whose costs were quoted exclusive of such charges.

It is certainly true that the four agency buildings did not provide as much space per floor as straight slab towers would have done, and thus even space defined more conventionally as "usable" cost more than industry norms for roughly equivalent structures at the time—though the difference was not in fact as great as Levitt implied. However, between 1967 and 1977, nationwide construction costs doubled; between 1977 and 1980, they increased again by seventy-five percent. This tremendous inflation, coupled with a concomitant rise in interest rates, in retrospect makes Rockefeller's arguments against a longer schedule look somewhat less extravagant.[24] Whether, in view of the 1974 fiscal crisis, the state could afford such extravagance is another question.

The Equitable Adjustment Act undoubtedly led to some abuses, but there was no grand jury indictment for the alleged contractor irregularities on the site. The one scandal that did break was in the OGS itself; in 1976 Martin Geruso, an assistant attorney, was indicted for accepting $22,000 in kickbacks. As for the lawsuits, an agreement about the office tower was arrived at with Foster-Lipkins, which was awarded some indemnification; an agreement was reached also with Carson, Lundin & Thorson concerning the motor vehicles building, the case being routinely settled when the problems with the marble cladding were found to be less severe than the press had indicated.[25]

Harrison & Abramovitz's ten years' work at the Mall netted the firm approximately $100,000 annually, less than the profit it made for a single building—such as its most recent one for U.S. Steel in Pittsburgh (1971).[26] There is no reason to believe that the Mall was any more profitable for the other architects who worked on it.

Harrison never charged a profit margin for the tremendous effort he personally spent on the project; and at the outset, the architects and engineers accepted a temporary twenty-five-percent reduction in their normal fees because of the state's lack of funds when they were engaged.

One of the most serious shortcomings of the Mall—and a real threat to all new superscale projects—was largely overlooked by its critics: the technology of the Mall was, on the whole, outdated before construction was anywhere near completion. The revolution in computer technology that had taken place since the design of the motor vehicles building meant that the agency would actually require only half the space it now occupies. The same is true of the large computer area in the concourse. And the enormous air-conditioning plant that serves the entire Mall, the capitol, and the Alfred E. Smith Building was already seriously outdated by 1978, as were many of the Department of Health's facilities.

Ironically, when properly executed, the very working method that created such chaos at the Mall can produce excellent results. The state's much-criticized letting of individual prime contracts at Albany on the basis of unrefined, and often incomplete, contract documents is now routine procedure for large, complicated jobs for which time and complex scheduling are critical factors. The method, sometimes referred to as phased design and construction, or more popularly as "fast-tracking," relies on a greatly condensed scheduling system that calls for early decision-making on design as well as for the "packaging" of various portions of the project into individual contracts—such as foundations or structural steel—and even for the advance purchase of materials and/or equipment (as OGS did for the Mall's structural steel). The use of "multiple prime contractors (or a single controlling general contractor who negotiates each of the subcontracts as the contract 'packages' are completed) who start work sequentially, before the construction documents are completed," can make this an efficient system when properly implemented.[27] It was precisely the absence of a logical sequence in coordinating the prime contractors that created one of the biggest problems at Albany.

The ideas and the technology for new construction management, or fast-tracking, systems, such as the Program Evaluation and Review Technique (PERT) and the Critical Path Method (CPM), came into existence in the late 1950s. Within a few years, the building industry had begun to experiment with these systems—but without the help of the computer technology that by the 1970s made phased design and construction a means to save time and money.[28] When the South Mall was being planned, the term fast-track was not often heard in the construction industry. Today, fast-tracking, when implemented by a new breed of professionals known as construction managers (CMs), can be used to reduce the overall time required for design and construction by as much as fifty percent.[29]

An essential principle in the success of a fast-track program is to arrive at, and strictly adhere to, an early design program, failing which the architects will find themselves struggling in effect to "remodel" a building as yet unbuilt. This principle was obviously not respected at Albany. The innumerable changes imposed on these designs, as well as the lack of strong management control, account for much that went wrong in the construction of the South Mall.

Has the Mall fulfilled Rockefeller's expectations for it? When one approaches Albany by any of the several superhighways that intersect there, its curious, modernistic structures suddenly appear, floating, as it were, like some futuristic mirage in the midst of the gently rolling hills of northern New York State. Because the Mall, and the platform on which it is elevated, are out of scale with the surrounding city, its buildings seem to stand alone, in splendid isolation. However, on sunny days the Mall is filled with people; depending on the season, they are strolling, picnicking, roller-skating or ice-skating on an outdoor rink. And in all seasons large crowds regularly assemble for the numerous celebratory events organized by the OGS (Figs. 242, 243).[30]

Almost all the people who work at the South Mall are enthusiastic about the new offices and appreciate their spectacular views of the rich surrounding countryside and distant hills. Instead of having to share offices, as they were required to do in their previous quarters, the

242. The South Mall at night.

243. The South Mall during the day.

legislators now occupy private, two-room suites; the senators' staffs claim to have increased their productivity by one-third since the move.[31]

Like most successful urban redevelopments, the South Mall has provided a tremendous stimulus to the neighborhoods surrounding it in downtown Albany. Between 1969 and 1979 over $200 million in public and private funds were spent on seventeen of a projected thirty-four projects for rehabilitation and new construction. Between 1972 and 1977 retail sales in the area rose over twenty percent. For the first time in its history, Albany has become a tourist attraction; restaurants have proliferated, and in 1980–81 a $19 million Hilton Hotel was constructed to accommodate the new influx of visitors, including those who are in the capital on business.

The revitalization of Albany's downtown has encouraged a new interest in the city's historical heritage. In 1974 the Committee on South Mall Environs established guidelines to protect approximately thirty square blocks of nineteenth-century town houses adjacent to the Mall. On the committee's recommendations, the City of Albany Building Code was strengthened and a Capitol Hill Architectural Review Commission was formed to pass on all proposed architectural changes in the area. The exterior of the capitol was cleaned and restored, and in 1977 a careful restoration of the building's interiors was begun.

In its scale and in the image it projects, the South Mall is in the tradition of the most imposing historical seats of power. In this respect it recalls cities such as Fatehpur Sikri in Mogul India and Saint Petersburg in eighteenth-century Russia. In the twentieth century the tradition continued with the creation of Brasília and of Chandigarh. From the time of the Imperial fora in Rome, the erection of a monumental municipal complex, planned as a whole and built in a relatively short period of time, was dependent on the political power of a single individual. Such power was common in ancient empires and dukedoms, but even within the democratic systems of modern-day Brazil and India, President Kubitschek at Brasília and Prime Minister Nehru at Chandigarh had ultimate control over the new government complexes that

were created during their administrations. Nelson Rockefeller exerted a comparable control at Albany.

When Harrison started to work on the South Mall in 1962, he was a robust sixty-seven years old. Broad-shouldered and standing to his full height, he conveyed an air of mature vitality. In a profession reputed for its longevity, and in which the first important commission is often received only after the age of forty, sixty-seven is a time of major productivity. By the time the Mall was inaugurated, fourteen years later, Harrison was eighty-one, old by any standard. He had lost a good deal of weight and his shoulders were slightly stooped. Physical frailty had replaced the vigor of his earlier years. Gone were the cigarettes, forbidden on doctor's orders; and a slight deafness made conversation difficult. But the keen intelligence and strength of character, the joyous enthusiasm for life, and for his own lifework, remained unchanged.

The young architect who had loved to build big had begun his career working with others on Rockefeller Center. How many times must Harrison have longed to be the sole designer of a comparable commission? A strange trick of fate gave him the commission he surely had dreamed of having, but under circumstances that severely constricted his design abilities. It seems paradoxical that Rockefeller Center's large group of Associated Architects maintained high design standards, whereas Rockefeller's Mall fell so far short of such standards. It is equally paradoxical that Harrison, who had consistently spurned the trappings of power, became the pliable architect of Rockefeller's monument to his own power. Nevertheless, in spite of the problems that plagued every aspect of the design and construction of the South Mall, he emerged from the experience as dedicated as ever to his profession, unscathed by the criticism, and despite his disillusionment, without rancor toward the governor. In contrast, these same years saw the breakdown of Rockefeller's private and public roles, his painful disappointment with politics, and, finally, his withdrawal from public life.

Chapter 22

The Last Years

For nearly fifteen years Harrison's work on the Albany Mall commanded his attention almost exclusively. It took him away from New York several days each month and occupied him constantly when he was in town. Inevitably, he lost touch with the daily business of Harrison & Abramovitz, just as he had during his wartime absence. Finally, in 1976, when completion of the Mall was in sight, Harrison could return his attention to the office. But the hiatus had been long; at eighty-one, with an energetic younger partner running the firm, it was considerably more difficult to pick up the pieces than it had been thirty years before.

By the time the firm had completed the Celanese Building in 1974, the last of its Sixth Avenue additions to Rockefeller Center, Abramovitz was working mostly outside of New York. He finished several large commissions in Pennsylvania, Ohio, and Illinois for John Galbreath, and he took on two important jobs in France. Because those of the firm's buildings that were currently going up across the country and in Europe were thus credited to Abramovitz, new clients who came to the office invariably asked for him rather than for Harrison.

It was assumed that Harrison accepted his role as an avuncular, background presence. Staff members who arrived one morning in the late summer of 1976 were therefore surprised to find the senior partner's office stripped of its contents. Harrison had had his things taken to an independent office in the old Time and Life Building, where he set up shop on his own. (In 1979 he moved back to the International Building, where he occupied a two-room office with one draftsman.) He had discussed the move with no one beforehand and refused to explain it after the fact. Abramovitz was away on vacation at the time and received the news only a few days later. He, too, refused to comment on what might have prompted the move. A few years later, in an unusual moment of expansiveness, Harrison gave his interpretation of the long relationship with Abramovitz: "It was like the competition between Ghiberti and Brunelleschi for the dome of Florence cathedral."[1] Was Harrison referring to the respective ambitions of his former partner and himself, to Brunelleschi's superior genius and dogged practicality, or even to Brunelleschi's eventual control of the cathedral project? Whatever his intent in making the comparison, there is no doubt which of the Renaissance architects Harrison identified with: it was a rare revelation of the self-confident sense of authority that still underlay the architect's modest demeanor. Such a man could not take a back seat at his own firm; his age, and his changed relationship with Nelson Rockefeller, may have made Harrison particularly sensitive to his position. For whatever reasons, the partnership was effectively terminated as of this time. Except for some additions and alterations at the U.N., no further communication passed between the two men whose names had been closely associated for more than three decades.

Harrison embarked on his one-man venture with two projects in progress: alterations to the Albany Mall's performing arts center and—a commission he had received twenty years before—a memorial to General Pershing in Washington, D.C. The career of John Joseph Pershing (1860–1948) had covered an extraordinary span of history, from fighting as a young cavalry officer against Apache and Sioux Indians to serving as commander in chief of the American Expeditionary Forces in World War I. Pershing's death in 1948 immediately elicited requests from veterans' groups across the country for a national memorial, but only in the winter of 1956–57 did Congress authorize the employment of an architect to prepare plans for the memorial.

At this time Harrison had been asked by the American Battle Monuments Commission (of which Pershing had served as the first chairman) to submit a scheme for the memorial; it was to occupy the entirety of a generous trapezoidal site one block from the White House on the south side of Pennsylvania Avenue between Fourteenth and Fifteenth streets. Harrison's first thought was to create a monumental marble portal to frame a statue of Pershing, an idea he said was inspired by a marble archway he had seen on the island of Naxos in the Cyclades. The archway, commonly referred to as the Gate of Apollo, was undoubtedly a ceremonial entrance to a temple or palace, and has been likened to "an enormous stone picture frame."[2] For Harrison, the appeal of this heroic form lay in its stance—"so solidly on the ground," as he described it. The idea of a modern triumphal arch

was appropriate to the original plan to place the memorial at the broad, westernmost side of the site, where it would provide a culmination point for a row of circular fountain-pools leading from Pennsylvania Avenue and serve as an important focal point for this end of the avenue (Figs. 244, 245). However, at the recommendation of various local review commissions, it was decided to reorient Pershing's statue to the narrower, eastern part of the site and to transform the triumphal arch into two twenty-foot-high walls; the fountains were to be replaced by a large reflecting-pool at the west (Figs. 246, 247). By 1959 the American Battle Monuments Commission was ready to go ahead with Harrison's adjusted design, but Congress had not yet voted the funds needed for its execution. Little did Harrison or anyone else suspect that the project would be subject to almost as much discussion as the 1982 Vietnam Veterans Memorial by Maya Ying Lin; six presidents would occupy the White House before it was completed.

One day in the winter of 1961, while he was riding down Pennsylvania Avenue, President John F. Kennedy remarked on the shabbiness of the ceremonial route between the capitol and the White House. Within a year, the temporary Pennsylvania Avenue Commission was formed, chaired by Nathaniel Owings. Under the Johnson Administration, the Commission formulated an overall plan for the avenue, but Congress failed to provide funding for its implementation. In the fall of 1972 all this changed. The Nixon administration transformed the Kennedy commission into the Pennsylvania Avenue Development Corporation, a government agency given by Congress the power of eminent domain, a budget of $38.8 million, and borrowing power of $50 million. Work was to begin at the avenue's north end with two parcels of land, one of which was Harrison's and the other an unoccupied rectangle diagonally across Pennsylvania Avenue from it to the south.

The Pennsylvania Avenue Development Corporation soon requested a new design for the Pershing Memorial. Instead of constructing a stately monument, the corporation wanted to use the Pershing site for a wooded park with popular attractions such as an ice-skating rink and hot dog stands. The Harrison project was set aside,

244. Harrison, preliminary sketches for Pershing Memorial, Washington, D.C. (1956).

a) Plan and monument.

b) Monument.

245. Harrison, first scheme for Pershing Memorial (1956). Artist's rendering.

246. Harrison, revised scheme for Pershing Memorial (1959).
Artist's rendering.

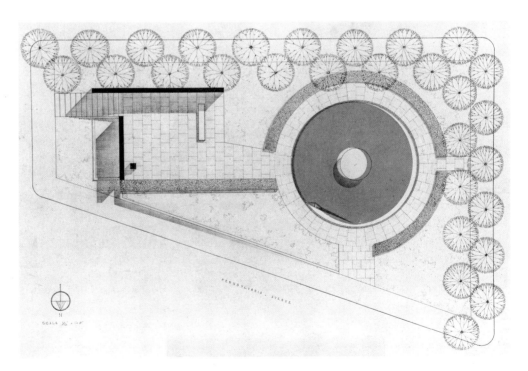

247. Harrison, revised plan for Pershing Memorial (1959).

and Venturi & Rauch, with landscape architect George E. Patton, were commissioned to design the park; M. Paul Friedberg, with Jerome Lindsey, a local Washington architect without previous experience with this kind of project, were asked to design the rectangular urban plaza across the way. Venturi & Rauch's first scheme seemed better suited for a plaza than a park, so after some discussion the assignments were reversed: the park was assigned to Friedberg, the plaza to Venturi & Rauch.[3]

According to Harrison, Friedberg, a New York landscape architect known for the severe concrete plazas and playgrounds he has built in Manhattan, was openly hostile toward him. But the Battle Monuments Commission supported Harrison and in June 1973 asked him to modify his design to accommodate the new concept. The architect now found himself with a site reduced from its original 400 by 240 by 160 feet to a small rectangle, measuring 47 by 49 feet, tucked into the eastern corner of Friedberg's park. How tempting it must have been for him to use one of these myriad changes as an excuse to quit the pitifully small project! Not one to give up, he altered his design a number of times to meet the aesthetic criteria of the Fine Arts and the National Planning commissions, as well as the stipulations of the Battle Monuments Commission and the Pennsylvania Avenue Development Corporation. He also accepted the need to cut the projected cost to approximately one-fifth of the original estimate. (When funding became a problem, he characteristically accepted a ten-percent reduction in his own fee.)

Despite the project's many irritations and his own failing strength, he persevered in relatively good humor. He recalled that he actually derived considerable pleasure from certain aspects of the work—for example, selecting lettering for the inscription that was to accompany the map of the Meuse-Argonne campaign on the longer wall. He had always delighted in combing his library for the historic precedent that might inspire the task at hand. His choice made, the octogenarian, helped by a student assistant, cut out the letters and stood on a chair to tack them on his office walls, just as he had done with his prolific drawings for so many vast projects in the past.

Harrison had been concerned for some time about the choice of the artist to execute the statue of Black Jack, as Pershing was called. Among his candidates had been Jacques Lipchitz, Marino Marini, Reuben Nakian, Isamu Noguchi, and Leonard Baskin; his strong preference had been for Lipchitz.[4] In the winter of 1977, the fifty-six-year-old sculptor Robert White, a grandson of Stanford White and an artist who worked in traditional forms, received a call from Ellen Harrison. She asked him for his curriculum vitae and for photographs of his work, explaining that these were requiried to qualify him for his official appointment to the Pershing project.

White had become friendly with Harrison in the early 1950s when the two men and their wives had enjoyed a short residence at the American Academy in Rome, and had maintained the contact in New York. As with his earlier designations of Mary Callery's abstract sculpture, Harrison evidently placed friendship before his preference for avant-garde art, when he endorsed this traditional artist of relatively little renown.

By the time Harrison's project was finally accepted in the summer of 1979, it had been reduced to a statue on a pedestal, partially enclosed by two ten-foot-high walls standing at right angles to one another at the southern and eastern boundaries of the site, and a stone bench facing the statue (Figs. 248–250). White recalls that "Wally was in despair but he never showed it, he would just laugh sadly."[5] It was precisely this willingness to compromise in order to see a job through that led to the severest criticism of Harrison's work.

The year that Harrison dissolved his partnership with Abramovitz also marked the end of Nelson Rockefeller's political career. After trying three times during his governorship to secure the presidential nomination, in August 1974 Rockefeller was finally given the vice-presidency by President Gerald Ford. It has been said that Rockefeller began to run for president almost as soon as he was elected governor;[6] and one could probably say that there was nothing he ever wanted as badly. But strangely, he was as inept in national politics as he had been astute in state government: public opinion turned so strongly against him in the 1976 campaign that he was forced to withdraw from consideration as Ford's running mate.

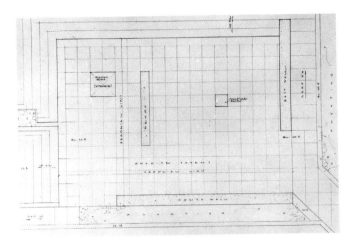

248. Harrison, revised plan (1979), Pershing Memorial.

249. Harrison in his one-man office working with a model for the Pershing Memorial. At the right is a photograph of the Trylon and Perisphere; outside, the RCA Building is visible.

250. Harrison, the Pershing Memorial (1983).

In 1977 Rockefeller announced his retirement from politics. He began to spend more time working on a book that he had talked about writing for over twenty years—on the architecture he and Harrison had built together. To assist him in his new endeavor, Rockefeller engaged Megan Marshack, a bright, outgoing young woman in her early twenties.[7] Members of Rockefeller's staff had assembled materials for the book, and Harrison had even written some sections. Shortly before his retirement, a summary of Rockefeller's state programs was submitted to the architect, who was shocked not to be credited. On the covering memo of this summary Harrison scrawled:

Oh my goodness
Absolutely no reference to my part in anything
in the state even when talking about the
Mall.[8]

Rockefeller's increasing commitment to politics in the 1970s had altered his relationship with most of the people who had been close to him; his office staff complained of a new distancing and irritability on his part. Still mindful, as he had been forty years earlier, of the essentially professional nature of their dealings, Harrison conjectured that the Rockefeller Center buildings on Sixth Avenue may have been the cause of his client's displeasure with him:

Before he died he told me again he didn't like them [the Sixth Avenue buildings]. He was very low in spirits. It was after he had lost the election [i.e., the nomination]. He felt that he might possibly get to be president; he was vice-president then. He started the buildings before he became vice-president. He started Sixth Avenue. He was the one who was always starting.

Usually Rockefeller had finished what he began, but with regard to Sixth Avenue, his political activities had prevented him from attending meetings with the architects, and he had relegated his responsibilities to other members of the family and to staff.

Added to the fact that he was still hard at work on the Mall when the Sixth Avenue buildings were completed, Harrison felt Rockefeller's criticism was terribly unfair:

Nelson criticized the Sixth Avenue buildings and said John [Rockefeller] didn't like them either. There was a complete change of attitude: Nelson said he wouldn't give me any more work.

After a lifetime devoted to building for the Rockefeller family, Harrison was faced with the kind of dismissal an unsatisfactory tradesman might expect:

I was broken-hearted about it. What the hell, I had done the very best I knew how. . . . I felt strongly that from the standpoint of Rockefeller Center, which had given so much in the early days, it was very important the Sixth Avenue extension be successful.

Rockefeller died suddenly on January 26, 1979. After his death, Harrison struggled until the end of his own life, two years and eleven months later, to understand why this long friendship had changed.

Professionally, Harrison was as much an achiever as Rockefeller: no amount of personal distress could deter him from his work. Unfortunately, by the time he dissolved the partnership with Abramovitz, the influential friends he had always counted on in the past for new commissions had either retired or, in some cases, had died. But even had they still been active, it is doubtful they would have provided the kind of commissions they had before. Architecture on the scale Harrison was accustomed to dealing with was now handled by methods associated with big business. Offices were run for maximum cost efficiency, and architects aggressively sought new work through public relations councils. Some large architectural firms had experimented with acting as their own developers. To the courtly Harrison, it was an altogether unfamiliar approach to the profession; the only remaining possibility for him seemed to be assignments for the alteration of his earlier work.

One such alteration was the design for the Metropolitan Opera House office atrium in 1978–79 described earlier (see chapter 18). At that time the Met also requested studies for remodeling the restaurant space on the top floor and for a café beyond the northern perimeter of the opera house (neither was executed). And from Albany there was an inquiry about increasing the capacity of the large auditorium in the performing arts center.

It was in connection with this last project that, toward the end of 1978, Harrison made the familiar trip to the state's capital; he was scheduled to address a group of approximately fifty people. The architect was now eighty-three years old, and in the bitter cold of the upstate winter he somehow appeared even frailer than usual. But no sooner had he mounted the small podium prepared for him in the theater of the performing arts center than he was transformed. Robert Klein, his draftsman, who had accompanied his employer, was astonished to see the old man draw himself to his full height and speak in the same firm voice and with the same engaging persuasiveness that he must have used at Rockefeller Center meetings half a century before.[9]

In 1979 another former client asked Harrison to work for him. Herman Krawitz, who had left the opera to become managing director of the American Ballet Theater, wanted him to design studio space in an old building he had just acquired at Broadway and Nineteenth Street. After making a few schematic studies, Harrison concluded that the difficulties of such a renovation were too great for the job to be worthwhile, and he turned it down.

During this time, Harrison remained actively involved with several institutions with which he was associated. From early 1977 until September 1978 he dutifully attended the intensive weekly meetings of the architect-trustees of the Museum of Modern Art with Cesar Pelli, the architect chosen to design the museum's renovation and new tower addition (1984). Pelli was grateful for Harrison's support in a difficult situation, remembering particularly the "extraordinary sense of responsibility" imparted by the older man.[10]

In the fall of 1979, Harrison enjoyed his role in helping several young architects at the Institute for Architecture and Urban Studies in New York prepare an exhibition of his lifework. The show was organized by Rem Koolhaas, a vocal Dutch practitioner and theoretician who had received considerable attention for his recently published book, *Delirious New York*. In it, Koolhaas dubs Harrison "the Hamlet of Manhattan." For Koolhaas, the Trylon and Perisphere marked the end of what he called Manhattanism: the daring imposition of surprisingly varied activities on a single site in a way that is best exemplified by Rockefeller Center. He believes that Harrison's design symbolized Manhattan before World War II—a place of architectural fantasy where "the impossible was inevitable"—and that by the 1950s Manhattan had succumbed to a joyless rationality devoid of this fantasy. For Koolhaas only Harrison remained, like Hamlet's ghost, to remind us of the fanciful earlier time. As one such reminder, he cites Harrison's first schemes for Lincoln Center.[11]

Harrison had always excelled in his designs for fairs or for projects that evoked the daring and fantasy associated with a fair. It was therefore fitting that his last large project was part of a plan as grand and as exotic as the most fanciful fair.

In January 1977, there arrived at Harrison's small office one of several thousand form letters sent to architects around the world announcing the forthcoming competition for the Pahlavi National Library in Teheran. Tied into the shah's attempts at a social reform program begun in 1962, the library was to be part of his monumental plan to create a whole new city in the Shahestan Pahlavi, Abbas Abad district by developing 1,359 acres of unbuilt hills in the neighborhood.

Iran was in the heyday of its newly created oil wealth, and its capital radiated what one observer called "the atmosphere of a Western boom town in the Gold Rush era."[12] The shah controlled enormous amounts of money, and he was determined to spend it on buildings for which he would be remembered. In 1974 he had obtained from Louis Kahn, in collaboration with Kenzo Tange, a scheme for improving the old city of Teheran and a plan for Shahestan Pahlavi. When Kahn died in March of that year, the shah had engaged the British planning firm of Llewelyn Davies in his stead. The new section's imposing north-south boulevard, lined with plane trees and approximately equivalent in length and width to Paris's Champs-Elysées, was now to be used as the project's spine, running uphill to the focal point of Shah and Nation Square. The square of almost twenty acres, set against the beautiful background of the Alborz Mountains to the north, was designed, according to the shah's specifications, as the largest square in the world; northeast of it were to be located a town hall, a museum, and a library.

To prepare for the library, Herman Liebaers, the former head of the Royal Library in Brussels, and a group of other international experts had begun in December 1972 a five-year investigation of major libraries throughout the world (including Harrison's libraries at Albany and the United Nations). Liebaers's three-thousand-page report was condensed into a two-hundred-page synopsis that provided the basis for development of the competition's building program. The complex project was as alien to the half-illiterate country as the enormous, unshaded new square was to the city, where nothing else existed of comparable scale and where temperatures could reach one hundred degrees Fahrenheit in the summer. The fully automated library, occupying a site of over 43,000 square feet and housing four million books with the same number of nonbook materials, was to be only one part of a vast research institution for resident scholars that would also include cafeterias and restaurants for the staff and the public and a children's library and recreation center. The Pahlavi National Library was intended to rank in importance with the British Museum, the Bibliothèque Nationale, and the Library of Congress; locally it was to serve as a "catalyst in the further cultural development of Iran."[13] An international jury of nine distinguished architects and librarians was appointed to judge the 3,056 entries submitted by architects from eighty-seven countries.[14]

Over six hundred American architects requested the competition's programs. Among them was Harrison's former firm, by then Abramovitz, Harris & Kingsland, consisting of approximately fifty people. After careful consideration, Abramovitz, Harris & Kingsland decided not to compete. In the words of James Kingsland, the program was "so immense and complicated we felt we'd better not do it."[15]

The size (a gross area of 1,291,116 square feet) and complexity of the building program were not the only difficulties. The north-south sloping site also presented a problem, broken as it was by a road into two parcels and further limited by strict regulation of height and setbacks. The competition's technical brief and spatial linkage diagrams were so sophisticated that they were comprehensible only with the help of a highly specialized technician. Finally, a minimal acquaintance with Iranian culture was essential to the sympathetic handling of a project in a country where traditionally the only public buildings were mosques and bazaars. Few, if any, of the competing architects had this kind of knowledge, and after the competition was judged, five out of six of the contenders complained that the program's contradictory requirements had been too complex to follow. This was the competition into which, at the age of eighty-two and with the assistance of only one draftsman, Harrison threw himself with the determination of an eighteen year old.

By April 1977 the competition's program had been distributed. After only a few weeks, it was clear to Harrison that he would need help in producing the elaborate presentation drawings, models, photographs, and written descriptions that were required. At first, he engaged one full-time and two part-time architectural students; after about five months' work, he added two more students. For the final three months, this little team, headed by Harrison, worked days, nights, and weekends to meet the deadline on January 20, 1978.

It was the kind of ordeal to which students submit in the preparation of an examination. The young Harrison had known similar trials, and the fact that he was willing to make such an effort at this stage of his life is revealing. He was still ready to meet a challenge: the making of buildings was life for Harrison, and his deep-seated need to design and to build prevailed over every conceivable deterrent.

Llewelyn Davies had planned a twelve-meter-high arcade to delimit Shah and Nation Square, and this was to be incorporated into the library's design. Harrison said he found the arrangement reminiscent of the way the lower arcade of Jacopo Sansovino's great library on Saint

Mark's Square in Venice relates it to other buildings on the square. For his Teheran design, Harrison divided the facilities among seven separate buildings oriented around the six-story main general-reference library (Figs. 251–253). A pedestrian street leading from Shah and Nation Square to the library's axial entrance was flanked by two three-story structures, of which one, at the west, contained an auditorium and conference rooms; the other, at the east, housed the Islamic studies department. Both buildings were organized around courtyards, and the main library itself was in a kind of larger courtyard created by the two long, low conference and administrative buildings to the west and east that met the two entrance buildings at right angles. The interior elevations of these buildings had wide terraces on alternating floors (Fig. 254). Across a narrow street at the north were three buildings: living quarters and the audio-visual department, the research center, and mechanical facilities.

Competition entries were judged between February 20 and March 2, 1978. The $50,000 first prize went to the West German firm of Von Gerkan, Marg & Partners of Hamburg, who had submitted a forbidding, megalithic project that reportedly appealed to the jury because "it incorporated everything into one massive structure with a logical continuity of the various functions."[16] While Harrison's design left much to be desired, his avoidance of precisely the type of monolithic solution the jury favored showed a far greater sensitivity to the city's architectural tradition and to current Western attitudes toward this kind of program than did the winning design.

Harrison received no acknowledgment of his entry's receipt, no reaction to it, and no notification that another architect had been chosen. His disappointment is understandable considering the enormous importance he attached to getting projects built, often against tremendous odds. He had little patience with the recent emphasis on theory; for him building was what mattered. In the end, the apparent futility of his effort applied to the winners as well, since less than a year after the results of the competition were announced, the shah fled the country, and his projects were wiped out overnight by the Ayatollah Khomeini.

Unlike many of the successful men he had known, Harrison never lost faith in what he was doing; despite setbacks, he never became disillusioned with his chosen profession. Early in his career, Harrison had had occasion to witness professional disillusionment at first hand. The lives of two of his mentors, Goodhue and Corbett, had been marred by serious reversals of fortune. Robert Moses and Nelson Rockefeller presented examples of even deeper losses of faith. They had sacrificed so much in terms of human values to their all-consuming ambition that when they fell from power, as in the case of Moses, or failed to achieve it, as in the case of Rockefeller, their lives were devastated. Harrison recalled:

> I was given the chance to enjoy power simply because Nelson couldn't handle it all. . . . But I never had enough power to corrupt me. I was always conscious of who I was: Mr. Harrison, watch your step. I was the little friend called the architect. But if I had had the controls I wouldn't have changed my attitude. Money didn't mean that much to me.

Certainly, Harrison's relationship with the Rockefeller family had provided him with many more opportunities for profit than he took. But probably equally true was the assertion of a former colleague, and one of Harrison's many lifelong friends, that the only power he ever really wanted was the power to create.[17]

Harrison was a designer of remarkably fertile imagination. For every new project, he came up with multiple solutions, many of which would have been viable and exciting. He was a master builder who learned quickly how to navigate skillfully the turbulent waters of political maneuvering, architectural intrigue, and design compromise that surround every large public building project. Because his largest projects often were vastly altered by budgets and committees, Harrison's virtues have been underestimated. Despite all, he emerges as a towering influence in the architecture of mid-century New York.

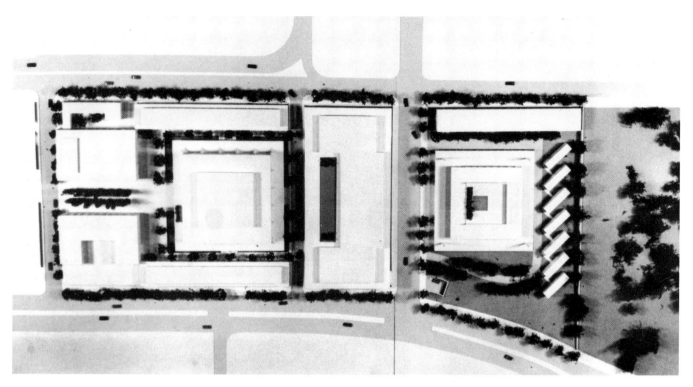

251. Harrison, early model, Pahlavi National Library Competition (1977). From left to right: Islamic studies department and auditorium, library (flanked by conference and administrative buildings), living quarters and audiovisual department, research center, and mechanical buildings.

252. Harrison, plan, Pahlavi National Library Competition.

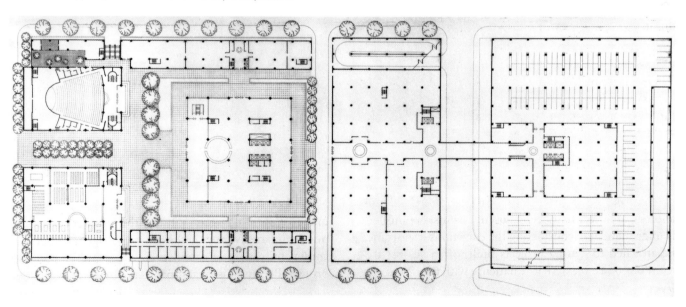

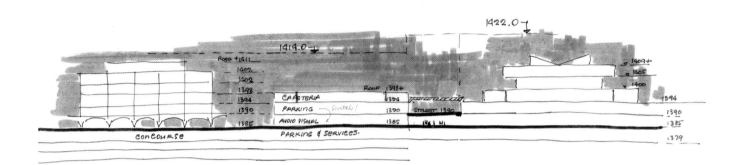

253. Harrison, elevations of library, service building, and
research center, Pahlavi National Library Competition.

254. Harrison, view of courtyard from above. At lower right:
sketch of east elevation, shown against mountain background.
Pahlavi National Library Competition.

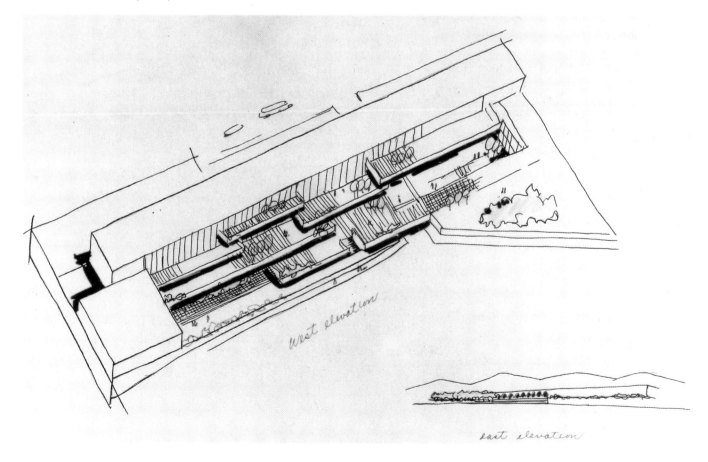

Harrison's luck remained with him to the end. Despite the frailty of his last years, his mind never suffered the indignities of old age, and he knew only a few weeks' physical discomfort before he died on December 2, 1981, attended faithfully by Ellen. Measured in terms of achievement, Harrison's life was a success. Disappointments at the end were slight compared with the extraordinary triumphs of preceding years. Friends, connections, monumental commissions—all seemed to have come naturally. If he was frustrated by design compromises made for the sake of expediency, there was consolation in the knowledge that some of his schemes were prophetic in concept and that he had made major contributions to building technology. While Harrison is firmly established as a modernist, with the climax of his career coming during the building boom of the 1950s and 60s, his long and colorful professional life reflected the dramatic changes of his time; from the conventional classicism to which he was introduced at McKim, Mead & White, to the eclecticism of the Goodhue office, the art deco modernism of Corbett, and finally the powerful personal modernism of his work from the United Nations on. With the Secretariat's glass curtain walls, Harrison provided an image that was to characterize large-scale architecture in the second half of the twentieth century. Through all, he greeted each new challenge with imagination and flexibility, but also with the patience and courtesy we now associate with an earlier, more gracious time.

Appendix A

After "The World of Tomorrow"

The fair opened on April 30, 1939, and by the time it closed on October 27, 1940, at the end of its second summer season, almost fifty million people had paid the admission fee (seventy-five cents the first year and fifty cents the second for adults and twenty-five cents for children) to bring in a revenue of about $48 million. The total investment, however, had been approximately $160 million, more than $67 million of which had been made by the Fair Corporation. The discrepancy between the corporation's expenditures and its receipts forced it to declare bankruptcy.[1] The fair's deficit was so large that backers were repaid only 39.2 cents on the dollar.[2]

The fair probably brought the city some of the business Whalen had hoped it would, but its specific impact on New York was impossible to evaluate: shortly after it closed, the economy was revolutionized by the nation's entry into World War II. Certainly, its political and socio-economic ideals remained in the realm of pure fantasy, yet the fair was without doubt a popular success (confirmed by the findings of George Gallup's recently established American Institute of Public Opinion). The machine technology of "The World of Tomorrow"—including television, to which the public was exposed for the first time—was viewed with fascination. It was no deterrent that twenty-three percent of the visitors who were on relief attributed their unemployment to increased mechanization.[3]

Appendix B

A Grand Approach to the United Nations

Zeckendorf had presented his idea, which anticipated—on an even more ambitious scale—elements of both the Markelius and the AIA proposals, to Moses, who turned it down in a letter dated April 1, 1947.[1] Despite the mayor's May announcement of the way in which he envisioned the city's relationship to the U.N. headquarters, on July 24 and 29 Zeckendorf presented his plan to the Board of Estimate.

Zeckendorf objected to Moses's endorsement of the city's meager solution of widening Forty-seventh Street on numerous grounds: it began nowhere and ended nowhere; it created two new bottlenecks of traffic at its entrance and exit; it exposed the unattractive backsides of the buildings facing the north side of Forty-sixth Street; it assured the continued existence of undesirable buildings that enjoyed prezoning rights; and it made no provision for parking or any other auxiliary access or service for the U.N.[2] The real estate man wanted to raze six city blocks: from the north side of Forty-sixth Street to the south side of Forty-ninth Street from First to Third avenues. Within this area, he envisioned a concourse 1,340 feet long and 320 feet wide—two-and-a-half times the width of Park Avenue—from First to Third avenues between Forty-seventh and Forty-eighth streets. Between First and Second avenues four sixteen-story structures would be set back as much as one hundred feet at either side of the concourse, the whole area becoming an uninterrupted park with buildings designed to stand on structural supports. An underground garage would provide up to eighteen acres of parking space for each floor excavated.[3] The concourse would culminate in a monumental steel pylon beside the river, which was conceived as a means of emphasizing the General Assembly building rather than the Secretariat. Recalling the earlier plan to incorporate the Metropolitan Opera House into Rockefeller Center, Zeckendorf now proposed a musical and theatrical center for the concourse. Broadcasting facilities would be located in twin forty-story office buildings that would face each other to form a giant gateway to the complex at Third Avenue. Flanking these towers to the north and south would be a concert hall and opera house, and to the east of these, eight theaters with rooftop restaurants and cafes.

Webb & Knapp held numerous parcels of real estate in the area in question (67,430 square feet of the total 1,138,800 square feet), together with an option to buy more. But for the firm to develop the project, the city would have had to exert its right of eminent domain, condemning the six-block site and reselling at public auction the two blocks to the north and the two to the south fronting the concourse. Zeckendorf offered to guarantee up to one hundred twenty percent of the current assessed value of land and buildings for all six blocks, thereby providing the two-block concourse to the city at no cost and possibly with a profit. As part of his proposal, he requested a multiyear freeze on the tax assessment for the six blocks, with full taxes to be maintained on improvements.[4]

The key to realizing any of these schemes was held firmly in the hands of Robert Moses, and Moses consistently vetoed each one of them. He claimed that all plans for a grand approach were unrealistic because the land to be occupied by the boulevard would present a tax loss of many millions to the city and such an avenue would conflict with the city's grid pattern of vehicular circulation. Abramovitz asserted that Moses adamantly opposed Zeckendorf's scheme on the grounds that city condemnation of land for resale to private interests would be a self-serving and dishonest attempt to confuse private and public interests.[5]

Zeckendorf's proposal and Moses's opposition to it turned into a bitter confrontation between two powerful men equally accustomed to getting their own way. In the course of a City Hall meeting on August 28, 1947, Zeckendorf became so outraged by the Board of Estimate's stubborn refusal to improve the Forty-seventh Street approach to the U.N. that he accused the Board of "abdicating to Mr. Moses." In an unfortunate loss of self-control, Zeckendorf called Moses a liar, thereby permanently sealing the fate of his project.[6] But Zeckendorf refused to give up. The following spring, an article in the *New York Sun* announced the sale of Webb & Knapp's holdings in the U.N. area as a step toward achieving Zeckendorf's monumental approach. Zeckendorf was quoted as saying: "The Mayor thought I was trying to pull a fast one because Webb & Knapp owned some property in the area. Well, we've sold it all. That ought to satisfy the city."[7] That fall Zeckendorf followed up with a series of full-page ads in the *New York Times* in which he explained that his plan was based on the AIA plan: both, he asserted, wanted an aproach to the U.N. that "New York could take pride in."[8] When even this extravagant gesture proved ineffective, Zeckendorf finally conceded that without Moses's endorsement the plan would never see the light of day.

Notes

List of Abbreviations

AIA Journal

American Institute of Architects Journal.

Caro

Robert A. Caro, *The Power Broker: Robert Moses and the Fall of New York* (New York, 1975).

Columbia Oral History

Transcript of ten interviews with Wallace K. Harrison conducted by R. Daum between 11 March and 4 November 1978, Oral History Research Office, Columbia University, New York.

Harrison Papers

Wallace K. Harrison. Papers, Avery Library, Columbia University, New York.

JSAH

Journal of the Society of Architectural Historians.

Krinsky

Carol Herselle Krinsky, *Rockefeller Center* (New York, 1978).

Plunz

Richard Plunz, "Institutionalization of Housing Form in New York City, 1920–1950," in *Housing Form and Public Policy in the United States*, ed. Richard Plunz (New York, 1980).

Spofford files

Charles Spofford's Lincoln Center files, Davis, Polk, Wardwell, One Chase Manhattan Plaza, New York.

Stern et al.

Robert A. M. Stern, Gregory Gilmartin, Thomas Mellins, "Rockefeller Center: From Metropolitan Opera to Miniature Metropolis," and "1939 World's Fair," *New York 1930, Architecture and Urbanism between the Two World Wars* (New York, 1987) pp. 617–71, 727–55.

Wind, with appropriate date

Herbert Warren Wind, Harrison Profiles, *New Yorker*, 20, 27 November and 4 December 1954.

Young

Edgar B. Young, *Lincoln Center, The Building of an Institution* (New York, 1980).

All references to the Metropolitan Opera Archive are to the Lincoln Center files, unless indicated otherwise.

Chapter 1
In Worcester and Boston

1. All quotations from Harrison in this chapter are taken from notes given to me by Harrison and from my interviews with him, 5 January, 26 February, and 11 March 1980.

2. "Project of Novel by Henry James," Appendix in Henry James, *The Ambassadors*, ed. S. P. Rosenbaum (New York, 1964), p. 377.

3. Other noteworthy buildings in Worcester included a number of private homes by leading architects of the day and the main railroad station (1877, demolished 1909), a magnificent low-slung, arched structure with a graceful, crenelated clock tower, by Ware & Van Brunt.

4. For the triple decker, see Marilyn W. Spear, *Worcester's Triple Deckers* (Worcester, 1977).

5. Worcester Board of Trade, *Worcester, the City of Varied Industries* (Worcester, 1909). Unpaginated pamphlet.

6. Wind, 20 November 1954, p. 62.

7. O. W. Norcross built more than half of Henry Hobson Richardson's designs, and nearly all his major works. James O'Gorman, "O. W. Norcross, Richardson's Master Builder, a Preliminary Report," *JSAH* 32, no. 2 (May 1973): 104–13.

8. Ibid., p. 109; and my interview with Harrison, 11 March 1980.

9. My interview with Harrison, 11 March 1980.

10. Letter of recommendation in Harrison Papers. Harrison was actually employed at Frost & Chamberlain from 22 February 1913 to 15 July 1916.

11. Henry-Russell Hitchcock, *Architecture: Nineteenth and Twentieth Centuries*, 3d ed. (Baltimore, 1968), p. 230.

12. America's first academic program in architecture was offered at the M.I.T. School of Architecture in 1865.

13. The club became the Boston Architectural Center in 1944 after it abandoned the Beaux-Arts system. It is presently at 320 Newbury Street.

14. Cross & Cross had been in existence for only eight years when it built the Park Office Building in consultation with D. H. Burnham of Chicago. The two brothers, John and Elliot Cross, continued their association until 1942, constructing a number of notable buildings in New York. Among these were the General Electric Company Building at 570 Lexington Avenue (1931), the City Bank Farmer's Trust Company Building at 20 Exchange Place (1931), and Tiffany's on Fifth Avenue and Fifty-seventh Street (1941).

Chapter 2
In New York; World War I

1. All quotations from Harrison in this chapter, unless otherwise indicated, are taken from my interviews with him, 26, 28 February, 3, 18, 31 March, and 4, 21 August 1980.

2. McKim agreed only reluctantly to allow his younger partners to enter the competition for a skyscraper—a building type which, like Henry James, he deplored as "a leggy weed in the garden of architecture." William H. Jordy, "The Renaissance in New York: The Buildings of McKim, Mead & White," *The New Criterion* 3, no. 2 (October 1984): 60.

3. Richard Guy Wilson, *The American Renaissance*, (New York, 1979), p. 75.

4. Ibid., pp. 97–98.

5. These were Madison Square Garden, the Morgan Library, the Washington Square Arch, Columbia University, the Municipal Building, and the American Academy in Rome.

6. My interviews with Harrison, 26 and 28 February 1980.

7. I am indebted to Christopher A. Thomas for the chronology of Bacon's career.

8. Wind, 20 November 1954, p. 66.

9. The church (1846), at 104 East Twenty-second Street, was built by James Renwick, Jr., at the same time as his more famous Grace Church. It included a Sunday school and a parish house. In this parish house the congregation's practical New England pastor let rooms for a nominal fee to the impecunious young men who studied for the clergy with him. Because of his special introduction, Harrison was granted the privilege of living in these modest but uplifting lodgings.

10. Wind, 20 November 1954, p. 67.

11. Irving Kolodin, *The Metropolitan Opera, 1883–1935* (New York, 1936), p. 229.

12. Wind, 20 November 1954, pp. 67–68.

Chapter 3
To Paris and back

1. Wind, 20 November 1954, p. 68.

2. Richard Chafee, "The Teaching of Architecture at the Ecole des Beaux-Arts," in *The Architecture of the Ecole des Beaux-Arts*, ed. Arthur Drexler (New York, 1977), pp. 62, 81–82.

3. All quotations from Harrison in this chapter, unless otherwise indicated, are taken from my interviews with him, 28 February, and 21 August 1980.

4. Gustave Umbdenstock's *Cours d'architecture* was published in Paris in 1930.

5. George Martin, *The Damrosch Dynasty* (New York, 1983), pp. 288–89; and my interview with Harrison, 26 February 1980.

6. Columbia Oral History, p. 391.

7. Thomas Tallmadge, *The Story of Architecture in America* (New York, 1927), p. 257.

8. For Goodhue's life and work, see Richard Oliver, *Bertram Grosvenor Goodhue* (New York and Cambridge, 1983).

9. For a description of Goodhue's office, see "Twelfth Night in Mr. Goodhue's Office," *Pencil Points* 3, no. 2 (February 1922): 21–26; and Ellen Harrison's private papers.

10. Oliver, *Goodhue*, p. 77.

11. W. K. Harrison, *The Building of the National Academy of Sciences and National Research Council*, unpaginated offprint from *Architecture*, vol. 4 (October 1924).

12. Oliver, *Goodhue*, p. 75. David De Long, chairman Historic Preservation, Graduate School of Fine Arts, University of Pa., has pointed out that Goodhue's modern classicism was also related to the work of Eliel Saarinen.

Chapter 4
The Grand Tour

1. The Rotch Traveling Scholarship still exists and now offers thirteen thousand dollars a year for eight months' study abroad.

2. All quotations from Harrison in this chapter, unless otherwise indicated, are taken from my interviews with him, 26, 28 February and 6 March 1980.

3. Notes for a book, *Report of the Rotch*, Box 16, Harrison Papers.

4. This and the following description of the American Academy in Rome are taken from Lucia and Alan Valentine, *The American Academy in Rome 1894–1969* (Charlottesville, Virginia, 1973), pp. 4, 39, 41, 82, 153–219.

5. Travel notes, Ellen Harrison's personal papers.

6. Travel notes, Ellen Harrison's personal papers.

7. Travel notes, Ellen Harrison's personal papers.

Chapter 5
New York:
the young partner

1. Oliver, *Goodhue*, pp. 196–99.

2. My interview with Harrison 4 August 1980.

3. All quotations from Harrison in this chapter, unless otherwise noted, are from my interview with him, 4 August 1980.

4. My interview with Harrison, 4 August 1980.

5. Andrew Saint, "Americans in London, Raymond Hood and the National Radiator Building," *Architectural Association Files* (London) 7 (1984): 37. Saint points out that Corbett's Bush Terminal Building provides an intermediary step between the Woolworth and American Radiator buildings.

6. Harvey Wiley Corbett, "Planning High Buildings on Narrow Streets," *American Architect* 119, no. 2369 (8 June 1921): 603–18.

7. Obituary, *New York Times*, 22 April 1954, p. 29.

8. Walter H. Kilham, Jr., *Raymond Hood, Architect* (New York, 1973), pp. 69–70. The museum was commonly referred to as the Roerich Museum and Master Apartments.

9. New York City Board of Education: *The First Fifty Years* (New York, 1949), pp. 86, 99, and *New York City School Buildings, 1806–1956* (New York, 1956), pp. 33–35.

10. Wind, 20 November 1954, p. 78.

11. The wedding took place at the Calvary Episcopal Church, in whose parish house Harrison had lived. Bobby Rodgers served as his best man. In marked contrast to Ellen's brother's wedding to Abby Rockefeller the preceding spring, the marriage was small and simple. Wedding announcement, *New York Times*, 14 February 1926.

12. My interview with Ellen Harrison, 18 June 1981.

13. Ellen Milton's travels had coincided with Harrison's before the two met. During the winter the architect spent in the Middle East on a Rotch Fellowship, Ellen had visited Egypt with her mother. While Harrison camped at the Engineer's Club at Luxor, spending grueling days making measured drawings of the temple, Ellen was living with her mother at the Luxor Palace Hotel.

14. My interview with Harrison, 4 August 1980.

15. After an unsuccessful marriage to Fritz Coudert, the socialite son of a founder of the Coudert law firm, Mary moved to Paris, where she lived a bohemian life with a handsome French sculptor from 1930 to 1940.

16. Arthur Gold and Robert Fizdale, *Misia* (New York, 1980), pp. 216, 271.

17. For a comparison of the Beaux-Arts method in France and in the United States, in particular at the BAID, see Rosemarie Bletter, "Modernism Rears Its Head," in *The Making of an Architect*, ed. Richard Oliver (New York, 1981), pp. 103–4.

18. Morris Lapidus, *An Architecture of Joy* (Miami, 1979), p. 54.

19. Ibid., p. 55.

20. Ibid.

21. My interview with Morris Lapidus, 14 September 1981.

22. W. K. Harrison and C. E. Dobbin, *School Buildings of Today and Tomorrow* (New York, 1931). Harrison also published several articles on school design: "The Functional Concept of School Architecture," *American School Board Journal* 93, no. 2 (August 1936): 31–32; "Placement and Size of Chalkboards," *The School Executive* 56, no. 5 (May 1937): 352–73; and "Movable Unit-Type Partitions," *The School Executive* 56, no. 6 (June 1937): 393–412.

23. For this and the following remarks about the significance of *School Buildings* in Harrison's evolution toward modernism, I am indebted to Charles C. Savage of the New York City Landmarks Preservation Commission, who lectured on the subject at the 1985 annual meeting of the Society of Architectural Historians in Pittsburgh.

24. I am indebted to Henry-Russell Hitchcock for calling this comparison to my attention.

25. See Harvey Wiley Corbett, "The Architecture of the Bush Buildings, London," *The American Architect* 120, no. 2372 (20 July 1921): 35.

26. The other two were the Milton House, Bermuda (1936), and the Avila Hotel, Caracas (1941). Because of his commitment to the U.N. Headquarters, Harrison was involved only peripherally with Harrison & Abramovitz's U.S. Embassy Office Buildings for Havana (1952) and Rio de Janeiro (1952), which were designed and built by Abramovitz and Charles Abbe.

27. *The Architects' Journal and Architectural Engineering* 51 (January–June 1920): 77.

28. Henry-Russell Hitchcock, *Architecture: Nineteenth and Twentieth Centuries*, p. 402.

29. The idea was first used by German expressionist architects and applied later in America by John Wellborn Root. I am indebted to David De Long for this information.

30. Krinsky, p. 178.

Chapter 6
Rockefeller Center: the beginning

1. All quotations from Harrison in this chapter, unless otherwise indicated, are taken from my interviews with him 21 August and 2 September 1980. A great deal has been written about the extraordinary venture that was to become Rockefeller Center, possibly America's greatest urban complex, and only the main points of the story, particularly those which pertain to Harrison's role, will be mentioned here. See Alan Balfour, *Rockefeller Center, Architecture as Theater* (New York, 1978); William H. Jordy, *American Buildings and Their Architects*, vol. 4: *The Impact of European Modernism in the Mid-Twentieth Century* (Garden City, 1972), pp. 1–85; Krinsky; Stern et al., pp. 617–672; Manfredo Tafuri, "The Disenchanted Mountain: The Skyscraper and the City," in Giorgio Ciucci, Francesco DalCo, Mario Manieri-Elia and Manfredo Tafuri, *The American City: From the Civil War to the New Deal* (Cambridge, Mass., 1979), pp. 461–86.

2. The proposed locations were Ninety-sixth Street and Park Avenue, Sixty-second to Sixty-third streets between Central Park West and Broadway, Columbus Circle, and the west side of Sixth Avenue between Fiftieth and Fifty-first streets. Ibid., p. 628.

3. The committee consisted of R. Fulton Cutting, president of the Metropolitan Opera and Real Estate Co., J. P. Morgan, Jr., Cornelius W. Bliss, Jr., Robert S. Brewster, De Lancey Kountze. Stern et al., p. 628.

4. Jordy, *American Buildings* 4:35–36.

5. Jordy, *American Buildings* 4:10–11.

6. John D. Rockefeller, Jr., founded the Palestine Archaeological Museum (now the Rockefeller Archaeological Museum) and financed the American Society of Classical Studies' excavation of the Agora in Athens; he financed construction of the new Protestant Riverside Church in New York (1930). Among the parks created as the result of Rockefeller donations are Acadia National Park on Mount Desert Island, Maine (1916); Grand Teton, Wyoming (1929); and the Great Smoky Mountains National Park, Tennessee (1930).

7. John R. and Dr. James M. Todd were the sons of a midwestern Presbyterian minister. After receiving his M.A. from Princeton in 1889, John R. Todd taught for two years at the Syrian Protestant College in Beirut, an experience that must account for his repeated appeals for a Byzantine or Romanesque style for Rockefeller Center. On his return, Todd entered New York Law School and was admitted to the bar in 1894. Like the brothers Todd, Hugh S. Robertson was also a minister's son. The partnership thus consisted of three ostensibly devout men of a type that was particularly congenial to Rockefeller. Geoffrey T. Hellman, "Profile, The Man Behind

Prometheus I," *New Yorker*, 14 November 1936, p. 36. Incidentally, Benjamin Wistar Morris 3d, the first architect involved with Rockefeller Center, was also the son of a churchman—in his case, an Episcopal bishop.

8. Medary had designed the relatively modern Bok carillon tower at Mountain Lake, Florida, which won the AIA Gold Medal in 1929.

9. Krinsky, p. 39.

10. Stern et al., p. 632; Krinsky, p. 39.

11. Krinsky, p. 40.

12. Ibid., p. 42.

13. Ibid., p. 44.

14. Jordy, *American Buildings* 4:36.

15. Kilham, *Hood*, p. 81.

16. Jordy, *American Buildings* 4:59.

17. *Architectural Forum* 56, no. 1 (January 1932): 1.

18. Krinsky, pp. 47–48.

19. My interview with Julian Street, Jr., 19 April 1982.

20. Ibid.

21. Jordy, *American Buildings* 4:39; Krinsky, pp. 50–52.

22. Krinsky, p. 59

23. *New York Herald Tribune*, 31 March 1931, p. 28.

24. Columbia Oral History, p. 95.

25. Krinsky, p. 73.

26. Jordy, *American Buildings* 4:46.

27. Carol Willis has pursued this aspect of setback design in her recent article, "Zoning and *Zeitgeist*: The Skyscraper City in the 1920s," *JSAH* 45, no. 1 (March 1986): 47–59.

28. Columbia Oral History, p. 73.

29. The aesthetics and function of the vertical and horizontal slab had intrigued architects for some time. In 1912 Frank Lloyd Wright sketched a thin twenty-five story building for the San Francisco Press, and in the 1920s and early 1930s Le Corbusier, Breuer, Gropius, and Aalto each designed either vertical or horizontal slab-shaped housing projects. With the exception of Aalto's Paimio Sanitorium, a building emphasizing horizontal lines, all of these early ideas for slab structures remained unexecuted. Winston Weisman, "Slab Buildings," *Architectural Review* 111 (February 1952): 119–20. David De Long has suggested that in making the east-west setbacks for the RCA Building, Hood may have been influenced—as he was for the Daily News Building—by one of Max Taut's designs in preparation for the *Chicago Tribune* competition, which showed setbacks on the sides of a tall building. The Philadelphia Saving Fund Society Building in Philadelphia (1932)

by George Howe and William Lescaze was one of the first approximations of a slab skyscraper in the United States. See Jordy, *American Buildings* 4:139.

30. Stern et al., p. 666.

31. "Building No. 11," *Architectural Forum* 72, no. 1 (January 1940): 23–28.

32. Jordy, *American Buildings* 4:77–78.

33. Wind, 27 November 1954, p. 68.

Chapter 7
Rockefeller Center: construction

1. Stern, et. al., p. 647.

2. Wind, 27 November 1954, pp. 60–61.

3. *Architectural Forum* 56, no. 1 (January 1932): 81–84.

4. In William Jordy's interview with Harrison in the early 1970s, he mentioned a fourth designer, John Walquist. Jordy, *American Buildings* 4:56.

5. All quotations from Harrison in this chapter, unless otherwise indicated, are taken from my interviews with him, 3, 6, 11 March and 21 August 1980.

6. Columbia Oral History, p. 97.

7. Ibid., p. 156.

8. Ellen Harrison's personal papers.

9. Krinsky, p. 56.

10. Eileen Simpson, *Reversals, A Personal Account of Victory Over Dyslexia* (Boston, 1979), p. viii. It was probably as a result of this disability that, throughout his life, Rockefeller favored visual over written presentations.

11. Frank Gervasi, *The Real Rockefeller* (New York, 1964), p. 64.

12. Heckscher was understandably antagonistic toward the Rockefellers. He had experienced a permanent congestion of traffic in his office building at 730 Fifth Avenue as a result of Mrs. John D. Rockefeller, Jr.'s, installation of the Museum of Modern Art's fledgling collection on its fourteenth floor; a few years later he witnessed the demolition for Rockefeller Center of the West Forty-ninth Street house in which he had grown up.

13. Krinsky, p. 66.

14. The Associated Architects may also have been influenced by Urban's recently published theater designs. Stern et al., p. 654.

15. *New York Journal*, 28 December 1932, p. 11.

16. Jill Lever and Margaret Richardson, *The Art of the Architect: Treasures from the RIBA's Collections*, exhibition catalogue (London, 1984), p. 125.

17. The scholars were: Ernest Martin Hopkins, president of Dartmouth College; George E. Vincent, a Rockefeller associate and president of the Rockefeller Foundation (1917–29); Michael Pupin, a physicist at Columbia University; and Hartley Burr Alexander (University of Southern California).

18. The second advisory group consisted of: Edward Waldo Forbes, director of the Fogg Art Museum; Everett V. Meeks, dean of the Yale University School of Fine Arts; Fiske Kimball, director of the Philadelphia Museum of Art; Paul J. Sachs, trustee of the Museum of Fine Arts, Boston; and Herbert E. Winlock, director of the Metropolitan Museum of Art. In his *New Yorker* profile of John Todd, Hellman claimed that Todd and Rockefeller made the final decisions on art in spite of the committee. Hellman, "The Man Behind Prometheus I," p. 35.

19. Balfour, *Rockefeller Center*, p. 148.

20. The following account of the Rivera mural for Radio City is based on Balfour, *Rockefeller Center*, pp. 181–91.

21. Winston Weisman, "Towards a New Environment," *Architectural Review* 108, no. 648 (December 1950): 402.

22. Balfour, *Rockefeller Center*, p. 35; Stern et. al., p. 639.

23. Balfour, *Rockefeller Center*, p. 36; and Krinsky, pp. 83–84.

24. Columbia Oral History, pp. 95–96.

25. Stern et. al., p. 639

26. Krinsky, pp. 84–85.

27. Ibid., pp. 85–86.

28. Russell Lynes, *Good Old Modern: An Intimate Portrait of the Museum of Modern Art* (New York, 1973), p. 190.

29. Goodwin was bitterly opposed by Alfred Barr and several trustees, who wanted a well-known European modernist—preferably Mies or Gropius—as the architect for the new museum building. Rona Robb, "1936: The Museum Selects an Architect," *Archives of American Art Journal* 23, no. 1 (1 November 1983): 22–30. I am indebted to Jennifer Licht Winkworth for calling this article to my attention.

30. Ada Louise Huxtable, "The Modern Prepares for Expansion," *New York Times*, Arts and Leisure Section, 29 June 1980, pp. 1, 26; and Paul Goldberger, "The New MOMA," *New York Times Magazine*, 15 April 1984, pp. 37 ff.

31. Lewis Mumford, "Mr. Rockefeller's Center," *New Yorker*, 23 December 1933, p. 30.

32. Lewis Mumford, "The American Tradition," *New Yorker*, 11 March 1939, pp. 37–40.

33. Jordy, *American Buildings* 4:84.

34. Krinsky, p. 90.

Chapter 8
Harrison, Fouilhoux, Abramovitz

1. Alex Gorlin, a New York City architect, has pointed out the motif's resemblance to draperies commonly found in rococo painting and wooden framing elements.

2. See chapter 7, n. 29.

3. My interview with Ellen Harrison, 18 June 1981.

4. Kilham, *Hood*, p. 73.

5. Richard Pommer, "The Architecture of Urban Housing in the U.S. during the Early 1930s," *JSAH* 37, no. 4 (December 1978): 249, 235.

6. My interview with Max Abramovitz, 30 July 1981.

7. James D. Kornwolf, Introduction, *Modernism in America, 1937–1941*, exhibition catalogue (Williamsburg, Virginia, 1985), p. 4.

8. The Aluminaire House may have been the first prefabricated house in the United States, and was certainly one of the first in this country designed in the International Style. Paul Goldberger, *New York Times*, 8 March 1987, p. 32 in "Arts and Leisure" section.

9. Harrison's Aluminaire House was never sheathed in canvas duck as claimed by Robert A. M. Stern in "IS: immediate effects," *Progressive Architecture* 63, no. 2 (February 1982): 106–9.

10. Ellen Harrison's personal papers.

11. My interview with Hester Diamond, the subsequent owner of the Huntington House, 3 January, 1984.

12. The Harrison & Fouilhoux office submitted two designs for this competition: one was Harrison's circular building that incorporated both the Senate and the House of Representatives, the other, by Abramovitz, consisted of two rectangular buildings, the narrow windowless sides of which were inscribed. See *Architectural Forum* 65, no. 7 (July 1936): 2–10.

13. My interview with Hester Diamond, 16 January 1985.

14. My interview with Ellen Harrison, 11 November 1983.

15. This and the following quotations from Julian Street, Jr., are taken from my interview with him, 19 April 1982.

16. Placement of the two Rockefeller apartment buildings parallel to each other at either side of a landscaped area (49 by 125 feet) adapts to the apartment block, row house plans that were common in England from the early nineteenth century. There were a few instances in New York City of this arrangement of large apartment houses a few years before the Rockefeller Apartments, as for example, the Parc Vendome Apartments at 330–360 West Fifty-seventh Street (Farrar & Watmouth, 1931) and 116 East Sixty-eighth Street (Andrew J. Thomas, 1932). See Stern et al., p. 421.

17. All quotations from Harrison in this chapter, unless otherwise indicated, are taken from my interview with him, 30 March 1980.

18. Lewis Mumford, "Modernity and Commerce," *New Yorker*, 3 October 1936, p. 48.

19. Rockefeller Apartments file, Rockefeller Family RG2, Real Estate Interests, Box 35, Rockefeller Archive Center, Pocantico, New York. In the minutes of a meeting on 3 July 1935 between Harrison and Mrs. John D. Rockefeller, Jr., she warned about keeping costs down.

20. The New York Zoological Society commissions came as a welcome challenge during Harrison & Fouilhoux's completion of the utilitarian Flower–Fifth Avenue Hospital (1939).

21. Allyn R. Jennings, "Planting the Plains of Africa-In-The Bronx," *New York Zoological Bulletin* 43, no. 6 (November–December 1940): 189.

22. The statement was made at a meeting between Harrison, Osborn, Laurance Rockefeller, and Moses. My interview with Harmon Goldstone, 3 May 1984.

23. In 1956 a nondescript building called Stage One was opened on the site: 216 feet long and 120 feet wide, it was a small fraction of Harrison's original scheme and bore little resemblance to it.

24. In the 1930s the Harrison & Fouilhoux firm executed a number of commercial renovations for which there is little documentation. One of these was the remodeling, in association with Harold Butterfield, of a store façade at 417 Fifth Avenue. At 417, as at its neighbor 415, shops were created at street level, with a series of display windows on the second floor. The Harrison & Fouilhoux storefront was distinguished by the boldness of its four-foot-high identifying numbers.

At the time of its completion, Lewis Mumford acclaimed these "new faces" as "the best piece of refurbishing on Fifth Avenue." Mumford, "New Faces on the Avenue," *New Yorker*, 9 September 1939, p. 62.

25. C. Grant LaFarge served as the committee's chairman; in addition to Harrison, it consisted of Charles Butler, William F. Lamb, and Ralph Walker. Judith Oberlander, "History IV 1933–1935," in *Making of an Architect*, ed. Richard Oliver (New York, 1983), p. 120. For the committee's recommendations, see "Architects' Committee Reports on Columbia's School of Architecture," *Architectural Forum* 62, no. 2 (February 1935): 163–65.

26. Oscar Nitzchke, who later worked for Harrison as a designer, is one of the few people who speak harshly—and with some bitterness—of his former employer, whom he accuses of appropriating the ideas of those around him as his own. When asked about Nitzchke, Harrison's terse rejoinder provided a glimpse of the tough, competitive side of his personality: "I was an obstacle to him; he always thought he would get a big thing, a whole building for himself, but no one would trust him to do a building on his own. I wonder why some guys get a building,

and others don't? Some fight and seem to put a lot into the thing they want and others just don't. I guess society has its own rules."

27. My interview with Porter McCray, 16 June 1982. In contrast with Harrison's dynamic effect on Yale's School of Architecture, Raymond Hood, Harrison's former employer and colleague at Rockefeller Center, served as design critic there from 1933 to 1934, and left no record of note.

28. Harrison's Yale students also included Benjamin Thompson, Norman Fletcher, and Robert MacMillan.

29. Wallace Harrison, "The Need for the Yale-*Life* Conference," in *Yale-Life Conference on Housebuilding Techniques* (New York, 1939), p. 9.

30. Philanthropic tenement housing for the poor had existed in New York since the 1870s. But with the exception of a few short-lived programs initiated in 1917 to house workers near wartime industries, the federal government was not directly involved with the problem until 1933, when the Housing Division of the Public Works Administration (PWA) was created. In 1937 passage of the Wagner-Steagall Bill, known as the United States Housing Act, empowered state and

local authorities to administer federal programs. Subsequently, the first federal and municipal housing developments began to go up in New York: in Manhattan's Lower East Side (Knickerbocker Village, 1934; First Houses, 1935; and Vladeck Houses, 1941); in Harlem (Harlem River Houses, 1937; and East River Houses, 1941); in Brooklyn (Williamsburg Houses, 1937; and Red Hook, 1939); and Queens (Queensbridge Houses, 1940). Richard Plunz, "Housing and Rehabilitation in New York City," in *Housing Form and Public Policy in the United States*, ed. Richard Plunz (New York, 1980), pp. 174–75, 179. James Ford, *Slums and Housing*, 2: pp. 635–36, 640 (Cambridge, Massachusetts, 1936).

31. Plunz, p. 184.

32. The other architects were Rosario Candela, Albert Mayer, Ethan Allen Dennison, William I. Hohauser, Ely Jacques Kahn, Charles Butler, Henry Churchill, and Clarence Stein.

33. Plunz, p. 184.

34. In 1922 the New York State legislature temporarily amended the Insurance Code to allow life insurance companies to invest in housing if rent did not exceed nine dollars monthly per room. By 1938 restrictions on insurance companies' investments were removed, and within a few years the companies became the major non-governmental source of housing money in New York. Plunz, pp. 163, 184.

35. I am indebted to Rosemarie Haag Bletter, director of interdisciplinary Modern German Studies, CUNY Graduate Center, New York City, for this observation.

36. Plunz, p. 179.

37. Ibid., p. 187.

38. Wayne G. Broehl, *IBEC* (Washington, D.C., 1968), pp. 203–9.

39. There are other claims for the invention of monolithic concrete, among them Grosvenor Atterbury (1904). See Donald H. Dwyer, Atterbury entry, *Macmillan Encyclopedia of Architecture* (New York, 1982). Edgar Chambless (1930s) worked on implementing production of monolithic concrete.

40. Kelly Burnham, *The Prefabrication of Houses* (New York, 1951), p. 242.

41. Broehl, *IBEC*, p. 235.

Chapter 9
1939: "The World of Tomorrow"

1. Doctorow, *The World's Fair* (New York, 1985), p. 250.

2. Joseph R. Cusker, "The World of Tomorrow: Science, Culture, and Community at the New York World's Fair," in *Dawn of a New Day, the New York World's Fair, 1939/40*, exhibition catalog (New York, 1981), p. 3.

3. Robert Moses, *The Saga of Flushing Meadow* (New York, 1970), p. 1.

4. Caro, pp. 1083–84.

5. Cusker, "The World of Tomorrow," p. 3.

6. *New York World's Fair Bulletin* (New York, January 1937) p. 12.

7. In addition to Michael M. Hare, the committee consisted of Louise Bonney, Harvey Corbett, Caleb Hornbostel, Albert Mayer, Harvey Zorbaugh, Lewis Mumford, Gilbert Rohde, Walter D. Teague, Ian Woodner-Silverman, N. H. Dearborn, and Henry Wright. Proposal submitted by a committee formed at the dinner at City Club, 11 December 1935, amended on 10 February and 13 May 1936. Box 7, A1–13, 1939, World's Fair Archive, New York Public Library, New York.

8. Cusker, "The World of Tomorrow," pp. 4–6.

9. Other members of the board of design were Richmond H. Shreve, Walter D. Teague, William A. Delano, Gilmore D. Clarke, Jay Downes, George Licht, Alfred Geiffert, Clarence Stein, William F. Lamb, Joseph Hartman, C. I. Lee, Louis Peixotto, and Louis Skidmore. Board of Design meetings 1936, Box 7, A1–13, 1939 World's Fair Archive.

10. Cusker, "The World of Tomorrow," p. 5.

11. Kenneth Reid, "World's Fair Competition," *Pencil Points* 17, no. 12 (December 1936): 655.

12. The first prize of $1,000 went to George Lyman Paine, Jr.; the second prize of $750 to Peter Copeland; and the third prize of $500 to Perry Coke Smith; the Harrison and Fouilhoux submission received an honorable mention. The competition jury included Stephen F. Voorhees, Gilmore J. Clarke, William A. Delano, Jay Downes, Charles Butler, Richmond H. Shreve, Walter D. Teague, Paul Cret, William F. Lamb, and Louis Skidmore. Among the better-known competitors were Warren & Wetmore, Cross & Cross, Chester B. Price, Frederick Hirons, George B. Post & Sons, William Van Alen, Percival Goodman, Ely Jacques Kahn, and Schultze & Weaver. The Architectural Competition, Box 44, CI, 1939 World's Fair Archive.

13. Wallace Harrison and André J. Fouilhoux, "The Theme Building," *Rockefeller Center Weekly* (30 April 1937).

14. Harrison & Fouilhoux press release, 5 March 1937.

15. All quotations from Harmon Goldstone in this chapter are taken from my interview with him, 7 July 1981. The sexual symbolism of the Trylon and Perisphere is obvious; Brenda Gilchrist, who helped edit this manuscript, suggests that Harrison's drawing next to a woman who was a symbol of sexual permissiveness reinforces this symbolism.

16. A number of other antecedents are attributed to the design. (See "1939 New York's World's Fair" in Stern et al., p. 752; commentaries posted at the exhibition, "Trylon and Perisphere, Icon of the Future," the Queens Museum, New York, 1981, cited *The Holy One*, a painting by Rudolf Bauer, and *Across and High*, a watercolor by Vassily Kandinsky, as design sources.) In my interviews with Harrison, he repeatedly disclaimed antecedents other than those I discuss in the text. See also Eugene A. Santomasso, "The Design of Reason: Architecture and Planning at the 1939/40 New York World's Fair," in *Dawn of a New Day*, pp. 33–34.

17. All quotations from Abramovitz in this chapter are taken from my interview with him, 23 September 1980.

18. Francis B. O'Connor, "The Usable Future: The Role of Fantasy in the Promotion of a Consumer Society for Art," in *Dawn of a New Day*, p. 62.

19. My description of the Trylon and Perisphere's structure is based on Helen A. Harrison's text on the wall panels for the exhibition "Trylon and Perisphere," Queens Museum.

20. Stern et al., p. 746.

21. Helen A. Harrison, "The Fair Perceived: Color and Light as Elements in Design and Planning," in *Dawn of a New Day*, p. 52.

22. Harrison also worked with Abramovitz and several of the firm's designers on the three pavilions that constituted the Master Pieces of Art Museum. It housed European paintings primarily from private American collections that included those of Samuel Kress, Robert Lehman, Mrs. Felix Warburg, Mr. and Mrs. Simon Guggenheim, Jules Bache, and Leon Schinas. *New York World's Fair 1939–40, Information Manual*, Box 1212, 1939 World's Fair Archive.

Chapter 10
With Nelson Rockefeller in Latin America and Washington, D.C.

1. Samuel E. Bleecker, *The Politics of Architecture: A Perspective on Nelson A. Rockefeller* (New York, 1981), p. 108.

2. Ibid., p. 109.

3. In this chapter, personal details and quotations attributed to Harrison are based on my interview with him, 3 March 1980.

4. The colors were criticized as garish, and the hotel was eventually repainted an off-white. My interview with Dudley, 17 July 1988.

5. A notable adaptation of a similar system of balconies and cross ventilation is Edward Durell Stone's El Panama Hotel in Panama City (1946).

6. Harrison included in the "junta": Beardsley Ruml, treasurer of R. H. Macy and chairman of the New York Federal Reserve Bank; Joseph Rovensky, vice-president of the Chase National Bank Foreign Department; Jay Crane, treasurer of Standard Oil of New Jersey; Hugh Robertson, who represented the Todd Company; William Benton, founder of the advertising company, Benton & Bowles, Incorporated; Robert Hutchins, and himself. Harrison's unpublished biography of Nelson A. Rockefeller, 1975, chapter 2, p. 9. Dudley adds to these: John Lockwood, Francis Jamieson, and Louise Boyer. My interview with Dudley, 17 July 1988. For Lockwood and Jamieson, see chapter 11; Boyer was for many years Nelson Rockefeller's personal secretary.

7. According to Ellen Harrison, the "little memorandum" consisted of a visual presentation, drawn up in the Harrison & Fouilhoux office, similar to the graphic displays Dudley produced later. Letter to me, 11 February 1984.

8. This was the first U. S. government money ever officially provided for a propaganda program. James Forrestal was to head the office, but two days after he received the assignment, he was asked to serve as Under Secretary of the Navy, whereupon he proposed that Rockefeller succeed him. Francis Jamieson, "Reminiscences," 1959, p. 91, Oral History Research Office, Columbia University.

9. My interview with Martha Dalrymple, Deputy Director of Information at the CIAA, 25 September 1981. After the war, Dalrymple continued to work for Jamieson, her boss at the CIAA, when he took over public relations for Nelson Rockefeller. See her *The AIA Story: Two Decades of International Cooperation* (New York, 1968), pp. 11–16.

10. Helping him in this task were the heads of the Guggenheim, Carnegie, and Rockefeller foundations: Henry Moe, Frank P. Keppel, and David Stephens, respectively.

11. The CIAA dispersed a great deal of cultural information, but its chief concerns were commercial and economic. The bureau was active in Latin American commodity problems and instrumental in persuading United States firms to continue spending their advertising money in Latin America, and it was probably the key agency carrying out research on economic development. By the end of the war, Venezuela still had a single-crop, single-product economy (with oil constituting ninety-five percent of its total exports); the country also had one of the lowest caloric intakes in the world. It became increasingly apparent that the CIAA would be unable to handle the long-range projects necessary to ameliorate the situation. By 1944, Nelson Rockefeller was pushing for an agreement with Latin America that would ensure continuation of the office's work.

12. These included the creation of two corporations: in 1947 the International Basic Economy Corporation (IBEC), a profit-making enterprise intended to create and energize business and to increase

the production and availability of goods and services, especially food and shelter (for Harrison's invention of the IBEC Housing Corporation's basic unit, see chapter 8), and in 1949 the American International Association (AIA), a nonprofit organization that would train people and develop institutions capable of continuing projects initiated by the Americans.

13. Within the traditional setting he exhibited, Harrison assembled materials and objects in an unconventional manner. The exposure of sporting goods, garden equipment, and clothing was noteworthy, as were the curvilinear effects of the focal lighting, by Kelly & Thompson.

14. Joe Alex Morris, *Nelson Rockefeller: A Biography* (New York, 1960), p. 76.

15. In 1941 the Harrison and Fouilhoux firm executed another domestic commission in Maine for Nelson Rockefeller: a sailing camp designed by Goldstone on a small island owned jointly by the Nelson Rockefellers and the Thomas Gates. (Mr. Gates was Secretary of Defense for President Eisenhower.)

16. As a result of a report Nelson Rockefeller requested on Axis airlines in South America, in June 1941 William Burden was appointed joint vice-president of the Defense Supplies Corporation, a subsidiary of the Reconstruction Finance Corporation. William A. M. Burden, *Peggy and I* (New York, 1982), p. 203.

Chapter 11
Toward the
United Nations

1. Wind, 27 November 1954, p. 51.

2. The figures related to William Zeckendorf's East River property are taken from William Zeckendorf, "X City Becomes the United Nations," chapter 6 in *Autobiography* (New York, 1970), pp. 63–78.

3. Ibid., p. 66.

4. Ibid.

5. "Real Estate: Mr. Knickerbocker's Face Lifting," *Time*, 14 October 1946, pp. 90, 92.

6. Robert Sellmer, "The Man Who Wants to Build New York Over," *Life*, 28 October 1946, pp. 67–74.

7. All quotations from and opinions attributed to Harrison in this chapter, unless otherwise specified, are taken from my interviews with him, 13 March and 9 November 1980.

8. Rem Koolhaas points out that the plans for X City specified horizontal separations of areas for diverse uses that had been superimposed vertically at Rockefeller Center; this was true also of the U.N. and of Lincoln Center. Koolhaas, *Delirious New York*, p. 238.

9. I am grateful to Philip Johnson for calling my attention to the flattened curve, and to Edgar Kaufmann, jr., for exploring the use of what he calls the "eyebrow curve." Other examples of Harrison's "eyebrow curve" are side walls and roof of the U.N. General Assembly, the main terminal at La Guardia Airport, the architrave of the Socony-Mobil Building, and the Lodge at Pocantico. See also Koolhaas, *Delirious New York*, p. 237.

10. Abel Sorensen's partial manuscript sent to Porter McCray, 6 February 1980. I am indebted to Porter McCray for making this manuscript available. Sorensen died on 12 January 1982, leaving this and additional material, which is being developed into a book by George Dudley, who helped me prepare the chapters on the United Nations.

11. Caro, p. 1085.

12. Wind, 4 December 1854, p. 58.

13. Jamieson, "Reminiscences," pp. 196–98.

14. Sorensen manuscript.

15. *Life*, 28 October 1946, pp. 67–74.

16. Wind, 4 December 1954, p. 60.

17. In his "Reminiscences," Jamieson recalls an interesting personal aspect of Nelson Rockefeller's relationship with his father regarding the U.N. In 1946, when the U.N. delegates were preparing to meet for the first time in the United States, as a member of the New York Committee for the United Nations, Nelson Rockefeller impulsively offered the Center Theater for the meeting. The offer, which was made public, became a source of embarrassment for Rockefeller when he found he could not deliver on his gesture; the Center Theater belonged to his father, who was unwilling—and perhaps unable—to change the existing lease. On signing the papers that committed him to the purchase of the East River site, Jamieson remembers that John D. Rockefeller, Jr., asked his son gently: "Will this make up for the Center Theater?" Jamieson, "Reminiscences," pp. 192–93, 204.

18. My interview with George Dudley, 9 April 1984. In an undated memo to the executive committee of the American Institute of Architects, Eric Gugler, the President, wrote:

"Whether you like the location or not, the imagination and ability, enthusiasm and friendship of Wallace K. Harrison are largely responsible for the choice of a site which has gratified the U.N. at least and certainly if you go along with the premises that actuated Wally in his effort, he must be given great praise and no doubt he will very likely become a party to future activity in relation to it." Eric Gugler Archive, Box R, folder 1, Avery Library, Columbia University.

19. Kenneth R. Stowell, ed., "A Competition for the World's Capital," and Edward Allen, "Capital for the UN," *Architectural Record* 99, no. 3 (March 1946): 65, 82–83.

20. Letter from George Howe to Eric Gugler, 22 May 1946, DAG 16/1.2.4., Box 1, U.N. Archive, New York.

21. Ibid.

22. Note from David Vaughan to Glenn Bennett, 11 April 1956, DAG 16/1.2.4., Box 1, U.N. Archive. A proposal was made at the annual convention of the American Institute of Architects for its sponsorship of an international design competition for the General Assembly building. The idea was rejected by the U.N. *New York Times*, 1 May 1947, p. 4.

Chapter 12
The United Nations: the battle of designs

1. *New York Times*, 7 January 1947, p. 6.

2. All quotations and opinions attributed to Harrison in this chapter, unless otherwise indicated, are taken from my interviews with him, 13, 17 March, and 3 April 1980 and 8 April 1981.

3. Wind, 4 December 1954, p. 67.

4. Le Corbusier, *United Nations Headquarters Report* (New York, 1946), p. 47.

5. Ibid., pp. 18–20.

6. Two years later, on 6 December 1935, Le Corbusier wrote to Harrison enumerating his subjects. He offered his services (1) for the design of model housing for the 1939 World's Fair and (2) for a study of New York's airport. He then asked if Nelson Rockefeller could be persuaded (1) to advance funds that were needed for publication of the English-language edition of his *La Ville Radieuse*; (2) to create a Rockefeller foundation for the friends of CIAM (Congrès Internationaux d'Architecture Moderne); and (3) to finance "a museum without walls" for the 1937 Exposition Internationale in Paris, as well as to purchase art to go into this museum. Harrison & Abramovitz files, Abramovitz, Kingsland & Schiff archive, 630 Fifth Avenue, New York.

7. This and the following references in this chapter to correspondence between Le Corbusier and Harrison are taken from the Harrison & Abramovitz files, Abramovitz, Kingsland & Schiff archive.

8. Memo from Le Corbusier to U.N. delegates to the General Assembly, 28 November 1948. Box 37, I_3 (II), Fondation Le Corbusier, Paris.

9. My interview with Michael M. Harris, then a Harrison & Abramovitz designer, 17 November 1981.

10. Dates related to activities of the Design Board, unless otherwise indicated, are taken from the diary kept by Glenn E. Bennett, DAG 16/1.2.4–4, Box 1, U.N. Archive.

11. Ad Hoc Committee on U.N. Headquarters, 26 September 1947, Harrison & Abramovitz files, Abramovitz, Kingsland & Schiff archive.

12. My interview with Goldstone, 23 November 1981.

13. Figures for the U.N. program are taken from Harrison's speech to the Technology Club and the Syracuse, New York, Society of Architects, 13 February 1950. Harrison Papers.

14. Wind, 4 December 1954, p. 69.

15. *This Week*, 23 March 1947, DAG 16/1.2.4., Box 1, U.N. Archive.

16. My interview with Dudley, 16 December 1981.

17. My interview with Harris, 17 November 1981.

18. Le Corbusier, "Declaration," No. 60, to Headquarters Planning Office, 15 April 1947, Harrison/Corbusier file, Abramovitz, Kingsland & Schiff archive.

19. My interview with Dudley, 30 March 1984.

20. Hugh Ferriss, account book, Avery Library Drawing Collection, Columbia University.

21. "The Secretariat, A Campanile, a Cliff of Glass, a Great Debate," *Architectural Forum* 93, no. 5 (November 1950): 96.

22. Stanislaus Von Moos, *Le Corbusier, l'architecte et son mythe* (Paris, 1971), p. 205.

23. Howard Robertson also gave credit to Ralph Walker for situating the tall building, "Obbligato to Architecture," *The Builder* 120, no. 6212 (8 June 1962): 1178.

24. My interview with Gordon Bunshaft, 6 November 1981.

25. Glenn E. Bennett diary, entry for 28 April 1947.

26. Sorensen-Dudley manuscript, transmitted by Dudley, 30 March 1984.

27. The General Assembly meets two to three months a year; the Economic and Social Council two to four times a year; the Security Council is in permanent session; the Trusteeship Council now meets infrequently, but its meeting rooms are in almost constant use by commissions and committees.

28. Draft of Le Corbusier report, 27 May 1947, DAG 16/1.2.3., Box 6, U.N. Archive.

29. Harrison's subsequent choice of Vermont marble reactivated what had been considered a dead industry in that state.

30. Bennett diary, entry for 30 April 1947.

31. My interview with Goldstone, 23 November 1981.

32. *Le Corbusier Sketchbooks*, Françoise de Franclieu, ed., vol. 2 (New York and Cambridge, 1981), p. 505 (written in 1951), p. 255 (written in 1950).

33. "U.N. General Assembly," *Architectural Forum* 92, no. 5 (May 1950): 97.

34. "U.N. General Assembly," *Architectural Forum* 97, no. 4 (October 1952): 144.

35. Ibid., p. 142.

36. I am indebted to Katrina Thomas, a former Harrison & Abramovitz designer, for drawing this analogy to my attention.

37. Quoted from the *Cleveland Plain Dealer*, in *Architectural Forum* 100, no. 1 (January 1954): 124. As the *Forum* article details, Oberlin had been given a bequest for the auditorium, Charles Martin Hall, in 1914 and had received proposals for it from a number of eminent architects including Cass Gilbert (1923), Richard Kimball (1937), Eliel Saarinen (1941), and Shreve, Lamb & Harmon (1943). Harrison obtained the commission through the intervention of Roy Hunt, with whom he was then working on the Alcoa Building in Pittsburgh (see chapter 14). My interview with Abramovitz, 4 February 1985.

38. Henry Stern Churchill, "U.N. Headquarters," *Architectural Record* 111, no. 7 (July 1952): 121.

39. My interview with Dudley, on 9 April 1984.

40. Churchill, "United Nations Headquarters," pp. 120–21.

41. Lewis Mumford, "U.N. Model and Model U.N." (1947) in *From the Ground Up, Observations on Contemporary Architecture, Housing, Highway Building and Civic Design* (New York, 1956), p. 54. Mumford's other Sky Line articles in the *New Yorker* on the U.N., "Buildings as Symbols" (1947), "Magic with Mirrors" (1951), "A Disoriented Symbol" (1951), "United Nations Assembly" (1953), and "Workshop Invisible" (1953) are also included in *From the Ground Up*, pp. 21–70.

42. Wind, 4 December 1954, p. 82.

43. "U.N. General Assembly," *Architectural Forum* 86, no. 6 (June 1947): 101.

44. Columbia Oral History, p. 288.

45. My interview with Harrison, 6 March 1980.

46. *New York Times Magazine*, 20 October 1946, p. 9.

47. Caro, p. 774.

48. Robert P. Wagner, Jr., and Robert Moses, *The U.N. and the City of New York, Report to Mayor Impelliteri and the Board of Estimate* (New York, 1951), p. 23.

49. Ibid.

50. The Carnegie Endowment Building was planned originally with the same green glass walls and aluminum mullions as the Secretariat. This project was published in the *New York Times*, 19 June 1951, p. 31. DAG 16/1.2.3., Box 6, U.N. Archive.

51. *The U.N. and the City of New York, November 1951*, p. 24.

52. One such proposal was made early in the design process by Markelius: he wanted to limit building heights near the U.N. and along First Avenue and to develop park belts on the Queens side of the East River, along with one beside the FDR Drive that would link the U.N.'s open spaces with green areas around riverside housing developments, hospitals, and residential sections. Markelius hoped eventually to connect the park belts on either side of the river. *The Secretary-General on the Permanent Headquarters of the United Nations, Official Records of the Second Session of the General Assembly*, supplement no. 8, New York, 1947, p. 79, and my interviews with Abramovitz, 23 September 1980, and Goldstone, 23 November 1981. Markelius also hoped to create a wide avenue between the headquarters and the center of the city (an idea already raised by the Design Board), setting aside four blocks between Forty-sixth and Forty-seventh streets from First to Park avenues and possibly two blocks between Forty-seventh and Forty-eighth streets from First to Second avenues. He planned to clear the area and transform it into a wide pedestrian walk one story above the avenues with two-story parking facilities below for four to

six thousand cars. Forty-sixth and Forty-seventh streets would have been lined with stores easily accessible from the nearby parking spaces and pedestrian area. Markelius, Report #59 on the U.N., n.d., pp. 4–6, Harrison Papers, and DAG 16/1.2.3., U.N. Archive.

53. The six parts of the plan were as follow: (1) Redevelopment of three blocks from the south side of Forty-eighth Street to the north side of Forty-fifth Street between Lexington and First avenues. (2) The creation of a 150-foot-wide boulevard connecting Park and Lexington avenues with one-way streets north and south of Grand Central Terminal. (3) To take advantage of the grade differences between Third and First avenues, the routing of vehicular traffic underground midway between Third and Second avenues to meet the levels of Second and First avenues. (4) The creation of a wide, central mall between Lexington Avenue and the point where traffic goes underground, with the continuation of the upper part as park strips with pedestrian access to the U.N. (5) The development of 285-foot-wide superblocks on either side of the approach. (6) The provision of parking facilities for 7,000 automobiles under the park strip and at the

lower level of the superblocks. *New York Times*, 25 August 1947, p. 19.

54. My interview with Bunshaft, 16 November 1981.

Chapter 13
The United Nations: the critics

1. *The Secretary-General on the Permanent Headquarters of the United Nations, Official Records of the Second Session of the General Assembly*, supplement no. 8 (New York, 1947), p. 79.

2. For the basic facts regarding financing and construction of the U.N. headquarters I am indebted to the third part of Herbert Warren Wind's three-part profile, "A Taxi to the U.N.," *New Yorker*, 4 December 1954, pp. 55–85.

3. The list of cutbacks is taken from the *New York Herald Tribune*, 1 April 1948, p. 13. As for the fence, Harris claimed that once it became a city expense Moses insisted on selecting the architect to design it. He chose Jacques Carlu, designer of the Palais de Chaillot and then head of the Massachusetts Institute of Technology School of Architecture.

4. Small countries that could not afford their own missions in New York, it was suggested, might locate their offices in such a building and share the

public space. In addition to problems of security, however, the countries in question were reluctant to make the financial commitment the project would have required, preferring to house their mission personnel in their own consulates. The idea eventually survived in embryo in the form of a few mission offices on the lower floors of 860 United Nations Plaza.

5. All quotations attributed to Harrison in this chapter, unless otherwise indicated, are taken from my interviews with him, 6 March 1980 and 17 March 1981.

6. My interview with Harrison, 6 March 1980.

7. I am grateful to Helene Lipstadt, curator of "The Experimental Tradition, Twenty-Five Years of American Architectural Competitions 1960–1985" exhibition, National Academy of Design, New York, 1988, for bringing this competition to my attention. The jury consisted of William Wurster (chairman), S. Herbert Hare, Fiske Kimball, Louis Labeaume, Charles Nagel, Jr., Richard J. Neutra, and Roland Wank. For sculpture, Harrison designated his old friend, Mary Callery. See *Architectural Group for the National Expansion Memorial Program* (St. Louis, Mo., 1947) and *Progressive Architecture* 29, no. 5 (May 1948): 51–75.

8. The ceiling in the U.N. Library's main reading room recalls Aalto's Municipal Library, Viipuri, Finland (now Viborg, U.S.S.R.). Harrison continued to be involved with alterations to the U.N. until the time of his death in 1981. In 1964 a $3 million expansion of the meeting areas was completed; in 1980 the General Assembly hall and all the large conference rooms were enlarged and the Security Council office and lounge were altered. Further additions were made by Abramovitz, Kingsland Schiff.

9. Wind, 4 December 1954, p. 78.

10. My interview with Harris, 7 November 1981.

11. Three months after the Secretariat was completed, a major hurricane blew into New York, striking the new glass building with all its force. Reports of window leaks revealed that water was being sucked into almost every floor from the window heads on the floor below. The problem was caused mainly by the building's north-south orientation. My interview with Street, 19 April 1982.

12. Draft of Harrison's reply to Le Corbusier, 19 November 1947, DAG 16/1.2.4., Box 2, U.N. Archive.

13. Harrison's speech to the Princeton Engineering Associates, 24 April 1947, p. 3. Harrison Papers.

14. The strike was called by the House-Wrecker Union, Local 95. Bennett diary, entry for 18 February 1947; *New York Times*, 2 October 1947, p. 16.

15. These exceptional conditions forced Fairless to break his agreement and raise the price of the steel he was supplying, necessitating further economies.

16. Reyner Banham, *The Architecture of the Well-Tempered Environment* (Chicago, 1969), pp. 220–26.

17. "Previews," *Architectural Forum* 90, no. 6 (June 1949): 81–85.

18. "The Secretariat," *Architectural Forum* 93, no. 5 (November 1950): 110.

19. Banham, *The Well-Tempered Environment*, p. 237.

20. Quoted in Bayrd Still, *Mirror for Gotham* (New York, 1956), p. 300.

21. Lewis Mumford, "The Quick and the Dead," *New Yorker*, 8 January 1949, p. 60.

22. *New York Times*, 17 September 1947, DAG 16/1.2.4., Box 5, U.N. Archive.

23. *New York Times*, 13 August 1947. DAG 16/1.2.4., Box 5, U.N. Archive.

24. Lewis Mumford, "U.N. Model and Model U.N." (1947), *From the Ground Up*, p. 21.

25. Lewis Mumford, "Buildings as Symbols" (1947), *From the Ground Up*, pp. 28, 29.

26. Ibid., p. 35.

27. *New York Times*, 7 January 1947, DAG 16/1.2.4., Box 5, U.N. Archive.

28. Gertrude Samuels, "What Kind of Capitol for the U.N.?," *New York Times Magazine*, 20 April 1947, p. 56.

29. Ibid. The terms "workshop for peace" were used repeatedly in different descriptions of the U.N. Headquarters project.

30. "The Secretariat," p. 95.

31. *New York Times*, 24 July 1949, DAG 16/1.2.4., Box 5, U.N. Archive.

32. Samuels, "What Kind of Capitol for the U.N.?," p. 57.

33. This and the following quotation are taken from Lewis Mumford, "Magic with Mirrors" (1951), *From the Ground Up*, pp. 36–44.

34. Churchill, "United Nations Headquarters," p. 121.

35. "The Secretariat," p. 98.

36. To execute the complex buildings, Harrison put together a network of construction technicians, many of whom he continued to call on throughout his career. Among these were Emil H. Praeger, a structural engineer; John Hennessy, of Syska & Hennessy, a specialist in mechanical equipment; William Mueser, of Mueser, Procter, Freeman, for foundations; and Louis Crandall, of Turner Construction, one of the biggest general contractors in the country.

Chapter 14
Big Buildings

1. Hitchcock, *Architecture: Nineteenth and Twentieth Centuries*, p. 403. In his description of Le Corbusier's attempt to build low-cost housing in Marseilles, Hitchcock points out what can happen without efficient office organization. The six years it took for the master's small atelier to construct the Unité d'Habitation made it a relatively expensive building by the time it was finished.

2. Ibid.

3. Historians and critics usually ignore the fact that, no matter how excellent a building's design, it remains a fantasy without the commission to build it. Throughout history the production of many accomplished architects was limited because they failed to obtain commissions. In sixteenth- and seventeenth-century Italy, personality problems limited the work of Serlio and Borromini;

the same was true of François Mansart in seventeenth-century France, and of Louis Sullivan in late nineteenth-century America. In the twentieth century, Henry Van Brunt's irascibility alienated many of McKim, Mead & White's longstanding clients, and Frank Lloyd Wright suffered from a painful period of inactivity as a result of social ostracism. At the opposite end of the spectrum was Hitler's architect, Albert Speer, who admitted that "he would sell his soul to the devil for a commission," (Barbara Miller Lane, "In Memoriam, An Architect Without Quality: Albert Speer 1905–81," *Skyline*, December 1981, p. 8), as indeed, he did.

4. Starting in the early 1930s, he served at various times as director or trustee of the New School for Social Research, Bennington College, the American Academy in Rome, the Equity Corporation, the 20th Century Fund, the Foreign Policy Association, the New York State Council of the Arts, Action, and the Solomon R. Guggenheim Foundation.

5. My interview with Goldstone, 7 July 1981.

6. My interview with Fritz Close, 2 February 1982.

7. "Alcoa Outlines Plan for Tower on Park Avenue," *Herald Tribune*, 14 April 1946, p. 8.

8. All quotations from Harrison in this chapter, unless otherwise indicated, are taken from my interviews with him, 3, 17 March and 7 October 1980.

9. Harrison became as relentless as his client in finding different applications for the metal, insisting on specially made aluminum nails and even designing a wavy motif for aluminum strips to be inlaid into the sidewalks surrounding the building.

10. My interview with Oscar Nitzchke, fall, 1980.

11. Aluminum pipes at this time cost less than half as much as copper and one-tenth as much as stainless steel. *L'Architecture d'Aujourd'hui* 24 (December 1953): 79–85.

12. Behind each panel was an air gap of two to eight inches and a four-inch wall of perlite—a special lightweight lath—and a plaster finish that was sprayed on from the interior.

13. After the panel's shape was decided upon, the question arose of a coating to protect the exterior surface during construction. Everyone agreed there should be such a coating, but because no precedent existed, it had to be made from scratch. Spurred on by the determination to find the right product, Alcoa's Roy Hunt (the son of Captain Roy Hunt, the company's principal founder), and two Alcoa engineers finally worked out a solution with Dupont de Nemours: a liquid plastic coating designed to wear off in five years. The system worked perfectly, with none of the "peeling" problems of more recent aluminum sheathing such as those suffered at the Citicorp Building in New York City.

14. Extrusion is a process applied to metal: a die is made in the desired shape and aluminum is squeezed through the die at very high temperatures (1,100 degress F).

15. My interview with Close, 2 February 1982.

16. "Alcoa," *Architectural Forum*, November 1953, pp. 124–126.

17. My interview with Abramovitz, 4 February 1985. Harrison also thought that Mellon might have been partial to him because of the work he did in the employ of Bertram Goodhue for the National Academy of Sciences in Washington under the watchful eye of Richard Mellon's uncle, Andrew, who was then secretary of the treasury.

18. The building's puzzling corner notches are explained by the parallelogram shape of the site, necessitating the same shape for the building, which had to be notched to join with the old, three-story-high Mellon National Bank next to it. See "The Ultimate Slab," *Architectural Forum*, April 1952, pp. 130–134.

19. Wind, 17 November 1954, p. 52. In the hands of the Federal Sign Company, engaged by Republic National to design the top as a support for a giant arc-light, the spike became an ungainly, rocketlike object.

20. Karl Hoblitzelle died of a heart attack before the building was completed. He was succeeded by James W. Aston, who dedicated additions of a new fifty-story tower and a one-story triangular pavilion on 25 January 1965, executed in the same style as the original building by George Harrel, a local architect. My interview with Aston, 5 November 1984.

21. Manuscript of Harrison's autobiography, with my editing, Harrison Papers.

22. Shortly after he completed the Corning Glass Building, Harrison used a similar glass sheathing for the Springs Mill Office Building (1962), just west of the Avenue of the Americas between Thirty-ninth and Fortieth streets. Abramovitz shares design responsibility for this building.

23. My interview with Rushmore H. Mariner, 6 January 1984.

24. Letter from Mariner to me, February 1984.

25. Members of the committee included the following men who had been connected with Rockefeller Center: Harrison, Hugh Ferriss, Walter H. Kilham, Jr., and Edward Durell Stone. Others on the committee were Leopold Arnaud, Stephen F. Voorhees, and Ely Jacques Kahn. Krinsky, p. 207, n. 150.

26. My interview, 16 February 1982, with Perry Prentice, who claimed that Harrison subsequently adapted several ideas developed for the Time, Inc. project to the U. N. Secretariat.

27. The new building cost more than two-and-a-half times the estimate for Harrison & Abramovitz's first proposal. In 1950 Time, Inc. sold the Marguery Hotel to Webb & Knapp; the Union Carbide Building (SOM, 1960), renamed Manufacturers' Hanover Trust Co. Building, now occupies the site.

28. Krinsky, p. 112.

29. *Architectural Forum* 108, no. 1 (January 1958): 96.

30. *Ibid.*, p. 98. In my conversation, 6 June 1986, with Alexander Hood, a Time, Inc. executive, he described the staff's amusement with the "jogs" in office partitions which inspired an office ditty: "I'll be happy as a bump on a log with my mullion to module job."

31. J. A. Morris, *Nelson Rockefeller* (New York, 1960), p. 287.

32. "Wallace Kirkman Harrison Designs Institute Buildings," *Rockefeller Institute Quarterly* 1, no. 2 (June 1957): 2.

33. See Krinsky, pp. 116 and n. 157.

34. My interview, 13 March 1985, with Robert Klein, a draftsman who worked with Harrison during the last decade of Harrison's practice.

35. My interview with Klein, 30 August 1983.

36. See "Recent Expansion," chap. 10 in Krinsky, pp. 116–29.

37. Peter Blake, "Slaughter on Sixth Avenue," *Architectural Forum* 122, no. 3 (June 1965): 16.

38. Plunz, p. 191.

39. Ibid.

40. The institutions were Barnard, Columbia, Corpus Christi Church, International House, Jewish Theological Seminary, Juilliard School of Music, Riverside Church, Teachers College, and Union Theological Seminary.

41. See Deirdre Carmody, "After 25 Years Co-op Endures as Stable Sign," *New York Times*, 16 October 1982, pp. 29–30.

42. For several years, Abramovitz remained involved as a consultant for the Battery Park City project.

Chapter 15
Small Buildings

1. Helen Dudar, "The Road to Success, Five Famous Men Take You Along," *New York Post Daily Magazine*, 4 December 1962, p. 37.

2. This and the following quotations about the new church, unless otherwise specified, are taken from my interview with Dr. Donald F. Campbell, 10 February 1982. Dr. Campbell was the church's pastor when the new building was designed and constructed.

3. This and the following quotation from Michael M. Harris are taken from my interview with him, 17 November 1981.

4. Harrison attributed the source of this first design to the Sainte-Chapelle in Paris. But instead of stopping the glass at the cornice line, as was done in the Sainte-Chapelle, he continued it overhead. He thought the result "looked like a greenhouse." My interview with Harrison, 1 April 1979. Another design, published in *Architectural Forum* 99, no. 6 (December 1953): 92–94, shows the glass and steel structure emerging from a rugged, irregularly shaped masonry base that rises almost to the roofline at one side.

5. One of two families who favored remodeling insisted that a new church could not be built within the $1 million budget. The sanctuary came to about $800,000, but the cost of the entire complex was close to $1.5 million.

6. Joan Miró and Jean Bazaine also contributed to the decoration of the church, which was constructed by the Peugeot auto factory workers.

7. The first letters of the words "Jesus Christ, God's Son Savior" form the Greek word "ichthys," or fish. The sanctuary's slate shingles have been likened to the scales of a fish (*Four New Buildings, Architecture and Imagery*, Museum of Modern Art, Art Bulletin 26, no. 2 [1959]: 13).

8. This and the following quotations from Harrison are taken from my interviews with him, 19 June 1980 and 29, 30 April 1981.

9. Shortly after the opening ceremonies, it was discovered that the enormous amount of new joining used in the church's structure had a degree of mobility that allowed rain to penetrate. Harrison insisted on rectifying the problem at his own expense.

10. My interview with the engineer, Paul Weidlinger, 21 August 1984.

11. Dan Kiley was the landscape architect.

12. Answer to UNESCO inquiry, 9 November 1955. Ellen Harrison's personal papers.

13. Public School 34 is one of a series of schools the Board of Education started to erect in New York in 1943 that broke with the traditionally bleak format of five-story buildings squeezed between tenements. Harrison's school was typical of the new approach: freestanding, no more than three stories high, and, together with its playground, occupying a whole block. The school's openness is a welcome relief amidst the oppressive highrise development in which it stands.

14. *The Academy Building; A History and Descriptive Guide* (Washington, D.C., 1980), pp. 21–25; and my interview with Cyril Harris, 4 May 1982.

15. Later additions to this second story were not designed by Harrison.

16. Harrison eventually built a beach shelter for Oppenheimer at Caneel Bay, St. John, in the Virgin Islands, which Ellen Harrison described as stunningly beautiful in its simplicity. Unfortunately, there is no visual record of it. Letter to me from Ellen Harrison, 27 September 1983.

17. 1961–64 files, Historical Studies and Social Science Library, Institute for Advanced Studies, Princeton, New Jersey.

18. The space above the acoustic-tile ceiling of the central corridor serves as a longitudinal duct connecting the lateral ducts in the beam system. This aesthetically pleasing innovation unfortunately proved to be impractical both because of a recurrent problem with leaks and, after the energy crisis, in terms of environmental control. "Light New Use—and New Form—for the Monitor Skylight," *Architectural Record* 141, no. 5 (5 May 1967): 151–58.

19. My interview with Mariner, 6 January 1984.

20. "Reflections on a Glass Museum." *Architectural Record* 169, no. 2 (February 1981): 68.

Chapter 16
Lincoln Center

1. Young, p. 14. By 1958 public opposition to the destruction of Carnegie Hall had saved the building.

2. Letter from Arthur A. Houghton, Jr., to me, 5 April 1982.

3. Letter from Ellen Harrison to me, May 1983.

4. Caro, p. 1013.

5. By participating in an urban renewal project with Lincoln Center at its core, he may have been consciously following in the footsteps of his father, who had created the Bureau of Social Hygiene in response to his horror at the condition of city slums. *Architectural Forum* 108, no. 3 (March 1958): 90.

6. Rockefeller's dependence on committee decisions also may have stemmed from family precedent, this time set by his grandfather's brilliant use of committee management at Standard Oil of New Jersey. (I owe this suggestion to my husband.)

7. For a personal account of the area in the early twentieth century, see Lewis Mumford, *Sketches from Life* (New York, 1982), pp. 3–9.

8. Ellen Manfredonia, "The Politically Viable Plan," Master's thesis, Columbia University, School of Architecture, May 1967, Avery Library, pp. 46–48.

9. Added to the Lincoln Square exploratory committee were: Devereux C. Josephs, chairman of the New York Life Insurance Company and a trustee of several cultural institutions, and Robert E. Blum, vice-president of Abraham & Straus and president of the Brooklyn Institute of Arts and Sciences. David M. Keiser, a trustee of the Juilliard School, soon replaced Floyd Blair, and the Met added to the committee two of its directors: Irving S. Olds, the retired chairman of U. S. Steel, and C. D. Jackson, publisher of *Fortune* magazine. Young, p. 21.

10. Ibid., p. 24.

11. Minutes of the meeting of advisory architects for Lincoln Center, 22 August 1957, Harrison & Abramovitz files, Abramovitz, Kingsland & Schiff archives.

12. Manfredonia, "The Politically Viable Plan," p. 82.

13. The twenty-two participants are listed in Young, chapter 2, n. 3.

14. John D. Rockefeller 3d (later elected chairman), Charles Spofford, Anthony Bliss, David Keiser, Arthur Houghton, Irving Olds, and C. D. Jackson were the incorporators. Young, pp. 19, 33.

15. The first board of directors of Lincoln Center for the Performing Arts included all members of the Exploratory Committee except Harrison (because his role as architect precluded his serving as his own client); plus Lawrence J. McGinley, S.J., president of Fordham University; Dr. George D. Stoddard, dean of the School of Education, New York University; and Frank Weil, a businessman active with the Federation of Jewish Philanthropies. Young, pp. 51–52.

16. The Los Angeles Board of Architecture and Design was made up of seven architects in addition to Harrison: William Pereira, Eero Saarinen, Henry Dreyfus, William W. Wurster, Gordon B. Kaufman,

Reginald D. Johnson, and Charles O. Marcham. *Los Angeles Times*, 3 January 1949, section 4, pp. 4–5. See also, *Southwest Builder and Contractor*, 23 July 1948, pp. 13–15. I am indebted to Richard Longstreth for bringing this article to my attention.

17. My interview with Abramovitz, 4 February 1985. In a letter of 1 May 1956 to John D. Rockefeller 3d, Arthur Houghton mentions William Wurster as another possible architect for one of the Lincoln Center buildings. He reports on Markelius, Belluschi, Wurster, and Philip Johnson, none of whose firms are large enough, he believes, to carry out "a big job on the east coast." Box 69, Architects' file, Rockefeller Family Archive.

18. Minutes of the conference of advisory architects, acousticians, and stage designers for Lincoln Center, 2–12 October 1956, pp. 4–5, Spofford files. Martin Bloom points out that, as built, Lincoln Center's attempted relationship to Broadway is unsatisfactory because its plaza intersects Broadway between Sixty-third and Sixty-fourth streets across the triangular green space of Dante Park rather than at Sixty-fifth Street, where Broadway crosses Columbus Avenue. "Cultural Colossi: Lincoln Center at 19," *AIA Journal* 70, no. 9 (August 1981):33.

19. Michael Kramer and Sam Roberts, *I Never Wanted to Be Vice-President of Anything* (New York, 1976), pp. 13–14.

20. Minutes of the conference of advisory architects, acousticians, and stage designers for Lincoln Center, 2–12 October 1956, p. 4, Spofford files.

21. Minutes of the meeting of advisory architects for Lincoln Center, 3 November 1956. Lincoln Center files, Abramovitz, Kingsland & Schiff archive.

22. Young, p. 66.

23. Ibid.; see also pp. 73–74, 77.

24. John W. Drye, Jr., Houghton, and Jackson were committee members; Spofford was added a year later. Edgar B. Young and Reginald Allen attended the committee's meetings to coordinate its activities with other aspects of Lincoln Center; General Otto L. Nelson, Jr., was responsible for implementing the committee's decisions. Young, p. 86.

25. *New York Times Magazine*, 8 February 1959, pp. 22–25.

26. "Eero Saarinen, Architect," *Time*, 2 July 1956, pp. 50–57.

27. My interview with Johnson, 25 March 1982.

28. My interview with Bunshaft, 6 November 1981; and minutes of the Lincoln Center for the Performing Arts meeting with the Collaborating Architects, 6 December 1958, pp. 1–2, Spofford files.

29. In asking d'Harnoncourt to replace his committee on design decisions, Rockefeller was undoubtedly thinking of d'Harnoncourt's tact as well as his expertise. The art critic John Russell wrote of d'Harnoncourt: "[He] operated as a European diplomatist who could play on other people as Segovia plays the guitar." "Revisiting the Mother of Modernism," *House & Garden* 156, no. 8 (August 1984): 160.

30. Minutes of the Lincoln Center for the Performing Arts meeting with the Collaborating Architects, 19 January 1959, p. 3, Spofford files.

31. *New York Times Magazine*, 8 February 1959; and my interview with Anthony Bliss, 16 April 1982.

32. Minutes of the Lincoln Center for the Performing Arts meeting with the Collaborating Architects, 22 November 1958, p. 1, Spofford files.

33. My interview with Johnson, 18 December 1981.

34. Young, p. 90; and minutes of the Lincoln Center for the Performing Arts meeting with the Collaborating Architects and John D. Rockefeller 3d, 26 August 1959, p. 1, Spofford files.

35. For example, when in the fall of 1960, Johnson's design for the dance theater met with severe criticism from the other architects because it did not relate to the design of the Philharmonic, he proposed a building with solid walls that would be interrupted solely by one glass bay on each side and one on the façade. Johnson argued in his defense that he could open the front only if he were allowed to leave the side walls solid, which he was finally allowed to do—despite the disparity his solution created between the Broadway elevations of the dance theater and the concert hall. He thereby achieved his original intentions in a trade-off that he alone had the savvy to pull off. Equally radical changes were made in the design of the museum-library, the theaters, and the opera. Minutes of the Lincoln Center for the Performing Arts meeting with the Collaborating Architects, John D. Rockefeller 3d, and Newbold Morris, Parks Commissioner, 3 November 1960, p. 2, Spofford files.

Chapter 17
The Metropolitan Opera House: beginnings

1. This brief summary of operatic history in New York City is based on Henry Edward Krehbiel, *Chapters of Opera* (New York, 1911), pp. 3–91. I am grateful to Richard Tuggle for drawing this book to my attention.

2. Cady's winning design was for a different site, and had to be adapted to the permanent Broadway location. As built, his opera house contained 3,765 seats with three tiers of boxes, a balcony and family circle, and twelve "baignoire" boxes (six at either side of the proscenium). Introductory text, with corrected number of seats, to the "Metropolitan Opera House" exhibition, National Academy of Design, New York, 1984.

3. Introductory text to the "Metropolitan Opera House" exhibition.

4. B. M. Steigman, "Precursor to Lincoln Center," *The American Quarterly* 13, no. 3 (Fall, 1961): 376–86.

5. Stern et al., pp. 618–19, 621.

6. For descriptions of Urban's designs and his relationship to Benjamin Wistar Morris and the opera project, I am indebted to Stern et al., pp. 621–25.

7. The Old House Committee included Chancellor Chase (chairman), H. Wendall Endicott, Colonel Joseph M. Hartfield, David T. Layman, Jr., and Thomas Sidlo, "New Opera Projects, 1927-file," Metropolitan Opera Archive.

8. The other members of the New House Committee were C. D. Jackson (chairman), Curtis Calder, William Keary, and Benjamin Strong; Charles Spofford was an ex-officio member of the committee, and Reginald Allen served as coordinator. Ibid.

9. These improvements were formulated the following year: 4,500 good seats; technical facilities; air-conditioning; facilities for the "practice and growth of music," television broadcasting; revenue-producing commercial facilities; and a 500–1,000-car garage. Report from New House Committee to board of directors, Metropolitan Opera House, 20 March 1950, Metropolitan Opera Archive.

10. Other schemes submitted at this time were for the existing site at Broadway and Thirty-ninth Street, Columbus Circle, Tudor City, and the Queensborough Bridge at Fifty-ninth to Sixtieth streets between Second and Third avenues. Report on Washington Square site, "New Opera House, 1949-file," Metropolitan Opera Archive.

11. A number of sites were available for approximately $2.5 million; the estimated cost of construction was $16 million. Sites available for the music center included Washington Square, Tudor City, and the west side of Sixth Avenue north of Forty-second Street; for the Opera House alone, Central Park South between Seventh Avenue and Columbus Circle, Tudor City, the Queensborough Bridge area, and Sixth Avenue. Report of New House Committee, 27 March 1950, "New Opera Projects, 1927-file," Metropolitan Opera Archive.

12. Ibid.

13. "Constituent Groups file," 1957, Spofford files. The Met's problems in dealing with others were long-standing. On 19 August 1929 John D. Rockefeller, Jr.'s, real estate aide, Charles Heydt, wrote to his employer about his protracted negotiations to sell a Rockefeller Center site to the Met: "I think it is outrageous that the Opera Group should be playing us as they have and making us wait on their convenience" (Balfour, *Rockefeller Center*, p. 11). One measure of the relative size and complexity of the opera house in relation to some of the other Lincoln Center buildings is the architects' fees. On 20 March and 8 August 1958, these are recorded respectively as $70,000 for the Juilliard School, $75,000 for the State Theater, and $300,000 for the opera. Memos from Mendes Hershman to Reginald Allen, Annual Report Correspondence, Box 47, Rockefeller Family Archive.

14. According to Krawitz, the Metropolitan Opera Building Committee consisted essentially of Bliss, Bing, and himself; he, in turn, relied heavily on the advice of Walther Unruh, a paid consultant, Rudolph Kuntner, and Lewis Edson, the Met's chief electrician and carpenter, respectively, and Herbert Graf, the stage manager. My interview with Krawitz, 6 October 1987.

15. All quotations from Anthony Bliss in this chapter are taken from my interview with him, 6 April 1982.

16. My interview with Abramovitz, 7 April 1982.

17. My interview with Krawitz, 31 March 1982.

18. In 1958 Krawitz became the Metropolitan Opera's Business and Technical Administrator, and from 1963 to 1972 he served as Assistant General Manager.

19. Sir Rudolph Bing, *5,000 Nights at the Opera* (New York, 1972), p. 290.

20. My interview with Katrina Thomas, who attended the architects' meetings for Lincoln Center as a member of the Harrison & Abramovitz staff, 19 July 1985.

21. Irving Kolodin, *The Metropolitan Opera 1883–1966* (New York, 1968), p. 40.

22. "The new Met and Its old master," *Newsweek*, 19 September 1966, p. 78.

23. These included the electronic, multi-preset lighting control system, the synchronous winch rigging system, and other analog and digital control systems that were labor-saving and therefore economical.

24. My conversation with George C. Izenour, 3 August 1985.

25. Letter from Krawitz to Day & Zimmerman, 27 September 1956, Metropolitan Opera Archive.

26. Unruh's final stage design in fact incorporated many aspects of the technology recommended by Izenour. See George C. Izenour, *Theater Design* (New York, 1977), p. 281.

27. Letter from Robinson to Bing, Gutman, Allen, and Rudolf, 17 November 1955, Metropolitan Opera Archive.

28. Harrison's memo to Bliss, 4 October 1956, Metropolitan Opera Archive.

29. The sail-like design resembles a 1915 drawing by Erich Mendelsohn and Otto Bartning's project for the Star Church (1924). The faceted design recalls Wassili Luckhardt's 1920 "Cinema Form Fantasy." I am grateful to Rosemarie Bletter for her help in making some of these comparisons. See Susan King, *The Drawings of Eric Mendelsohn* (Berkeley, 1969), p. 58; Julius Posener, *Otto Bartning* (Berlin, 1983), p. 16, and Ian Boyd Whyte, *The Crystal Chain Letters* (Cambridge, Mass., 1985) p. 33.

30. My interview with Harrison, 17 March 1981.

31. In recent years this arched motif has been reproduced *ad nauseum*. One of its first progenies was for the auditorium at the University of Baghdad by Walter Gropius and the Architects' Collaborative (1960).

32. Ada Louise Huxtable, "The Met as Architecture," *New York Times*, 17 September 1966, p. 17.

33. In an updated letter from Krawitz to Graf, official note was taken of Harrison's unhappiness with his clients. June–July 1958 file, Metropolitan Opera Archive.

34. Peter D. Franklin, "Lincoln Center Design: 'A New U.S. Landmark,' " *New York Herald Tribune*, 25 May 1958, p. 1. Harrison's proposal for the interior had been accepted at the opera board meeting of 4 September 1957. Minutes of the meeting of the board of directors, Metropolitan Opera House, Metropolitan Opera Archive.

35. Minutes of the meeting of advisory architects, 29 January 1958, p. 2, Metropolitan Opera Archive.

36. Young, p. 69.

37. Letter from Krawitz to Bliss on dismissing Harrison and Abramovitz, November 1958, Metropolitan Opera Archive.

38. Minutes of the meeting with representatives of the Metropolitan Opera, Harrison, and Abramovitz, 18 February 1959, p. 1, Brothers' Interests, Box RG UMR, Rockefeller Family Archive.

39. Ibid., p. 2.

40. Minutes of the meeting with the Collaborating Architects, 28 October 1959, p. 11, Metropolitan Opera Archive. Although sheathed by a flat roof, the structural arches of the first proposal were kept: each arch is thirty-four feet in diameter and stretches from the front of the stage to the building's façade. The arches were built simply and economically by using a form five times: after the concrete was poured into a form, it was moved back on rails and poured again. Columbia Oral History, p. 333.

41. The opera house was not the only building at Lincoln Center to change radically from the architect's original intention. At a meeting of the architects on 26 February 1960, Eero Saarinen presented a model of the repertory theater with a graceful glass façade hung from a catenary concrete roof. Bunshaft relates that after the meeting, he and Saarinen decided to add columns at the building's corners. My interview with Bunshaft, 6 November 1981.

42. Columbia Oral History, p. 252.

43. Minutes of the meeting of Lincoln Center directors with the Collaborating Architects, 7 January 1960, Metropolitan Opera Archive.

44. *New York Times*, 1 December 1955, p. 44.

45. Johnson said recently of Kirstein: "He was as scary then as he is now." *New York Times Magazine*, 20 June 1982, p. 26.

46. Young, p. 188.

47. Minutes of the meeting of the Collaborating Architects, 15 April 1960, pp. 1–2. Harrison & Abramovitz files, Abramovitz, Kingsland & Schiff archives.

48. My interview with Bliss, 6 April 1982.

49. Minutes of the meeting of the Collaborating Architects, 13 July 1960, p. 1. Spofford files.

50. Memo to Harrison from Allen, 17 November 1960, Metropolitan Opera Archive.

51. Minutes of the meeting of the Lincoln Center board of directors, 15 May 1961, Metropolitan Opera Archive.

52. My interview with Harrison, 18 March 1980.

53. My interview with Bliss, 6 April 1982.

54. Minutes of the meeting of the executive committee of the Metropolitan Opera Association, 8 June 1961, Spofford files.

55. Letter from Louis Crandall, chairman of the Fuller Construction Company, in charge of constructing the opera house, to Young, 14 June 1962, Metropolitan Opera Archive.

56. Minutes of the meeting of the executive committee of the Metropolitan Opera Association, 7 July 1961, Spofford files.

57. Minutes of the meeting of the executive committee of the Metropolitan Opera Association, 14 December 1961, Spofford files.

58. Frank Lloyd Wright said that "the physician can bury his mistakes, but the architect can only advise his client to plant vines." Wright seems to have first used this often-quoted idea publicly in a lecture on 2 October 1930. Frank Lloyd Wright, "To the Young Man in Architecture," in *Two Lectures in Architecture* (Art Institute of Chicago, 1931), p. 62. I am indebted to Edgar Kaufmann, jr., for this information.

Chapter 18
The Metropolitan Opera House: completion

1. Memo from Unruh to Bing, 18 May 1962, Metropolitan Opera Archive.

2. Memo from Unruh to Bing, 10 October 1963, Metropolitan Opera Archive.

3. Ibid.

4. Anticipating that Lincoln Center, Inc. would assume responsibility for construction interrelationships between its buildings and the adjoining plaza, park, and garage to be built by the city and supervised by Harrison & Abramovitz, Moses wanted to use the same general contractor for the private and public work; he pushed for a joint venture of several builders. In response to Moses's urging, the Turner, Fuller, Walsh, and Slattery companies were retained on 5 December 1958 by Lincoln Center, Inc. Young, p. 94.

5. Ibid., p. 69.

6. Minutes of the meeting of Collaborating Architects, 26 January 1961, p. 2. Spofford files.

7. This and the following quotations from Carl Morse are taken from my interview with him, winter 1981–82.

8. On 26 July 1962 Lincoln Center, Inc. and the Lincoln Center Building Committee terminated its contract with the joint venture after completion of the Philharmonic Hall and the central mechanical plant. Young, p. 144.

9. My interview with Abramovitz, 30 March 1982.

10. My interview with Carl Morse, winter 1981–82.

11. My interview with Bliss, 6 April 1982.

12. Columbia Oral History, p. 320. The Auditorium Theater in Chicago (Adler & Sullivan, 1889) provides a famous precedent for a movable hinged ceiling.

13. Harris denies ever working with Jordan at the State Theater, as stated in Young, p. 93.

14. Thus, if the model was built on a scale of one-quarter inch to one foot, a frequency of twenty-four thousand cycles would correspond to a sound of five hundred cycles in the room. Cyril M. Harris and Vernon O. Knudsen, *Acoustical Designing in Architecture*, rev. ed. (New York, 1978), p. 182.

15. Letter from Harris to Jordan, 14 May 1963. A copy of this letter is in the possession of Cyril Harris.

16. My interview with Cyril Harris, 4 May 1982.

17. Letter from Harris to Harrison, 22 June 1965. A copy of the letter is in the possession of Cyril Harris.

18. This and the following quotations from Harris, together with technical details, are taken from my interview with him, 4 May 1982.

19. Unless otherwise indicated, this and the following quotations from Harrison are taken from my interviews with him, 25, 26, and 27 March 1981.

20. Columbia Oral History, p. 256.

21. Raymond Erickson, "New Metropolitan Opera House to Have Some Limited Views of Stage," *New York Times*, 28 June 1963, p. 26.

22. Columbia Oral History, p. 256.

23. The committee is referred to in the minutes of the meeting of the board of directors, Metropolitan Opera House, 16 April 1959, Metropolitan Opera Archive.

24. William H. Jordy makes this distinction for the Music Hall in *American Buildings*, 4:82.

25. Columbia Oral History, pp. 267–68.

26. My interview with music critic Irving Kolodin, 21 April 1982.

27. Ada Louise Huxtable, "A Dream Unfulfilled," *New York Times*, 17 September 1966, p. 17.

28. Minutes of a special meeting of the Metropolitan Opera House Building Committee, 8 October 1964, J. D. Rockefeller 3d papers, Box 47, Rockefeller Family Archive.

29. Minutes of the meeting of the Metropolitan Opera House Building Committee, 17 May 1966, p. 2. J. D. Rockefeller 3d papers, Box 47, Rockefeller Family Archive.

30. The remaining drops by Dufy for this production are in two of the opera's rehearsal rooms.

31. Charlotte Curtis, "The Metropolitan Opera House Opens in a Crescendo of Splendor," *New York Times*, 17 September 1966, p. 1.

32. Letter from Ellen Harrison to me, 27 September 1982.

33. My interview with William Schuman, 17 June 1982.

34. The Colón Theater in Buenos Aires comes next, with 3,432 seats, followed by the Chicago Civic Opera, with 3,400. European houses are considerably smaller: the Paris Opera, 2,347; Milan's La Scala, 2,135; the Vienna Opera, 1,620.

35. *Newsweek*, 19 September 1966, p. 70.

36. Financial Statements, 31 July 1986 and 1985. *Metropolitan Opera Association*, and *Metropolitan Opera Association, Inc. Financial Statements*, 31 July 1986 and 1985.

37. Irving Kolodin, "Opera on the American Plan," Opening Night Program, Metropolitan Opera, 16 September 1966, pp. 21, 28. My discussion of the seating is based on this article.

38. Ada Louise Huxtable, "The Met as Architecture," *New York Times*, 17 September 1966, p. 17.

39. Ada Louise Huxtable, "Lincoln Center: Adding Up the Score," *New York Times*, 25 September 1966, p. 29.

40. Mildred F. Schmertz, "For Concerts, Dance, and Drama: Flexible Design," *Architectural Record* 141, no. 2 (February 1967): 115–30.

41. My interview with Abramovitz, 8 July 1982.

42. Brendan Gill, "Welcoming the Muses," *New Yorker*, 28 September 1981, p. 92. My description of the Kennedy Center is based on this article, pp. 79–116.

43. Ibid., pp. 108–9.

44. Andrea O. Dean, "Cultural Colossi: Kennedy Center at 10," *American Institute of Architects Journal* 70 (August 1981): 27.

45. "The damage wrought by the World's Fair will last for half a century from its date, if not longer. It has penetrated deep into the constitution of the American mind, effecting there lesions significant of dementia." Louis Sullivan, *The Autobiography of an Idea*, rev. ed. (New York, 1956), p. 325.

46. John Jacobus, "Philip Johnson, His Work, His Times," *Progressive Architecture* 65, no. 2 (February, 1984): 99.

47. Philip Johnson's New York State Theater was one of several classicizing buildings that he designed in the early 1960s, beginning with the museum in Utica, New York (1960). Ibid.

Chapter 19
Commissions of the 1960s: the World's Fair and New York City's airports

1. From *The Mighty Fair, New York World's Fair 1964–1965, a Retrospective*, exhibition catalogue (New York, 1985), p. 2.

2. Minutes of the meeting of Collaborating Architects, 13 July 1960, p. 2. Lincoln Center files, Abramovitz, Kingsland & Schiff archives.

3. For a complete account of Moses's involvement in the fair, see "Off to the Fair," chapter 45, in Caro, pp. 1040–66.

4. My interview with Bunshaft, 6 November 1981.

5. Edith Evans Asbury, "Designers Quit Fair in a Dispute on Plan," *New York Times*, 3 December 1960, p. 21.

6. Asbury, "Designers Quit Fair," p. 21.

7. Ibid.

8. John Brooks, "Onward and Upward with the Arts, Diplomacy at Flushing Meadow," *New Yorker*, 1 June 1963, p. 41–59.

9. As Brooks points out, there were no exhibits by the U.S.S.R. or by any other country of the Communist world.

10. "Pop Art Fair," *New York Herald Tribune*, October 1964, shown in "The Mighty Fair, New York World's Fair 1964–1965," exhibition, Flushing Gallery, New York, 1985.

11. The other two were the Port Authority's heliport and Philip Johnson's New York State Pavilion.

12. Ada Louise Huxtable, "Romantic Science Hall," *New York Times*, 10 September 1964, p. 27.

13. All quotations and opinions attributed to Harrison in this chapter are based on my interviews with him, 4 September 1980 and 1 April 1981.

14. The Hall of Science's relationship to Minoru Yamasaki's neo-Gothic Federal Science Pavilion at the Seattle 1962 World's Fair has also been pointed out. Huxtable, "Romantic Science Hall," p. 27.

15. Ibid.

16. Caro, pp. 1102, 1107.

17. Moses, *Public Works*, p. 602.

18. It was the biggest salary Moses had ever received—$75,000 per year plus $25,000 per year in expenses for seven years, as well as an annuity of $27,000 per year for an additional seven years. Caro, pp. 1060, 1090, 1108.

19. Marc Solomon, "The Fair that Never Knew its Own Strength," *The Mighty Fair*, p. 22.

20. My interview with Brad Clark, the Harrison & Abramovitz civil engineer and office manager from the mid-1960s to 1976, 12 August 1982.

21. New York World's Fair Corporation, *Post Fair Expansion Hall of Science*, (New York, n.d.), New Opera projects 1927-file, Metropolitan Opera Archive.

22. The discussion of airport design in terms of three generations is based on Edward G. Blankenship, *The Airport* (New York, 1974), pp. 28–30.

23. My interview, 4 February 1984, with Charles Abbe, who worked as a designer for the Harrison & Abramovitz office on La Guardia; my interviews, 20 and 23 July 1984, with Warren Kenn and Lawrence Schaefer of the New York Port Authority.

24. The design also relates to a scheme for a high school, published in 1935, which Harrison prepared with the assistance of W. K. Oltar-Jevsky, who worked with him on the 1939 Fair, Max Abramovitz, and Ellen Harrison, who occasionally helped her husband with interiors. See *Architectural Forum* 62, no. 2 (January 1935): 56. The high school design is, in turn, strikingly similar to Otto Haesler's Fredrich Ebert School, reproduced in Harrison's *School Buildings*, pp. 46–49.

Chapter 20
The Albany Mall: beginning

1. Kramer and Roberts, *I Never Wanted to Be Vice-President of Anything!*, p. 10. In addition to the South Mall, Rockefeller's accomplishments included ninety thousand new housing units; twenty-three new mental health facilities; one hundred nine new or expanded voluntary and municipal hospitals; fifty-five new state parks; an innovative new water pollution control program, which resulted in the construction of two hundred waste treatment plants; an increase in agricultural research; the development of a regional mass-transit system; the expansion of the state university system from twenty-eight campuses with 38,000 students to seventy-one campuses with 246,000 students; and, extending from Long Island to Buffalo, the construction of twenty-nine major state office buildings. Ibid., pp. 145–46.

2. Gervasi, *The Real Rockefeller*, p. 258.

3. My interview with Martha Dalrymple, 25 September 1981. For Dalrymple, see chapter 10, n. 9.

4. This and the following quotations from Harrison in this chapter, unless otherwise indicated, are taken from my interviews with him, 21 August 1980 and 1, 10 April 1981.

5. Stone's solution was the polar opposite of Harrison's. His inflexible Beaux-Arts plan flattened out the landscape to create uniformity rather than diversity. See Paul Turner, *Campus: An American Planning Tradition* (New York and Cambridge, 1984), chapter 7.

6. Quoted in Eleanore Carruth, "What Price Glory on the Albany Mall?" *Fortune*, June 1971, p. 92.

7. Rockefeller named as chairman of the commission Lieutenant Governor Malcolm Wilson, formerly a conservative state assemblyman from Yonkers, who had been a key factor in the gubernatorial campaign. Frank Wells McCabe, a leading Albany banker, was named vice-chairman; the commission had seven additional members, and within six weeks, nine others had been appointed: three by the president pro tem of the state senate, three by the speaker of the state assembly, and three by the mayor.

8. Bleecker, *The Politics of Architecture*, pp. 178–79.

9. Columbia Oral History, pp. 245–46, with my editing.

10. Ibid.

11. My interview with Dudley, 25 September 1981.

12. Ibid.

13. Ibid. The strange figure cut by the blue-haired Rotival, who regularly napped through every meeting at Albany, was much commented upon. My interview with John Byron, 31 October 1983.

14. *Plan for a Capital City*, Report Prepared by the Associated Planners for the Temporary State Commission on the Capital City (Albany, 1963), section 13, p. 1; section 14, pp. 1–3.

15. Louise Savell, assistant to Nelson Rockefeller, typescript of Albany Mall chapter for Nelson Rockefeller biography. Harrison & Abramovitz file. Harrison, Kingsland & Schiff archive.

16. New York State Constitution, Article 7, Section 11.

17. In this respect, the bonds differed from the "moral obligation bonds" introduced by Rockefeller, for which the state legislature is committed to appropriate money to pay the bond holders, but which future legislatures could conceivably vote against paying. At the time, State Comptroller Arthur Levitt questioned the legality of the state's contract to pay Albany County rent with Attorney General John Mitchell, who had approved it. Richard Karp, "Albany Mall," *Barron's* 56 (22 March 1976): 5, 14.

18. My interview with Emerich Levatich, New York State attorney, 14 July 1983. Four million dollars of this were spent on computerized central security and climatic control equipment, which were designated in the original plans.

19. All quotations from Byron in this chapter are based on my interviews with him, 14 July and 15 August 1983. On 24 April 1963 local press coverage of the official unveiling of a model of the South Mall

reported the $250 million figure with an equally erroneous estimate of twenty-two years for completion of the project.

20. Nelson A. Rockefeller, "At the Cornerstone Ceremony for the South Mall Projects, Albany" (21 June 1965), in *State of New York, Public Papers of Governor Nelson A. Rockefeller, 53rd Governor, Albany 1959–1973*, p. 951.

21. Alvin Moscow, *The Rockefeller Inheritance* (New York, 1977), p. 340.

22. Columbia Oral History, p. 338.

23. My interview with Klein, 10 November 1983.

24. Columbia Oral History, p. 359.

25. Bleecker, *The Politics of Architecture*, p. 200.

26. My interviews with Dudley, 25 September and 4 November 1982.

27. Bleecker, *The Politics of Architecture*, p. 220.

28. Lena Williams, "The Footlights Begin to Lend a Glow to the Egg," *New York Times*, 18 January 1981, p. 44.

29. My interview with Dudley, 3 April 1981.

30. The Egg was planned originally to house a 975-seat auditorium and a 300-seat conference room. John Byron, *Empire State Performing Arts Center*, press release, 18 April 1978.

31. Columbia Oral History, p. 349.

32. My interview with Michael Mostoller, assistant designer to Dudley at the time of this meeting, 30 September 1982.

33. The 900 units were part of a potential 6,500 housing units that were slated for Albany's downtown renewal. The South Mall housing got as far as the pylons (which still stand on the site), but when a $40,000 per unit estimate came in, the project was abandoned.

34. My interview with Abramovitz, 12 August 1982.

35. My interviews with Dalrymple, 25 September 1981 and with Ellen Harrison, 7 September 1983.

36. My interview with Byron, 31 October 1983.

37. My interview with Diamond, 7 November 1983.

Chapter 21
The Albany Mall: construction and completion

1. My interview with Dudley, 3 April 1981.

2. This and subsequent quotations from Byron in this chapter are taken from my interview with him, 14 July 1983.

3. A total of ninety-nine prime contractors were employed by the OGS for the South Mall. My interview with Byron, 14 July 1983 and his letter to me, 22 July 1988.

4. Carruth, "What Price Glory on the Albany Mall?," p. 166.

5. My interview with Walter Relihan, former attorney for New York State, 13 July 1983.

6. The description of the Equitable Adjustment Act and of the events that led up to it are based on my interview with Relihan, who drafted the bill.

7. This and the following quotations from Harrison in this chapter, unless otherwise indicated, are taken from my interviews with him, 3 March 1979, 21 August 1980, and 1, 10 April 1981.

8. Wolf Von Eckardt, "Rocky's Monumental Error, or the Billion-Dollar Misunderstanding," *New York Magazine*, 20 April 1970, p. 29.

9. Columbia Oral History, p. 356.

10. My interview with Byron, 24 August 1983.

11. Among the many program changes in the Department of Health space, probably the most disruptive was the decision in November 1970 to install what was then the largest electron microscope in the world dedicated to biological research. Coming eight months after the platform foundations had been completed, this addition required structural changes that cost almost $1 million. There were also tenant

changes of a somewhat less drastic nature made in the justice and legislative buildings. In the latter, offices were enlarged when assemblymen complained that their quarters were smaller than those of the senators', and an entire floor was redesigned to accommodate an extravagant dining room, which was then dismantled.

12. For the discussion of changes in the Department of Health, I am indebted to Byron, Dr. David Axelrod, who was in charge of the infectious disease department at the time of the Mall's construction, and Dr. Hollis Ingraham.

13. Concrete corridor floors covered with carpeting were substituted for terrazzo, and dry wall for plaster, and a number of other simplifications were made that, had they been planned at the outset, could have saved money, but as changes, ended up costing more. The discussion of changes in the Mall design is based on State Comptroller Levitt's audit of 1970; on my interview with General William W. Wanamaker, 9 August 1983; and on his letter to me 10 August 1983.

14. The governor's political popularity gave him tremendous power, and for years no one dared to question his procedures. Finally, at a meeting with Rockefeller and Harrison at the governor's New York City

offices on West Fifty-fourth Street, Byron could contain himself no longer. In response to Rockefeller's persistent questions about delays and deadlines, the steely, six-foot-six-inch engineer blurted out: "We'll never get it done if you don't stop making changes!" To Byron's astonishment, Rockefeller responded with deadpan assurance: "I never make changes." My interview with Byron, 14 July 1983.

15. *Progressive Architecture* 44, no. 9 (September 1963): 70; and Martin Filler, "Halicarnassus on the Hudson," *Progressive Architecture* 60, no. 5, (May 1979): 106–7. At midpoint of its construction, Lewis Mumford was equally damning of Rockefeller Center in "Mr. Rockefeller's Center," *New Yorker*, 23 December 1933, pp. 29–30.

16. State Comptroller's Audit, 31 March 1971, filed 27 May 1971, pp. 45, 47, 50.

17. *New York Times*, 31 January 1971, sec. 4, p. 3.

18. Hilton Kramer, "Mall's Immensity Overwhelms Art Works," *New York Times*, 24 June 1976, p. 35.

19. A total of ninety-two pieces was acquired at a cost of $1,887,610 (C. R. Roseberry, *Capitol Story*, rev. ed. [New York, 1982], p. 147). In 1985 the collection was valued at $12 million (*New York Times*, 4 May 1985, p. 13).

20. Henry-Russell Hitchcock, *The Architecture of H. H. Richardson and His Times*, (New York, 1977), pp. 167–70.

21. William Kennedy, "Everything Everybody Ever Wanted," *Atlantic Monthly* 251, no. 5 (May 1983): 78.

22. Ada Louise Huxtable, "The Rayburn Building: A National Disaster," in *Will They Ever Finish Bruckner Boulevard?* (New York, 1970), p. 156.

23. In 1976 Harrison completed a $24 million house in Princeton, New Jersey, for Mrs. Seward Johnson, who changed so much of Harrison's design that he excluded the house from his list of buildings. See Shawn Tully, "Mr. Johnson's $21 Million Palace," *Town & Country*, October 1977, pp. 16–46.

24. The first three bond issues in 1966–67, totaling $140 million, were at the rates of 3.90, 3.80, and 3.75 percent. In 1969 a $70 million bond was issued at 6 percent. By 1976 the interest rate had risen to 8.9 percent, and the last issue, in 1982, was at 9.38 percent.

25. In the effort to ensure that the Mall would last for a hundred years, unusually thick marble was used for the facings. On the motor vehicles building, where these heavy slabs were anchored with nonstainless steel, a slight shifting of the

marble took place; it was quickly adjusted. At the Cultural Education Center a few small marble crescents became detached because of insufficient joining material between the slabs; this problem was also remedied.

26. My interviews with Abramovitz, 11 August 1983, and with Clark, 12 August 1982.

27. The discussion of construction management systems is based on my interview with Richard Rose, architect, New York City, 1 September 1983. Rose also made extensive comments on this aspect of the discussion in a letter to me, 13 December 1983.

28. The Associated General Contractors of America, *The Use of CPM in Construction* (Washington, D.C., 1976), pp. 7–8.

29. My interview with Edwin Stevens, New York State's architect in charge of campus construction, 4 August 1983. Stevens claims that probably the first conscious applications of the method took place during construction of the buildings erected at the state university at Stony Brook (1967).

30. The Empire State Institute, housed in the performing arts center, has been referred to as one of the most interesting theatrical groups in the nation. Harold C. Schonberg,

"Have Cultural Centers Benefited the Arts?" *New York Times*, 10 July 1983, sec. 2, p. 26.

31. M. A. Farber, "Albany Mall Proves Dazzling to Inhabitants," *New York Times*, 25 January 1973, p. 43. At the time the project was planned, one million additional square feet of office space for government employees was allocated to space outside the Mall. In accordance with the well-established fact that active bureaucracies soon outgrow their assigned quarters, the need for even more space has grown considerably since the Mall was completed.

Chapter 22
The Last Years

1. All quotations and opinions attributed to Harrison in this chapter, unless otherwise indicated, are taken from my interviews with him, 27 March, 17 December 1980 and 25 March, 8 April 1981.

2. E. Forbes-Boyd, *Aegean Quest* (New York, 1970), p. 201.

3. Suzanne Stephens, "Monumental Main Street," *Progressive Architecture* 65, no. 5 (May 1979): 110–13.

4. List in Pershing Memorial folder, Harrison & Abramovitz files, Abramovitz, Kingsland & Schiff archive.

5. My interview with Robert White, 27 September 1983.

6. Kramer and Roberts, *I Never Wanted to be Vice-President of Anything!*, p. 221.

7. Marshack was replaced in 1978 by Samuel Bleecker, who subsequently authored *The Politics of Architecture*.

8. Manuscript in Wallace Harrison file, Abramovitz, Kingsland & Schiff archive.

9. My interview with Robert Klein, 10 November 1983.

10. My interview with Cesar Pelli, 23 October 1984.

11. Koolhaas, *Delirious New York*, pp. 236–40.

12. My interview with William L. Hanaway, Jr., chairman, Oriental Studies, University of Pennsylvania, a former consultant to the Library Competition Committee, 9 November 1983.

13. *Pahlavi National Library Project, Published Exhibition of Projects*, 16 March–16 April 1978, Teheran, Iran, p. 4.

14. The committee was composed as follows: chairman, Nader Ardalan, architect (Iran); vice-chairman, Natalia I. Tyulina, librarian (U.S.S.R.); voting members, Lili Amir-Ardjomand, librarian (Iran); Charles M. Correa, architect (India); Trevor Dannatt, architect (Great Britain); Giancarlo De Carlo, architect (Italy); K. L. Liguer-Laubhouet, librarian (Ivory Coast); Fumihiko Maki, architect (Japan); and Poori Soltani, librarian (Iran).

15. My interview with James Kingsland, 16 August 1983.

16. My interview with François Lombard, the architect in charge of the building program, 19 October 1983. Second and third prizes of $25,000 each went respectively to Engelbert Eder, Rudolf F. Weber, & Reiner Wieden of Vienna and to William O. Meyer of Johannesburg. See François Lombard, "Bibliothèque Nationale Pahlavi," *L'Architecture d'Aujourd'hui* 197 (June 1978): v–vi.

17. My interview with Goldstone, 13 September 1983.

Appendix A
After "The World of Tomorrow"

1. Stanley Applebaum, *The New York World's Fair 1939/40* (New York, 1977), pp. xi, xvii.

2. *New York Times*, 31 October 1940, p. 25. Caro gives the figure as 30¢ on the dollar, p. 1085.

3. Warren I. Sussman, "The People's Fair: Cultural Contradictions of a Consumer Society," in *Dawn of a New Day*, pp. 21–22.

Appendix B:
A Grand Approach to the United Nations

1. Letter from Moses to Zeckendorf, 1 April 1947, William Zeckendorf, X City files.

2. Statement by Zeckendorf to the Board of Estimate, p. 4, Zeckendorf, X City files.

3. Ibid.

4. Ibid.

5. My interview with Abramovitz, 23 September, 1980.

6. *New York Times*, 29 August 1947, pp. 1, 6.

7. Harold Brown, "Plan for Monumental Approach to the U.N. East Side Site Praised," *New York Sun*, 20 May 1948, p. 3.

8. *New York Times*, 13 November 1948, p. 12.

Wallace K. Harrison
List of Buildings

Project	Location	Completion Date	Associated Architects
Office Buildings			
Alcoa	Pittsburgh, PA	1953	Mitchell & Ritchie, Pittsburgh, PA
Bush Building Addition	London, England	1927	Harvey Corbett
Carnegie Endowment	New York, NY	1953	
Corning Glass	New York, NY	1959	Charles Abbe
I.B.M. World Trade	New York, NY	1958	
Marine National Exchange	Milwaukee, WI	1962	
Three Mellon Bank Center	Pittsburgh, PA	1951	W. Y. Cocken
Republic National Bank	Dallas, TX	1954	
Rockefeller Center Buildings	New York, NY		
Associated Press		1938	Michael M. Harris
British Empire		1935	
Celanese		1974	Michael M. Harris
Center Theater		1932	
Eastern Airlines		1939	
Exxon		1973	Michael M. Harris
Garages		1939	
International		1935	
Maison Française		1935	
McGraw-Hill		1973	Michael M. Harris
Music Hall		1932	
R.C.A.		1933	
R.K.O.		1932	
Time and Life		1937	
Time and Life		1960	Michael M. Harris
U.S. Rubber		1940	
U.S. Rubber Addition		1955	
South Mall (Nelson A. Rockefeller Empire State Plaza)	Albany, NY		
Agency Buildings 1, 2, 3, 4		1974	
Corning Tower		1973	
Cultural Education Center		1977	
Health Department Laboratories		1974	
Justice Building		1972	
Legislative Office Building		1972	
Motor Vehicle Building		1972	
Performing Arts Center		1975	
Platform		1974	

Educational Buildings

Hall Auditorium	Oberlin, OH	1952	Eldredge Snyder
Hopkins Center, Dartmouth	Hanover, NH	1962	
Library for History and Social Sciences, Institute for Advanced Studies	Princeton, NJ	1965	
P.S. #34	New York, NY	1956	

Exhibits

Corning Glass Center	Corning, NY	1951	
New York World's Fair 1939–1940	Flushing, NY		
Consolidated Edison Electric Utilities Exhibit			
Electrified Farm Master Pieces of Art			
Trylon and Perisphere		1939	
New York World's Fair 1964–1965	Flushing, NY	1965	
Hall of Science			

Government Buildings

Central Intelligence Agency	Langley, VA	1961	Frederick King
U.S. Embassy Office	Havana, Cuba	1951	
U.S. Embassy Office	Rio de Janeiro, Brazil	1952	
U.S. Navy: Jobs in U.S. and U.S. Possessions			
Fifty-six different jobs: Engine Laboratories, Overhaul Buildings Test Cells, Boiler Plants, Paint Shops, etc.		1941–43	
U.S. Submarine and Air Base	Panama Canal Zone	1942	

Hospitals

Flower–Fifth Avenue	New York, NY	1939	

Hotels & Apartments

Avila Hotel	Caracas, Venezuela	1941	Harrison & Fouilhoux
Nurses Residence for Sloan-Kettering Memorial Hospital	New York, NY	1962	
Rockefeller Apartments	New York, NY	1936	

Housing

Astoria Houses	Astoria, NY	1951	
Clinton Hill Apartments	Brooklyn, NY	1943	Abramovitz and Irwin Clavan
Fort Greene Houses (now called Walt Whitman and Raymond V. Ingersoll Houses)	Brooklyn, NY	1944	
Morningside Gardens	New York, NY	1957	

Laboratories & Industrial

Corning Glass Works	Corning, NY	1957	
Laboratory			
Office Building			
Pilot Plant			
Additional Corning Buildings		1965	
"B" Building			
Cafeteria & Auditorium			
Fundamental Research Buildings			
Pepsi Cola Plant	Long Island City, NY	1941	

Churches

First Presbyterian Church	Stamford, CT	1958	
First Presbyterian Church, Carillon		1968	

Public Buildings

African Habitat, Bronx Zoo	New York, NY	1940	
Aquarium, Coney Island	New York, NY	1957	
Lincoln Center for the Performing Arts Opera House	New York, NY	1966	
Pershing Memorial	Washington, D.C.	1983	
United Nations Headquarters	New York, NY	1953	

Miscellaneous Buildings

Auditorium, Oberlin College	Oberlin, OH	1952	
Branch Banks: Chase Manhattan–Carnegie Endowment	New York, NY	1953	Eldredge Synder

La Guardia Airport Buildings and Approaches	New York, NY	1964
National Academy of Science Addition: two wings		
Research Auditorium		1962
Symposia	Washington, D.C.	1965
Rockefeller University: Offices, Dormitories, Residence and Auditorium	New York, NY	1958

Residences

Burden Residence	Northeast Harbor, ME	1947
Wallace K. Harrison House	Huntington, NY	1935
Albert Milton Residence	Washington, CT	1936
David Milton Residence	Bermuda	1936
Nelson A. Rockefeller, The Anchorage	Seal Harbor, ME	1941
Nelson A. Rockefeller, Hawes Guest House	Tarrytown, NY	1939
Nelson A. Rockefeller, The Lodge	Tarrytown, NY	1960
Julian Street, Jr., Residence	Scarborough, NY	1938

Max Abramovitz
List of Buildings

Project	Location	Completion Date	Associated Architects
Office Buildings			
Akron Center	Akron, OH	1969	
Alcoa Administration	Davenport, IA	1949	
Banque Rothschild	Paris, France	1970	Pierre Dufau, Paris
Borden	Columbus, OH	1973	
Breguet	Versailles, France	1977	Jean-Pierre Bisseuil, Paris
Cincinnati Center	Cincinnati, OH	1969	
Columbus Center	Columbus, OH	1966	
Commercial Credit	Baltimore, MD	1957	
Commercial Investment Trust	New York, NY	1957	
Daily News Addition	New York, NY	1960	
Dayton Power and Light Company	Dayton, OH	1977	
Equitable Life Assurance Society (Gateway 4)	Pittsburgh, PA	1960	
Erie County Bank	Buffalo, NY	1969	Charles Abbe
Erieview Plaza	Cleveland, OH	1965	
Fiberglas Tower	Toledo, OH	1969	
First National Bank Building	Louisville, KY	1972	
Groupe Des Assurances Nationales	Bordeaux, France	1978	Jean-Pierre Bisseuil, Paris
International Business Machines	Boston, MA	1959	
Mead Tower	Dayton, OH	1977	
Nationwide Plaza	Columbus, OH	1977	James Kingsland
Newspoint Rotogravure Plant– Daily News Publishing Company	Long Island City, NY	1974	
Ohio Bell Telephone	Cleveland, OH	1969	
Phoenix Mutual Life Insurance	Hartford, CT	1964	
Porter	Pittsburgh, PA	1958	
Springs Mill	New York, NY	1962	
Tour GAN, Groupe Des Assurances Nationales	Paris, France	1976	
Union Bank Square	Los Angeles, CA	1967	
U.S. Steel Building	Pittsburgh, PA	1971	Charles Abbe
Wachovia National Bank Building	Pittsburgh, PA	1958	
Westinghouse Building	Pittsburgh, PA	1970	

Educational Buildings

Brandeis University	Waltham, MA		
Adolph Ullman Amphitheatre		1951	
American Jewish History Society		1960	
Bio-Chemistry Laboratory		1965	
Commuter Student Center		1960	
Goldfarb Library		1959	
Goldman-Schwartz Art Studios		1970	
Mailman Hall		1958	
Men's Dormitories and Dining Center		1959	
Olin-Sang Center		1959	
Rabb Graduate Center		1958	
Rose Art Museum		1963	
Science Center		1967	Gerald Schiff
Slossberg Music Center		1960	
Springold Theater		1965	
Stoneman Infirmary		1956	
Wein Faculty Center		1960	
Columbia University	New York, NY		
Amsterdam Plaza		1964	
East Campus Law School		1962	
School of International Affairs		1970	
New York University	New York, NY		
Loeb Student Center		1959	
Radcliffe College	Cambridge, MA		
Currier Hall Housing Complex		1970	
Hilles Library		1966	
University of Illinois	Urbana, IL		
Assembly Hall		1963	
Hillel Foundation	Champaign, IL	1954	
Hillel Foundation	Evanston, IL	1954	
Krannert Performing Art Center	Champaign, IL	1969	
University of Iowa	Iowa City, IA		
Fine Arts Center (Hancher Auditorium and Music School)		1972	
Museum		1969	

University of Pittsburgh	Pittsburgh, PA		
Learning Research and Development Center		1974	
United Nations School	New York, NY	1972	Charles Abbe

Monumental Buildings

Benjamin M. Frankel Memorial	Champaign, IL	1951	
Lincoln Center for the Performing Arts	New York, NY		
Garage Complex and Central Plant		1962	
Philharmonic Hall (now Avery Fisher Hall)		1962	

Exhibits

New York World's Fair 1964–1965	Flushing Meadow, NY	1964	
American Telephone and Telegraph Exhibit			Henry Dreyfuss

Government Buildings

Central Intelligence Agency	Langley, VA	1961	Frederick King
U.S. Embassy	Havana, Cuba	1952	
U.S. Submarine and Air Base	Panama Canal Zone	1942	

Housing

Battery Park City, second phase (design unexecuted)	New York, NY		
Clinton Hill Development, eleven units	Brooklyn, NY	1947	
Marlboro Houses	Brooklyn, NY	1958	

Laboratories and Industrial

Alcoa Research Center	Merwyn, PA	1965	
Continental Can	New York, NY	1961	
Corning Glass Works: Laboratory, Pilot Plant, Office Building	Corning, NY	1957	
Duke Laboratories	Norwalk, CT	1958	
Educational Testing Laboratories	Princeton, NJ	1958	Charles Abbe

Public Buildings

Bronx County Courthouse	New York, NY	1976

Religious Buildings

Jewish Chapel, West Point	West Point, NY	1985
Temple Beth Zion	Buffalo, NY	1967
Three Chapels, Brandeis University	Waltham, MA	1955

Residences

Eastchester Houses	Bronx, NY	1951
R. E. Lawther Vacation House	St. Lucia, British West Indies	1966

Index

Picture Credits

Endsheets: Harrison's parallels of architecture, a Beaux-Arts tradition after J.N.L. Durand (1760–1834)

Detail and plan redrawn by Eric Marshall: 162, 185

Motif drawn, and plan redrawn, by Alex Gorlin: 27, 83, 87

Plans redrawn by Anne E. Lacy: 14, 16, 37, 41, 83, 88, 113, 114, 230, 231

Where the photographer's name appears alone, he or she is located in New York City.

Abramovitz, Kingsland, and Schiff: 110,116

Abramovitz, Max: 30, 100

Architectural Review, December 1950, 402:23.

Avery Library, Columbia University: Drawing Collection 4, 8, 19, 23, 24, 36, 58 (photo by Michael Vest), 62, 222 (photo by Michael Vest from *Construction des formes d'architecture et des machines*, Leningrad, 1931, p. 201), 69, 91, 93–95, 101 (photo from Le Corbusier, *UN Headquarters*, New York, 1947 p. 31), 105, 161, 166–70, 180–82, 183, 189, 200 (photos by Eric Pulitzer), 186, 187, 219, 244a (photo by Michael Vest), 248, 251–54.

Barrows, Wendy: 53, 54, 130, 141, 142

Beville, Henry B., Annapolis, Maryland: 245–47, 250

BILD Service, Göteborg, Sweden: 214

Bleecker, Samuel E., *The Politics of Architecture*, New York, 1981, p 185: 225

Brant, Mrs. Peter: 42

British Architectural Library, RIBA: 22

Brown Brothers: 15

Buk, E., Collection of, New York City (photo by McKay): 179

Central Intelligence Agency, Langley, Virginia: 131

Clements, Geoffrey, Staten Island, New York: 149

Consolidated Edison: 72, 73

Corning Glass: 163, 164

Dartmouth College Archives: 193

Dudley, George (photos for *Architectural Forum*, June 1946, 113–16): 76–78

Goucher College: 31–32

Harrison, Ellen, Collection of: endpapers, 1, 5, 6, 7, 10, 20, 25, 28, 29, 40 (photo by Jean Bohne, Inc.), 43 (photo by F.S. Lincoln), 44, 45, 80, 82 (photos by Shirley C. Burden), 48, 49, 50, 55–56 (photos by Photo Craftsmen, Inc.), 57, 60 (photo for *Architectural Forum*, May 1937, 392), 61, 63, 64, 65–68, 71, 74 (photo by Robert M. Damora), 79 (photo Pan American Airlines), 81 (photo by Akron Studios), 83, 85, 86, 89, 90, 92

(photo by Drix Duryea), 98–99 (photos United Nations), 99, 106 (photo by Acme News-pictures), 107, 109, 118–20 (photo United Nations), 122, 126 (photos by Todd Webb), 125, 127 (photos by Photo Associates), 128 (photo by John R. Shrader, Pittsburgh), 129 (photo by Ulrig Meisel, Dallas), 132, 137, 138, 143 (photo by Louis Checkman), 145–46, 153, 157 (photo by Corona Color Studios, Inc.), 159, 171, 172, 174, 175, 188, 191, 196, 197, 201, 203–4, 210 (photo by Tod Papageorge), 215, 221, 223, 226–28 (photos by Patrick W. Sturn), 236, 237, 241

Hirsch, David, Brooklyn, New York: 194a

Horch, Nettie S, Hallandale, Florida: 11

Horst: 249

Jefferson, National Expansion Memorial/National Park Service: 124

Kinne, Russ, Stamford, Connecticut: 150

Le Corbusier, Fondation, Paris: 108

Metropolitan Opera Archive: 165, 176, 177, 202, 205–209, 213 (photo by Louis Melançon)

Metropolitan Opera Association: 12, 13, 198, 199, 212 (photo by Louis Melançon)

Milton, Albert, Washington, Connecticut: 39

National Academy of Sciences, Washington, D.C.: 158

New York City Mayor's Committee on Plan and Scope, *Plan for Permanent World Capitol at Flushing Meadow Park*, New York 1946, pp. 16–17:96

New York Public Library, Manuscript and Archive Division: 59, 70

New York Zoological Society: 51, 52

Office of General Services Albany, New York: 224, 233, 240, 242 (photo by Donald Doremus), 229, 234, 235, 238, 243

Papadaki, Stamo, *Oscar Niemeyer*, New York 1960, Fig. 13: 111.

Rockefeller Archive Center: 47

Rockefeller Center, Inc.: 17, 18, 21, 26, 135, 136, 184

Rockefeller University Archives: 155, 156

Rosa, Joseph: 33à

Scherschel, Frank, *Life Magazine* © Time Inc.: 34, 144

Schnall, Ben: 84

Schulenburg, Fritz von der, London: 9

Sher, E. Fred: 211

Thomas, Katrina: 33b, 35, 36, 38, 151, 152, 173

Time Inc. Archives: 134, 136

Worcester (Massachusetts) Historical Museum Collection: 2, 3

Zeckendorf, William, Jr.: 97, 123